THE ONE YEAR®

WORSHIP

THE KING

DEVOTIONAL

365 DAILY BIBLE READINGS TO INSPIRE PRAISE

chris tiegreen

WALK THRU THE BIBLE®

TYNDALE HOUSE PUBLISHERS, INC.
CAROL STREAM, ILLINOIS

Visit Tyndale's exciting Web site at www.tyndale.com

TYNDALE and Tyndale's quill logo are trademarks of Tyndale House Publishers, Inc.

The One Year is a registered trademark of Tyndale House Publishers, Inc.

The One Year Worship the King Devotional: 365 Daily Bible Readings to Inspire Praise

Copyright © 2008 by Walk Thru the Bible. All rights reserved.

Cover photo of thorns copyright © by Jill Fromer/iStockphoto. All rights reserved.

Cover photo of crown copyright © by Hans Caluwaerts/iStockphoto. All rights reserved.

Designed by Julie Chen

ISBN-13: 978-1-4143-2395-4

ISBN-10: 1-4143-2395-6

Printed in the United States of America

13 12 11 10 09 08
6 5 4 3 2 1

WALK THRU THE BIBLE®

Lasting life change through transferable
biblical teaching, training, and tools.

For more than three decades, Walk Thru the Bible has created discipleship materials and cultivated leadership networks that together are reaching millions of people through live seminars, print publications, audiovisual curricula, and the Internet. Known for innovative methods and high-quality resources, we serve the whole body of Christ across denominational, cultural, and national lines. Through our strong and cooperative international partnerships, we are strategically positioned to address the church's greatest need: developing mature, committed, and spiritually reproducing believers.

Walk Thru the Bible communicates the truths of God's Word in a way that makes the Bible readily accessible to anyone. We are committed to developing user-friendly resources that are Bible centered, of excellent quality, life changing for individuals, and catalytic for churches, ministries, and movements; and we are committed to maintaining our global reach through strategic partnerships while adhering to the highest levels of integrity in all we do.

Walk Thru the Bible partners with the local church worldwide to fulfill its mission, helping people "walk thru" the Bible with greater clarity and understanding. Live seminars and small group curricula are taught in over 45 languages by more than 80,000 people in nearly 100 countries, and more than 100 million devotionals have been packaged into daily magazines, books, and other publications that reach over five million people each year.

Walk Thru the Bible
4201 North Peachtree Road
Atlanta, GA 30341-1207
770-458-9300
www.walkthru.org

Introduction

What is worship? What does it mean to present yourself as "a living sacrifice"? Is there a set time and place for it, or does it encompass all of our lives? Considering the priority the Bible places on true worship—and Jesus' declaration that real worship is what God is after—these are enormously important questions. If we want to fulfill the purpose God has for us, and in fact to *be* fulfilled, we need to know how to love and adore Him.

The readings in *The One Year Worship the King Devotional* explore the heights and depths of worship. We'll look at it from many angles: God's perspective and humanity's, passions and practicalities, outward form and inward function, words and actions. Through the course of this year, you will be urged to purify yourself from false worship and to let the Spirit of God fill you with truth. And in the process, you'll grow to be more like the One who created you in His image.

Worship defines the relationship between God and His people and touches every aspect of our existence. These devotionals are drawn from all portions of Scripture, which is only natural, since God's story is filled with encouragement and exhortation about the affections of our heart. The full range of human expression is found in its pages. If you'll let His Spirit work through His Word to sink into your life, you'll find your relationship with Him deepening in every way. May that purpose be fulfilled in your life as you explore His heart this year.

In Spirit and Truth

**God is spirit, and his worshipers must
worship in spirit and in truth.**
JOHN 4:24

In Word

We are worshiping creatures by nature. It's why we were made. A glance around our world reveals a panorama of worship. Our culture alone includes an abundance of styles, a plethora of deities, a multitude of definitions, and myriad motives.

Considering the central role of worship in the life of a human being—it is our entire reason for being, as well as the eternal activity of the saints in heaven, according to the Word—we might do well to consider what God wants it to be like. Does He prefer informal or formal? Ritualistic or spontaneous? Noisy or quiet? Dignified or recklessly passionate? Nearly everyone has an opinion on these alternatives, but they aren't really the heart of the issue. What God desires most has less to do with how we express our worship than with the spirit behind it. In our adoration of our Creator, God seeks inspiration and integrity, sincerity and a spirit of sacrifice. He wants our outward expression to match our inward attitudes. He wants us not to worship ignorantly, but to know who He is. He wants it to be real.

That's hard for us. We fall into error so easily: We're either too emotional or not emotional enough, too rigid or too unstructured, too self-conscious or not self-aware enough. Most of all, we're apt to turn a worshipful heart into a routine behavior in the blink of an eye. What was sincere devotion yesterday is a performance for God's approval today. What was once an act of passion is now an act of obligation. Our hearts can grow cold faster than we ever thought.

In Deed

What is your worship like? Is it a Sunday ritual or a frenzied emotion that you can put on and take off? Is it limited to one style of music or a particular church? Most important, is it more than skin-deep?

God seeks those whose worship emanates from deep within. He desires legitimate praise and integrity between heart and mouth. He wants to be the One we treasure most. Most of all, He wants you. All of you.

To worship God is to realize the purpose
for which God created us.

—HERBERT CARSON

Chosen for a Reason

You are a chosen people . . . that you may
declare the praises of him who called you.

1 PETER 2:9

In Word

This is a remarkably encouraging passage of Scripture. It tells us of our chosenness, our royal role in this world, and our inheritance as children of the
most high God. We read verses like this and are amazed at the high and holy
nature of our calling. We realize that mercy has been lavished upon us and
we're in a privileged place. We are the ultimate rags-to-riches story.

But the amazing story doesn't end there. God hasn't just saved us and then
written "the end." There's more to the plot than that. We are chosen so that
we might declare His praises. As verse 9 continues, we have been transferred
from a kingdom of darkness to a kingdom of light. We were blind, but now
we see. We were hidden and then revealed. We were lost in a dark, murky
wilderness, then plucked out of it and placed on streets of gold glimmering
under the perpetual radiance of the Son. And according to this verse, there's a
more ultimate purpose to our salvation than ourselves. We are bestowed with
the honor of chosenness with the specific purpose of declaring His praises.

If you've never seen your worship as the ultimate purpose of your salvation, you're missing the best part of salvation. The place of glad worship is the
place of greatest blessing, of richest fellowship, and of true fulfillment. Salvation isn't complete until we praise Him for His mercy—daily, passionately,
honestly. We were bought with a price for a reason.

In Deed

Many believers get caught up in getting the most out of their salvation. Few
move on to giving the most out of their salvation. But those who do will realize one of the many paradoxes of the Kingdom: Giving it all results in getting
it all. A heart poured out in praise results in a heart filled with purpose. The
way of sacrifice leads to great gain. Losing your life in worship ends with
fulfilling your life in God. And that's exactly the reason for which you were
redeemed.

We are saved to worship God. All that Christ has done for us
in the past and all that He is doing now leads to this one end.

—A. W. TOZER

A Living Sacrifice

**I urge you, brothers, in view of God's mercy, to offer
your bodies as living sacrifices, holy and pleasing
to God—this is your spiritual act of worship.**
ROMANS 12:1

In Word

Since the days of the Exodus, wherever a tabernacle or temple stood, faithful Jews would bring the best of their flocks and herds to a priest standing at the altar of God. It was an act of devotion, a commandment handed down by God Himself. There were various reasons for the command: The offering would, at times, serve as a symbol of sin and its ugly consequences; as a sacrifice of gratitude, acknowledging that every good gift comes from God; or as an act of devotion and worship, a gift from a loving heart. Regardless of the reason, the origin of the sacrifice was always God—human beings clearly never created a ram or a bull—and the sacrifice was always a reminder of the horrible gap between the Creator and the created.

God bridged that gap with His ultimate sacrifice, of course—the body of Jesus on an altar made of Roman lumber. The wages of sin were paid in full. There are no more guilt offerings. All that was left for us to do is to place our lives in Him. Never before had such a gift been given, and never since. Those who accept it have no sin to work off, no condemnation to dread. We're left standing with nothing but our gratitude.

In Deed

There is, however, an appropriate response. It has nothing to do with merit or guilt, but only with the thankfulness that should naturally flow from a redeemed heart. It is our spiritual act of worship.

The response is for us to walk to that tabernacle or temple as the Israelites did in days of old, approach the Priest, and hand Him the sacrifice that we brought out of our gratitude: ourselves. We are to envision our Priest doing His duty by taking the sacrifice, placing it on the altar of God, and accepting it in His name. But unlike the old sacrifices, this sacrifice lives. It lives a dedicated life, an altar life. It now belongs to the Priest. We are in His hands.

> If Jesus Christ be God and died for me, then no
> sacrifice can be too great for me to make for Him.
> —C. T. STUDD

On the Altar

I urge you, brothers, in view of God's mercy, to offer
your bodies as living sacrifices, holy and pleasing
to God—this is your spiritual act of worship.
ROMANS 12:1

In Word

What does it mean to lay our lives on God's altar? Imagine a scene from the movies: In some distant tribal culture, one man saves another's life. According to custom, the saved now belongs to the savior. And why not? If not for the rescuer, the rescued one would be dead. His life rightfully belongs to the one who preserved it. He might as well spend the rest of his days for the one who actually gave him the rest of his days.

So it is with Jesus and His sheep. We were lost and, for all practical purposes, dead. That's not our preferred assessment of ourselves, but it's what the Bible says. Without Jesus, we'd be forever lost and lifeless. But He rescued us. And in His culture, we now belong to Him. We are to live out the rest of our days—the days He mercifully gave us—for Him.

That's what being a living sacrifice is all about. It means that when Jesus tells us to turn the other cheek, we don't have the right to say, "No, not this time." When Jesus tells us to give all we have—our time, our talents, our money, or even our deepest desires—to some aspect of His work, we don't have the authority to decline. We are not our own; we have no claim on our own lives. We were bought with a precious, heavy price. We were saved for the One who saved us.

In Deed

Just as Jesus laid Himself on God's altar for our sin, we are to lay ourselves on that altar for His righteousness. We don't earn His righteousness, of course. But practically, God puts it into us—He works it into our spirits— to the extent that we lay down our tainted lives in exchange for His resurrected one.

The implications of that relationship are astounding. Radical. Relentless. It was an "everything" purchase for a "forever" promise. Living sacrifices don't live for themselves. They live for Another. That's their service of worship.

Precisely because they have been redeemed at
such a cost, believers must be God's men.
—LEON MORRIS

Nonconformity

**Do not conform any longer to the pattern of this world,
but be transformed by the renewing of your mind.**
ROMANS 12:2

In Word

Imagine a culture in which there is no word to describe deception. No lie has ever been told and no one has even considered deviating from the truth. This culture has such clear lines of authority that it would occur to no one to assert his own rights—or violate another's. It has a complete absence of conflict, a perfectly united fellowship, and a plan that everyone single-mindedly pursues. There's no discord there, only harmony. It's the utopia that human beings have instinctively envisioned, yet never achieved.

Such was the culture of heaven before Satan fell like lightning from his high estate. As far as we can tell from Scripture, Lucifer's rebellion was an isolated incident. It drew many followers—one-third of heaven's hosts, according to many interpretations of Revelation 12:4—but was not in any way typical of the remainder of heaven's inhabitants. No, heaven's culture was perfect. Who—except for a being as prideful as Satan—would have wanted to mess it up?

We can't relate to a society in which evil is foreign. We're not nearly innocent enough for that. We've grown up with sin all around us, showing up in violence, bitterness and anger, lust and greed, and all sorts of idolatries. But in the enormous span of cosmic history, our earth has gone tragically wrong for only a well-defined moment—a brief sliver of eternity. What we've accepted as normal is drastically abnormal. God's eternal kingdom will not accept any elements of rebellion. Regardless of how comfortable we've been in the past with the human rebellion, we need to be terribly uncomfortable with it now. We have to change.

In Deed

Our worship of God is to involve a radical transformation to His culture—a society in which all disobedience is a horrifying thought. No lying, no lust, no discord, no rebellion. Our minds must fit the eternal patterns of heaven, not the momentary aberrations of earth. We are citizens of a very different kingdom than we've ever known. The ways of this world hold nothing for us anymore. Our conformity is over. Transformation must begin.

Measure your growth in grace by your sensitiveness to sin.
—OSWALD CHAMBERS

A Sacrifice of Love

Love the LORD, all his saints!
PSALM 31:23

In Word

Being a living sacrifice is more than a holy obligation; it is a holy passion. It's the lover who says, "I would do anything for you. I'd sacrifice my life, my dreams, my everything for your welfare." Few of us love God like that with any consistency, but that's our goal. And the only way to get there is to ask Him for that kind of love. It's supernatural. Only He can offer it and maintain it in our hearts.

How do we know if we have it? We'll know by what fills our minds when we lie down at night and when we wake up in the morning. We'll know it by where we direct all of our resources and all of our abilities. And we'll know it by the things we pray for.

If a stranger were to pick up the ledger of our checkbook and read it, would he know that we are lovers of God? If he were to examine our calendar, would he be able to tell that we have a holy desire for a beloved Savior? If he were to hear our prayers, would he find that we're wholly dedicated to the will of Another? We're reluctant to answer, because we know our shortcomings. We know how fickle our hearts and how self-directed our desires are. We know we have more than one agenda—God's plus our own. We know we have a long way to go to be filled with a holy, God-centered love.

In Deed

That's okay. God's grace is more than enough to cover our lukewarm hearts. But He doesn't want us to remain ambivalent toward Him. He wants to stir us up to a consuming obsession with His goodness, His love, and His plans. He wants us not just to try hard to please Him—we've done that and failed so many times—but to delight in Him. Like any lover of another, He wants to be our joy. Like a wife who craves evidence of her husband's affections, or a husband who looks expectantly for affirmation from his wife, our God—though never needy—wants to be adored.

Can we adore Him? We must—it's our created purpose, and it's the only love we'll ever have that will leave us completely satisfied. All others fall short, but passion for Him always fulfills.

> Love unites the soul with God; and the more
> love the soul has, the more powerfully it enters
> into God and is centered on Him.
>
> —JOHN OF THE CROSS

We Surrender All

If anyone would come after me, he must deny
himself and take up his cross daily and follow me.

LUKE 9:23

In Word

When you were first saved, or as you grew in your walk with Christ, you probably told God that you surrendered all of your desires, plans, skills, talents, relationships, and resources to Him. (If not, stop reading and consider doing that now.) That pledge is a serious one, and most of us have made it with all sincerity and even enthusiasm. We've begun to see ourselves as His possession, available for His purposes. We gave Him the keys to our lives—keys that we wrongly held as our own. And, according to His plan, He probably began to test our devotion.

That's the catch. The thought of letting Jesus have our all was liberating and relaxing when we first had it. But when He began to take our word for it, we balked. Did He remove a loved one from you? Let your peaceful circumstances erupt in chaos? Threaten your financial security? Limit the use of your time or talents? It hurt. It had to. He has to make our devotion more than theoretical. He will not let us live under an illusion that we have surrendered all to Jesus when we haven't. In our hearts, we have to let everything go but Him.

It's often a shock that God would actually take us up on some of our offered sacrifices. When we tell Him we'll go anywhere and do anything for the glory of His name, we have to mean it. He already knows whether we're authentic in our devotion, but do we? No, we have to notice our own reactions to be sure. When we develop hard feelings toward Him because He has not given us what we wanted, He has opened our eyes: We wanted some things more than we wanted Him.

In Deed

Did you mean it when you told God, "I give my life to You"? Then His removal of your props should be no surprise. We cannot "give" Him our lives and then complain when He takes them—or painfully touches them, or seemingly deprives them. Our lives are His. What business is it of ours if we are uncomfortable under His management? He has higher purposes than we do, and we trust Him. We've surrendered all.

No sin is small.

—JEREMY TAYLOR

Mysterious God

Clouds and thick darkness surround him.
PSALM 97:2

In Word

Can we worship someone we can't see clearly? It stretches us to try. We describe God's greatness in our praises and we give gratitude for the good things He has done, all the while knowing that we're missing the mark. Whatever we can conceive of when we think of God is going to fall woefully short of who He really is. The biggest, greatest, most awesome being we can imagine is an insufficient image of God. If our minds can come up with it, it won't measure up.

Perhaps that's why we are so prone to idolatry: We like to worship things we can see. Our adoration seems to beg for specifics. When we fall in love with a person, we adore the way she smiles or the way he walks. But when we fall in love with our God, what do we have to hang on to? His ways are mysterious, His thoughts higher than ours. Clouds and thick darkness surround Him.

That's why God sent us Jesus. "The Son is the radiance of God's glory and the exact representation of his being" (Hebrews 1:3). Though we can't completely comprehend Him, we can "see" Him. Even if we didn't walk Galilee and Judea all those years ago, we can see Him through the eyes of His disciples. We can know what He has said and how He has related to other human beings. We don't have to wonder, as did a popular song a few years ago, "What if God was one of us?" For a moment in time and through the eternal Word, He was. And is.

In Deed

Why do clouds and thick darkness surround God? Because seeing Him fully would blow a poor creature's circuits as completely as a million-volt current running through a 110-volt appliance. And also because there's this problem called sin. We are too small to comprehend Him naturally, and too unholy to comprehend Him righteously.

But we worship a God who has made Himself accessible. We take that for granted, but the rest of the universe is amazed. Avoid the idolatry that our limited vision craves. Jesus has pierced the cloudy darkness and invited us higher.

> Behold, the Heaven of heavens cannot contain thee, and thou sayest, Come ye all unto me.
> —THOMAS À KEMPIS

Beneath Rebellion

**The heavens proclaim his righteousness,
and all the peoples see his glory.**
PSALM 97:6

In Word

Beneath every skeptic's protests against the existence of God is a desire to be autonomous. Their objections are often a transparent mask. To acknowledge God and His righteousness would be to admit that humanity must bow down. That's an unappealing option for many, so the intellectual arguments come out and the clarity of truth gets obscured.

How do we know that pure, objective logic does not guide the skeptic? Because the Bible is clear: "The heavens proclaim [God's] righteousness, and all the peoples see his glory." The psalm was written at a time when many thought that only Israel saw His glory. But God has written the evidence for His existence—and His righteousness—into every human culture and into every dark corner of this world. The smoke-and-mirrors approach of agnostics and atheists will not hold water; even if their theories span centuries, they are still short-lived. And the misdirection strategies of those who worship idols will not hold water either. Tailor-made gods may appear to spring from religious sincerity, but they are simply one more human attempt to avoid the Righteous One. Our Sovereign has not spoken as subtly as many think.

In Deed

Be careful not to get drawn into religious issues as the world has framed them. There are only two categories of religion: the religion of those who accept the Righteous God, and the religions of those who avoid Him.

What does that mean in the daily life of the average Christian? It means that the bottom line in every conversation you have with a non-Christian about your faith is an authority issue. You don't have to point that out; just know that it's there. And it also means that the doubts you may struggle with are probably not an intellectual crisis. A question of authority often underlies them as well. Will you trust in God's sovereignty or strive for your own autonomy?

Doubts are normal for believers and unbelievers alike, but understand the battle of wills that is their source. His righteousness has been abundantly proclaimed, and all have seen His glory.

*Every revelation of God is a demand, and the
way to knowledge of God is by obedience.*
—WILLIAM TEMPLE

Opposed to Evil

Let those who love the LORD hate evil.
PSALM 97:10

In Word

God is relentless in His hatred of evil. We may think He tolerates it awfully well to let the world go on as it has for century upon century. But He hates evil. He has demonstrated at every turn His opposition to anything that conflicts with His character and corrupts His work. His judgments are certain. God and evil will not forever coexist.

We must ask ourselves if we love this God. We would hardly admit that we don't, but the biblical witness is clear: Those who love Him will hate evil. Those who love evil have opposed God. There can be no double-mindedness in the heart of man—not legitimately, and not permanently. The unredeemed cannot help but accept some form of evil, whether it is ideological or moral. And the redeemed cannot tolerate any form of evil—at least not in the long run. Our true love will tell on us. Sooner or later, we will demonstrate either a love for God or a love for corruption.

That doesn't mean a Christian can't vacillate between the two. But one of them will eventually win. Jesus told this truth to His disciples: "If anyone loves me, he will obey my teaching. . . . He who does not love me will not obey my teaching" (John 14:23-24). It doesn't get any clearer than that.

In Deed

An obedient Christian may or may not have love for God in his heart. But a Christian who loves God will necessarily be obedient. You can fake obedience, but you cannot hide love. It will come out in actions, and those actions will be increasingly marked by an absence of evil. Those who love the Lord will love His values.

Most of us have grown up in a society that has a high tolerance for evil. Our late-night shows laugh at it, our advertisements flaunt it, and our leaders wallow in it. We dismiss gross corruption because, after all, no one's perfect. We allow our own bad habits to become more deeply ingrained because, after all, we're not legalistic Puritans. And all the while God grieves. He hates evil and is zealous about purging it from the hearts of His people. May His righteous zeal become ours.

> The destined end of man is not happiness
> nor health, but holiness.
> —OSWALD CHAMBERS

Joy and Light

**Light is shed upon the righteous and
joy on the upright in heart.**
PSALM 97:11

In Word

We want our lives to be filled with light and joy. Yet so often, they aren't.
Discouragement, depression, and darkness threaten regularly. Why? Are we
targets of the dark enemy? Are we victims of circumstance in a fallen world?
Or might we be contributing to the problem ourselves?

There are many possible sources for our dark days, but one of them is a
possibility we'd rather not face. We don't want to think that we're responsible
for our downcast hearts, but we may be. God has given a promise. Those who
are righteous see light, and those who are upright in heart have joy. The blessings of a life that is right with God are certain.

Why don't we experience those blessings as often as we'd like? It can't be
that the promise of God has failed. Perhaps we have. Perhaps we are not righteous or upright in heart. Perhaps what is stealing our joy is a struggle within
us for dependence on Jesus' righteousness and victory over sin.

Think about it: We are most discouraged when we feel defeated. And
when do we feel defeated? When we know that God has commanded an obedience or an attitude that we just can't seem to comply with. In other words,
sin gets us down. The primary struggle in the human heart is a battle of the
will. When we lack joy, it may be because we're losing that battle—or, more
accurately, winning it when we shouldn't. The heart laments its own unbelief
and disobedience, and when it does, all peace leaves.

In Deed

Do you lack joy? It probably isn't a fault of your circumstances or your brain
chemistry, although those can certainly have their effects. Look first at your
heart. Is it questioning promises that God has emphasized? Is it reluctant to
surrender all your cares to Him? Does it trust His will and comply with His
purposes? Is it able to say, even when life is tough, that God's grace is greater?
Those are hard questions, but our internal struggles demand answers. We
can't know peace until these are settled. He has promised: Joy and light come
to those who are unreservedly His.

*The surest mark of a Christian is not
faith, or even love, but joy.*
—SAMUEL SHOEMAKER

Present in Praise

*While they were worshiping the Lord and fasting,
the Holy Spirit said, "Set apart for me Barnabas and
Saul for the work to which I have called them."*
ACTS 13:2

In Word

A lot can happen when people worship God. Many disciples were gathered together in Acts 2, presumably for worship, when the Holy Spirit came upon them in wind and fire. The church was born, the first sermon was preached, and amazing things began to happen in Jerusalem and beyond. In Acts 13, the Holy Spirit spoke with instructions: Send out Barnabas and Saul.

There seems to be a connection. When people worship God—really worship Him with love in their hearts and truth in their minds—the Holy Spirit is there. That's no coincidence. He inspires our worship, and the more we worship, the more deeply He dwells with us. The God who is enthroned on the praises of His people (Psalm 22:3, NASB) is mightily and manifestly present when we worship Him. If we want Jesus to be in our midst, all we need to do is follow His instructions: Gather two or more in His name. Worship brings the throne room of heaven into the company of our fellowship.

But He does more than just show up. He also fills us and gives direction. God may hesitate to instruct people who aren't serious about following Him. But a group of worshipers who have made it clear that He is their desire will hear Him. The volume of His voice grows louder when we worship. At this point of genuine worship in the early church, a mission to a lost world was launched.

In Deed

Have you ever wished for such specific direction from God? Be careful what you wish for; an obedient heart is a prerequisite for hearing His voice. But given such a heart, worship Him. Praise Him in the company of others with similar hearts.

This gathering of the Antioch leaders to worship and fast is too infrequently repeated in our age. But if we will spend our lives in worship, He will direct us in how to spend our lives.

*Be not afraid of saying too much in the praises
of God; all the danger is of saying too little.*
—MATTHEW HENRY

High Conformity

Be imitators of God.
EPHESIANS 5:1

In Word

A trap of the human conscience is to think that God wants us to be loving, gracious, generous, and all those other good things because He wants us to behave ourselves and get along with each other. That would, in fact, be a wonderful by-product of our spiritual maturity, but it isn't the goal. No, the goal is much deeper than that: It's to be like God.

As creatures designed to reflect His image, we've fallen tragically short of the goal. God's restoration offered in the Cross of Jesus and the gift of His Spirit puts us back on the image-of-God track. God wants us to be loving, gracious, generous, and all those other good things because He is all of those things. Any good father would want to instill his values and his character into his children. And our God is a very good Father. He wants us to be like Him.

That's a different approach to maturity than many of us usually take. We want to fulfill the requirements—at least the minimum—and get by with better-than-average growth. We seek a Christianized form of self-improvement. But God has so much more for us than self-improvement. His greater desire for us is God-conformity. We are being drawn by His Spirit into a new role—from servants to children. Both must comply with the Father's wishes. Only one can really inherit His genes and grow in His character.

In Deed

Have you approached the fruit of the Spirit as items on a list—a list that's primarily about you and your growth? Look higher than that. They are aspects of God's character that He is fully intent on having you share. He is relentless in pursuit of His image being found in you. He won't diverge from that goal. Neither should we.

God wants us to love because He is love. He wants us to be pure because He is pure. He wants us to forgive because He has forgiven. He wants us to give because He has given. The list could go on. And, in fact, it should. Everything we do should be done with one question in mind: Does this look like my Father?

We are shaped and fashioned by what we love.
—JOHANN WOLFGANG VON GOETHE

No Ordinary Love

Live a life of love, just as Christ loved us
and gave himself up for us as a fragrant
offering and sacrifice to God.

EPHESIANS 5:2

In Word

Nowhere in the New Testament is love defined simply as a common human emotion. Biblical love is much more radical than that. It extends farther than the world's love—to enemies and strangers; and it also goes deeper—to sacrificial offerings of adoration. We love because God adamantly insists that we be like Him. But if human experience isn't the template for biblical love, where do we go to take our cues? Jesus is our example.

Jesus loved us and gave Himself as an offering. He considered His own human feelings of no account; a higher consideration than self took Him to the Cross. He defined love for His disciples as laying down one's life for a friend, and He gave them an object lesson they would never forget. The visual illustration of this kind of love sticks with us as well. It's the example Paul gives to the Ephesians: We are to love in the same way that Christ loved us. Paul wrote to the Romans of the call to be a living sacrifice. Using Jesus as our model is a reiteration of the same theme.

Think of Jesus' kind of love: He embraced cheaters and prostitutes. He touched lepers and dead people. He was sometimes very tender and sometimes very harsh. He always told the truth, even when it hurt. He loved sinners but hated sin. He let people self-destruct—Pharisees, insincere seekers, Peter in his denial—never compromising principles for the sake of sentiment. He was incredibly patient with hardheaded disciples. And He bled.

In Deed

Does that description of Jesus' love reflect the kind of love we show each other in the church and in the world? Probably not. We have a long way to go. But there's no way we can worship this God without a desire to be like Him—especially in His love.

Paul frequently makes Jesus our prime example. So much for attainable goals! But a God worth worshiping would never settle for mediocrity anyway. We must press on. His love compels us.

He who is filled with love is filled with God Himself.

—AUGUSTINE

The Vineyard

My loved one had a vineyard on a fertile hillside.

ISAIAH 5:1

In Word

Long ago, God specifically told His people not to make images of Him because they would end up worshiping something less than who He is. But when God presents an image of Himself, His people should carefully take notice. The self-portraits He draws reveal who He is better than any other description. As is often said, a picture is worth a thousand words. At least.

One of the first images God presents of Himself in the prophets is as the owner of a vineyard. This vineyard is precious to Him. He planted it on the side of a fertile hill, and He tends it with great care. He expects great things of it, because it isn't just any vineyard. It's His. It's an expression of the heart of the Creator.

The vineyard, in an immediate sense, is God's description of Israel. In an eternal sense, it's a picture of all of His people. Humanity's first habitat was a garden because God is a Gardener. When God created this world, He planted human beings to grow and spread. When He chose Abraham as the father of faith, He planted a chosen nation to establish His praise in all the earth. When He sent Jesus into this world, He planted a Vine from whom all His branches could grow. God's gardening is a universal theme. He cultivates hearts for love and fruitfulness.

In Deed

If you have come into a relationship with Jesus by grace through faith, you are in the vineyard. You are a branch growing from the Vine, carefully cultivated, pruned, and nurtured by the Vinedresser. If you ever thought you were wandering aimlessly through life, surviving on your own, here is a clear affirmation from God that your life isn't aimless in the least. You were planted to grow and bear fruit.

Remember that when you get discouraged. There's nothing random about your existence. In fact, the Gardener who tends to all aspects of your life is known for His attention to detail. When God gave us this self-portrait, He showed how much He cares.

> The only priority that drives the Master of the vineyard is to bring us to fruitfulness. He will do whatever it takes to make that happen.
>
> —WAYNE JACOBSEN

The Vinedresser

**He dug it up and cleared it of stones and
planted it with the choicest vines.**

ISAIAH 5:2

In Word

The owner of the vineyard tends to it carefully. He clears it of stones, plants it with the very best vines, prunes it precisely, and harvests it with great enthusiasm. The fact that Isaiah's image of the Vinedresser is presented in the context of futility and frustration should not distract from this revelation of God. Regardless of our sin, He is still the Gardener who cares, who relentlessly cultivates, and who will not be disappointed in the end.

Historically, the point of this parable for Judah was that the Vinedresser was going to have to prune His vines severely. The sins of the nation were too great and the repentance too slow in coming for God to let the vines grow at will. This parable of the vineyard informed His people that His discipline would fall; Babylon would come and sack the holy city, and Judah's captivity would be devastating. The fruitless vineyard required drastic measures.

From an eternal view, however, the parable of the vineyard points more to the nature of God than to the nature of His people. Yes, we have sinned and need a Savior, and the Vinedresser has provided that. But in the heart of this master cultivator, we can also see His relentless pursuit of abundance—growth, fruitfulness, prosperity, and the finest finished product in the field. And His efforts never fall short.

In Deed

Though the parable of the vineyard was written to a nation, it has a personal application as well. We can legitimately view God as our personal vinedresser, the Gardener who is patiently, precisely, and effectively cultivating us for the best fruit possible. He's a master at His trade, so He knows exactly what He is doing with you—even when it hurts. He can be trusted.

Rest in His care today. Trust Him with the time and weather, the harsh elements of your surroundings, the other branches on the vine—with everything. Realize that He's even more committed to your abundance than you are.

*You—one magnificent branch in the Father's
vineyard—were made for abundance.*

—BRUCE WILKINSON

The Vine

Then he looked for a crop of good grapes.
ISAIAH 5:2

In Word

God is looking for a good crop in the lives of His people. He has planted, cultivated, and watched over His vineyard, and He anticipates a bountiful harvest. Before Jesus died on the cross and was resurrected, that harvest was often meager, as in the case of Isaiah's audience. Jesus Himself demonstrated the unfruitfulness of God's people by causing a fig tree to wither and telling His own parables of disappointing vineyards. But He also spoke of abundant life, rivers of living water, and branches that bear much fruit. His life—as He lived it on earth and as He now lives it in us—is the good crop God is look-ing for.

We sometimes lose that insight in the details of our daily lives, and that causes us to stumble. We begin to think that God defines a good crop as more productivity: more time in prayer, more Bible verses memorized, more people served, more church services attended, and more good deeds done. All of those can be part of a good crop if—and only if—they flow through a branch that is intimately attached to the Vine Himself. Grapes that come by any other means are not really grapes at all.

Grapes that come from the true Vine, however, are sweet and succulent, nearly bursting as they are harvested. They have drawn their flavor and aroma from the life of the Vine, and they are exactly what the Vinedresser had in mind when He planted His vineyard. He looks at them with delight.

In Deed

Believe it or not, that's God's plan for your life: to look at you with delight. You might have thought His plan was entirely about being a better, more productive disciple, but those are poor words that pale in comparison to the picture of the vineyard. God's ultimate intention in your life—today and forever—is to look at your Vine-fed heart with utter delight.

That should remove your pressure to perform and free you to love and flourish. As the Vinedresser watches you today, let Him see your beauty.

> As the vine sends its energy through the branch to bear fruit, so Christ can send His energy through you.
> —JOHN MACARTHUR

The Vinedresser's Sacrifice

What more could have been done for my vineyard than I have done for it?
ISAIAH 5:4

In Word

"I had planted you like a choice vine of sound and reliable stock," God says to Israel (Jeremiah 2:21). "How then did you turn against me into a corrupt, wild vine?" Jeremiah's refrain is a haunting echo of the song of the vineyard in Isaiah. The Vinedresser was incredulous. How could such agricultural expertise have resulted in so little fruit? It just didn't make sense.

But in a way, God's question in Isaiah 5:4 is rhetorical. There was something more the Vinedresser could do, and He did it in the Gospels. In one of Jesus' parables, He said that the owner sent His Son into the vineyard to hold the tenants accountable, but the tenants killed Him (Matthew 21:33-40). The Son made the ultimate sacrifice for the harvest.

Harvests don't come cheaply. Any farmer can tell you that. A good harvest requires a lot of labor, wisdom, and love, and that's exactly what God has provided on our behalf. Paul addressed this concept in Romans 8:32: "He who did not spare his own Son, but gave him up for us all—how will he not also, along with him, graciously give us all things?" In other words, a serpent's lie in the Garden notwithstanding, God has not withheld anything from His people. He has paid extraordinary costs for extraordinary blessings. He was determined to have His harvest.

In Deed

Jesus knew exactly what He was doing when He told that parable in Matthew 21. He was boldly and bluntly pointing to Isaiah 5 and telling the Jewish leaders that they had not borne the fruit God intended; but even their fruitlessness would have been forgiven if they had accepted the Vine. The key to fruitfulness is to accept it.

Make Isaiah's question personal: "What more could God have done for me than He has already done—or than He will continue to do?" The answer is, "Nothing." God would not have made such a high sacrifice for you to abandon it now. He will see fruit in your life. Ask Him for it today.

He offered His cross to God as a sacrifice in order to make us all rich.
—EPHREM

The Vineyard Song

I will sing for the one I love a song about his vineyard.
ISAIAH 5:1

In Word

We should all end where the parable of the vineyard begins: singing a song for the One we love. This vineyard song is a sweeping story of tender love and bitter betrayal, of sin and redemption, of power and purpose. In a few short verses, it summarizes the entire Old Testament and sets up the New. It reveals the heart of the Creator.

Somehow the song of the vineyard captures God's heart so much better than a prose description of Him. So do the other images presented in the prophets; God is a Husband, a Father, a Potter, a Refiner, a Builder, a Lion, and much more. These images are prophetic poetry, and they remind us again and again that a picture is worth a thousand words. So when God describes Himself to us, He uses pictures. And when we describe Him to others, we would be wise to do the same.

You can present many pictures of God to others by telling them how He relates to you as your Father, your Beloved, your Teacher, and more. But there's one picture God gave us of Himself that stands out above the rest, and it's a pattern for us as well. God gave us the picture of Jesus—the Son is the exact representation of the Father's nature (Hebrews 1:3). Likewise, Jesus told each of us to be a picture of Him. We are being conformed to His image because (1) we were made in that image on day six of creation and (2) we are to reflect the glory of His image forever. In other words, when you want to present a picture of God to your world, consider being one.

In Deed

Your life can be prophetic poetry, you know. God doesn't give the world a fact sheet about you; He gives it a story, a biography. You are an epic of triumphs and tragedies, of dreams and disappointments, and of sin and salvation. In a very real sense, you are a song of the vineyard.

Sing that song, and sing it well. Your epic isn't a private matter; it's a picture that reveals the heart of the Vinedresser. And it's a picture that the rest of the vineyard desperately needs to see.

> The Christian should resemble a fruit tree, not a Christmas tree. For the fruit grows on a fruit tree, whereas the decorations are only tied on to a Christmas tree.
>
> —JOHN STOTT

God-Man

My Lord and my God!
JOHN 20:28

In Word

The resurrected Jesus showed His wounds to the doubting disciple, and flood-lights filled Thomas's mind with truth. He couldn't restrain his reaction: He not only called Jesus "Lord"—he had likely done that many times before—but he called Him "God." That doesn't flow easily from the mouth of one human being to another. Only a crisis of the soul can lead us to such a conclusion. Thomas had such a crisis. He had doubted the Resurrection and then was confronted with the incarnate Word about the matter. It blew his mind.

The same thing happened to Paul on the road to Damascus. Initially, Paul didn't know whom he had seen, but he knew enough to call Him "Lord" (Acts 9:5-6). The response must have been staggering: "I am Jesus, whom you are persecuting." Like Thomas, it blew Paul's mind.

This world isn't very comfortable with God-men. We've only had one— the only One—and He didn't fare too well in public opinion polls. Neither have His disciples. We've had a hard time convincing the skeptics that there really are holes in the hands and feet, and that there really is a dazzling Lord who can appear to His persecutors whenever He wants. Many in the church are not exactly comfortable with the deity of Jesus, either. Teacher, Healer, Prophet, and such titles are generally not a problem. Even "Lord" seems to fit. But God Himself? In human flesh? A rabbi in the Middle East a couple of millennia ago? We're not sure we want to go that far.

In Deed

The story of Thomas's moment of truth is noteworthy because of Jesus' silence on the subject of His deity. Thomas calls Him "God" to His face—and Jesus never corrects him! Angels who are mistakenly worshiped in Scripture correct their worshipers, but not Jesus. He let it go. He let it go because Thomas wasn't wrong. His moment of truth was entirely true.

And that's critical for us to grasp. We can't worship the Father in truth without worshiping the Son. Maybe it takes a crisis of the soul to get there, but we must. Jesus is our God in the flesh—and that blows our minds.

> If Jesus Christ is not true God, how could He help us?
> And if He is not true man, how could He help us?
> —DIETRICH BONHOEFFER

Ends of the Earth

**Ask of me, and I will make the nations your
inheritance, the ends of the earth your possession.**

PSALM 2:8

In Word

This psalm is about the Messiah, and it emphasizes a solid biblical theme: From the call of Abraham to the praises of Revelation, God's Kingdom is a worldwide promise. His heart is global in scope. Worship is appropriate in every culture, every language, and every corner of this planet. God has a holy agenda for the ends of the earth.

Let that sink in, and then ask yourself a question: Why is it that you can go to a backwoods village in the forbidding mountains of Bhutan and find icons of Western culture—but no church? Why does the neon glow of soda logos shine brighter there than the image of the Cross? Why do so many of the remote citizens of this world know the name of our tennis shoes but not the name of our Savior?

Our message is more compelling than soft drinks and sportswear. It changes lives more drastically than blue jeans and pop music can. It is more profound than our advertising jingles. And yet our quest for a global market has driven us farther and faster than our quest for a global salvation.

Perhaps it is not our fault. Logos and songs have fewer enemies than Jesus does. There is greater resistance against a gospel of repentance and grace than against a gospel of pop culture. American idols don't demand a radical change of heart; Jesus does. The obstacles to His mission are great.

In Deed

Even so, there must be more we can do. When we read Psalm 2 and worship our Savior, we must be struck by the magnitude of our apathy. His heart extends to the nations. Does ours? His mission will not let Him rest until every lonely goatherd in every remote valley is reached. Will ours? Corporate executives have figured out how to saturate their market. Why haven't we?

These are hard questions. Many Christians have a heart for all nations, but not one that will sacrifice anything to see the Savior there. But a heart that really loves Him will be passionate about His mission. Are you?

Christian mission is the only reason for our being on earth.

—ANDREW MURRAY

Here I Am

[God] said to him, "Abraham!" "Here I am," he replied.
GENESIS 22:1

In Word

God called upon Abraham with a test. It was perhaps the most difficult test any of us could think of. Did the thought of sacrificing his own son horrify Abraham? Did he weep all night before he got up and went to Moriah? The text doesn't say. All it says is that Abraham obeyed. And that obedience began with a simple statement of readiness: "Here I am."

The army recruit learns to say "Here I am" when the drill sergeant barks out his name. But his availability is born out of fear. The consequences are more undesirable than the obedience. There is no love in his readiness, no real respect—just fear. He is available, but the relationship means nothing.

The employee learns to say "Here I am" when the boss calls her name. But her availability is born out of duty. It isn't bad, just superficial. Negative consequences or not, an allegiance to the cause will prompt the right response. She obeys because she should. She is available, but the relationship isn't warm.

A romantic naturally says "Here I am" because of love. Availability isn't induced by fear or duty, and negative consequences aren't an issue. There's a desire to please. There is an implicit trust in the other's wishes. There is a respect that goes beyond obligation; it has been both earned and invited.

In Deed

We know that Abraham feared God and that he was obligated to God. But somewhere wrapped up in his reverence and duty was the simple desire to please the Lord who had graciously provided the son. His response was more than that of a slave or a subordinate. It came from the heart; it had to, considering the command. It meant that Abraham had cast his affections on a very trustworthy God.

When God calls, do you say "Here I am"? Probably so. But here's a deeper question: How do you say it? Let your response flow from a loving, reverential faith in your Provider. Trust Him. His loving command is an invitation to love Him in return.

> Love for God and obedience to God are so completely involved in each other that either one of them implies the other too.
> —F. F. BRUCE

A Godly Hunger

"My food," said Jesus, "is to do the will of him who sent me and to finish his work."

JOHN 4:34

In Word

How do we honor God? One of the best ways is to breathe His desires and to crave His will. There aren't many of us in His body who do that consistently; it isn't very natural, and it doesn't appeal at all to the fallen self. But if we knew the glory and the peace of being at one with His will, we'd have no greater craving. God's desire for us is for us to desire only Him.

To desire God goes beyond the need for His fellowship that we so desperately seek. It is a desire with feet. It works. It isn't content with only the emotional side of the relationship; it must put godly emotions and allegiances into action. Our desire for Him necessarily includes a desire to work with Him. There's no way to separate our love and our will.

Jesus didn't seek to do His Father's will only from a sense of obligation. There was no drudgery in it. It wasn't a matter of gritting His teeth and getting it done so He could go about His other business. There was no other business. This was His food—His life, His breath, His passion. Doing the Father's will was the entire preoccupation of His life. And at the end of John's Gospel, Jesus tells His disciples that they are sent out in the same way the Father sent Him (20:21). His food is their food. His love of the Father's will was to be theirs. And ours.

In Deed

How can we accomplish such a thing? There's no way other than God's way: He fills us with His Spirit. It is He who is working in us, both to will and to work for the Father's purposes (Philippians 2:13). Not only does He give us what our hearts desire, He gives us the very desires in our hearts (Psalm 37:4). He puts them in there, if we've submitted our hearts to Him with delight.

Is God's will your food? Do you seek to accomplish His will as a bonus to pursuing your own, or is His the only one you really care about? The single-mindedness of being passionate about His will is liberating. Crave His will alone.

The will of God is the measure of things.

—AMBROSE

Glorified in Need

Those troubled by evil spirits were cured, and
the people all tried to touch him, because power
was coming from him and healing them all.
LUKE 6:18-19

In Word

What would we know of Jesus if everyone had taken care of their own problems? What would Jesus have done if all of His hearers had been self-sufficient? Would He have been proud of them? Given His blessing and moved on? Sadly, the nature of Jesus would have remained unrevealed in any place with a high standard of health and welfare.

That fact should not escape us. We often try to clean ourselves up for God so that He won't have to expend so much time, so much effort—so much mercy—to keep us going. We sometimes feel guilty about needing so much from Him. We don't want to be the problem child.

But God specializes in problem children. The parable of the Prodigal Son in Luke 15 should be enough to convince us: The good older brother who complained about the favor given to his younger, more rebellious sibling actually turned out to be the greater problem for the father. That son's self-sufficiency made him harder to reach and caused him to question the father's mercy. And throughout His ministry Jesus' response to the religious authorities should convince us as well: Those who "have it all together" don't really have it at all. And God can do little for them.

In the four Gospels, it was the sinners, the prostitutes, the tax collectors, the lepers, and the demon-possessed who glorified Jesus. How? In their need. They became the platform for Him to demonstrate His mercy. We can do that too.

In Deed

Are you aware that your neediness honors God? Well, in our experience it isn't always an occasion for His glory; but it can be—if you will present it to Him humbly and without using your own devices to supersede His. Don't catch yourself lamenting that you are a high-maintenance disciple. We need to be high maintenance. We need to realize that we can't—and shouldn't—maintain ourselves. He is glorified in the way that He keeps us, heals us, restores us, and builds us up.

O God, never suffer us to think that we can
stand by ourselves, and not need Thee.
—JOHN DONNE

The Artist

Like clay in the hand of the potter,
so are you in my hand.
JEREMIAH 18:6

In Word

We're involved in a lifelong art project. We want our lives to turn out the best possible way for us, so we are consumed with crafting circumstances, people, work, and dreams to our advantage. We plan for the best education, the best job, the best family, the best neighborhood, the best everything we can think of, constantly trying to shape ourselves into the right form. Whether consciously or not, we are diligent craftsmen.

There's a Craftsman more skilled than us, though, and if we would trust Him to shape us into something more beautiful, He would. After all, clay can't really do much on its own. When we try to make art of ourselves, we end up with slightly reshaped clay. But when the Master Artist makes art of us, His work can be breathtaking. He has a grander vision of beauty than we do.

We are reluctant to relax in the hands of the Potter for one main reason: We forget why we exist. We assume that clay exists for the sake of its own feelings or dreams. We focus on "clay esteem," "clay actualization," or "clay fulfillment," oblivious to the infinitely larger purpose of our formation. Clay really exists for the Potter alone. When the Artist is allowed to do His work, the clay displays the creativity of His heart and mind.

In Deed

Are you allowing the Potter to do His work? Never resist it, even though there's no guarantee that it will be a comfortable process. In fact, it almost certainly won't be; if clay could feel, the bending and twisting would likely be excruciating.

The trials of your life are like the tools of a potter. They gouge you for the sake of beauty. But the finished product is glorious. It has to be; it comes from the heart of the Potter. Trust Him completely. There's nothing more beautiful than His artwork.

God's fingers can touch nothing but to mold it into loveliness.

—GEORGE MACDONALD

The Artist's Design

The pot he was shaping from the clay was
marred in his hands; so the potter formed it into
another pot, shaping it as seemed best to him.
JEREMIAH 18:4

In Word

A potter isn't very emotionally engaged with mass-produced pottery. In fact, in mass production, the potter is usually a machine. But our Potter is deeply invested in His work. He crafts each piece individually with a specific design in mind, and He loves what He does.

Our Potter, however, has a problem that no other potter has. The clay in His hands has a mind of its own. It should be thrilled to be touched by the Master, but it develops its own ideas of beauty and comfort. It wants an identity of its own, largely independent of the Craftsman who put it on the wheel in the first place. Clay with a mind of its own has the potential to be astoundingly beautiful—a living, breathing masterpiece. Sadly, it also has the potential to be stubbornly, ignorantly insistent on its own ugliness. And when that happens, the Potter weeps.

That happens a lot. The Potter's plan is to display His artistry, but if a piece of clay isn't allowing His craftsmanship, He'll contrive some pretty drastic measures. He'll press it into a ball and start over. He'll take the same clay and use a different approach. His goal is beauty, and He will stop at nothing to achieve it.

In Deed

Ask yourself two questions today: What does the Potter dream of doing in my life? and What is He actually doing right now? Don't answer too quickly. Consider the heart of the Potter—His ultimate goal, His tender care, and His exquisite artistry. And then apply His heart to your present circumstances.

Those questions will launch you into a reorientation that every piece of clay needs to go through: a shift from a clay-perspective to a potter-perspective. We need to see our circumstances today in light of eternal glory. We need to see ourselves as expressions of His delight. When we do, our hardness will turn to softness, our stubbornness will give way to compliance, and our trials will become much more meaningful.

When a man is wrapped up in himself, he
makes a pretty small package.
—JOHN RUSKIN

The Artist's Mercy

If that nation I warned repents of its evil, then I will relent and not inflict on it the disaster I had planned.
JEREMIAH 18:8

In Word

Repentance is a much-maligned word. It sounds so hard and painful, even condemning. Those connotations don't go over well in a laid-back, life's-a-beach culture of tolerance like ours. Repentance implies that something is wrong with us and we're going to have to deny ourselves something we treasure in order to change. That's a biblical truth we don't enjoy memorizing.

Maybe it would help us to think about repentance in terms of clay. Clay that has lost its moisture, that is hardening and no longer pliable, is unrepentant clay. If that thickening process isn't too far along, the Potter can add some water and soften it up. But if the clay is too dry and stiff, there's nothing to be done. It has to be tossed out.

Based on that illustration, repentance sounds like a good plan, doesn't it? It is a matter of regaining pliability in order to be useful to the Master Artist. David demonstrated it when Nathan confronted him about his sin with Bathsheba, and Nineveh demonstrated it when its citizens repented after Jonah's prophecy of destruction. In both cases, the Potter was merciful and the clay became useful again. Repentance was a very worthwhile event.

In Deed

Our Potter's grand design depends on the malleability of His clay. If we are too stiff and unyielding, God has no compassionate alternative to informing us of our impending uselessness—the disaster the prophets proclaimed. If we accept the warning, however, we become soft and easy to reshape, and the Potter enjoys us again. He always has a good plan for clay that bends.

Are there any areas in which your heart needs to bend? Yes, it sounds painful, but the alternative is far worse. Softening the substance of your life makes the Potter delightfully willing to make something beautiful. His blessings come to those who bend.

> One of the first things for which we have to pray is a true insight into our condition.
> —OLIVE WYON

The Artist's Integrity

If at another time I announce that a nation or
kingdom is to be built up and planted, and if it does
evil in my sight and does not obey me, then I will
reconsider the good I had intended to do for it.

JEREMIAH 18:9-10

In Word

The Potter is focused on outcomes. While He is spinning the wheel, softening the clay, cutting the design, and firing the kiln, He is preoccupied with one thing: what the piece will look like in the end. He may enjoy the process with some lumps of clay and find others tedious, but the process is insignificant in light of the value of the final image. The beauty of the art is in His mind the whole time.

In verses 7 to 10 of Jeremiah 18, God is focused on how His people finish. Not where we start, but where we end. If we start with apathy or rebellion but respond to His warnings, He blesses. If we start with responsiveness and end with rebellion or apathy, He reconsiders His blessings. Jesus made that clear in His parable of the two sons: one said he wouldn't work in the father's vineyard, then did; the other said he would, then didn't (see Matthew 21:28-32). Only one, Jesus said, fulfilled his father's plan.

That principle applies to nations—as in Jeremiah and Isaiah—and to individuals, as in every biblical call to obedience. Our Potter is known for His extravagant mercy toward His clay. But clay meant for glory can end up in the trash. Extravagant mercy can be taken for granted and squandered.

In Deed

There's a difference between faith and presumption, but Christians confuse them often. We take God's promises for granted. True faith leads to gratitude and service; presumption leads to complacency. And God's mercy is rarely grasped by the complacent.

Don't presume on grace. If God has promised you blessing—and He has, you know—meet the conditions of the promise. Love Him, comply with Him, trust Him. In every detail of your life, follow His heart. In His integrity, the Potter will shape you not only according to His will, but also according to yours. Finish well.

Complacency is a deadly foe of all spiritual growth.

—A. W. TOZER

The Artist's Workshop

**Go down to the potter's house, and
there I will give you my message.**
JEREMIAH 18:2

In Word

When God spoke to Jeremiah, He didn't just give him some information to pass on to Israel. He sent him to a potter's house to get the full impact of an illustration. It goes back to God's practice of sometimes giving us pictures rather than words. If Jeremiah could see a potter at work, he would know God's heart in a way that nothing else could show him.

That's true for us too. If our lives are to have any message at all, it isn't going to come from an exchange of information with God. It's going to come from experience—God at work in our lives, showing us what He is like, giving us visual aids to things like His mercy, purpose, and power. That has always been His way. He didn't just tell Israel He was their deliverer; He actually delivered them from Egypt. He didn't just tell them He was a holy judge; He judged them all the way to Babylon. He didn't just give us a description of Himself; He came in the flesh as Jesus. When God wants to get a point across, He speaks the language of experience.

That should be a pattern for us as well. The world will not be changed by Christians who speak a lot of words (though the gospel in the form of words is important). Words won't mean much unless there's a picture to go with them: a picture of Jesus, of faith, of Christianity, of changed lives. With Jeremiah, God spoke of Himself through a visual illustration of a potter. With us, He often speaks of Himself through a visual illustration of a redeemed child of God.

In Deed

God is speaking to your world. How could He not? He's the living Word. The living Word is not interested in being silent; He's interested in calling a lost world to Himself. And His voice—His illustrations, metaphors, pictures, and descriptions—are found primarily in the people who have experienced Him and who worship Him. Those who have gone down to the Potter's house— who have spent an extraordinary amount of time intently watching God and admiring His work—are those who are entrusted with this message: the Potter will take any lump of clay and make it beautiful.

Witnessing is not something we do; it is something we are.
—ANONYMOUS

The God Who Wounds

**He wounds, but he also binds up; he
injures, but his hands also heal.**

JOB 5:18

In Word

Have you suffered wounds from God? We'd prefer never to know pain at
His hands, but the Bible gives us no such promise. What we are promised is
comforting, but much less relaxing than what we'd like to hear. We want a
god who will always give us what we want and will never teach us hard les-
sons. We want to be conformed to the image of Jesus without the chisel that
shapes us. But God's hand, though always good, isn't always easy. He takes us
through not only joys and comfort, but also pain. A quick survey of Scripture
should be enough to convince us. Just ask Job—or Abraham, Joseph, David,
Jeremiah, Daniel, John the Baptist, John the disciple, Peter, Paul, Stephen, or
any other character God used. The godly life is joyful but painful.

Or we could just ask our living Lord. That sacred head once wounded
has a testimony for us: Those who worship God yet live in this world will be
traumatized by the contradictions between the two. Count on it. And it isn't
just an unfortunate spiritual dynamic; the God we worship has ordained it.
Whether for correction or character, it's from Him.

Is that unsettling? Don't worry; His wounds are never deeper than they
must be, and never beyond His ability to heal. In fact, He has promised to heal
them. But we must have them if He is to shape us. There's no way we can be
like Jesus and yet wear no scars in this world.

In Deed

Did you think the Christian life was going to be without pain? No. Look at
Jesus. Look at His disciples. Look at two thousand years of church history.
Or, closer to home, look at the headlines. The crucified Lord has a crucified
church. It's the only path to resurrection.

No, the Christian life is by no means without pain. It can't be, not if it's
real and if it exists in a hostile world. And not if we're going to be like Jesus.
But neither is it without comfort and healing. That's why we can worship the
God who wounds as well as the God who restores. He knows what He is
doing; He is preparing us for glory.

> No pain, no palm; no thorns, no throne; no
> gall, no glory; no cross, no crown.
>
> —WILLIAM PENN

Image Reflectors

So God created man in his own image.
GENESIS 1:27

In Word

As the culmination of His creation, God made man. Why would He do such a thing? What was He lacking in His heaven? There were angels who worshiped Him, worked for Him, and served Him faithfully. We hear of cherubim and seraphim, but only God knows how many other orders of created beings there were before He created us. He could have anything He wanted. Why humanity?

Have you ever considered what it means to be made in the image of God? It doesn't mean that we're omniscient or omnipotent. That's all too clear. It also doesn't mean that we're pure and holy. That's clear as well. What did He want from us? Why did He find it meaningful to create a being who resembled—in some manner and in some degree—Himself?

Perhaps the angels cannot feel the pleasure and passion of God. Perhaps they do not know the many kinds of love that God has made us capable of. Perhaps they can't express the grief and anger over sin and destruction that we can. Perhaps there was no one in this heaven who knew anything substantial about mercy and grace. So God made man.

Think about what it means to resemble God—spiritually, emotionally, and at levels we may never fully understand. The angels can worship God; in fact, they do that all day long where it is always day. But they cannot reflect Him. Only someone made in His image can shine His glory back to Him. It may only be a glimpse or a spark of glory, but millions of images of God can make a dazzling display from where He sits. We are, in essence, little glory reflectors. Only creatures that resemble the Creator can do that.

In Deed

That's perhaps why sin so angers a holy God. Not only is it so unlike Him, it is such a tragic loss. It represents a wasted opportunity to shine glory. It clouds the mirror that would reflect the image of God.

But God has cleaned us up. His image was exactly expressed in Jesus, and He has put Jesus' Spirit within us. In Adam we were made in God's image; in Jesus we are remade in His image (2 Corinthians 3:18). Reflect Him well.

> You and I were created to tell the truth about God by reflecting His likeness. How many lies have you told about God today?
>
> —IAN THOMAS

For His Honor

He must become greater; I must become less.
JOHN 3:30

In Word

People had been flocking to John in the wilderness, seeking the baptism of repentance and soaking up the words of a bona fide prophet. John had even gotten the attention of Judea's most influential classes, as both Pharisees and Sadducees came to hear his teaching (Matthew 3:7). His ministry had gathered steam, and he was on a roll. Clearly, God was working in his life. The man in whom the Holy Spirit had dwelled since the day of his birth (Luke 1:15) was popular among the masses and a threat to the elite. He was a rising star.

No wonder, then, that his disciples were a little concerned with the Galilean who was starting up His own ministry. Their rising star had a rival, at least in their eyes. They had hitched themselves to a prophet whose influence was rapidly declining while Another's rose. Israel needed John's message; his disciples were just sure of it. So they approached John with this serious problem: This Galilean that John had testified about was stealing John's sheep.

John assured his disciples that the sheep were now following the right Shepherd. He also confirmed their insecurity over John's status. The other Teacher was, in fact, the greater one. His influence must rise at all costs—even if it meant the end of John's prophetic ministry. Jesus must become greater, and John must fade away.

In Deed

John put words to the attitude that every believer should maintain: In every situation, we must defer to Jesus. He is God incarnate, and God does not yield His glory to others (Isaiah 48:11). Nor should He. It's a travesty when our service points to us and not to Him. It's shameful when our words give credit to human beings and not to Him. It's tragic when the world looks at us and sees only us. Instead of our being the supporting actors and Jesus being the star, we often get the roles reversed. But Jesus is more than a supporting actor, and we are not rightfully stars. Every day, repeat John's words: He must become greater; I must become less.

> The soul stands at salute when Jesus passes by.
> —ANONYMOUS

The Cheerful Giver

God loves a cheerful giver.
2 CORINTHIANS 9:7

In Word

Is God short of funds? If so, whatever happened to His power and His sovereignty? Why is He always trying to drum up support for His work? And if not, why does He expect us to give? If the coffers are already full—if He truly owns the cattle on a thousand hills (Psalm 50:10)—why in the world does He ask for our resources?

Because God loves a cheerful giver. If we ever wanted a heart that beats with God's, this is the way to get it. We who have freely received enormous grace and extravagant mercy ought to have liberal generosity flowing from our hearts. Heaven's riches have been poured out on us. Sometimes it is a financial windfall, sometimes it is material or experiential, sometimes it is the giftings of His Spirit. And it is always grace—the forgiveness of our most grievous sins and the unmerited favor of receiving all we ever need in every area of our lives.

But not all of us experience such favor. Why not? There may be many reasons, but one of them is thinking that God's gifts to us end with us. We aren't just to be recipients, accepting what God has given for our own use, minus the 10 percent tip we owe Him. No, we are to be streams of blessing to others in every area that God has blessed us. That includes financially. If money flows liberally out, God will, in principle and with rare exceptions, ensure that our sufficiency flows liberally in. He gives so that we'll give. And He gives cheerfully so that we'll give cheerfully.

In Deed

The Greek word for "cheerful" in this verse is the same word from which we get "hilarious." God loves a hilarious giver—someone who is not just comfortable with generosity but delighted with it. Not just someone who will answer an appeal for funds, but one who will seek out ways to bless with them. If our outflow in His name is great, our inflow in His name will be greater still.

But there's a higher motivation than that. We are to give because we are children of the chief Cheerful Giver. Is He the only One who loves a cheerful giver? No. So do we.

A cheerful giver does not count the cost of what he gives. His heart is set on pleasing and cheering him to whom the gift is given.
—JULIAN OF NORWICH

God-Centered Worship

The LORD reigns, let the nations tremble.
PSALM 99:1

In Word

If we are to be true worshipers of our God, we must undergo a radical change of perspective. All humans have grown up self-centered in this world, looking out for our own concerns and planning our own agenda. We aren't necessarily selfish, just self-directed. From our first cry in the cradle to our complaints of today, we have made it clear: We're all about us.

But the Bible points us in a different direction. From Genesis 1 to Revelation 22, it's all about Him. He created the world for His purposes, and He will fulfill them. The books of Moses are really the books of God. The psalms of David are really the psalms about God. The Acts of the Apostles should really be called the Acts of God. And our lives, too, end up with inappropriate names: The biography of "so-and-so" is nothing more than the story of what God did—or didn't do—in a person's life. We aren't independent creatures. We exist for a greater purpose—a greater Person, actually.

That's why, while our worship will always express gratitude for what God has done in our lives, it must first and foremost be about what God has done—period.

In Deed

How do we know when we have the right perspective? When we're able to praise God for His holiness, even though it resulted in His discipline to correct our unholiness, we're there. When we're able to praise Him for His healing power, even though someone else received it while we remain sick, we understand. When we're able to worship His righteous judgments, whether or not they fall favorably on us, we get it.

Are you there? Not many people are. But that's the goal of God-centeredness. It delights in the victories God has won, the lives He has touched, the diseases He has healed, the failures He has forgiven—even if they're not our victories, lives, diseases, or failures. If we rejoice that He reigns, even when His reign makes us tremble, we can know: God is the center of our worship.

> You awaken us to delight in Your praise.
> —AUGUSTINE

God-Centered Prayer

For your sake, O Lord, look with favor
on your desolate sanctuary.
DANIEL 9:17

In Word

"Glorify Your name." That was essentially the prayer of Moses when God offered to destroy the idolatrous Israelites and bless Moses' descendants (Exodus 32:9-14). That was the prayer of Ezra when asking the king for protection would have contradicted Ezra's claims that God was Israel's security (Ezra 8:21-23). That was the prayer of Jesus just days before the Crucifixion (John 12:28). That was the prayer of David in many of the psalms. And that was the prayer of Daniel as he confessed Israel's sins and asked for the fulfillment of Jeremiah's prophecy of deliverance.

In fact, that is essentially the prayer of everyone who prays with power: that God would glorify His name. It isn't that asking God to meet our needs is wrong; there's just a greater issue at stake. God's reputation comes first. His renown should be a greater concern than our immediate needs. We should be entirely focused on what He is doing in this world and how our needy situation relates to it.

That doesn't mean that we should never ask God to meet our needs— spiritual, physical, emotional, material, psychological, relational, or whatever else we truly need or even desire. It does mean, however, that even in our deepest crises, our prayers should be God-centered. There's a huge difference between praying, "Lord, please give me what I need so I can be content and fulfilled," and "Lord, please give me what I need so You can be honored as the Giver of all good things." Both are okay; the latter is clearly more in line with a Christian's worship.

In Deed

If your prayers are filled with your concerns and little else, try a different approach. Pray that God would glorify Himself by meeting your needs, delivering you, healing you, comforting you, or whatever you are asking for. That perspective keeps us from deifying ourselves and from becoming completely self-absorbed. And it turns our attention to the One who is worthy of it. Ask Him to glorify His name in you.

For every one look within, take ten looks at Christ.
—ROBERT MURRAY M'CHEYNE

God-Centered Ministry

I eagerly expect and hope . . . that now
as always Christ will be exalted in my
body, whether by life or by death.
PHILIPPIANS 1:20

In Word

The highly active apostle Paul was languishing in a Roman prison, observing how the gospel had impacted the empire in just a few short years. Christ was being preached, even with wrong motives, and that was encouraging to him. For all he knew, Paul was approaching death by execution, and he didn't view that as catastrophic. His ability to preach freely wasn't the issue, and neither was his survival. In both ministry and life, Paul's concern was the gospel and the name of Jesus.

That's a foreign perspective for many of us. We assume that God's goal for us is survival, and that He has teamed up with us to ensure a happy, healthy life. But God's definitions of happiness and health are far removed from ours. While we are busy trying to survive and maybe even accomplish something for ourselves or our loved ones—or even our Lord—God has a change of heart in store for us. This life we're living isn't about us; it's about Him. We're not to be preoccupied with our survival. We're to be preoccupied with His reputation in this world. The name of Jesus should be the food we eat and the air we breathe.

In Deed

That sounds as if it will lead us into a dismal slavery, but it won't. Just the opposite, in fact. It leads us into a glorious freedom. When we're centered on God, we no longer need to obsess about our work, our children, our lifestyle, or our image. We can obsess about His name and let Him take care of the rest. Do you see how that relieves the pressure? We are to be wholly concerned with something that is certain to be victorious. The name of Jesus will be exalted. That's a given.

Playing on a team that's guaranteed to win and having no other ultimate responsibility in life is liberating. It doesn't mean we don't care about the other things; it means that if we concern ourselves entirely with His mission, He concerns Himself entirely with our needs. There's no simpler, freer way to live.

Provided that God be glorified, we must not care by whom.
—FRANCIS DE SALES

God-Centered Victory

**All those gathered here will know that it is not
by sword or spear that the LORD saves.**
1 SAMUEL 17:47

In Word

It was an appalling situation. A nine-foot giant would stand out in the open every day and taunt the armies of Israel. The people chosen by the almighty God were in the land promised by the almighty God, fighting a battle ordained by the almighty God, and they were intimidated. By an offensive loudmouth—albeit a very big one. But their God was bigger. They should have known that.

David did. He didn't come upon the situation and challenge his elders' courage or their battle skills. He didn't offer a better strategy or suggest an opportune moment to strike. No, he was simply outraged by the absurdity of the scene. The soldiers of the living God cowering in fear? While the name of the merciful, mighty God of the universe was slandered? Why?

David didn't go to the front lines to make a name for himself. He went to serve his brothers lunch. But while he was there, he could not tolerate the situation. God's reputation was at stake. The army's fear did not honor Him; the enemy-occupied Promised Land did not honor Him; and the gorilla of Gath did not honor Him. Something had to be done.

In Deed

Do you take that attitude into your world every day? No, you need not carry a slingshot and stones. And you need not be offensive about it. But your God— the merciful, mighty God of the universe who has chosen us and equipped us for every good work, even guaranteeing us ultimate victory—is being slandered by an unseen enemy. That enemy's propaganda has been swallowed by a gullible, hard-hearted world. And we're the only army God has redeemed for service.

Goliath is an appropriate image for Satan—big, noisy, intimidating, . . . and doomed. David is first an image of Christ, but also an appropriate image for the Christian—concerned mainly with serving bread and defending the name of his God. Can you follow his footsteps of faith into battle? Will you?

We're in spiritual combat—cosmic combat
for the heart and soul of humankind.
—CHARLES COLSON

The Everywhere God

Where can I go from your Spirit?

PSALM 139:7

In Word

The omnipresence of God is not a foreign concept to us. We're quite familiar with the idea that He is everywhere at all times. A more relevant issue for us involves the practicality of that notion. God's presence needs to be more than an intellectual understanding. Deep down, we want to ask the vital question: So what?

There are times in our lives when God's presence is an uncomfortable reality—those independent times when we don't necessarily want Him to be watching us. But most of the time, we need to know He's there. We struggle with anxiety, fear, uncertainty, loneliness, and discouragement. When we do, we don't only want to know that He is observing; we also want to know that He is intensely involved.

God's presence is welcome news to us fallen creatures. It wouldn't be if He were first and foremost a God of judgment, but He is not; His mercy takes precedence over His judgment (James 2:13). Grace is His preference. Knowing that, we can rest in the presence of God. He has demonstrated that He is in His element anywhere in our world other than in the company of sin (for which He has a radical remedy). A dazzling throne is not too glorious, a smelly manger not too humble, and a criminal's cross not too shameful. Every corner of His universe is "room temperature" for Him.

In Deed

Does that reality mean anything to you? It won't, as long as God's presence is a theological issue of "omnipresence." But this psalm is not talking about omnipresence; it's talking about companionship. This is no cold stare of watchfulness; it is for the believer a warm fellowship with the divine Friend. Our Creator—the One who molded us, breathed life into us, and painfully redeemed us—is, at this moment, wherever you are. Are you in a strange, lonely place—physically, emotionally, spiritually, or in any other way? A dungeon of the soul? An exile of the heart? A steep, long path? He is right there, really there, and remarkably sympathetic.

> You need not cry very loud; He is nearer to us than we think.
>
> —BROTHER LAWRENCE

Fear Not

**Fear not, for I have redeemed you; I have
summoned you by name; you are mine.**
ISAIAH 43:1

In Word

God's Word through Isaiah tells us what kind of God He is. Granted, this prophecy was given to Israel, but logic applies it to everyone He has redeemed. Those whom He has purchased and summoned by name are His.

That has plenty of implications. We might read it as our obligation to serve Him and depend on Him to the neglect of our own sense of autonomy. And it's true; as His redeemed ones, we are obligated to Him. We were bought with a price. But there's a warmer, more encouraging side to this verse: God doesn't go to the trouble to save and cultivate a people only to let them flounder in their own troubles. Even in their rebellion, He saves.

Think of what that means. When we pass through the waters—and we will pass through them—He will be there. When we walk through the fire, no matter how hot it feels, we will not be burned. The Holy One of Israel is the Holy One of all He has bought. He didn't redeem us to then leave us alone.

In Deed

Do you see how that changes everything for us? The knowledge of what God has already invested in us ought to be enough to convince us that He will not give up on the investment. A shortsighted, double-minded god might drop his precious investments when they go bad, but not the eternal God of well-laid plans. He knew the day He redeemed you what your future would look like. And He committed to it.

That means there is nothing you are experiencing now that was not part of His foresight in your redemption. God does not fly by the seat of His pants, picking up those whom He can and abandoning those who have become too difficult. You were redeemed; you are His. That's a huge obligation, but it's a huge relief. You are His. He will watch over you as a treasured possession because that is what you are. He is never careless with His property. There is nothing more secure in the world.

There is never a fear that has not a corresponding "Fear not."

—AMY CARMICHAEL

A Living Savior

**"You are . . . the Son of the living God." . . .
"On this rock I will build my church."**
MATTHEW 16:16, 18

In Word

What is the church? To someone who worships God in spirit and in truth, the church becomes more than an institution. Before that, it can be any number of things: a service organization, a social club, an educational institution, an obligation, a hobby, or even a passion. But as worshipers of Jesus, we know there is something more supernatural about it. It is His body.

Do you see it that way? Many don't. Many see it as one way among many other ways to serve humanity. Others see it as a fellowship of like-minded friends, akin to a fraternity or a country club. Still others see it as a place of learning, responsible for teaching religion to those who can't get it in public places. But it is more. It is not just a service organization, though it absolutely must serve others. It is not just a social outlet, though it absolutely must have fellowship. And it is not just a school, though it absolutely must educate. No, above all of these functions is the church's essence: It is a living organism, the actual physical body of Christ in this world. Jesus lives in us—not just individually, but corporately. Especially corporately.

That only makes sense. Any one of us is insufficient to embody His fullness. So is the church, but a body of millions does it better than a body of one. In our spiritual fellowship, Jesus dwells. Not just the teaching of Jesus, but Jesus. Not just the philosophy of Jesus, but Jesus. Not just His goodwill or His good works, but Jesus. Yes, there will be teaching, a Christian worldview, goodwill, and good works. But that's because He really lives there, not because we live simply as a memorial to our Founder.

In Deed

Do you realize the significance of the body of Christ? Do you realize also your significance as a part of it? We do not live simply in remembrance of a Savior. A Savior actively lives in us. We don't just ask what Jesus would do, we ask what He is doing—right now, in us. Together.

*There is only one organism of the new creation, and
we are members of that organism, which is Christ.*
—LIONEL THORNTON

WIJD

**Through him you Gentiles are also being made part
of this dwelling where God lives by his Spirit.**
EPHESIANS 2:22, NLT

In Word

It's not quite as catchy, and you won't find any bracelets or bumper stickers
with the acronym WIJD on them. But it perhaps asks a better question than
its more familiar counterpart. "What would Jesus do?" is a good question,
but it doesn't have life. The heart of the matter is similar, but more pointed:
"What is Jesus doing?"

The WWJD phenomenon has turned the attention of millions toward
the character and works of our Savior, so it is certainly a useful question to
consider. But there's a subtle implication in it: Jesus is our example, a teacher
who lived long ago whom we are left to emulate. In a sense, that's true. Jesus
is our example: "Be imitators of God . . . and live a life of love, just as Christ
loved us," we're told (Ephesians 5:1-2). There's more, however: "If a man
remains in me and I in him, he will bear much fruit" (John 15:5). "I no longer
live, but Christ lives in me" (Galatians 2:20). We don't just have an example,
we have an Inhabitant. There's a world of difference.

In Deed

Do you see Jesus as your example or as your life? He is both, but asking the
question is more than a matter of simple semantics. It will profoundly affect
how we approach every day, every decision, every act of character or impulse
of the heart. If we see ourselves as imitators of the divine Example, we will
find ourselves failing often and growing ever more frustrated with our inability to live as He did. But if we see ourselves as vessels in which the Spirit of
the living God dwells, we're inclined not to try harder but to trust more.

So what would Jesus do? We should ask this; He is the way. What would
He think? We should also ask this; He is the truth. And what is He doing? We
should especially ask this; He is the life. No one comes to the Father except
by Him. Not just by His example, but by His life. He indwells us to take us
where we should go and lead us away from where we've been. It's an amazing
thought: We live by means of a living Lord.

> One person works upon another person from outside
> inwards, but God alone comes to us from within outwards.
>
> —JAN VAN RUYSBROECK

The Shepherd

You my sheep, the sheep of my pasture, are people,
and I am your God, declares the Sovereign LORD.

EZEKIEL 34:31

In Word

"The LORD is my shepherd. . . ." It's a familiar psalm and a familiar concept. When God gave the prophets the image of Himself as a shepherd, it was an image every Jew could relate to. In an agrarian society, everyone knows what a shepherd does.

Most of us today know simply that a shepherd tends sheep. We may not realize how important the job is—that a sheep that strays is a disastrous blow to the family income in terms of wool, milk, meat, and generations of off-spring. It might not dawn on us how much danger wolves and jackals pose to a flock, or how acutely a sheep needs to be able to hear its shepherd's voice. We might not consider how vigilant and enduring a shepherd's task is as he works around the clock to guard his sheep from all kinds of dangers and provide for their every need. And, if we haven't been around sheep very much, we might not understand, frankly, how obstinate and stupid sheep can be.

But all of these aspects of the shepherd role are common knowledge in more pastoral cultures. When God called Himself a shepherd—through David's psalm; through the prophecies of Isaiah, Ezekiel, Hosea, and Micah; and through the words of Jesus—He gave us a very loaded image, a picture worth far more than a thousand words. He painted a self-portrait of treasured ownership, loving care, intense vigilance, patient endurance, and extreme generosity and sacrifice.

In Deed

Read through that last sentence slowly and deliberately. Think of God's self-portrait as a shepherd, and specifically of that self-portrait as it has applied to your life in the past and today. Why? Because many of your struggles today are larger than they ought to be, larger than they would be if you were convinced of how diligently your Shepherd watches over you. The Shepherd is deeply, intensely focused on your wandering, even if He seems to be strolling at the rear of the flock. He will never cease to keep you safe and well.

Savior, like a shepherd lead us; much
we need Thy tender care.

—DOROTHY A. THRUPP

Affection for Sheep

I myself will tend my sheep and have them lie
down, declares the Sovereign LORD. I will search
for the lost and bring back the strays. I will bind
up the injured and strengthen the weak.
EZEKIEL 34:15-16

In Word

The heart of the Shepherd is a deep mystery. Why would someone choose such a thankless job for such oblivious creatures? For most shepherds, the task falls on them as an obligation, not a career choice. But our Shepherd relishes the position. He expects something more than a family income from His flock—something much, much more—so the tedium isn't all that tedious to Him. A passionate heart will endure an awful lot in order to obtain the object of its affection.

That's how our Shepherd views His flock, both as a whole and as individual sheep. We are, according to Scripture, the object of His affection. We can wonder what would draw Him to such mangy creatures and argue that we're not worthy, but that doesn't change what He has declared of Himself. He's a Shepherd who loves His job, and He loves it because of His affection for the sheep in His flock.

This is one of the hardest truths for Christians to grasp. For all our talk about God's love, we don't really understand it—or believe it. We dissect the Greek words for love and come up with a sterile sort of agape—selfless love—that feels more like an obligation on God's part rather than a delight. But God doesn't define *agape* that way, and He doesn't portray His love as obligatory. He delights in His sheep. Treasures them. Adores them. Swells with torrential passion over them.

In Deed

Don't believe it? He makes it clear in other prophetic images, like His self-portrait as a Husband, for example. Consider this: repeated calls for love over the course of several millennia and through a vast spectrum of hardships do not come from a dispassionate heart. And yet our Bible is a veritable love song from beginning to end. Know that love. Embrace it. Never, ever doubt it again.

The person you are now, the person you have been, the
person you will be—this person God has chosen as beloved.
—WILLIAM COUNTRYMAN

Sheepish Tendencies

**They will live in safety, and no one
will make them afraid.**
EZEKIEL 34:28

In Word

Handel set Isaiah 53:6 to music in a memorable way, but we hardly needed reminding: "All we like sheep have gone astray" (KJV). We know that straying is the tendency of our hearts, and it always has been. With eyes that focus on our surroundings more than on the Shepherd, and ears that listen to other voices indiscriminately, we are prone to wander according to our mood of the moment. That can be very dangerous.

So the promise that we will "live in safety" is not just a comforting statement that God speaks through Ezekiel. It's a matter of urgency and desperate need. With aimless hearts that lead us through a countryside full of vicious hyenas and gaping crevices, this is no small promise.

It is, however, a promise that is easy to forget. The world doesn't seem very safe. And, being sheep, we usually focus on the world, not the Shepherd. That puts us in a tentative, even petrified, state of mind. We feel defenseless against the predators, and the slopes seem awfully slippery. The more we consider how frightened we ought to be, the more frightened we become.

In Deed

The Shepherd, however, doesn't want us to be afraid. From His perspective, we're perfectly safe already. He won't let us wander into crevices too deep for us, He can see the predators coming from miles away, and He knows exactly where He is leading us. At the end of wandering, there's a safe pasture with flowing streams and ample grass. The fears that seem so large to us are extremely small to Him.

Living with that understanding is a huge part of what faith is all about. When the sheep get a glimpse of the Shepherd's perspective, fear vanishes. More than that, when the sheep get a glimpse of the Shepherd's heart, fear becomes completely illogical. A sheep that remains in ignorance spends its life in fear and apathy. A sheep that trusts its Shepherd implicitly becomes a noble creature of confidence and purpose. And every member of the flock must decide which it wants to be.

> The best answer to fear is to have a firm grasp
> of what it means to be accepted by God.
> —JOHN GUNSTONE

The Good Shepherd

I will bless them and the places surrounding
my hill. I will send down showers in season;
there will be showers of blessing.

EZEKIEL 34:26

In Word

The Shepherd loves to bless. Most Christians don't know that and approach
Him with the intent to bribe Him with good behavior or twist His arm with
whining. And while persistence and boldness in prayer are good attributes,
they should never be implemented without a prior understanding of the nature
of God: He is good, and He blesses us abundantly—without reservation.

Intellectually we know that, but that knowledge is rarely visible in the
lives of God's people. We crave more intimacy with Him and lament the
separation we feel, never realizing that we feel it because we refuse to believe
in His generosity. Deep down inside, we're just sure that God would have us
jump through certain hoops to obtain His blessings or overcome every hint of
fallenness before we're worthy. But those impressions are not from God; in
fact, they're kind of arrogant. They assume that the key variable in obtaining
God's favor is us. It isn't. The key variable in receiving the goodness of God
is the goodness of God.

In Deed

Do you live with the assumption that God is extravagantly generous, waiting
to do something good for you, and delighting in your happiness? If not, it's
probably because you haven't experienced His extravagance and delight like
you want to. But God wants you to turn the equation around. You haven't
experienced that generosity because you haven't assumed it—i.e., really
believed in it. Those who approach the Shepherd as a reluctant giver will
experience a reluctant giver. Those who approach Him as a blesser will see His
blessings. According to your faith, that's how it will be (Matthew 9:29).

That does not mean that faith will eliminate trials and pain from our lives.
Sheep still have to go through a lot. It does, however, mean that we don't have
to live our entire lives without showers of blessing. The Shepherd who blesses
us promises to make sure of that.

God's gifts put man's best dreams to shame.

—ELIZABETH BARRETT BROWNING

A Distinctive Voice

**Then they will know that I, the LORD
their God, am with them.**
EZEKIEL 34:30

In Word

Every shepherd has a distinctive call that his sheep can recognize. That's particularly helpful when several flocks are mingled together at one watering place; the shepherd needs only call his sheep, and they will separate themselves from the rest.

Our Shepherd has a distinctive voice, and Jesus said His sheep will be able to recognize it. In John 10, that voice was the miracles Jesus did in the Father's name. The skeptics didn't acknowledge the character or the work of God, so they couldn't hear the voice of God. But those who are of His flock can distinguish His character, marvel at His work, and therefore hear His voice.

We need to keep that in mind. We cannot live in this world without diligent attention to discernment. There are quite a few flocks mingling around the watering holes of this world, and an ear-shattering din of shepherds calling to their sheep. If we can't distinguish our Shepherd's voice from theirs, we're liable to end up in the wrong flock and headed in the wrong direction. In fact, that's where most sheep are headed, indiscriminate in their choice of shepherds to follow. They hear the smorgasbord of appealing voices and choose the one that sounds most promising at the moment. Sadly, they end up in one of many flocks headed away from the Good Shepherd's pasture.

In Deed

Make discernment a priority. In eternal matters, sheep cannot coast through life. They have to be able to hear the Master's call, and they aren't going to hear it merely by going with the flow of their culture. Hearing our Shepherd requires diligence, persistence, and constant attentiveness to the subtleties of His ways.

At all costs, avoid being like the Pharisees who saw the works of God and didn't recognize them. Culture, the habits of tradition, and false assumptions called to them at the same time the Shepherd did, and they listened to the wrong things. When you sense the God of the Bible at work, hear His voice. Follow Him always.

*The voice of God is a friendly voice. No one need fear to
listen to it unless he has already made up his mind to resist it.*
—A. W. TOZER

Love Comes First

Be very careful to love the LORD your God.
JOSHUA 23:11

In Word

As the aging Joshua gave his farewell address to the Israelites, he reminded them of everything God had done for them. The appropriate response to God's faithfulness, Joshua said, was to "be very careful" to love Him. It is an act of the will, an intentional response to who He is. But have you ever thought about what it really means to love God?

Many who set out to love God focus on theology. But theology, while important and necessary, makes God an academic subject to study or a philosophical argument to prove. It may be a product of our love for God, but it does not define love. Discussions abound in which God is a premise—a subject viewed through a theologian's microscope or a philosopher's telescope—but in which there is no affection. Doctrine is critical for us to grasp, but it is not love. Ask any Sadducee.

Many who set out to love God focus on works. But works, while an essential outgrowth of love for God, can easily become an attempt to gain His approval. In truth, they are not acts of devotion but acts of self-interest. We want to gain higher esteem in His eyes, something that makes us one of His "insiders." We end up with a self-righteousness that fills us with brief satisfaction but leaves us empty of love. Ask any Pharisee.

Many who set out to love God focus on emotions. But emotions, though a desirable and essential outgrowth of love, cannot define our love. They are far too fleeting. We end up riding waves of feeling or missing out on them altogether. Love remains constant. Feelings don't. Ask any zealot.

In Deed

So how do we love God? We lie at His feet and tell Him we are His. We seek to honor Him in all we do. We want to be like Him. We crave His fellowship. We pray His desires. We are consumed with, obsessed with, and filled with His ways, His works, and His will. The theology, the works, and the feelings will come. They are good—but only after the devotion. Love always comes first.

I would hate my own soul if I did not find it loving God.
—AUGUSTINE

Dependence

Apart from me you can do nothing. . . . This is to
my Father's glory, that you bear much fruit.

JOHN 15:5, 8

In Word

The disciples must have been scratching their heads. Jesus told them that God
was honored when they bore much fruit. Because just a few sentences earlier,
He told them that they couldn't bear any fruit. At least not on their own. Two
thousand years of commentary have given us plenty of time to grasp what
Jesus is saying, but the disciples had only had three years with Him. This surely
was confusing to them.

We might share their confusion, to a degree. We know that we are to worship God with everything in us, and that includes living a fruit-bearing life.
But we easily slip from the spiritual realm into a very natural translation. We
think we're called to go out and work for God. He is honored by fruit, so we
intend to bear fruit. We forget a very key element of Jesus' teaching: We can't.
We don't have that ability. Unless we're abiding in the Vine—in Him—we're
just dead branches.

We know the answer, of course, at least in our minds. Jesus is to bear
fruit in us and through us. He is the producer, and we're the branches through
whom He produces. But it is remarkably easy to forget that we need to depend
on Him as the source of production. We realize eventually that we're only
spinning our wheels by our busywork, but our inclination is only to work
harder. We have to train ourselves in an unnatural pose: spiritual, emotional,
and even physical dependence.

In Deed

The element of dependence is why God is glorified when we bear fruit. If we
achieved things for God, we would be glorified, not Him. But our incapability
gives Him a platform to work in the Spirit. He can work in an insufficient life
to much greater honor than He can in a self-sufficient life. Our inabilities can
be turned into an act of worship, if we'll offer them up to His power.

Have you learned yet that your dependence on God—your manifest
weakness, in fact—is an occasion for His glory? Let Him be honored in you.
Learn dependence.

The more we depend on God, the more
dependable we find He is.

—CLIFF RICHARD

Insufficiency

**My grace is sufficient for you, for my
power is made perfect in weakness.**
2 CORINTHIANS 12:9

In Word

We tend to think of our weaknesses as failures. Perhaps we feel that we've
let God down by our bungling attempts at righteousness or service, or that
we've disqualified ourselves from the circles of the spiritual elite. We forget
that every disease is an opportunity for Him either to heal us or to comfort
us; every problem is an opportunity for Him either to display His power or
to shape our character; and every sin is an opportunity for Him to demonstrate His mercy (if we're repentant) or to display His righteous judgments
(if we're not). Whatever failures we come up with, He can redeem. And that
brings Him glory.

That doesn't mean that we should fail intentionally, especially if that failure is sin. There's plenty of insufficiency to go around; we don't need to create
more for Him. But it does mean that we should intentionally avoid successes
that aren't birthed by Him. Our independent victories are failures in His eyes,
while our failures that lead to dependence are His victories. As always, the
Kingdom is a paradox.

That's a radical perspective for us. The world gives us clear definitions of
success and failure, strength and weakness. But if we look closely at God's definitions, we discover that anything that points to Him—even our inability—is
a great success. Anything that doesn't—even our ability—is not.

In Deed

Instead of considering your weaknesses as failures, try considering them as
occasions to worship. Offer them to God. Remember that a few loaves and fish
were all that was offered to Jesus to feed a large crowd, and He was glorified.
A leprous hand was offered to Him, and His power to heal was honored. The
tomb of a dead brother became a scene of awesome praise. And a disgraceful
cross, as well as the horrendous sin behind it, became God's greatest glory.

God is used to taking humility, brokenness, and even failure, and magnifying Himself in them. Are you weak? humble? a broken failure? Then He's
ready to work. Let Him magnify Himself in you.

*It's the nature of God to make something out
of nothing; therefore, when anyone is nothing,
God may yet make something of him.*

—MARTIN LUTHER

Humility

Everyone who exalts himself will be humbled,
and he who humbles himself will be exalted.

LUKE 18:14

In Word

The worshipful heart will have its struggles. One of its greatest is combating the natural human desire to establish our own success, status, and security. We easily become self-focused, wanting to become good in order to represent God well. Have we forgotten? God is already represented well by Jesus—especially in the company of lepers, sinners, and thieves on a cross.

The selfward heart doesn't get it. It can't be transparent about its weaknesses and failures because it is too busy masking them. There is a personal reputation to maintain. The Godward heart, however, is busy with God's reputation. It can easily confess sin and sickness, because it knows that God is glorified by His treatment of such things. The selfward soul runs around saying, "I'm doing my best for the glory of God." The Godward soul can relax and proclaim, "God's doing His wonderful work in the wreck that is me."

Both perspectives come from good intentions. But deep in the heart of man is a reluctance to enhance God's reputation at the expense of our own. We don't want to own up to our weaknesses, failures, brokenness, and sin. We want to demonstrate God's grace in our respectable lives. But God's grace shows up best in the honesty of a tax collector like Zacchaeus or a prostitute who weeps for mercy. Honest souls know what's inside of them. They alone can showcase a Savior.

In Deed

This parable isn't just about Pharisees; it's about all of us. Do you really want to worship God with every aspect of your being? Then let Him be your everything—your Savior, Healer, Provider, Judge, Refuge, and Strength. Acknowledging your ultimate dependence and need isn't always easy. It will require honesty before Him and an honest testimony before the world. Will that reflect well on you? Probably not, but it will reflect incredibly well on Him. And that's what worship is all about.

Humility is nothing else but a true knowledge
and awareness of oneself as one really is.

—THE CLOUD OF UNKNOWING

False Worship

You were once darkness, but now you are light in the Lord. Live as children of light.
EPHESIANS 5:8

In Word

We just love the end of the gospel, but we hate its beginning. We don't dwell there long. Why should we? It includes everything we hate about ourselves.

The beginning of the gospel, of course—at least our experience of it—is the fact that we desperately need a Savior. Our original condition is never sugarcoated by the Bible, or even by our gentle Jesus. No, the human heart is "desperately wicked" (Jeremiah 17:9, KJV); "there is none righteous, no, not one" (Romans 3:10, NKJV); and here in Ephesians we were objects of wrath (2:3) and not only children of darkness, but darkness itself (5:8). As such, we were idolaters. False worshipers. People who gave glory and honor to things that were not worthy, while neglecting the glory and honor that should go to the One who is. That hurts.

It's a brutal assessment, but we have to own up to it. We don't like to think of our flirtation with impurity or materialism as idol-worship, but it is (5:5). It places value on something that is ultimately without value, and it ignores the ultimate worth of the One who created everything we lust after in the first place. The absurdity of our misplaced affections is mind-boggling in heavenly places. We just don't notice the absurdity because it is so common in our world.

In Deed

Is it really false worship to enjoy things and people and ideas? That depends. If we enjoy them as gifts from God in their proper place in our lives, then the answer is no. But if we seek them with a higher priority than we seek the mind and will of our Creator—and we often do—then yes, we are idolaters. Whatever we pursue with a passion greater than our love for our God is a false form of worship.

But then there's the end of the gospel to encourage us. There is sufficient grace to cover our every idolatry. We must not let those false adorations persist, but they have been covered by grace. What's our response to such a liberating thought? To live as children of light.

Idolatry: trusting people, possessions, and positions to do for me what only God can do.
—BILL GOTHARD

Anti-Worship

Search me, O God, and know my heart; test
me and know my anxious thoughts.

PSALM 139:23

In Word

It's a little disturbing to us that David equates anxious thoughts with an "offensive way" (v. 24) in this psalm. We're anxious by nature, frequently wondering how things will turn out for us. We know bad things happen to all kinds of people, and it's only natural for us to worry that they might happen to us. Life can be stressful. So what's wrong with being stressed?

Think of what our anxiety says about God. When we harbor anxious thoughts, we are saying that the One who has promised to take care of our future (Jeremiah 29:11) might not do a good job of it. It says that the One who has promised to walk us through the waters and not to allow the fire to burn us (Isaiah 43:2) might abandon us to the waters and the fire. And it says that His presence in the valley of the shadow of death (Psalm 23:4) might not be enough to calm us. We don't realize it, but our emotions often tell our Provider that we don't think we'll have enough provision, tell our Savior that we're afraid of not being saved, tell our Comforter that we're uncomfortable, and tell our Deliverer that we're sure we'll remain captive. Our hearts actually slander Him when we don't trust His protection, His strength, and His love. We don't mean to; we're just anxious. But our anxiety can be awfully offensive.

In Deed

Imagine a son lying awake at night wondering if his parents are going to feed him tomorrow. Or a daughter wondering if she will have something to clothe herself in. That might happen in some homes, but what does it say of the parents? Nothing complimentary.

But we who worship God cannot praise Him with such insecurities. Our fears are a form of anti-worship—a clear declaration that our God might not have promised us enough, or might not be able to follow through on what He has promised. Yes, He will let us go through hard things, but never outside of His timing or beyond His protection. So worship Him. And don't worry about it.

Anxiety comes from strain, and strain is caused by
too complete a dependence on ourselves.

—THOMAS MERTON

Majesty

**How precious to me are your thoughts,
O God! How vast is the sum of them!**
PSALM 139:17

In Word

We're amazed at human ingenuity: the planning and talent put into a work of art, a successful business, or a dazzling performance. We're mystified by the scientific discoveries of our age that have revealed more and more intricacies and design than we ever thought. We're easily impressed with our findings.

Yet we rarely appreciate the Founder who created this universe. Have we become convinced by the lie that it may have "just happened"? Or is creation just too overwhelming to even begin to understand? Whatever the reason, the complexities of time and space, matter and energy, and life and relationships are mind-boggling. We find order and design wherever we turn. We discover a Master Intelligence behind everything we see, whether we see it through a microscope or a telescope.

Think about the amount of planning that went into creation. Our God is the mastermind behind both macro-majesties and micro-marvels. Our understanding stretches millions of light-years, but still to only a fraction of all there is. Our insights discern distinct atomic particles, but we still don't really know what makes them spin. We cannot begin to comprehend the extremes that we can imagine. Eternity without time? Space with undiscovered limits and irregularities? An infinite God with infinite attributes? Unlimited wisdom, power, and love? Boundless grace? We just don't get it. We can't. We're too small, too finite, and too confined by our natural senses. The things of eternity elude our understanding.

In Deed

Get comfortable with that. We will spend an eternity exploring God, and we should begin now. Let yourself be in awe. Think about the imagination and power that went into a sunset, a mountain range, our human physiology, the wisdom of Scriptures, or the plan of the Kingdom of God. Stand amazed in His presence. Worship begins with an understanding of our inability to understand. It silences our complaints and captures our hearts. It believes God is astoundingly precious.

We seem to have lost the vision of the majesty of God.

—JOHN STOTT

A Clear Direction

I have set the LORD always before me.
PSALM 16:8

In Word

David pursued a lot of interests: his sheep, victory over the Philistines, the kingdom of Israel, Bathsheba, Absalom, and more. Most of his intentions were good; some were not. Regardless, he was governed by one overriding interest, one passion that superseded all others: He wanted to know the heart of God.

David set the Lord continually before him. Or, to say it another way, David continually set himself in the direction of God. Regardless of the intermediate pursuit—whether it was a kingdom, a military victory, a temple, or whatever—the intermediate was only a means to a higher purpose. David was consumed with knowing God. No, he didn't follow his passions perfectly, and sometimes they were misdirected. But they were always brought back to this one. God's ways, His character, and His will were paramount. The heart of any worshiper knows this.

According to Psalm 16, this one overriding passion was relevant to David's security, his inheritance, his wisdom, and more. It affected everything. But all of these benefits were only side effects; they were not the main attraction. God was the main attraction, and in a worshiper's heart, He always will be. A greater Example, foreshadowed in this psalm, reinforces the message with even more purity and single-mindedness. Jesus more completely and passionately set the Lord before Him. If David is a worshiper's great example, Jesus is the great fulfillment of our desire. His Spirit in us worships God as He worshiped God on earth. David tried to make everything in his life point to God. Jesus not only tried, He succeeded.

In Deed

Our lives often seem like a conglomeration of multiple goals and pursuits. Positions, possessions, places, people, and plans—all will occupy our thoughts from time to time. Our priority, according to Scripture, must be God Himself. Not the things God gives us, but God. Not the ways God leads us, but God. Not even the worship of God, but God. It's so easy to understand, so hard to grasp. Be relentless about it. Set the Lord always before you.

Worship is not a part of the Christian life; it is the Christian life.
—GERALD VANN

A Worthy Hope

Though he slay me, yet will I hope in him.
JOB 13:15

In Word

How do you react when your circumstances are difficult? Do you try to maneuver your way out of them? Do you blame other people? Or worse, do you blame God? It's a common response that nearly everyone has given in to. Even when we know that blaming Him is wrong and misguided, we still sometimes nurse resentment that He let us go through the trial. We just don't see the big picture when we're struggling with the small one.

God has a multitude of reasons for allowing our troubling situations. Perhaps He is working on some of the people in our lives. Maybe He is working out His timing to reap the maximum harvest when His solution comes in the end. Or He could be proving a point to His enemy about His glory, as He did with Job—and our reaction is the key. Maybe He is even working on us—our character flaws, personality issues, or spiritual growth. Unpruned trees bear less fruit, so He must shape us differently. But we're surprised—and angry—when His pruning hand is not as gentle as we'd like.

The question we need to settle in our hearts is whether we believe God is good. It isn't hard to hold such a belief when His blessings seem bountiful. But the blessing of hardship? We wonder where His favor has gone. We grow distant, resentful, and bitter over the harshness of His loving hand. Like a child who has just been spanked—or simply told no—we pout. God just doesn't seem fair.

In Deed

If we really believe our circumstances are under the hand of a sovereign God—and that God is always good—then bitterness, anger, and resentment can have no hold on us. A vengeful, sovereign God is no comfort, and neither is a good but impotent God. But a firm belief in both His goodness and His sovereignty over our every circumstance is an incredibly relaxing trust. An all-powerful, good-hearted God gives us absolutely nothing to fear except our own disobedience—and He even has a plan for that. We can always hope in Him.

Let God do with me whatever He will; whatever it be,
it will be either heaven itself or some beginning of it.
—WILLIAM MOUNTFORD

Eyes for Glory

**As for me, I will always have hope;
I will praise you more and more.**

PSALM 71:14

In Word

The psalmist is in the midst of a crisis. He needs rescuing. We don't know the exact trial he is going through, and it doesn't really matter. We know his response. Though he has enemies who conspire against him (v. 10), he knows where to find help. His problem leads to praise.

God is looking for those who will worship Him not only in spirit and in truth—as Jesus says in John 4:23—but also in crisis. He seeks those who can look beyond the clouds that threaten and hover over them to His radiance that thoroughly surrounds them. And when He finds them, He blesses them.

That's a difficult maturity for most Christians to learn. Our natural reaction in a trial is to flee, or to beg for relief. And we have plenty of biblical examples; asking God for deliverance is thoroughly recommended throughout the Word. But is there panic in the asking? Our weak souls are easily unnerved, but there's a better pose: We can praise God, knowing that when we call, He will answer. He may not answer exactly the way we expect—though often He does—but He will answer, and His answer will be good. We can count on that. Those who do will pray for deliverance not in a panic, but in a rock-solid trust. God will save. It's His nature.

In Deed

God has not given us a spirit of fear, and He has commanded us to be anxious for nothing (Philippians 4:6). The apostle who penned those instructions would know. He went through all sorts of trials and tribulations, and he always found God faithful. He and Silas were able to sing praises from the depths of a Philippian prison. We should be able to do the same.

God went to great lengths to redeem us and call us His children. He did not intend for us to live in anxiety, wondering where each new threat will drive us. He gave us eyes for His glory; we are to see Him in every circumstance. After all, seeing the resurrection beyond the shroud is what our faith is all about.

Hope can see heaven through the thickest clouds.
—THOMAS BENTON BROOKS

A Now and Future Kingdom

Be glad and rejoice forever in what I will create.
ISAIAH 65:18

In Word

God has promised a new Kingdom. It will be dramatically different than the kingdom we've grown up in. In fact, He has already begun it. Jesus gave us glimpses of it whenever He taught, healed, and forgave. He gives us glimpses of it even now, whenever He answers our prayers and grants us the pleasure of His presence. The new heavens and the new earth are a future promise with a present taste. Still, we often live a lot like captive citizens of this fallen planet.

Are we? Of course not. We know God's promises and we depend on them. We've seen His mercy and known His love. We know there's more to look forward to than the status quo. The King is coming, and what He does when He comes will be amazing.

The problem for many of us is living the future glory in this present world. Basing our lives on one-day promises doesn't seem very realistic today. But doing so is one of the clearest ways for us to honor God. We can go ahead and live His Kingdom's ethics, count on His Kingdom's plans, fit into His Kingdom's culture, and learn His Kingdom's language. Most of all, we can rejoice, worshiping as if we were living in Revelation 22, even when we're still only lingering after the end of Acts.

In Deed

In fact, we must. Worshiping that way is our witness that He is who He says He is, that He will do what He says He will do, and that it will all be good. When we joyfully live as citizens of the coming Kingdom, conforming to all of its character and falling in line with all of its plans, we are a visible sign to this world that: (1) it is fallen and there's a more glorious purpose for it; and (2) God is real and His Kingdom is coming.

Yes, others may think we're strange. They don't understand this Kingdom's ethics, and they don't grasp its values. No matter. The joy they observe in the lives of its citizens will be a testimony to them, and they will have to choose. If we are glad in what God will create someday, He is glorified now, as well as then.

Solid joys and lasting treasure none but Zion's children know.
—JOHN NEWTON

Unlimited Wisdom

. . . Christ the power of God and the wisdom of God.
1 CORINTHIANS 1:24

In Word

We live in a world where wisdom is obscured. There are heavenly places where the wisdom of God is clearly visible, but not here. No, the Bible calls our home a place of spiritual darkness. There are multitudes of competing philosophies and perspectives, worldviews that give different definitions to the meaning of life and how we got here. We have distorted emotions that make us strive after things that aren't really important, or that cause us to be blind to the things that are. We set goals for ourselves that may or may not coincide with eternal truth. Why? Because eternal truth is a matter of debate in the dark world in which we live.

But when we embrace the God who has called us and drawn us to Himself, we begin to learn from Him. We may have internal debates with ourselves—with the morals and traditions of those who reared us, with the philosophical agendas of those who schooled us, or even with our own desires and impulses. But deep down we know: God has a monopoly on truth, and if we want truth, we need Him.

In an age of relativism, that means a lot. It means that no matter how much our society tells us that truth is a matter of one's own opinions and all perspectives are valid, we know that there are absolutes. We can fix our lives on them. We can build on solid foundations. We can be guided confidently into our future even without knowing it. Why? Because we know the One who does.

In Deed

Think about what God's unlimited wisdom, revealed to us in Jesus, actually implies. If Jesus is the wisdom of God that was expressed in terms we can comprehend, we can base our lives on humility, service, sacrifice, love, and faith without any shadow of doubt that these things will prove utterly worthy in eternity. We can act in ways that are contrary to our culture because we know God's ways will last and our culture will not. We can tap into truth that has no depth limits. We can know everything we'll ever need to know.

True wisdom is gazing at God.
—ISAAC THE SYRIAN

Unlimited Power

**Proclaim the power of God, whose majesty is
over Israel, whose power is in the skies.**
PSALM 68:34

In Word

The power of God is an amazing thing. We can scarcely even begin to understand it. We strain to comprehend the vastness of our own solar system or
the intensity of our sun's heat, and then are overwhelmed by the thought that
there are thousands of such systems and millions of hotter stars. We try to
understand the infinitesimally small measurements of an atom, and then are
flabbergasted to think that our smallest known particles may have smaller
particles still. And to think: The hand that created such vast mysteries and such
detailed intricacies is the hand that holds our lives.

We know people who do not believe the miracles of the Bible but readily
accept the miraculous nature of the known universe. But we who know the
power of God have no trouble accepting parted seas, burning bushes, a virgin
birth, or even a resurrected body. And an even greater miracle is the life that
He breathes into a dead, sinful soul. Dry bones get up and dance, and we usually take it pretty casually; but if we really thought about the miracles of God's
hand—the everyday, ordinary ones as well as the dramatic, unusual ones—
we'd constantly be in awe. The power of God—and especially the power of
God in Christ—is amazing to behold.

In Deed

Try not to lose that sense of amazement. It's easy, having a fallen nature in a
fallen world, to see life as being mundane and ordinary, but it never is. It is
being sustained by One who is all-powerful. Whenever you begin to lose sense
of that, try this exercise: Contemplate the vastness of this creation; then contemplate the amazing details of it; then consider all the things God has done
in redemptive history and also in your life. Then realize the awesome truth:
The God of all that power, who has done all those things, and who continues
to sustain it all, is the God who is watching over you.

He who sees the infinite in all things, sees God.

—WILLIAM BLAKE

Unlimited Love

How great is the love the Father has lavished on us!
1 JOHN 3:1

In Word

First Corinthians 13 is a familiar passage to many. It is read at weddings and any other time someone wants to define love from a biblical point of view. For most of us, it is the surest description of how we are to love. But think about the passage's foundational idea: love is not an out-of-the-blue emotion. It is a choice that takes its cues from the very nature of God. And if God loves, we can know that His love, like all of His attributes, is infinite.

That's an amazing thought. God doesn't just love us; He loves us infinitely. When He forgives, He forgives completely. When He saves, He saves thoroughly. When He makes a covenant with us, it's a forever covenant. The eternal, infinite God does not express His core attributes in temporary, partial ways. He is an extreme God with an extreme love.

That's good for us to know, because we question His love often. Things don't work out as we planned, and we wonder if God loves us. He doesn't give us what we asked for, so we speculate that He might be withholding His affection. When we harbor such thoughts, we are underestimating God. We are applying our finite experience to an infinite being. The result is a distorted view.

In Deed

Read 1 Corinthians 13:4-7, making a couple of slight assumptions. Instead of seeing it as your instructions on how to love others, see it as God's unlimited expression of Himself. To paraphrase: God's love is infinitely patient, infinitely kind. It is completely devoid of envy, boasting, and pride. It is never rude, self-centered, or easily angered, and it keeps no record—none at all—of wrongs. God's love could not possibly delight in evil, and it always rejoices with truth. His love is extremely zealous to protect, trust, hope, and persevere.

Having read that as a description of God, now envision that kind of love as the subject of today's verse, 1 John 3:1. That's the kind of love God has lavished on us—unlimited, amazing, and free. We can never exhaust it.

> Jesus, Thou art all compassion, pure,
> unbounded love Thou art.
> —CHARLES WESLEY

Unlimited Grace

. . . that you may be filled to the measure of all the fullness of God.

EPHESIANS 3:19

In Word

God is unlimited in wisdom, unlimited in power, and unlimited in love. Whenever we try to imagine the greatness of any of His attributes, we fall short. We just can't picture it. We can let our imaginations run wild, but they will never run as far and as wide and as deep as He is. He's an infinite God. Finite minds will never fully grasp Him.

But think of the blessing of having access to this infinite God! Winning a national lottery would make us rich, but the riches, though vast, would be limited. Becoming a globally popular entertainer might make us feel loved, but there are limits to global popularity—both in quantity and in quality. And what if we had global power? The wisdom of a thousand Solomons? The resources of every national economy? All would pale in comparison to the resources of God. His wisdom, His power, His love, and all of His other attributes are infinite. And when they're applied to us, they are grace. Unlimited grace.

Paul prays an incomprehensible prayer in Ephesians: that the church would experience God's glorious riches, His spiritual power, His presence, and His love. And Paul's summary statement is mind-boggling: "That you may be filled to the measure of all the fullness of God." In other words, he asks that the measure God uses to dispense His grace to us would be as immeasurable as His own attributes. It's a brave prayer, one that we rarely dare to ask.

In Deed

Think of the privilege of being a child of God: unlimited wisdom, power, and love poured out on us in one gracious act of salvation. If we really understood that, could we ever pray casually again? Could we ever doubt? Would we ever worry about our future or stress about our present? No, all such frailties come from a lack of understanding on exactly this point: The God who is unfathomable, incomprehensible, and boundless in everything He does or can do, is the God who has chosen to dwell within us. Amazing.

> To Him no high, no low, no great, no small; He
> fills, He bounds, connects, and equals all!
> —ALEXANDER POPE

In Awe of God

The fear of the LORD is the beginning of wisdom.
PSALM 111:10

In Word

You've sinned. Perhaps it was intentional, or maybe it was just a casual slip-up. Either way, you're frustrated about your shortcomings—how you try to overcome them but can't, or how you can be godly some of the time but not consistently. Is your sin a repeated behavior? If so, it may be particularly frustrating. If you have a heart for God, you've probably confessed it a thousand times and then fallen into it a thousand times. Focusing on your sinfulness—even obsessing about it—hasn't helped. What can break you out of this guilty cycle?

There are several answers: the Holy Spirit, the Word of God, and the fellowship and accountability of other believers are all elements of our growth in Christlikeness. But there's a root to our problem that perhaps we haven't acknowledged and confessed. The real problem—the first sin that led to our behavior—is that we were not in awe of God enough to stop and think about our actions. We forgot that we were on holy ground—and in holy company. We forgot that the utterly transcendent God, awesome in majesty, is always with us and even in us. That would have changed everything.

In Deed

Most of us sin repeatedly—we all have our various "weaknesses." Usually, our first step in dealing with them is to focus on them, trying to avoid them and even to flee from them. That's part of the process, but we need to try something else first: Focus on God. Realize that if you are aware of His holiness, conscious of the enormity of His presence, and recognizing the sacredness of every moment and every thought, your sinful behavior is much less likely to happen.

That takes mental and spiritual training. We don't naturally live with a sense of the Holy One's inspiring, terrifying, loving presence. We forget that pointing out our sins after the fact isn't His preferred remedy for us. No, He gives us reminders of His majesty all the time, and learning to be aware of them will make all the difference. Fearing Him will lead to wisdom in all we do.

> It is not the constant thought of their sins, but the vision of the holiness of God that makes the saints aware of their own sinfulness.
> —ANTHONY BLOOM

The Architect

**Jerusalem will be a city without walls because of
the great number of men and livestock in it.**
ZECHARIAH 2:4

In Word

God is building a city. The New Testament is full of His building plans—Jesus
as the cornerstone, believers as the living stones, the city of Zion (in Hebrews),
and the new Jerusalem (in Revelation)—but the New Testament writers got
the image from the prophets. The precious Cornerstone was prophesied in
Isaiah, the rebuilding of ancient walls was foretold in Isaiah and Jeremiah, and
both Amos and Zechariah speak of plumb lines and measuring rods that will
ensure a well-constructed city. Behind every phase of salvation history, there
is an Architect with a plan.

The great promise of Zechariah is that the city will be huge, and walls
won't be necessary. That sounds commonplace to those of us who live in a
modern metropolis, but in Zechariah's day, a city without walls was unheard
of. It would have been a sitting duck on the Middle Eastern landscape, vulner-
able to anyone with a mind to raid and pillage. But the Architect inspired His
prophet to give His people a picture they could hardly fathom. He gave them
a glimpse of radical building plans.

For a Jew carried off into captivity in Babylon—a Jew whose city walls
had been breached one miserable day decades earlier—a huge city with no
need of walls seemed like a heavenly vision. Jerusalem would be rebuilt bigger, better, and safer than ever, and its people would dwell in peace. It would
be a fulfillment of their deepest hopes.

In Deed

That's the message of God's self-portrait as an Architect. The dreams we have
of peace, safety, abundance, rest, and overflowing happiness are part of the
design of a city currently under construction. We are stones in the city's centerpiece, the temple of God, and we will reside on property far greater than
any beach house or ski chalet we can dream of. And without any walls in the
way, the view will be magnificent.

Peace reigns where our Lord reigns.

—JULIAN OF NORWICH

His Pet Project

Whoever touches you touches the apple of his eye.
ZECHARIAH 2:8

In Word

In Revelation 21:2, the new Jerusalem, the city of God, is portrayed as a beautiful bride. That should tell us plenty about God's view of His people. The Architect has specified living materials in the plans He has drawn up, and He is personally invested in the project. He loves whatever He makes.

God's affection for Jerusalem as revealed in the Old Testament was applied by New Testament writers to the church, a melting pot that included Jews, Gentiles, slave, free, male, female—everyone who believed. While many religions depict a god who is capricious, uninvolved, or stern and strict, there's no such portrait of God in the Bible. He is intimately involved in His work, and He is zealous about completing what He started. When the prophets show us a God who designs and builds, they are revealing a direction and purpose to this world that few people recognize. And that purpose comes from an extremely good heart.

In Deed

Meditate on that today. Spend some time thinking about the direction not only of the world, but also of your life. Don't focus on the process, but on the finished product. See if you can envision yourself in the eternal city, a key member of the cherished bride of Christ, one of the beloved whom He calls "the apple of His eye." You may not be comfortable with such intimate affection from your Lord, but you'll have to get used to it. Spend some time getting used to it today.

It is imperative for every Christian to understand the diligence of the Architect over His plans. He does not waste materials, He does not treat His designs casually, He is not sloppy in His work, and He is never deterred from completing His project. This is why He created the world to begin with, and He will not fail to use you exactly as He planned.

> That tender love completely surrounds us, never to leave us.
> —JULIAN OF NORWICH

Your Place in the Plan

Shout and be glad.
ZECHARIAH 2:10

In Word

Joy is a serious problem for Christians. Actually, the real problem is our lack
of it. Believers feel oppressed, depressed, stressed, and burned-out at alarming levels. Why? Because we feel disconnected from God's plan and purpose.
We don't comprehend how our daily to-do lists fit in the eternal landscape,
or how our month-to-month survival leaves time for an everlasting vision. We
want every moment to count and every activity to bear fruit, but we don't see
how they do. And worst of all, we don't see how His desires for our lives fit
our desires for our lives. We get discouraged because we lose our vision.

Two proverbs give us insight into human depression: "If people can't see
what God is doing, they stumble all over themselves; but when they attend
to what he reveals, they are most blessed" (Proverbs 29:18, The Message);
and, "Hope deferred makes the heart sick, but a longing fulfilled is a tree of
life" (Proverbs 13:12). In both cases, whether from impaired vision or denied
gratification, discouragement is a result of the disconnect between human
hope and God's design. When we're on the construction site while the Architect's plans are hidden away in an office somewhere, we're lost.

But the Architect's plans are not hidden away. If we think they're going to
be posted on a billboard, we'll be disappointed, but if we search them out like
treasure on a scavenger hunt, we'll find life an adventure. And an adventur-
ous life is a joyful life. The exhilaration of being led by God, specifically and
fruitfully, is the sure antidote to a life of discouragement. It leads to shouting
and gladness.

In Deed

How would you describe your life today? Are you in glad shouting mode, or
are you in burnout survival mode? If the latter, why? You have access to the
Architect's design and an open invitation to be a part of it. Not only that,
you can rest assured that His desires for you line up with the deepest needs
and appetites of your heart. The disconnect between your will and His and
between your hopes and His is an illusion. He crafted you to fit your place in
the plan. That should be worth a joyful shout.

> There is not one blade of grass, there is no color in
> this world that is not intended to make us rejoice.
>
> —JOHN CALVIN

Where He Dwells

Be still before the LORD, all mankind, because
he has roused himself from his holy dwelling.

ZECHARIAH 2:13

In Word

When God is ready to occupy His human dwelling, we'll be speechless. In fact, we already should be. The message of the prophets is astounding: the God of heaven and earth, the Holy One of Israel, the King of kings and Lord of lords, the One who occupies a glorious throne room beyond all comprehension, is crafting a dwelling in the hearts and community of people who trust Him.

Though the context of the prophetic words in Zechariah is the restoration of Jews from captivity, the principle is to be fulfilled on a cosmic scale. The New Testament writers were clear that God is the Architect and Builder of an eternal Jerusalem in which all His people will dwell (Hebrews 11:10). His construction applied to Judah as its captives left Babylon. His role applies forever.

That means that the words of the prophets have profound implications for your life. It is imperative to ask yourself what God is building in your relationships, what He is building in your work, and what He is building in your personal ministry. Your life is not a random process; it's integral to the entire plan. Your gifts are needed to complete God's project, and if you understand them correctly, you'll see how they fit into the overall scheme.

In Deed

You may not consider your life that critical to God's plan. After all, the mass of humanity is huge, and it seems plausible that God could replace anyone at will, like a football coach substitutes players. But God is building a dwelling place, and your uniqueness is integral to it. God is efficient with His materials. You need to find out what kind of material you are and where you are to be placed.

How do you do that? Ask. Specifically and repeatedly ask God to guide you into place, and don't stop asking until He has revealed His design for you. The Architect will show you His plans—you can be sure of that. This is His dream home.

The Holy Spirit has promised to lead us step
by step into the fullness of truth.

—LEON SUENENS

The Occupant

"I myself will be a wall of fire around it," declares
the Lord, "and I will be its glory within."
ZECHARIAH 2:5

In Word

Marie Monsen, a Norwegian missionary to China years ago, was in a village under siege by bandits. In her bed one night, she awoke to the sound of the bandits breaking through the village walls. As she prayed, Zechariah 2:5 came to mind, and she saw a wall of fire around her. Remarkably, she was untouched—even undiscovered—by the bandits all through the night.

That's a personal application of God's promise to His people. Whether dealing with individuals or churches, God functions as a wall of fire around those who believe that He will. His people are His habitation, after all. He has calculated us meticulously with a plumb line (Amos 7:7-8) and a measuring line (Zechariah 1:16). He does not work such precision only to leave it unguarded, where vandals can deface and destroy. You and the church are much too vital to His plan—and to His heart—to be left alone.

You are also much too vital to be left vacant. God fills His human city with divine glory. You may not see it right now, or only in glimpses if you do, but His glory is part of the plan. The Architect's design will glow from without and within; it's a beautifully lit structure.

In Deed

If you tend to worry a lot, you are slandering the wall of fire that surrounds you. You are questioning His strength (or willingness) and are suspicious of whether His glory really dwells within. That may sound harsh, but we all do it. And God's response is to assure us—repeatedly, emphatically, and intensely—to trust Him.

"We must protect this house" is a common battle cry for sports teams in their own stadiums. How much more is God zealous for His house! His city, His well-crafted dwelling, is to be the seat of His glory. He protects it and He fills it with Himself—you, your family, your church, everything—at all costs.

O Comforter, draw near, within my heart appear,
and kindle it, Thy holy flame bestowing.
—BIANCO DA SIENA

Depths of Glory

The Son of Man did not come to be served, but to serve.

MATTHEW 20:28

In Word

Where is God glorified? Is it in our stylish appearance on Sunday mornings? Our impressive displays of talent and skill? Our ability to influence others? Maybe sometimes, but most of us know that's not where the God of glory dwells. Despite His majestic splendor, He's much more humble than that. Ours is a God who, during His incarnation, dwelt in a feeding trough at birth and rode a donkey at the height of His popularity. The exalted Lord Jesus has never really appeared "exalted" to our worldly eyes.

Why is that? He could certainly impress us all the time with parted seas and with blazing fires by night. He could clearly fill a temple with His awesome presence. Why did the Everlasting Father clothe Himself as a Suffering Servant?

Because glory is about His character, not about His appearance. And character shows up best when circumstances are worst. It's the same with us. Nobody really judges us by the way we appear at our best; they size us up when we're under a burden. The contrast between light and darkness shows up when we're one and our environment is the other. So it is with God.

Many think the glory of God is reflected in the great cathedrals, and perhaps it is. But it is also reflected in the slums of third-world megacities and the mental hospitals of postwar generations. The cathedrals make it possible for observers to praise the ingenuity of man; the slums and the wards are so dreadful that any evidence of God in them is clear. No one has trouble finding a light when all else is dark.

In Deed

Don't strive for the glory of God by reaching for the heights. Seek it by plunging into the depths. That's what Jesus did, leaving eternal majesties for the corrupt environment of earth, and oh, how God was glorified. That's the direction in which He calls us as well. Go down. Show His love to broken sinners; proclaim His mercy in trash-filled streets; and shine your light in dark ghettoes. Jesus dove deep for us. He calls us to dive deep for Him.

If Christ were here, He would help them, and so must I.
—TOYOHIKO KAGAWA, ON HIS MISSION TO KOBE'S SLUM-DWELLERS

God in the Flesh

Honor God with your body.

1 CORINTHIANS 6:20

In Word

One of the first heresies the church had to face was gnosticism. Its proponents believed that the physical world was either evil or irrelevant. God, being Spirit, was believed to be concerned only with our spiritual life. Gnostics insisted that He relates to us only spiritually, He redeems us only spiritually, and He gives us only a spiritual eternal life. What we do—and what Jesus did—in the flesh does not matter. Or maybe it didn't even happen. So said the gnostics.

But our God is intensely involved in physical things. Though He is Spirit (John 4:24), He expressed Himself through His creation of a very physical universe. And our Savior—God in the flesh—thirsted, hungered, wept, bled, and died. He was a Spirit-God in a human body. Why? Because physical bodies mattered.

God did not relegate the physical world to irrelevance after Jesus' ascension, either. Soon after Jesus' glorified body rose into heaven, the Holy Spirit filled human flesh in power. Our Spirit-God no longer calls tabernacles and temples His home. Instead, He pours Himself into human hearts and He dwells in the body of Christ—the church. Why? Because physical bodies still matter.

In Deed

Do not make the mistake of thinking that God is only concerned with our spirits. It's true that Jesus said we are to "worship in spirit and in truth" (John 4:24). But there's a context. We worship the God who indwells mortal flesh. We are His temple. And those who carelessly degrade His temple, either through immorality or irreverence, are being careless about their worship. Praising God with physical mouths and then treating our bodies with little concern for our health or morality is a gross contradiction. Worshiping God while discounting His chosen dwelling place does not make sense.

How do you regard God's temple? Are you aware that wherever you go, you are walking on holy ground? Accept the absurdity of an infinite God who inhabits your flesh. Consider your earthen vessel sacred.

> Every cell in my body is a hymn to my Creator and a declaration of love.
>
> —ERNESTO CARDENAL

Called to Endure

**We put up with anything rather than
hinder the gospel of Christ.**
1 CORINTHIANS 9:12

In Word

Living in a culture that emphasizes rights, we are naturally inclined to insist on
them often. American founding documents regard certain rights as "inalien-
able" and God-given. We feel a moral obligation to insist on human rights
around the world. It's the right thing to do in an oppressive world.

One of the drawbacks of being in a rights-based society is that we cultivate
a sense of entitlement. We have trouble switching from rights-based thinking
to grace-based servanthood. For social functioning in a free democracy, rights
are important. But for serving in a Spirit-filled theocracy—the Kingdom of
God—rights are almost irrelevant. All that matters is the gospel.

That's hard for us to grasp. In this radical reorientation from self-centeredness to God-centeredness, we carry the foundational principles of the
former into the practice of the latter. We forget that in the grand scheme of
eternity, our temporary liberties in a human society don't mean a lot. They
aren't eternal either in duration or in importance. They can be sacrificed—
they must be, in fact—for a greater good.

Paul frequently called himself a slave and bond servant of Christ. Whether
he was chained in prison or preaching in open air, he considered himself
bound to the good news of salvation and the glory of Jesus. No assertion of
rights was appropriate. The overriding concern was the eternal destiny of
human souls—even at the expense of freedom.

In Deed

Most of us can admit that we're not quite that God-centered. We like our
freedoms; they are good, and God has blessed us with them. But He has not
guaranteed them—yet. He has promised us eternity instead. As His creation,
we do not deny that we are born with rights. But as His servants, we lay them
down willingly for the sake of the gospel. Whatever we must endure will be
worth it.

Nothing is really lost by a life of sacrifice; everything
is lost by failure to obey God's call.
—HENRY P. LIDDON

Diligent Discipleship

Run in such a way as to get the prize.
1 CORINTHIANS 9:24

In Word

Imagine showing up for the Boston Marathon without ever having run a race. Or worse yet, imagine showing up without ever having even practiced. How far would you get? A mile? Maybe two? That would be impressive, but it's still only a fraction of the race. Athletes who do not train but still show up for the competition are in for an embarrassing time. Those who really want to compete do what it takes to be competitive.

Some people may enter discipleship casually, but those who do will not get very far. The Christian life must be an all-out proposition, a marathon that demands intensive training even to finish well, much less win. Those who do not approach it as such will become mediocre and ineffective in their relationship with God. Spiritual growth doesn't just happen by accident. We are runners in an intense training program.

God is not going to crown a single winner—a discipleship champion, so to speak. He will, however, hand out prizes to those who finish well. What are they? A "well done" from the Master? A greater capacity to serve Him? More responsibility? More eternal treasure? We can only speculate about some of these. But we know His desire: He wants His followers to follow to the end. He wants them to press hard in their training for the eternal Kingdom. He wants spiritual success through the power of His Spirit.

In Deed

What can be said for someone who praises God loudly and with enthusiasm but will not run His race in like manner? Is there any greater contradiction? It makes no sense to say we follow Jesus and then to lag behind. Jesus is intense; casual discipleship won't keep up with Him.

That doesn't mean that there's no grace for all of our weaknesses and insufficiencies. No, God delights in such frailties, showing Himself strong in them at every turn. But only when we depend on Him as we run the race. Halfhearted running wins no prizes. Wholehearted running cannot fail.

Nothing great was ever done without much enduring.
—CATHERINE OF SIENA

Our Strength

I do not trust in my bow, my sword does not bring me victory.
PSALM 44:6

In Word

Strong warriors have been reduced to weak, desperate souls on the battlefield. There comes a time in every human fight when strength is exhausted and fatigue sets in. That applies to battle-weary soldiers as well as to ambassadors for Christ. Whether the battle is over land or souls, the fighting can be intense. When it is, human weakness shows itself. No one is invincible.

Every person reaches that point, especially those who are fighting the real battle—the warfare that rages between the people of God and the enemy of God. Whether the issue is discipleship, evangelism, or anything else of an eternal nature, the stakes are higher than anything a skilled swordsman or a battleship commander has ever fought for. Yes, this Christian life is a fight to the death. And it is exhausting.

Are you weary? Feeling defeated? Overwhelmed by the odds against you? Don't be. This isn't about odds, and it isn't even about your strength. Our weakness is no problem to God; in fact, it's His golden opportunity to show Himself strong. If you are feeling weak, you are in a good place. God can now do His work with less hindrance. The stage is set for His might.

In Deed

The only power that will ever really accomplish anything eternal in this world is God's. But He insists on operating in a power vacuum. He won't compete against our own strength. He may use us—our strengths, gifts, and talents— as He wills, but He won't share His glory with us. He waits for us to exhaust our resources; then He works through us for His own glory to whatever degree we're surrendered to His will and His power.

Do you have the tendency to trust in your bow and your sword? Maybe the images are a little outdated, but we know what our strengths are, and we trust in them far too often. We forget that our greatest power is infinitely weaker than God. Which would we rather depend on in a battle? Trust God's power. He is always the Victor.

Fight the good fight with all thy might; Christ is thy strength, and Christ thy right.
—JOHN SAMUEL BEWLEY MONSELL

The Obedience of Joy

Rejoice in the Lord always. I will say it again: Rejoice!
PHILIPPIANS 4:4

In Word

Depression is one of the most universal psychological maladies. On every continent, in every culture, people get depressed. Why? Perhaps life doesn't go the way they want it to; maybe there's a chemical imbalance in their brain; or maybe they just lack the social support and affection that people should provide one another. Regardless of the reason, our fallen nature often results in sadness and emptiness.

Paul gives us a remedy. It may not solve everything for every depressed person, but it has a lot to do with how we approach life. He tells us to rejoice. Not only that, he tells us to rejoice in the Lord. There's a basis for it: we're His children, and He has done great things for us—whether we feel it or not. Regardless of how we perceive our lives or the things around us, God has done things for us that are worthy of exuberant celebration. So Paul's instruction is simply this: to celebrate.

Notice that Paul does not say that only those people whose circumstances are encouraging should rejoice. He's writing the Philippians from prison, after all. And notice also that he does not say that only those people with favorable genetics, brain chemistry, upward mobility, economic status, or any other specific result of a healthy ancestry are to rejoice. No, the implication is that everyone in His church, at all times and in every circumstance, is to rejoice—in the Lord.

In Deed

The knee-jerk reaction of most people to such an imperative is to whine about why we can't. We can't rejoice because Paul just doesn't understand the situation we're in. We haven't had the good fortune that other rejoicers have had. For some reason, God hasn't dealt with us as bountifully as with others. The excuses are limitless, but the command remains the same. Rejoice.

Can you? Regardless of what is going on in your life right now, can you find it in you to praise God for His blessings? When you do, you'll be amazed at the result: Life somehow grows more worthy of our joy.

Happiness depends on what happens; joy does not.
—OSWALD CHAMBERS

Not to Us, O Lord

Not to us, O LORD, not to us but to
your name be the glory.
PSALM 115:1

In Word

We don't like to think of ourselves as self-centered. The word has such negative connotations, implying an egotistical selfishness that is repulsive everywhere from the preschool playground to the church sanctuary. But we came into this world as babies who have demands in the middle of the night, completely unaware of their parents' needs. And we have carried our self-orientation into our adulthood. We are often wholly preoccupied with our own lives.

What are the signs of a self-centered life? An obsession for our own success, perhaps; an overriding concern for our own security, whether financial or relational; a zealous pursuit to satisfy our own emotional needs; and the list could go on. God wants all of those things for us: fruitfulness, security, emotional stability, and more. But He never tells us to pursue them. He tells us to pursue Jesus.

Most likely, you showed up somewhere on that list of self-centered characteristics. We all do. It's who we are by nature and as a product of our sinful fall. We seek our own kingdom, in a sense, obsessing about our accomplishments, our welfare, and our needs. We want success and status. And rather than trusting God to take care of those things—which He has promised to do in His own time and way—we seek to satisfy them ourselves. We seek our own dominion.

What are the signs of a Jesus-centered life? A preoccupation with His glory, for one thing; a dependence on His ability to provide and protect; and a pursuit of His kingdom and His dominion alone. It's radical, but it's our calling. A Jesus-centered life is a life that fits with God's plan.

In Deed

Have you been seeking your own kingdom? That's a heavy burden to bear, and it will lead to frustration. What's the solution? Lay it down and ask God to help you submit more fully to His Spirit. The self cannot overcome the self-centered life. Only God can make us God-centered. Ask Him. Seek His glory alone.

True glory and holy joy is to glory in Thee and not in one's self.
—THOMAS À KEMPIS

A Tragic End

**Those who make [idols] will be like them,
and so will all who trust in them.**

PSALM 115:8

In Word

False worship has a horrifying result: It shapes us into the object of our idolatry. The psalmist who observed the worship habits of Philistines and Canaanites saw that the end result of idolatry was a state of senselessness—eyes that do not see, mouths that cannot speak, ears that cannot hear, and hands and feet that cannot feel or walk. In other words, idolatry leads to numbness and death.

Our idols today are more sophisticated, but they dull our senses just the same. When we give undue attention to the gifts of God, distorting them, we close our eyes and ears to the vision and voice of our God. We see Him less clearly and hear Him more faintly. In our pursuit of the things we think will bring us life at its fullest, we drift away from the Source of life Himself. The fullness we seek always eludes us until we return to Him and worship Him alone.

What an irony. Those who pursue pleasure in place of God become less able to sense it. Those who seek success as a validation of their own worth end up feeling worthless. Those who chase after sexual or romantic passion eventually find themselves numb to its greatest blessings. The gifts of God never seem like gifts to those who pursue them instead of the Giver. But to those who seek only God, all other gifts become even greater blessings.

In Deed

Be careful about what you pursue. It will eventually define you. Your addictions to pleasure, to substances, to ideas, or anything else eventually become your identity. What begins as a deep interest can easily become a personality-altering obsession. Those who "worship" falsely begin to look like the objects of their worship. Whatever your passions are, the result can be scary.

Many people seem to believe the Bible prohibits our enjoyment of God's gifts. It doesn't. In fact, it blesses such. But it gives strong warnings: Enjoyment can turn to idolatry in subtle, dangerous ways. Be very careful; idols are a heavier burden than they appear.

*We easily fall into idolatry, for we are inclined to it by nature;
and coming to us by inheritance, it seems pleasant.*

—MARTIN LUTHER

Sacred Trust

The highest heavens belong to the LORD,
but the earth he has given to man.
PSALM 115:16

In Word

The psalmist has given us ample reason to praise God, not just with the words of our mouths, but with every inclination of our hearts. In fact, we are not just to praise Him; we are to be zealous about His glory and completely unconcerned with our own. We are to seek the glories of His Kingdom and not the glory of ours. We are to trust Him in everything and turn away from the false comforts of idols. We are to be completely His.

But the psalmist makes a curious observation at the end of his poetic praise. The highest heavens, he says, are God's—but earth is man's. In other words, there is no doubt in heaven about the glory of God. There may or may not be doubt in our own minds about the glory of God. But there is most certainly doubt in this world about the glory of God, and it is mankind's holy responsibility and sacred trust to declare His worth. Dead men sing no praises in this world. If God is to be glorified at all on this fallen planet, it is through our mouths and our actions. Worship does not—it cannot—end in our hearts.

It's an overwhelming thought: Though the heavens and earth declare the glory of God, according to Scripture, the hardened hearts and minds of an unbelieving world require an interpretation. And God has given this world interpreters: us—those who believe in Him. It is our sacred obligation to reach this generation with the news of our good God. We are given the job of reflecting His light. We are the evidence of God for an unbelieving culture.

In Deed

It's a shame when evidence remains hidden. It's a tragedy when the people of God, who have been entrusted with the authority of Jesus in the world, do not realize that they are instruments of His Kingdom. But we are. We are messengers, ambassadors, voices of praise and glory on a vainglorious planet. He has given us this world for His own purposes. What have we done with the gift?

We are mirrors of God, created to reflect Him.
—ERNESTO CARDENAL

God Laughs

**The One enthroned in heaven laughs;
the Lord scoffs at them.**

PSALM 2:4

In Word

We live in an age of turmoil, but that's nothing new. Everyone since Adam and Eve in the Garden of Eden has lived in such an age. Sin has ravaged this planet, and history has witnessed empire against empire, fighting to the death. The back halls of legislatures and parliaments, the high offices of presidents and kings, and the war rooms of generals have long been filled with plotting and planning. Everyone has an agenda, and it doesn't matter much whether that agenda is based on nationalism, ideology, vengeance, security, or cultural conflict: No one's agenda but God's will enthrone the Lord of glory.

God sits in heaven and laughs—not because He thinks it's funny, but because He knows the truth of the future. His plan will be carried out, and His Son will be exalted. Despite the schemings of men and nations, despite the massive presence of massive weapons, despite the political philosophies of ancient Greece, Machiavelli, Stalin, Hitler, Pol Pot, or even Washington and Jefferson—good or bad, free or dictatorial—humanity's devices will fail and God will reign. That's certain.

In Deed

That's good to know in an age of terrorism and ethnic hostilities. Wars and rumors of wars may rattle us, but there's no need to be rattled. The One enthroned in heaven laughs. He knows. There is an end to this story, and it is unquestionable. Not only that, it is unquestionably good. Righteousness will be established and peace will prevail. It will take a miraculous intervention, but that's exactly what we're promised. It will come through the clouds when few expect it.

Our response to this violent world is not to look scared, but to look up. Our final redemption is coming because our Redeemer has been promised an inheritance. The King has assured us: We have nothing to fear.

Do you live in fear in this age of uncertainty? Don't. Let the nations roar, and remember that God laughs. Our greatest threats are nothing compared to His strength.

Tomorrow's history has already been written—at the name of Jesus, every knee must bow.

—PAUL KAUFFMAN

The Spring

I will pour water on the thirsty land, and streams
on the dry ground; I will pour out my Spirit on your
offspring, and my blessing on your descendants.
ISAIAH 44:3

In Word
The Israelites wandered through the desert criticizing God for leading them
into a place of no water—until God miraculously gave them water. Elijah
prayed that God would withhold rain, and God did—until he prayed again for
rain, and God gave it. In any age, droughts are serious business, taking liveli-
hood and even lives from a water-dependent world. And the Israelites were
well acquainted with them; both physically and spiritually, they had lived in
some pretty dry places.

So whenever God promised to pour out water in those dry places, it
painted a vivid picture of His mercy. He promised to rain righteousness on
His people (Isaiah 45:8); He promised that those who trusted Him would be
like trees planted next to life-giving streams (Psalm 1; Jeremiah 17:8); and,
best of all, He declared Himself to be the rain that refreshes and the spring
that brings life (Isaiah 44:3; Jeremiah 17:13).

That's nowhere clearer than it is in Jesus' ministry. He offered a woman
at a well the kind of water that would satisfy her thirst forever (John 4), and
He told a hostile crowd that all who believed in Him would have rivers of
living water flowing out of them (John 7:38). The image of God as a spring is
a refreshing picture of salvation.

In Deed
God rains down on His people. Sometimes it's a rain of judgment, but even
then it has redeeming life in it. But more often, the falling rain and the bub-
bling spring are pure mercy, the righteousness and salvation of God saturating
the people who need it most.

Where do you need it most? All of us have parched places in our lives,
and there's nothing that will bring them to life but the streams of God. Fortu-
nately, we have a holy Spring from whom all blessings flow. Plant yourself next
to Him, let your roots grow deeply into Him, and watch your life flourish.

God is more anxious to bestow His blessings
on us than we are to receive them.
—AUGUSTINE

Receptive Soil

This is what the LORD says—Israel's King and
Redeemer, the LORD Almighty: I am the first and
I am the last; apart from me there is no God.

ISAIAH 44:6

In Word

The people of Judah were having a hard time choosing between gods made of wood and stone, which could do basically nothing, and the God of the universe, who holds all power in His hand. On one hand, the man-made gods required very little effort, were quite popular with the neighbors, and probably provided a hint of intangible psychological benefit. On the other hand, the real God, while requiring quite a bit, had also delivered them from Egypt, displayed mighty miracles among them, and had never wavered in faithfulness. For some reason, this was a difficult choice.

We can be that logic-impaired too, sometimes, and it always grieves God. The fact that the all-powerful, all-wise, and always-good God, full of mercy and perfect in every way, has to constantly defend Himself to us is a sad statement on human fallenness. He told us very early in Scripture that He is a jealous God (Exodus 20:5; 34:14; Deuteronomy 4:24). Still, the King, Redeemer, and Lord often has to sit in the backseat while we entertain those we consider more honored guests.

Why would anyone in his right mind forsake the spring of living water (Jeremiah 2:13)? He wouldn't, but we didn't come into this world in our right mind, did we? We came in with a rebellious streak, our inheritance from our most ancient ancestor. As a result, it takes a whole new seed to produce a God-loving organism—a seed watered by a supernatural spring.

In Deed

That Spring was available to rebellious Judah, and it is still available to us. God waters what He plants in this world; all that's required is the kind of soil that will soak in the moisture.

Examine the soil in your life. Test your receptivity to living water from above. Make sure that the God who is jealous never has to defend Himself to you.

There is nothing so abominable in the eyes
of God and of men as idolatry.
—BLAISE PASCAL

Inner Delight

One will say, "I belong to the LORD"; another will call
himself by the name of Jacob; still another will write on
his hand, "The LORD's," and will take the name Israel.

ISAIAH 44:5

In Word

The prophet says that there will come a time when God's people are unabashedly open about their identity in Him. They will call themselves by His name and by the names He has given His treasured ones. They will wear their relationship with God on their sleeves.

To a degree, that has happened; many people are quite open about God's work in their lives. But they may be the exception. Jesus gave His disciples several warnings about being ashamed of Him; the implication is that the pressures of the world would inhibit God's people and keep them quiet about Him. There are few Christians who exude the joy of bearing His name.

When God rains righteousness on His people—when His Spirit is poured out like a rushing river or a cascading waterfall—secrecy is not an option. The world may marvel or it may express contempt, but it will not remain oblivious to the Christian's life. Wearing Jesus on our sleeves does not allow for neutrality.

That doesn't mean wearing Him obnoxiously. The eternal Spring is refreshing, not annoying. Those who soak in His mercy do not come out of it with a bad odor. They come out with a vitality that is observable and contagious. People want to find out what it is.

In Deed

How would you characterize your level of pleasure and delight at being one of God's own? Would you describe yourself as a blooming rose? Or are you more like a shrinking violet? To what degree does your time inside the prayer closet cause you to beam with joy when you're out of it?

If you aren't happy with the answers, don't try to muster up more pleasure. See your lack of it rather as a symptom of a deeper need—a need to come closer, grow in intimacy, and enjoy Him more. Let the eternal Spring nourish you more deeply.

All earthly delights are but streams. But God is the ocean.

—JONATHAN EDWARDS

Significance

They will spring up like grass in a meadow,
like poplar trees by flowing streams.

ISAIAH 44:4

In Word

One of the deepest human needs is a sense of significance. We want to know that our life counts for something. The thought that we might be "dust in the wind" or small fish in a big pond can be utterly depressing. We all want to count for something and do things that will last. Everyone wants to be fruitful.

God promises that. He says that those who live for Him, who are planted by His streams, will flourish. They will bear fruit in season and the fruit will last forever. While the whole world feels as if it is chasing after wind, wondering if there's any meaning to life, we can rest confidently in the fact that we have been planted by a master Gardener and watered by a living Spring. We are offered a far greater significance than we ever thought we craved.

Contrast that promise with the promises of our age. Our advertisements tell us what matters most in life, and the list is depressingly superficial. Our common wisdom tells us that just being happy is enough, but deep down inside, we know that earthly happiness is temporary and will never be enough. We are led to believe that working hard and saving for a comfortable retirement is the epitome of true success, but we weren't wired to be content with such short-term success. Whatever values our world instills in us, we still can't be ultimately content until we break out of the cage that keeps us confined to time and space. We want to last forever.

In Deed

We will. God has promised. And not only will we last forever, the work we are able to do in this short time and small space can be planted and watered in a way that will make it eternally fruit-bearing. We can leverage our time, our talents, our money, our relationships, our spiritual gifts—everything God has given us—as seeds that sprout forever. In the landscape of life, that means one thing: your search for significance is over.

Work designed for eternity can only be
done by the eternal Spirit.

—A. W. TOZER

The Rock That Flows

You are my witnesses. Is there any God besides
me? No, there is no other Rock; I know not one.

ISAIAH 44:8

In Word

Twice between Egypt and the Promised Land, the Israelites grumbled about
their lack of water in the wilderness and complained that God was going to
let them die of thirst. Both times, God brought water out of a rock, satisfying the thirst of a whining people. It was a merciful response to a slanderous
charge. When God's people are dehydrated and grumpy about it, God rains
grace on them anyway.

Hundreds of years later, when Israel was turning to man-made idols, God
promised another "pouring out," this time of His Spirit. And then He gave
them a not-so-subtle reminder with this essential message: "I'm the same
God who can satisfy your thirst from a rock. In fact, I am your Rock. I may
appear stolid and stagnant, but life comes out of Me. I'm a Rock that flows
with whatever you need to flourish."

We live in a world that craves life but seeks it in idols. It complains about
its suffering and turns to things that are emotionally satisfying for nothing
more than a brief moment. All the while, God the Rock is ready to gush with
life. All He waits for is a reasonable acknowledgment that temporal things
can't satisfy eternal desires. Only He can do that.

In Deed

Don't be drawn into the world's idolatry. Our culture, entertainment, trends,
styles, material prosperity, transient relationships, and recreational pursuits
may bubble over with promises of life, but they are false promises. Our life-
giving sustenance comes from a Rock. Only eyes of faith can see that.

Walk through this world with eyes of faith. There's no other way to avoid
the bitterness and disappointments of the wilderness, and there's no other
way to recognize all the false promises of counterfeit springs. Survive the wilderness by drinking deeply from the Rock that flows. Immerse yourself in His
mercy, wash yourself in His promises, and always let Him satisfy your thirst.

I have always drunk of that water of life, and have
never been athirst in the sandy desert of this world.

—SUNDAR SINGH

Citizenship

Our citizenship is in heaven.
PHILIPPIANS 3:20

In Word

The Christian life depends heavily on perspective. Trials are suddenly bearable when we have an eternal point of view. Plans come into focus when we see things in the light of God's Kingdom. Relationships are cultivated when we realize their godly purposes. Nearly everything we think and do depends on how we identify ourselves.

Paul tells us to think of ourselves as citizens of heaven. On earth, we were born in a particular country and we have a particular ethnicity. Our economic status may determine our circle of friends, the neighborhoods in which we live, and the schools our children attend. Our careers may be the first piece of information people ask for when we're introduced to them. But none of these things are our true identity. None of them define us. We are not Americans, Europeans, Africans, or Asians. We are not upper class or middle class or lower class. We are not white-collar or blue-collar, employed or unemployed. We are heaven's citizens. That is our only valid ID.

Think of what that means. We no longer have to impress anyone. The titles on our business cards and our mail have no real significance. The municipalities we live in will be redrawn when His Kingdom comes in its fullness. Our Kingdom passports declare that we are children of God whose address is in heaven. We are not to have our feet planted in this world.

In Deed

When your feet are planted in heaven, you can quit striving for status in this world. You can live with a godly sense of abandon because you aren't attached to material things or even your own physical life. You can take some risks, although nothing God calls us to do is really risky by eternal definitions. You can follow Him without fear.

Where do you feel at home? Scripture tells us that our home is in heaven. That means heaven is where we are to invest ourselves wholeheartedly. If not, we will have all kinds of competing desires and emotions in this life. But if so, we can move forward with perspective and purpose. We're headed home.

> Our duty as Christians is always to keep heaven
> in our eye and earth under our feet.
> —MATTHEW HENRY

Every Breath

I will extol the LORD at all times; his
praise will always be on my lips.
PSALM 34:1

In Word

What would happen if we decided to let every thought and every breath bless God? Imagine the result if His name were affectionately on our lips as we lay down at night, as we turned over in our sleep, as we awoke in the morning, and as we went about our daily business. Would such a perspective radically change our hearts? Probably. Would it change our world? It's likely. Anytime in the Bible someone gives himself to worship, God does amazing things through that person. Blessings abound. God's work is done. He is honored.

What prevents us from such a pervasive sense of His worth? Are our schedules just too busy? Or is it deeper than that? Perhaps it's a suspicion that He hasn't been as good to us as Scripture declares that He is. Or maybe it's a subtle resentment that He has not paved our paths with gold and has allowed us to taste the bitter trials of life.

Whatever reasons we can come up with, we should ask ourselves if a worship-filled heart is worth sacrificing to the gods of busyness, apathy, and disappointment. If we really got a glimpse of God, we would never be too busy; we would never be too apathetic; and we would never be disappointed with His will for us. We would understand that underlying everything we go through and every responsibility we're given is the loving hand of a God who is leading us closer to Him. The end result is a greater blessing than any earthbound human can possibly imagine.

In Deed

The angels surrounding God's throne cry out day and night, "Holy, holy, holy is the LORD Almighty; the whole earth is full of his glory" (Isaiah 6:3). Perhaps we were not created with exactly the same role as those angels were; but then again, perhaps they are pictures of the praise all creatures—including us— owe Him. We at least have a similar purpose: to honor God and ascribe glory to Him. What prevents us? Nothing should. What would result? Everything our heart truly desires.

Let your first "good morning" be to your Father in heaven.
—KARL MAESER

Radiant Faces

Those who look to him are radiant.
PSALM 34:5

In Word

Psalm 34 is about David's ongoing saga of running from trouble. He had just fled from King Saul; next he was in the presence of a Philistine king, one of Israel's archenemies. He feigned insanity, and then went and hid out in a cave. Not an easy place to be. Compared to David's troubles, our troubles often seem petty.

Or do they? Regardless of outward circumstances, we often feel pursued by enemies, questioned by rivals, and maybe even on the verge of insanity. We may feel that our only refuge is the darkness of a cave. When life gets tough, sometimes we just want to hide.

That's not forbidden. God allows it. His only request is that we hide ourselves in Him. David and others throughout Scripture refer to God as their refuge. We even sing a hymn, "Rock of Ages," that asks God to let us hide under His protection.

Psalm 34 is one of the most encouraging passages in the Bible. Its promises are extravagant, and its message is comforting. Its priorities are our pattern; we are to praise God first, seek Him second, and then look to Him in gratitude and love. Those who follow this prescription, according to the Word, will never—never in the scope of all eternity—be disappointed. The refuge of the Righteous One is all the refuge anyone needs—from anything.

In Deed

Those who look mainly to other people for their security or their direction will one day be disappointed. No one can live up to our expectations; no one can be "God" for us. Those who look to possessions or personal wealth for their security or status will one day be sadly lacking. Nothing in all of creation can satisfy our deepest, longest-lasting needs; only the Creator can do that. Those who look to anything other than the fullness of God, whether in times of ease or times of adversity, will end up tragically empty.

Those who look to God, however, will be radiant. It's the promise of this psalm. There will be no shame, only vindication and satisfaction. No one has ever sought the true God and been disappointed. And no one ever will.

Rock of ages, cleft for me, let me hide myself in Thee.
—AUGUSTUS TOPLADY

Needing God

**Taste and see that the LORD is good; blessed
is the man who takes refuge in him.**
PSALM 34:8

In Word

Most of us have been to the emotional depths. We've been desperate about
a situation—relational, economic, physical, spiritual—and we've cried out
to God with every ounce of energy we have. At such times, we hardly think
we're honoring Him; we may even think we're a bother to His busy schedule,
with all the taking care of the world that He does. Maybe next time we're at
such a low point, we'll be encouraged to remember that when we pray this
way, we're worshiping.

Desperate prayers are, in fact, one of the clearest ways for us to honor
God. Saying "Lord, I need You," acknowledges His importance to us. He is
essential, after all, and the desperate soul is not afraid to say so.

There's a repeated dynamic in the Bible: God's people have a great need,
they come to Him with it in faith, He provides by meeting that need, and they
presumably (though not always) give Him thanks and sing songs of praise. The
Word gives us songs of deliverance, of victory, of gratitude, and more. Why?
Because needy people sought Him, He answered, and they praised Him. He
was glorified in the dynamic of human need. No wonder He lets us go to those
low places so often.

In Deed

The dynamic is distorted, of course, when (1) we don't take our needs to
Him; (2) we don't believe He'll answer us; or (3) we don't give Him glory
after His gracious response. Perhaps that's why we so often miss it; we mis-
understand the whole point.

But God has chosen to create a planet of needy people as a stage for His
great supply. In our depths, His heights are more visible. In our depravity, His
righteousness shines brighter. In our poverty, His riches are so much more
appreciated than they ever would have been otherwise.

Do you see your deep, desperate needs as occasions to worship Him? They
are. Even the very act of crying to Him is to His glory. It recognizes who He
is: the essential God.

A groan is a matter about which there is no hypocrisy.
—CHARLES SPURGEON

Deliverance

**The righteous cry out, and the LORD hears them;
he delivers them from all their troubles.**
PSALM 34:17

In Word

Whenever times get tough, we crave deliverance. We cry out to God and ask Him to get us out of whatever situation we're in. It's human nature; we're not conditioned to enjoy pain.

God knows that. That's why He promises deliverance. We want Him to get us out of trouble, and this psalm promises that He will. That seems simple, except for one nagging question—a huge one: Despite our cries for deliverance, and despite the promise that it will come, we still seem awfully stuck. All our troubles seem to persist, even in the face of desperate prayer. Why?

God desires a deeper deliverance than we crave. Or, to turn it around, we look for the shallow way out and ask Him to give it to us. Sometimes He may, but that's not usually His first response. First and foremost, He wants to deliver us from the internal captivity we face—the emotional anguish, the sense of dread, the worries about our future, the idols that we clutch. Giving us the shallow way out would leave all of those things intact. We know God better than to think He's obsessed with our circumstances without giving attention to our hearts. The heart is where He delivers first. The circumstances almost always follow afterward.

In Deed

Have you noticed the attributes of the person God delivers? In this psalm, He delivers the righteous—not the perfectly sinless (though the Savior who has come to live in us certainly fulfills that requirement), but the one whose heart is constantly, repeatedly leaning in God's direction. Those who gravitate toward sin have to be broken from that attraction.

And that's the second attribute of the one God delivers: brokenness. Being "crushed in spirit," as verse 18 mentions, sounds painful, but it's the only way to freedom. God is close to the brokenhearted, the crushed—those who are utterly undone. Our weakness is an occasion for His strength. And His strength always delivers us more deeply than we could have imagined.

Our extremity is God's opportunity.
—REES HOWELLS

Begin with Gratitude

**Who am I, O Lord God, and what is my
family, that you have brought me this far?**
1 CHRONICLES 17:16

In Word

David has gotten some good news and some bad news. The news came from God Himself, so David understands its finality. The bad news is that a dream of his has been denied; he will not be the one to build a house for God. The good news is that God will build David's house, establishing his throne forever.

For most of us, the good news would far outshine the bad. It probably did so for David, too. But his prayer seems to have just a touch of bittersweet flavor, a disappointment that though God has richly blessed His servant with lavish promises, He has not promised that a temple will be built during David's reign. So David has bowed in reverence, humbled at the plan of God.

David's opening line (v. 16) would be a good one for us to use whenever God has denied us our plans. Yes, we will be disappointed sometimes when our will for serving God does not match His plans for us. The disappointment could be overwhelming if not for one thing: God has given us promises as lavish as the ones given to David. We have been grafted into that very same eternal Kingdom that has come through David's line. David's house has been established forever through the Messiah, and so has ours. We're in the same house—the Kingdom of the One who has redeemed us. We can say with David: "Who am I . . . that you have brought me this far?"

In Deed

Perspective is the key to our disappointments. No matter what prayer God leaves unanswered, He has promised us an eternity with Him. And it will be more than just an existence; it will be an eternity of unimaginable quality. The riches of our God have been poured out on us in Jesus! An awareness of that wealth is where all prayers should begin. Every disappointment will pale in comparison to what He has already blessed us with.

> When thou hast truly thanked the Lord for every blessing sent, but little time will then remain for murmur or lament.
>
> —HANNAH MORE

Out of the Depths

My tears have been my food day and night, while men say to me all day long, "Where is your God?"
PSALM 42:3

In Word

Sometimes it seems as though we suffer while the rest of the world parties. You probably know the feeling: Advertisements offer us the high life, peers put on a good show of confidence and success, and bookstores try to sell us everything we need to know to be healthy, emotionally balanced, and satisfied in all areas of life. Meanwhile, life for us has lost its luster. We see the corruption of fallen humanity, we have witnessed broken relationships, and we are faced with illness and death. The crushing weight of life reminds us that "Eat, drink, and be merry" is a completely empty philosophy. It offers us nothing in the end.

Navigating the heavy issues of relationships, debts, burdens, and human mortality without the comfort of God is the source of nearly every human neurosis. How do people get by without Him? The truth is that they don't. They can ignore Him for a time, and they can pretend that they are satisfied and happy. But their pursuit of pleasure, ideology, or some other empty agenda will catch up to them with a nagging reminder: We live in a fallen world, we will suffer pain, and we will die. No amount of partying can change that.

In Deed

This weighty reminder is the reason that so many have rejected the Christian faith. They want nothing to do with negatives: no sin, no corruption, no death. Health and happiness in all things is the golden calf they seek, never knowing the true health and happiness that a relationship with Jesus can bring.

The psalmist is right. Though his soul is downcast, though he suffers mockery and feeds on his own tears, he knows where to turn—"a prayer to the God of my life" (v. 8).

Never seek comfort in pleasure or possessions. Let people comfort you only if they offer the comfort of God. In your lowest points in life, realize the emptiness of those who are living the high life. Put your hope in God.

As sure as God puts His children in the furnace
He will be in the furnace with them.
—CHARLES SPURGEON

Washed and Broken

**Deep calls to deep in the roar of your waterfalls; all
your waves and breakers have swept over me.**
PSALM 42:7

In Word

Life with God is rough on us. It's a tremendous blessing and a light burden, but it can also be a violent overhaul. A life reoriented from self to God, from human impulse to Holy Spirit, and from sin to holiness implies a traumatic event. The change we experience is radical and relentless. We will forever be glad for it; but it might hurt for a while.

The writer of Psalm 42 is experiencing pain—"mortal agony," he declares in verse 10. His soul is downcast. God has allowed him to be in a difficult place. His response is correct: He thirsts for God and trusts Him as his Rock. Still, he must look forward to the future with hope, because the present is excruciating.

You've probably been in a similar state of mind. Pain is part of human experience. It's also part of the life of worship. Being a living sacrifice means that we live through the painful part of devotion. We give up treasures to the One we love in gratitude for the blessings of His love. It's worth it, but it hurts sometimes. Especially when He puts us in a hard place.

Perhaps the hardships are simply to develop our strength of character. Or perhaps God is rearranging our lives so we're really living for Him. It's hard to sacrifice dreams and goals for His greater plans, but if we belong to Him, it's inevitable. He always puts our hearts in their proper place.

In Deed

If you have entered into a relationship with God—if the Breath of Life is alive in you—then He will painfully touch you at your deepest levels of desire. That's a given, an integral part of the discipleship process. It isn't that your desires and attachments are wrong; they simply may not hold the proper place in your affections. But reordering your priorities to match God's is what being conformed to the image of Christ is all about. Like a violent waterfall, God sometimes hurts. Like rushing water, He also purifies. If His work hurts, let it. Your hope is in Him.

> We often learn more of God under the rod that
> strikes us than under the staff that comforts us.
> —STEPHEN CHARNOCK

Raw Nerves of the Soul

**By the rivers of Babylon we sat and
wept when we remembered Zion.**
PSALM 137:1

In Word

The captive Jews could not sing. Their city—their lives—lay in ruins at the hands of the Babylonians. Now they were slaves in a foreign land. All those promises from God about establishing Jerusalem forever seemed tragically obsolete, forfeited by their own disobedience. Did God live in Babylon? They weren't sure. He seemed so far away. And there was no song left for them to sing.

Psalm 137 is a lament by someone whose life had been struck by catastrophe. All seemed lost; hopelessness and despair had set in. There is anger in this psalm, along with disappointment and frustration. And bitterness—perhaps the most brutal emotion a human being can have. Bitterness obsesses about what could have been and despairs that it now isn't even possible. It eats away at all sense of hope and leaves us feeling awfully hollow.

Emotions are one of humanity's most powerful attributes. They can incite a crowd, sway a nation, distort our values, affect our decisions, inspire great works of art, and move us to serve God and others. They can have both positive and negative implications—even simultaneously. And the Bible is an emotional book. There is joyful dancing before the Lord, loud lament over broken lives, and everything in between. There is no hint in God's revelation that He desires sterile, calculated religion. We were created as beings of passion.

In Deed

Are you emotional before God? He put this bitter psalm and others into His Word, and its raw nerves are unashamedly bared in His presence. Clearly, it is okay with Him for us to dance, to lament, to weep, to laugh, to be excited, to be moody—to express whatever our hearts are feeling. Does He want us to be ruled by such moods? Of course not. But if we have them, He wants us to be honest about them—just as the writer of Psalm 137 was.

Take whatever emotions you have into the presence of God. It doesn't matter how raw they are. Sincerity honors His grace. There's healing in our honesty before Him.

You cannot have real religion without emotion.
—DONALD GEE

Justice Deprived

In his humiliation he was deprived of justice.
ACTS 8:33

In Word

The Ethiopian was reading from Isaiah 53, and the prophecy was confusing to him. Who was this sheep led to the slaughter? Who would undergo such treatment without opening his mouth? Who could possibly have his life taken in such degrading fashion and still be so highly honored in the prophetic Word? The Ethiopian had ears to hear; now he needed someone with a mouth to speak.

God sent Philip, who explained the good news about Jesus. We may have a hard time understanding what it was like to hear such strange truths for the first time. Some flesh-and-blood Person was cruelly executed because that was what we deserved. That's hard to swallow unless the Holy Spirit has done some groundwork in the hearer's heart. And He had; the Ethiopian embraced the Good News right away.

It's so sad, this good news. A righteous Savior was deprived of justice so that a wicked world might be spared from it. The Judge could have rightfully vindicated Jesus with glorious blessing while condemning us with well-deserved wrath. But this God switched justice around on His own Son. Jesus absorbed the shock of wrath so that the world wouldn't have to. All in all, justice was done; wrath was poured out on mankind. But the ones who deserved it were forgiven while the only One who didn't—the only One ever—felt it all.

In Deed

We won't ever get to the bottom of that mystery. It's too deep. We understand what we need to know about it, but God hasn't told us everything that went on behind the scenes in that transaction. All we know is that if we accept it, we are blessed by it. We have to accept it at face value like a child would accept an extravagant gift—without ever really understanding its cost.

But that shouldn't stop us from meditating on the mysterious sacrifice of the Lamb who didn't open His mouth. It's amazing. What a Savior.

Well might the sun in darkness hide, and shut his glories in,
when God the mighty Maker died for man, the creature's sin.
—ISAAC WATTS

The Refiner

For he will be like a refiner's fire or a launderer's soap.
MALACHI 3:2

In Word

Silver and gold do not come out of the earth in complete purity. In fact, sometimes precious metals are hardly recognizable in the mines; they look just like the earthy minerals around them. But an experienced eye can spot them amid the dirt, and a careful miner can extract them. That, however, is only the beginning of the process.

In order for a precious metal to be purified, its corruptions must be burned out of it. It has to be extracted from its ore by melting, which separates the impurities from the valuable elements. It's a rough process, and if the metal had feelings, it would scream in pain. But the finished product is magnificent—a rare treasure of beauty. People pay extravagantly for such treasures.

God presents Himself through the prophets as a Refiner. He can take any precious metal, no matter how corrupt and indistinguishable from its environment, and extract what is precious and beautiful. It's a traumatic process but extremely worthwhile. The result is something that shines with the glory God intended it to have.

In Deed

No one really wants the Refiner to do His work in his or her life, but those who welcome Him anyway are very wise. The refining process is never comfortable, but there is absolutely no way to experience the glory of God without it. We usually don't see past the choice between comfort and the crucible, but it's really a choice between mediocrity and beauty, or between boredom and fulfillment. If we really knew what God was doing in the refining, we would choose it every time.

Let that attitude shape your response to the difficulties in your life. You don't have to accept what the enemy tries to dish out, but you would be wise to let your trials do their deep work in your character and your spiritual growth. God has a purpose for the things we go through, and it's always good. The Refiner is extracting your beauty.

God never strikes except for motives of love,
and never takes away but in order to give.
—FRANÇOIS FÉNELON

A Pure Heart

He will sit as a refiner and purifier of silver; he will purify the Levites and refine them like gold and silver.
MALACHI 3:3

In Word

Imagine a person with absolutely no impure motives—no selfishness, no manipulation, no unworthy desire. Imagine that person having never functioned from any driving force other than love—an intense desire to seek the best for everyone. Imagine this person having the patience to wait for eons, the mercy to cover all mistakes, and the generosity to pour out kindness after kindness. Now imagine a person like that finding someone to relate to intimately.

That would be a hard task, wouldn't it? A person like that is one of a kind, and there are no true counterparts for one-of-a-kind people. Yet that's a picture of the God who made humanity in His image for the purpose of intimacy. We were designed to be pure, loving, generous, kind, and enduringly patient. We were formed to be like Him so that we could relate to Him emotionally, spiritually, mentally, and even physically as creative beings. The only problem is that God's pure image became corrupted in human rebellion. His counterparts became decidedly unlike Him.

That's why God is in the business of extracting silver and gold from common ore. The Refiner has a greater purpose than the purity of the metal. He means for it to fit His taste and match the glory of His heart. The master metallurgist is creating something dazzling for Himself.

In Deed

Maybe you never thought of yourself as "dazzling." Maybe that's because you, like all of us, are still in the refining process, where impurities still mingle with the treasure being extracted. But just because the unappealing process is highly visible doesn't mean that the end result shouldn't be beautiful. Keep your eyes on it and trust the Refiner. He knows exactly what it takes to make you shine.

If there is joy in the world, surely the man of pure heart possesses it.
—THOMAS À KEMPIS

A Deep Desire

**Suddenly the Lord you are seeking will
come to his temple; the messenger of the
covenant, whom you desire, will come.**
MALACHI 3:1

In Word

Most of us don't understand our own desires. We all want fulfillment, and we
think we know how to get it, but we don't. Nearly everything we expect to
be fulfilling is a temporary fix. It may scratch some itches, move us deeply,
or even satisfy our longings temporarily, but ultimately it all falls short. Deep
down, we want to be fulfilled completely and forever. We've never come up
with a solution for that.

God has. Malachi prophesied that the messenger of the covenant, the Messiah, was actually the desire of our hearts. He is the Lord we were seeking,
the One we delight in. And, Malachi says, He will come.

Impure hearts like ours don't necessarily find that comforting. We want
our desires to be fulfilled, and to a person, we all seem to think that God
doesn't quite understand our desires. Our assumption is that He has a great
plan for us—as He defines "great"—but that it will be harder or more noble
or less satisfying than we want it to be. Somehow we got the message that
God's plan is best, but not fulfilling—or fun.

We're wrong. We didn't get that message from God or His Word. In fact,
it sounds suspiciously like a lie once told by a serpent in a garden. "There are
better things than what God has offered you," the lie says. But according to
God and the prophets He inspires, we have a destiny that will thrill us from
our head to our toes.

In Deed

When we understand that, we become willing participants in the process.
We understand what the refinery produces, so we submit ourselves to the
Refiner Himself. We take humanity's biggest hang-up—the desires of the
fallen heart—and let them be purified into something that matches the heart
of the Father. And we embrace the most fulfilling promise ever given: the One
whom we seek will come.

Every promise God has ever made
finds its fulfillment in Jesus.
—JONI EARECKSON TADA

In the Crucible

Who can endure the day of his coming?
Who can stand when he appears?
MALACHI 3:2

In Word

We might think that the coming of our true desire, God's promises in Jesus, is a peaceful event, but it's not. It's very traumatic. There are two reasons for that: first, the world isn't ready for a righteous Refiner to do His work; and second, frankly, neither is the church.

We often fail to realize that the accomplishment of our true desires requires the incineration of our false ones. That's a painful process, not just because our impurities suffer intense heat, but also because our true selves do too. The smelting puts everything under the flame; that which is impure is burned away, and that which is pure is melted. But everything experiences the flame.

You've probably noticed that, probably even resisted it. We want our desires to come, but we want them to come painlessly. In a fallen world, that's not the way of God's Kingdom. The Refiner comes to save, and part of the saving is purging. When Paul writes about the judgment seat of Christ, when everything is burned and only what is good will remain, we can see the principle at work in our lives even today. The crucible of life is a judgment of sorts; every decision comes at a critical point of contact between metal and dross.

In Deed

Begin to think of your life in these terms, if you don't already. As you approach major decisions, relationships, directions in career or ministry, and investments of time, talents, and wealth, ask yourself whether your decision will result in molten purity or mineral waste. Examine your motives, your resources, your plan, and your process in every area of your life. The outcomes you envision should have an eternal glow to them.

That may be hard to decipher sometimes, but God will give you insight if you ask Him. The Refiner is very invested in the final product; He wants your life to shine like a brilliant trophy of glory. He is determined to bring you through the crucible.

> God can never make us wine if we object to
> the fingers He uses to crush us with.
> —OSWALD CHAMBERS

At the Altar

Then the LORD will have men who will
bring offerings in righteousness.
MALACHI 3:3

In Word

Everyone has an altar. It can be visible or invisible, holy or profane, elaborate or ordinary, but it's always there. It can be based on ideologies, dreams, or simple pleasures, but we can always find a foundation. We have to; everyone's life needs to revolve around something.

Because everyone has an altar, everyone brings offerings. Some people offer their bodies to people and pleasure. Others offer their minds to areas of study. Still others offer their emotions to a trend of the day or a relationship of the month. We can offer finances to gods of materialism and exploitation, time to gods of entertainment and apathy, and talents to gods of fame and fortune. We have no shortage of gifts to bring to our altars, because the world has no shortage of altars. All human beings are drawn to a cause, even if the cause is themselves.

Part of the Refiner's purpose is to get to the bottom of those causes and burn all of them away except one. That's why people often come to Christ when they're in the midst of a crisis or when they've lost everything they once thought mattered to them. In a world of false altars, the only way God can establish true praise in His people is to break down His rivals. His Word calls that "refining." We call it pain.

In Deed

Yes, it's painful to live in this crucible. But before you despair, try this exercise: Offer your pain on the true altar. Bring all of your trials, your temptations, and your disappointments to God; place them on the altar and worship. Ask God to use every hard thing in your life to display something of His glory—in your sin, mercy; in your impossibilities, miracles; in your sickness, healing; in your turmoil, peace. Realize that every situation in your life is a platform for God to show something of Himself. In the end, the beauty of the metal will demonstrate the beauty of the Refiner.

All along the Christian course, there must be set up
altars to God on which you sacrifice yourself.
—ALEXANDER MACLAREN

God of the Impossible

**Do you think I cannot call on my Father,
and he will at once put at my disposal
more than twelve legions of angels?**
MATTHEW 26:53

In Word

God can do impossible things. Just look at the revealed testimonies to His power: "Is anything too hard for the LORD?" (Genesis 18:14); "Do I lack the strength to rescue you?" (Isaiah 50:2); "Is anything too hard for me?" (Jeremiah 32:27); "With God all things are possible" (Matthew 19:26); and, "Everything is possible for him who believes" (Mark 9:23). We may pray and wonder what God's will is in a situation, but we should never—under any circumstances—wonder if He can meet our needs. The Creator of heaven and earth can do anything.

As He approached His Passion, Jesus had no doubts about the Father's power. The only question was God's will in the situation, and to that, Jesus submitted willingly.

When we pray, we want God's power to be at our disposal. We want the power first, and our submission afterward. That's not God's way, and that's not what Jesus did.

He spent years demonstrating submission before He demonstrated miracles. Answers to prayer were not the ultimate goal for Him; obedience was. God's will was. The plan of salvation and the Kingdom of God were. Miracles were only a small part of the bigger purpose.

In Deed

Do we pray with that kind of focus? Not usually. We sometimes seek answers to prayer without settling our commitment to Kingdom purposes first. But if we can be firmly allied with God's great plan—even when it hurts our short-term interests—we can pray with the power of Jesus. We can call on the Father, knowing that He'll put angels and His Spirit at our disposal. We will have demonstrated that "at our disposal" is a trustworthy place to invest His unlimited resources.

Have a firm commitment to God's Kingdom at whatever cost to your agenda. Then pray. Pray with power and with faith. With God, nothing is impossible.

*The world appears very little to a soul that
contemplates the greatness of God.*
—BROTHER LAWRENCE

False Promises

Let him come down now from the cross, and we will believe in him.
MATTHEW 27:42

In Word

This had to be an awfully tempting offer. Jesus came into the world to save sinners through their faith. What could possibly be wrong with coming down off the cross in order for people to believe? But we know the answer: Sin had to be paid for with holy blood. Jesus knew that answer, too.

We'd do well to use Jesus as our model. Temptations often look reasonable to us—even seeming to fit the will of God. But just because something appears to accomplish God's ultimate purposes doesn't mean it fits with God's ways. God's will always conforms to His character. In God's plans, the ends do not justify the means. In God's plans, ends and means work together for the ultimate goal. Whenever they don't, we can be assured that we're being tempted.

Jesus knew their taunt was false. We're given no evidence that He considered the crowd's dare. As satisfying as the demonstration of self-deliverance would have been, there was a greater demonstration going on: the mercy of God. Justice was being done on our behalf. Jesus could see ahead to the glory beyond the grave, and He knew that in retrospect He would be utterly vindicated. Temptation has no grip on those who live with an eternal perspective.

In Deed

Satan's methods throughout Scripture are consistent. He promises good things if we'll accomplish them in disobedient ways. Adam and Eve were promised knowledge and godhood; in the wilderness, Jesus was promised all the world's kingdoms; and here, He was promised the faith of the mockers—if He would just prove Himself. But He knew the hearts of men. "They will not be convinced even if someone rises from the dead," He had once said (Luke 16:31).

Beware of the promise of good things. God's offers of abundant life always imply obedience. Satan's offers of the high life never do. Like our Savior on the cross, know the difference.

Be thoroughly acquainted with your temptations and the things that may corrupt you.
—RICHARD BAXTER

Amazing Grace

**Father, forgive them, for they do not
know what they are doing.**
LUKE 23:34

In Word

This statement from Jesus ought to have a dramatic impact on the way we live. Perhaps it loses impact because we assume that Jesus is in a league of His own in the forgiveness game; there's no way we could match His grace. Or perhaps we see this as an example of how God forgives without realizing the implications it has for us. Meanwhile, we forgive those who are sorry for their sins—which does not describe these crucifiers at all; and we forgive those who haven't hurt us too badly—which also does not describe these crucifiers. Somehow we've confined our mercy to definitions that Jesus never embraced. We've limited grace.

Think of the drama of Jesus' statement. These aggressors were committing the ultimate crime: an unjust execution of their own holy Creator. There has never been a more evil act. And yet, Jesus forgave. Without their asking. Without their even being remotely sorry.

Do you understand what that means for us? It means that those grudges we hold are horribly illegitimate. We will have to answer for them to the Savior of unlimited grace. We will have to explain why we accepted His painful blood-purchase while hardly lifting a finger for those who have hurt us.

Or, if we're wise, we can go ahead and try to understand the gospel better. We can realize that God's kind of grace—which He expects us to emulate—is meant not just for insults and oversights, but for spouses who have betrayed spouses, for thieves who have bankrupted their victims, for traitors and rapists and killers. The infinite God has infinite grace.

In Deed

That's a hard truth to embrace. We love it when it applies to us, but we just can't accept it when it applies to those who have offended us deeply, violated our trust, or even killed our loved ones. But if grace doesn't go far enough to cover sins against finite humans, it can't cover our sins against an infinite God. Thank God, it does. Thank God that He forgave us when we didn't know what we were doing. And He enables us to do so for others.

The glory of Christianity is to conquer by forgiveness.
—WILLIAM BLAKE

The Passion of Jesus

**When Jesus had cried out again in
a loud voice, he gave up his spirit.**
MATTHEW 27:50

In Word

The movies often portray a calm, collected Jesus—sad and in pain, but always glassy-eyed and dignified—in their depictions of the Crucifixion. And certainly we don't doubt His confidence. He came into this world to die and rise again, and He knew that. He did not hang on that cross with doubts about His identity or God's plan. No, He hung there only with pain.

But what pain it was! This was no dignified event; it was raw and excruciating. And the incarnate God—the One in whom infinite feelings were embodied in one frail, fleshly being—suffered. It wasn't a calm, quiet suffering; it was loud and tortured. He screamed out the first line of Psalm 22: "My God, my God, why have you forsaken me?" He thirsted. He refused sedatives that would have lessened the pain (but also the judgment). And then He yelled out again. The agonizing cry of Matthew 27:50 was His last shout before His resurrection. But it wasn't His last shout forever. He will shout again (1 Thessalonians 4:16). And when He does, it will be exciting.

Do you know the emotional, joyful Jesus? He is passionate from His cross to His return. He is coming again with a loud command, a shout—a noisy, triumphant declaration of final victory. Jesus never just went through the motions—never. He is not a dispassionate Savior.

In Deed

Why should that matter to us? Because we're often given a false picture of Jesus. Our traditions imply that God created us with deep emotions but never shared them while He was in the flesh. We often envision a Lord who is robotic and matter-of-fact, not a Lord who is in excruciating pain on one end of the emotional spectrum and noisily celebrating His victory on the other. But our Jesus is enthusiastic about His plan and exuberant about those He has redeemed. His joy is unbridled. As you think about His resurrection and His Kingdom this week, it's okay if yours is, too.

Catch on fire with enthusiasm and people
will come for miles to watch you burn.
—JOHN WESLEY

The Living Lord

Why do you look for the living among the dead?
LUKE 24:5

In Word

The women who had followed Jesus waited until the Sabbath was over, and then went to the tomb to care for Jesus' body. They were completely startled by what they saw: two gleaming angels questioning their task. It would disorient any of us, and it certainly disoriented them.

The angels' question is loaded with meaning. In one brief sentence, they have told the women that Jesus is alive, that death has not contained Him, that their Lord is still their Lord, and that life will never be the same. It couldn't have all sunk in right away, but at least the women knew that something incredible had happened. They were looking in the wrong place for the Lord of life. He doesn't dwell in cemeteries.

That's old news for us, isn't it? We celebrate it annually—and contemplate its meaning even more frequently. It's not exactly a startling question to us. With twenty centuries of celebration, it has sunk in: Jesus is alive. We know that.

But imagine God, whether by His Spirit or by angelic messengers, asking you the same question: "Why do you look for the living among the dead?" Would it apply? Do we not do that often? We begin to read the Bible as a historical document rather than as a living Word. We begin to follow Jesus as our example rather than listening to Him as our living Lord. We take our cues from our denominational traditions rather than from the Spirit of life. In other words, we turn our faith toward dead things rather than toward the Living One.

In Deed

That doesn't mean that the Bible isn't good history, or that Jesus is not our perfect example, or even that our denominational traditions are off base. It simply means that those things aren't the substance of our faith. Jesus is. Not Jesus the historical figure, but Jesus our constant companion. Not Jesus the martyr, but Jesus the still-living sacrifice and High Priest. Not Jesus our founder, but Jesus our leader. Knowing the life that He still lives—that powerful, present life—we must ask ourselves: Why do we look for the living among the dead?

[Jesus] is the greatest influence in the world today.
—W. H. GRIFFITH THOMAS

Jesus, the Visible Image

He is the image of the invisible God.
COLOSSIANS 1:15

In Word

We've heard it all before: Jesus was just a good teacher, a moral philosopher, a social revolutionary, a martyr—anything but divine. Unfortunately for the skeptics, there's no evidence of a Jesus who did not claim deity for Himself. And in the culture that was prepared for Him, He was certainly not claiming to be one of many deities. No, He implicitly claimed to be the one true God— Yahweh, the God of Abraham, Isaac, and Jacob. That's the stumbling block of the gospel. This suffering servant, this humble man of Galilee, this relatively poor man from a relatively poor family, taught with authority, forgave sins, allowed people to worship Him, claimed unity with the Father, and invoked for Himself the divine name of deity: I am.

Think of that. The invisible God became visible. The mystery of the ages was revealed. For a brief time in this world, the vague and often distorted speculations of ancient Greek philosophers, Persian magicians, and Oriental sages were answered. God showed up in the flesh. And He wasn't at all what we expected.

But we have come to love Him, haven't we? Though we haven't seen Him in the flesh ourselves, we read the testimonies of those who have. And our belief in those testimonies has opened doorways of experience for us in which His Spirit has proven to be alive and powerful. The invisible God has a visible image, and we are drawn to Him. Our worship is an enigma to an unbelieving world, but to us it is life. Jesus is God.

In Deed

Is Jesus an integral part of your worship? If not, you are missing something. You may be worshiping a vague concept of God—a life force, a cosmic power, a God who works in mysterious ways. And our God is all of those things. But He has given us more specifics than that. He has opened the curtain on much of the mystery. His ways have been demonstrated on the very earth we live on. He has had human blood pulsing through His veins. He has shed human tears. And He has died a human death. Worship Him. He was made visible so we can.

The only Christ for whom there is a shred of evidence
is a miraculous figure making stupendous claims.

—C. S. LEWIS

Jesus, the Ultimate Purpose

All things were created by him and for him.
COLOSSIANS 1:16

In Word

One of the primary sources of depression, we are told, is a sense of meaning-lessness. Meaninglessness is the powerful vacuum behind the angst of secular society; it is the tragic result of false theories of our origins; and it is the number one cause of suicide. If life as a whole has no ultimate purpose—if it means nothing—then we as individuals mean nothing. And if we mean nothing, we can hardly bear to go on living. Life without meaning is a tragedy we cannot endure.

But life does have meaning. We are told so in the Word. Despite the persistent questions of philosophers—questions like "Why are we here?" and "Where are we going?"—we have been given a revelation. The questions were answered centuries ago. We are here because of Jesus. He was the hand of creation, and He is its ultimate goal. It was all done by Him, and it was done for Himself.

If you have ever struggled to find meaning in your life, consider this amazing truth: You were created for Jesus. You weren't created incidentally as a by-product of the rest of creation. You were specifically designed for Him. You are a bride, handpicked for the Bridegroom; or an adopted son, chosen specifically by his Father. You were intentional.

In Deed

That's a comforting thought for a society on the edge of despair. Though we once wandered aimlessly in this world, God had a plan for us. Here in Colossians, the plan is specifically identified. We are made for Him.

That's a blessed truth with a huge responsibility: Territory in our lives that is not given over to Him amounts to a refusal to worship. If we were made for Him, and we aren't giving ourselves to Him, we have some adjustments to make. But what a truth! We have been betrothed. There's no greater security and no greater blessing. And for those of us who are looking for purpose, this is it. There's no greater meaning.

> The seed is choked in our souls whenever
> Christ is not our all in all.
> —CHARLES SPURGEON

Jesus, the Exalted Head

He is the head of the body, the church.
COLOSSIANS 1:18

In Word

Human beings can be ridiculously foolish, even after God has redeemed us. We have available to us the image of the invisible God, the One by whom and for whom all creation came into being. And whom do we choose as our head? Other people. Committees. Our own feelings. Our own agenda. Majorities. Minorities. Influential leaders. Humanistic philosophies. The list is nearly endless. We, even as Christians, are influenced by myriad people and things, even when we are aware of the corruption of our entire species.

We could be guided and managed by the completely omniscient, wholly benevolent Lord of all creation. Why would we refuse such an opportunity? Is it that we don't believe we'll hear from Him clearly? Do we mistrust His motives? Have we forgotten that He is on our side—and has demonstrated His sympathy for us as dramatically as anyone ever could? Somewhere in our thinking, something is wrong. We are promised a direct link with the living Head, and we end up so, well, misdirected. What happened?

Perhaps we have missed the end of verse 18: "so that in everything he might have the supremacy." Was his supremacy our goal from the beginning? If so, He would have gladly guided us. But we have mixed motives; we want to maintain a little autonomy here, a touch of self-will there. And in wanting Jesus to be the Head over most of our lives, we are rejecting Him as the Head over all of our lives. And He won't make that compromise.

In Deed

How do we become more submitted to Jesus? We stop asking Him to compromise His lordship. We need to become so much more enraptured with the thought of His headship than we are with our own agendas that we gladly sacrifice the latter for the former. Think of the thrill! The be-all and end-all of creation is accessible to our churches! to our families! to our own lives! The beginning, the end, and every authority in between is available—and He loves us! Who would refuse such an offer?

Jesus Christ will be Lord of all or He will not be Lord at all.
—AUGUSTINE

Created to Shine

You are the light of the world.
MATTHEW 5:14

In Word

The apostle John tells us that Jesus was the true light coming into the world (John 1:9). He shone into our darkness, but the darkness did not understand Him. Jesus takes His identity a step further. He tells His disciples—He tells us—that we are also lights in the world. The One who came to shine uses lanterns He has Himself redeemed. We have a bright, holy purpose.

We often think that we are called to shine as lights because this world needs light. That's true, but we have an even higher calling than that. We are to shine as lights because Jesus is light. Our holy calling is to reflect Him, to display Him, and to worship Him by being the vessels by which He reveals Himself to others. Radiating Jesus is the highest honor we can give Him, not just because the world needs Him, but because He is beautiful. If that's hard to believe, consider our future: We will be shining His light and reflecting His glory long after this world has passed away. It won't be because someone needs convincing; it will be simply because of who He is. Our shining is more for the sake of His eternal glory than for the needs of this present darkness.

Worship brings God's rule—and even better, His comfort and joy—visibly into a rebellious world. It represents His Kingdom here and now. It brings heaven and earth into a sacred meeting, letting the Kingdom of God invade our lives and our environment. It shines the light of heaven into a dark, dismal night.

In Deed

Do you reflect Jesus? Have you ever been able to put your agenda aside—even the good parts of it—simply to be like Him? There is no greater task. Our primary responsibility in this world, as His servants and His children, is to show His kind of mercy, do His kind of works, pray His kind of prayers, tell His kind of stories, and seek His kind of justice. The grace, forgiveness, and love of Jesus are to permeate everything we do. Why? Because He is light, and we were created to shine.

Our great honor lies in being just what Jesus was and is.
—A. W. TOZER

A Pleasing Aroma

Even if I am being poured out like a drink offering
on the sacrifice and service coming from your
faith, I am glad and rejoice with all of you.
PHILIPPIANS 2:17

In Word

Accompanying many of the Old Testament sacrifices is the rite of a drink offering—a liquid sacrifice on the altar of God. It often symbolizes blood—the spending of one's life for the Giver and Sustainer of life. Over and over again in the Old Testament, the drink offering is "an aroma pleasing to God."

Paul envisioned himself as just such an aroma. Here in Philippians 2:17 and in 2 Timothy 4:6, he speaks of the goal of his life: to wholly serve God as a living sacrifice. That's the purpose of any worshipful heart—which leads those of us who love Him to a deeply personal question: How do we "spend" ourselves?

The resources of your life—your money, your time, your talents, your skills, and your relationships—will naturally flow in the direction of what you love. If you find that your offerings to God, in whatever form they take, are a distraction from your greater interests, then you can know the painful truth and acknowledge your humanness: You have placed some of your passions above your love for Him.

In Deed

We always spend ourselves on something. Perhaps we make great sacrifices of our resources in order to satisfy ourselves and our own pleasure. Or we might invest ourselves in people, in creative expressions, in pastimes, in work, in appearances, and even in service. Regardless of our efforts, we must remember our highest purpose: the Kingdom of God.

Do you really love God? Then you'll often find yourself entirely preoccupied with Him, His work, and His people. It usually won't be a painful effort, but rather a joyful endeavor. You will gladly pour out your life, and it will be a wonderfully pleasing aroma to Him.

You will always give effortlessly to that which is your salvation.

—TIM KELLER

The Honor Competition

God exalted him to the highest place and gave
him the name that is above every name.
PHILIPPIANS 2:9

In Word

We live in a competitive world. Brothers and sisters cultivate rivalries against brothers and sisters. Spouses argue with spouses. Businesses compete for limited shares of the market. Nations war against nations. Civilizations clash against civilizations. And what is at stake? Personal plans and dreams? ideology? resources? power? Maybe. But something else is involved in every competition. There is one key concept that can turn a petty disagreement into a lifelong feud, one treasure that can prompt armies to sacrifice thousands for small parcels of worthless land: Honor.

Have you noticed how integral honor is to human relationships? Our spirits are easily wounded from our—or someone else's—sense of honor. Egos are stroked and rivalries deepened over honor. Sports teams spend their last drop of energy on a field over the honor of winning. Honor shapes a lot of what we do.

Drop it. Lay it down. It's a pride issue, and in the end, there is only one winner in the honor competition: Jesus. Every knee will bow and every tongue will confess that Jesus is Lord. That is the direction this whole creation is moving—though it hardly knows it now. Eventually, though, every heart, every knee, every cell, every atom, will point toward the throne of God.

In Deed

Are you there yet? That's what worship is. It is letting every corner of your world bow toward God. It is turning every aspect of your life to Him—your dreams, your goals, your fears, the people and things that feed your life, and the people and things you feed. Every relationship, every thought, every impulse you have, whatever you can consider as "yours"—does it confess Him as Lord? If not, think of something specific today—just one thing—that you once withheld but can now give to Him. Do that every day until you can find nothing else in your life that refuses to call Him Lord. The honor is rightfully His.

There's not a thumb's breadth of this universe about
which Jesus Christ does not say, "It is mine."

—ABRAHAM KUYPER

The Sincerest Worship

**Be perfect, therefore, as your
heavenly Father is perfect.**
MATTHEW 5:48

In Word

The Little Leaguer steps up to the plate, swings the bat a couple of times, knocks the dirt off his shoes, and spits in the direction of third base. Where did he get that routine? Did he come up with it on his own? No, he had simply watched a little baseball on TV and had come to admire some of the big-league players. He is acting like the person he wants to be.

You've heard the saying, "Imitation is the sincerest form of flattery." And it's true. We rarely, except in jest, imitate someone we don't like. No, the way we pattern our behavior says a lot about whom we admire and respect. If we look across our culture, we can see millions of those Little League athletes—as well as men and women who dress, behave, and think like the most popular figures in Hollywood. We have become a culture of movie posters and CD covers. Why? Because not only does art reflect culture, culture is shaped by art. We are imitators at our core.

Imitation is not just the sincerest form of flattery; it's also the sincerest form of worship. We shape ourselves to be like either our idols or the God we adore. It isn't that our words of praise are meaningless on any given Sunday morning or whenever we meet for worship. But God knows what most of us have already experienced: Words of praise can be faked. So can emotions. Even when our minds and mouths are honoring God, our hearts can often be disengaged. But imitation of the character and ways of God reflects a deeper praise.

In Deed

Examine your thoughts and your behavior. After whom are they patterned? Maybe you've never considered that they are patterned after anyone, but you've grown up in a culture that has given you a lot of cues about what is acceptable and admirable. And if you're like most human beings, you've sought acceptance and admiration.

But now your heart wants to engage with God. Praise Him with your words and emotions, but look deeper. Don't just praise your Father for His love, purity, and grace. Be like Him. It's the sincerest worship you can give.

All love . . . casts the mind into the mold of the thing beloved.
—JOHN OWEN

Saved for a Purpose

His intent was that now, through the church, the
manifold wisdom of God should be made known to
the rulers and authorities in the heavenly realms.

EPHESIANS 3:10

In Word

From a human perspective, life is all about us—our welfare, our accomplishments, our plans, our cultures and social systems. Even when we bring God
into the picture, we describe Him as being concerned for us, sacrificing for us,
loving us, and caring for us. And He is concerned and loving, making His relationship with us clear throughout Scripture and our experience. But sometimes we get a little too "us-focused." We forget that God's ultimate goal, the
very purpose of creation, is not for a fallen race to be loved and saved. It is to
demonstrate His wisdom and mercy by saving a fallen race. The visible result
in both cases is the same. But the ultimate purpose is His glory, not ours.

It makes sense to us to approach life from a very human point of view.
That's because we're very human. The point of view comes naturally. But our
perspective isn't really logical in the grand scheme of things. From heaven's
view, it's extremely self-focused. If we think the Cross was all about us, we're
right—to a point. But it's all about us in order to demonstrate something
about God: He is merciful and kind, forgiving and gentle, the Just and the
Justifier. As the first chapter of Ephesians tells us repeatedly in its description
of our salvation, it's all for the praise of His glory (vv. 6, 12, and 14).

In Deed

That doesn't mean, of course, that God is really only saving us for His own
reputation and not out of a sense of selfless love. Of course He loves us. We're
promised that, over and over again in Scripture. But this whole creation—the
one that fell into sin and rebellion under the watchful eye of its Creator—
exists as a divine demonstration of His very genuine love. That's why we're
saved. It's all about Him.

The glory of God is a living man; and the life
of man consists in beholding God.

—IRENAEUS

In the Coming Ages

**God raised us up with Christ . . . in order
that in the coming ages he might show
the incomparable riches of his grace.**
EPHESIANS 2:6-7

In Word

Do you view spiritual growth as God's intention for you? Most of us do. We want to fulfill God's design for us, realize the plans He has for our lives, and be fulfilled. But a strange thing happens when fallen human beings begin to view their salvation and their ensuing growth as a path to their own maturity, or worse, as a self-improvement technique. When we get discouraged, we decide that the goals we have for our growth aren't worth the extra strain or the intense devotion that they require. We take a break.

That's a natural result when we think our fruit-bearing and our maturity are "our" issues. And certainly God means for us to have great benefits from godliness. But our growth is not just ours. It's also His. He desires it for our good, but He also desires it for His reputation—His glory. As Paul says in Ephesians, we were saved not just so we would grow and be fulfilled people. We were saved so that "in the coming ages he might show the incomparable riches of his grace." Once again, the Scripture reminds us: Our lives are all about Him.

In Deed

What does that mean in real life? It means that God has a huge stake in whether or not we bear fruit. It means that the reflection of His image in us is affected by the level of our spiritual growth. It means that when we're tired and decide that we don't have the energy for any spiritual disciplines today or this week or this month, we're overstepping our authority. We don't have the right to decide that. Our spiritual disciplines aren't exclusively for our own good; they're for God's glory.

Salvation and sanctification, the birth and growth that result as we are shaped to be like Jesus, are certainly gifts from God. But we are so used to calling them gifts—our "possessions"—that we miss their higher purpose. We are a display of God—His mercy, His image, His love. We aren't just saved to be saved; we're saved to be mirrors of Him. His beauty is our ultimate purpose.

The glory of God is man alive, supremely in Christ.
—LEON SUENENS

Powerful Prayers

**I pray . . . that the eyes of your
heart may be enlightened.**

EPHESIANS 1:18

In Word

The church is to be a body that always points to its Head. In our exploration of worship, we realize that we are in a life-changing process between self-centeredness and God-centeredness. The transformation is radical; it changes everything we think and everything we do.

Paul knew that when he prayed this prayer for the Ephesian church and others who would read it. The apostle's heart for Asia Minor is expressed in these verses: that God would reveal Himself to them more clearly, that the "eyes" of their hearts would be opened to glorious visions, and that they would understand the vast inheritance they've been given and the sheer power of the God and the gospel they have come to believe. Paul's prayer is really a request for their transformation to God-centeredness—seeing life and salvation from a heavenly perspective, understanding His purposes in creation and redemption, and becoming a willing, grateful part of that dramatic display of mercy.

We marvel at the depth and the beauty of Paul's prayers. Sometimes we wish he had prayed those things for us, and we speculate that perhaps he looked down through future generations and applied his prayers to all who would follow in faith. We want that kind of growth that he desired for the Ephesians. We crave full hearts and enlightened eyes.

In Deed

There's a very practical way to have these prayers applied to ourselves: We can pray them for each other. We might have tried praying them specifically for ourselves, and God has surely accepted those prayers. But there's a better way: Think of ten Christians in your family and circle of friends for whom you can pray this prayer. Pray it daily. Ask God to pour out His Spirit of wisdom and revelation on them. Plead for their eyes to be enlightened even more than they already are. Ask for His power to explode into the lives of your fellow believers. And watch the body of Christ realize the promise of verse 23: "the fullness of him who fills everything in every way."

The greatest thing anyone can do for
God and for man is to pray.

—S. D. GORDON

A Particular Savior

**I live by faith in the Son of God, who
loved me and gave himself for me.**
GALATIANS 2:20

In Word

How personal is the Cross to you? It's a question that shouldn't be answered
too quickly. Many of us have heard for years—decades, even—that "God so
loved the world," and that Jesus is "the Lamb of God who takes away the sins
of the world." We've sung songs about how Jesus loves all the children of the
world, and we may have even told others, "Jesus loves you." All of that is easy
to accept for those who believe the gospel. But there's a harder question we
have to ask ourselves: Does Jesus love me—personally and individually? Did
He die for me? Does His blood apply specifically and directly to me?

Imagine being one of the disciples speaking with Jesus after His resurrection. In your mind's eye, envision sitting down with Him in the shade of a
building or on a couple of rocks on a hillside, asking Him this question: "Why
did You go to the Cross when You didn't have to?" Listen to His answer: "It is
God's glory to redeem you, to give you life with Me forever. I did it because
I love my disciples: Peter needed it; so did James and John. And so do you. I
did it for you."

It's not a far-fetched conversation. He is alive and He still speaks to us.
He says such things today. It is critical that we open our ears to hear Him. The
gospel is for the whole world, but it is also deeply personal. Salvation is a gift
from God to an individual.

In Deed

Many Christians have a gnawing gut feeling that while Jesus died for other
people, He wouldn't have necessarily done it for them alone. Some of us feel
as though we just jumped on a bandwagon that was really meant for other
sinners—more sinful, more righteous, more worthy, better able to live up to
the gospel after their salvation, etc. We believe the gospel and even proclaim
it. We praise God for it. But what we really want to know is this: Does this
really apply to me?

It does. Let it sink in. You aren't just worshiping the Savior of the world.
You're worshiping the Savior of you.

> The essential fact of Christianity is that God thought
> all men worth the sacrifice of His Son.
> —WILLIAM BARCLAY

A Global Savior

He is the atoning sacrifice for our sins, and not only
for ours but also for the sins of the whole world.
1 JOHN 2:2

In Word

Some Christians go to extremes in their understanding of personal salvation.
It becomes too individualized and not broad enough to include many others.
The Pharisees made that mistake: They thought salvation was for the Jews
alone, not just as a chosen vehicle of revelation to the world, but as revelation's
final destination. They had forgotten God's promise to bless many nations
through Abraham (Genesis 12:3). And we can do the same thing. Though we
won't say it, we often think of salvation as being for those who look like us or
think like us—whoever "us" happens to be. Our horizon isn't broad enough,
and our tent isn't large enough. We need to remember: When Jesus told His
disciples to go to the ends of the earth (Acts 1:8), He really meant the ends
of the earth.

Jesus' parable in Luke 14:15-24 gives us a picture of God that many of us
believe in our minds but not in our hearts. The God in this parable searches
hedges and highways for those who will come to His banquet. The "preferred"
guest list isn't sufficient. Even the riffraff are invited.

In Deed

How exclusive is your salvation? Do you find it satisfying enough just to have
it? Or do you burn with a desire to share it and to see it spread both next door
and around the globe? The Gospels tell us that God is like a woman searching
for a lost coin, or a shepherd going to great lengths to restore his wayward
sheep. The value of the coin isn't the issue, and neither are the distance and
the dirtiness of the sheep. All that matters to this God is finding people with
open hearts and hearing ears.

True worship of God will always embrace His global mission. No place
on this planet is beyond the great commission (Matthew 28:19). No class or
caste is beneath His grace. He is relentless in the offer of His salvation. So
must we be.

My parish is the gutter.
—DAVID WILKERSON

The Husband

**As a bridegroom rejoices over his bride,
so will your God rejoice over you.**

ISAIAH 62:5

In Word

"Your Maker is your husband." That's how God inspired Isaiah to describe His relationship with His people. In the prophetic books, God used a lot of metaphors to describe that relationship, but this one is the most prominent. He is the Husband of His people, the Lover of the beloved, the Bridegroom who delights in His bride. Like a smitten man who cherishes his sweetheart, God cherishes us.

God could have described His love for His people in the form of a fact sheet or a news report. He could have simply inspired the prophets to write, "God loves you and He wants what's best for you." But somehow that just wasn't descriptive enough. When God speaks, He often uses pictures. And in Scripture, the picture of God's love is very often a husband's love for the woman of his dreams.

We should be ecstatic that God used such a picture. "Love" can mean a world of things, from our superficial feelings about preferences and pastimes to our deepest emotions of passion and purpose. "Love" by itself wouldn't tell us much about God's desire for us. But the love of a bridegroom, a husband, a suitor—that's exhilarating. That sky-high feeling of budding affection as it develops into deep, consuming passion is a feeling we all understand. This picture tells us that God's love for us isn't an obligation. It thrills Him.

In Deed

Have you ever tried to imagine God rejoicing over you? Have you ever envisioned Him as madly, deeply taken with you? If the imagery of the prophets means anything at all, God's love isn't calculated and formal. It's wild and wonderful. His affection is like that of a groom for his bride; it sends Him soaring.

If you think about that, it will send you soaring too. People who have found their true love are on an emotional high, completely absorbed with each other. God wants that kind of relationship. Let yourself fall in love with the One who loves you deeply.

Romance is at the heart of the universe
and is the key to all existence.

—PAUL BILLHEIMER

Agony

**No longer will they call you Deserted,
or name your land Desolate.**
ISAIAH 62:4

In Word

Some couples break up easily. In a day of casual love, when many relationships are seen as temporary, a parting of the ways is often uneventful. People have found that uncommitted hearts don't break very easily.

God's heart doesn't work that way. In the prophets' descriptions of the Husband, God's pain is agonizing. When the bride becomes a prostitute—yes, the metaphor for Israel's and Judah's idolatry is just that graphic—the Groom suffers. To illustrate His pain, God told Hosea to marry a prostitute as a prophetic illustration, He inspired Ezekiel to describe Judah as a harlot, and He had Jeremiah proclaim a divorce decree. The King of glory, deeply in love, watched His treasured bride leave the palace bedroom and go sleep with vagrants.

That's why Judah found herself "deserted" and "desolate." Not many husbands are content with harlotry in the house, so Judah was expelled from the house. The most loving heart in all of existence had been pierced by betrayal and rejection.

In Deed

But true love never gives up, and God's love is always true. So after the exile of the bride, the Husband restored her. That's the story of Israel, that's the story of humanity, and that's the story of each one of us who has been redeemed by His grace. We have all been unfaithful, we have all experienced alienation from our God, and we have all been offered reconciliation.

That's what God's heart is like. It loves passionately, it wounds deeply, and it persists eternally. God told Israel through the prophets that His love is forever, and He has told us the same thing through Jesus. The piercing of the Groom's passionate heart was made visible one day on a hill outside of Jerusalem, and now creation waits for the revelation of the bride. And from the wedding day on, we will never hear the words "deserted" and "desolate" again.

I have asked but this of you, He cried. That
you love Me . . . love Me . . . love Me.
—GENE EDWARDS

Ecstasy

The LORD will take delight in you.
ISAIAH 62:4

In Word

Picture a young man and woman on their wedding night. For years, they have loved each other and longed for the consummation of their relationship, and now their longing is fulfilled. The sheer delight of togetherness—of knowing they will be in each other's arms for the rest of their lives—is overwhelming. There is no better feeling than that.

That's how the bridal imagery in the prophetic books describes God's love for us. We may have a hard time believing that—for centuries, people have seen God as a hard taskmaster or cosmic cop, bent on indicting His people—but the Groom's love is a thoroughly biblical picture. The only thing missing in Scripture is the bride's passionate love for her husband. Sometimes it's there, though often it isn't. But it's always encouraged. God always welcomes the fervent love of His people. We are never told to maintain emotional distance from Him.

The tragedy of many Christians' lives is an unbalanced marriage. Many of us are living in a relationship where the Groom is madly in love and the bride is ambivalent. That makes for an awkward marriage—awkward worship, awkward prayers, and awkward service. The tragedy is that it doesn't have to be that way. If we really understand the heart of the Lover, being the beloved becomes a lot more natural.

In Deed

Is your relationship with God living up to the image of the Husband who rejoices over His bride? The intimacy and the ecstasy of wedded bliss is God's design. He gave us that kind of human relationship as an illustration of the divine. All of those dreams we have about falling in love and being completely satisfied in intimacy with another are there for a reason. God wove them into our design for Himself.

Don't let that design go unfulfilled. If you are casual about the God who delights in you, seek a balanced relationship. God has made the first move; there's no chance of your love being rejected. Let your passion for Him run as wild as His passion for you.

> There is nothing sweeter to the Bridegroom or the bride than hallowed and unhindered communion.
> —HUDSON TAYLOR

The Husband's Crown

You will be a crown of splendor in the LORD's hand.
ISAIAH 62:3

In Word

The wedding language in the prophetic books is emphatic. Perhaps in a culture far removed from ancient Near Eastern wedding customs, we don't get the full impact today. But when Isaiah tells Jerusalem that its people will be called Hephzibah and its land Beulah (v. 4), the names are loaded with meaning. Hephzibah means "my delight is in her," and Beulah means "married." God makes it clear that He gets excited about intimacy with His people.

Those names come right after a powerful description: "You will be a crown of splendor in the LORD's hand." In other words, the King holds His bride proudly. In matters of romantic love, the nature of the beloved usually reveals quite a bit about the heart of the one who loves her. A bride represents a groom's tastes and pleasures, his deepest desires. The fact that our King calls us His bride is astounding. Those who were made in His image are meant to be a delightful expression of who He is.

What does that mean in real, everyday life? It means that we are soul mates with the One who redeemed us. When Jesus told the disciples in John 14 that He would come for them, He used wedding terms. In the greatest Cinderella story of all time, the King has graciously taken a woman dressed in rags and made her the apple of His eye.

In Deed

If you knew that—if you really felt that in the deepest corners of your heart—how would it change the way you live? Christians who don't know that God delights in them live as paupers and prisoners, serving God out of obligation rather than out of intimacy. But that kind of lifestyle is not a worthy representation of the marriage of the King.

Live regally—not arrogantly, not excessively, but regally. The prophets call God's people into intimate union with the King. To live as strangers or menial servants is to spurn the best proposal we'll ever get. Let your prayers and worship be sweet whispers of a person madly in love. Let the King have you as His crown of splendor.

> The courtship that began in the Garden culminates
> in the wedding feast of the Lamb.
> —JOHN ELDREDGE

The Husband's Glory

**The nations will see your righteousness,
and all kings your glory.**
ISAIAH 62:2

In Word

We get hung up on the word *righteousness*. It points to moral perfection, and we know we don't have it. But the biblical word isn't just about morality; it signifies a fulfillment of a covenant. So when God says the nations will see the righteousness of His people, He means that the world will see the marriage covenant of God fulfilled in the bride He has chosen. When the bridal veil is removed, we, His beloved, will shine with His glory.

A few verses earlier, Isaiah says that God has clothed him with garments of salvation and arrayed him in a robe of righteousness (61:10). He gives God's people a poetic image of a couple getting dressed for the wedding. There will come a day—the biggest day of our lives and one that we've dreamed about as long as we can remember—when we will walk the aisle and be presented to our divine Groom. We'll be a little nervous, because everyone in that situation is. And we'll have plenty of reason for our nervousness, as the whole world has been given a mandatory invitation to the big event. The revelation of the bride's glory is for the entire Kingdom to see.

Meanwhile, the engagement is to be very visible. The preparation for the nuptials is not a secret process. The righteousness—the expression of the covenant—"shines out like the dawn" (62:1). The nations are to see it, and they'll know it not by how we behave ourselves, but by how we love. We are to be models of propriety, of course, but that's not the righteousness that will impress them. The righteousness they need to see is the kind that fulfills the covenant: with our extravagant, blushing adoration of the Bridegroom.

In Deed

Does the world see that in your life? If not, why not? If you're like most of us, you easily get caught up in the wedding details and forget the passion that won your heart in the first place. Whatever it takes, recapture the passion. Let the people around you wish they were as in love as you are—and tell them how they can be.

> The finished product of all the ages is the spotless
> Bride of Christ, united with Him in wedded bliss.
>
> —PAUL BILLHEIMER

Frugal Extravagance

I have received from Epaphroditus the gifts
you sent. They are a fragrant offering, an
acceptable sacrifice, pleasing to God.

PHILIPPIANS 4:18

In Word

Ben Franklin had it half right. A penny saved is a penny earned. But that's
not the whole story for us believers in Jesus and worshipers of our Provider.
There's a follow-through left out of that sequence: A penny saved is a penny
earned, and a penny earned is a penny available for the Kingdom. God is all
for our saving, but there's a purpose to it. We're to save so we can give.

Think about what our expenditures tell us about ourselves. Whether we
mean it or not, our use of money says a lot about what we think of God. Is His
agenda important to us? Our ledgers will reflect it. Do we have His sacrificial
love? Our checkbooks will tell the truth.

God has always done amazing things with people whose financial priorities were all about His work. Hudson Taylor was exceedingly frugal, and God
used him to found one of history's most effective mission agencies. George
Müller and his wife sold everything they had in order to minister to others,
and God poured millions of dollars through their hands as they ran orphan-
ages in nineteenth-century England. Millions have given their 10 percent and
found God's blessing. A smaller number have given their all and found God's
more abundant blessing. Their faithfulness in finances honored their Provider.
He poured out honor in return.

In Deed

What does God want from His people who live in a consumer society? Perhaps He wants a generation of frugal Christians who earn pennies by saving
them, and by earning, give. Maybe He wants to establish a visible community of people whose sacrificial giving honors Him and furthers His work.
A community that society can observe but can't explain. A community that
demonstrates the most curious economic phenomenon: The more they give,
the more they have.

Gain all you can, save all you can, give all you can.

—JOHN WESLEY

What the World Needs

**Love the LORD your God, listen to his voice, and
hold fast to him. For the LORD is your life.**
DEUTERONOMY 30:20

In Word

It is the greatest commandment: Love the Lord with everything you've got (Deuteronomy 6:5; Matthew 22:37). It may take us a lifetime to figure out exactly what loving Him should look like, but it doesn't take us long to realize one sad truth: We don't love Him that way very often.

Have you ever tried to determine what the backbone of your faith is? Is it doctrine? If so, you've probably found that, though necessary and important, doctrine runs dry pretty quickly, even for those who decide to spend their lives in theological scholarship. Is it emotion? You'll find that a faith that not only includes emotions, but is based on them, will be an up-and-down experience. Is it understanding? No, we all need it, but we'll never have enough. So what is our faith about?

It's about love. God makes that clear. Scripture tells us to study doctrine, express emotions, and seek understanding, but it never tells us to make those things our foundation. A consuming love for God, though, is foundational. If we don't have that, we don't have much of a relationship with Him. Not a meaningful one, anyway.

In Deed

An old song tells us "What the world needs now is love, sweet love." It's exactly right, although not in the context that the songwriter probably intended. What the world really needs now is a generation of believers who are deeply, madly in love with their Savior—and who live like it. That is what the church, in its simplest definition, is supposed to be—a people in love with Jesus. That includes understanding His revelation, experiencing His grace, and studying His truth; and those endeavors are surely necessary. But without a love for Him, those endeavors are, well, boring. Or irrelevant. They carry no weight in God's presence, and they have no impact on our world.

Do you really want to commune with the heart of God? Then love Him.

Love Him totally who gave Himself totally for your love.
—CLARE OF ASSISI

Convenient Discipleship

**Any of you who does not give up everything
he has cannot be my disciple.**
LUKE 14:33

In Word

Too many Christians consider their discipleship an obligation—a behavior
that Jesus wants us to follow or an image that He wants us to live up to.
Behavior and image are certainly involved, but our walk with Him is more
than that. It is better. It is the result of being a living sacrifice, and it is our
act of worship.

Have you considered your motives for discipleship? Is your Christianity
the product of God's law or of God's love? Is it an act of your responsibility or
of your love? If love is not the beginning and end, discipleship will fall short
not only in its outcome—as all discipleship does while we are in this fallen
world—but also in its essence—which never needs to happen. And as an act
of love, discipleship will inevitably involve sacrifice.

Think of how human beings show devotion to one another. Is it always
convenient? Love stories of convenience make neither good movies nor good
real-life relationships. Romantic partners know they are in love when each can
sacrifice freely for the other. Why, then, do we seek a convenient relationship
with God? If our walk with Him involves no sacrifice, it might easily have no
love in it. He has demonstrated His love for us with a horribly painful sacrifice.
What is the condition of our love for Him? Here's how we can know: Love is
clearly revealed when its costs are high.

In Deed

Test yourself: How much does it cost you to follow Jesus? If your discipleship
involves little or no sacrifice, it isn't worship. It isn't really even discipleship. Both worship and discipleship imply being "living sacrifices" (Romans
12:1); sacrifice is an essential element in our walk. There's no such thing as
discipleship without a cross, though we often seek a painless relationship with
God. But if we're in tune with His Spirit—and if we really love Him—we'll
frequently find ourselves out of our comfort zones. He stretches us, molds
us, bends us, and expands us. And, like any of our other loves, He requires
sacrifice. Always.

The principle of sacrifice is that we choose
to do or to suffer what apart from our love
we should not choose to do or suffer.
—WILLIAM TEMPLE

Radical Sin, Radical Mercy

To the King eternal, immortal, invisible, the only
God, be honor and glory for ever and ever.
1 TIMOTHY 1:17

In Word

We live in a world that understands rebellion. Not only has this world rebelled against its Creator, but all of its alleged sovereigns have had to quash rebellions of their own. We may cringe at the thought, but we understand why medieval kings felt they had to eliminate all their rivals for the throne. We consider the subjugation of dissidents throughout history, from ancient kingdoms to modern states, a relatively common and expected outcome, if a distasteful one. We don't like chaos and anarchy, and we even rejoice when those who threaten our peace are suppressed. In a war-torn world, we tend to embrace survival over mercy.

That's why Paul's praise of the Father in this verse is more than a tip of his hat. It is a statement of love. Something radical has happened to this recovering Pharisee. He has encountered the kind of mercy the world simply cannot fathom.

Paul doesn't bless God just because it's the right thing to do. His praise is the natural conclusion of the verses leading up to it. Paul was "a blasphemer and a persecutor and a violent man" (v. 13). He had a reputation as a holy-war terrorist, proud of his righteous indignation toward this festering sect of heretics known as Christians. In serving the God of his tradition, he was blaspheming the God of his salvation. Still, he was shown mercy. This rebel didn't die. He wasn't cast into prison, and he wasn't eliminated in the name of peace. Instead, he was powerfully transformed. Mercifully transformed. In his mind, the world's worst rebel had been pardoned (v. 15).

In Deed

That kind of mercy—that kind of God—is worth praising. A world of rebels like us would expect our treason to be punished, and rightly so. We have all threatened the divine order, the peace of the heavenly Kingdom. And what did we receive? Mercy. Even the worst of us. The unlimited patience of Christ has been displayed. In addition to giving Him honor forever, give Him honor today.

God doesn't just give us grace; He gives
us Jesus, the Lord of grace.
—JONI EARECKSON TADA

The Highest Worship

With what shall I come before the LORD and
bow down before the exalted God?

MICAH 6:6

In Word

Micah's question is a critical one to answer, isn't it? We are told that God desires our all-or-nothing love, expressed with everything in us: our heart, our soul, our mind, our strength, our all. This creation was designed for worship. The universe knows it well (Psalm 19:1); mankind does not (Romans 1:21). We are sorely lacking when it comes to the one thing God created us to do: honor Him.

So Micah's question is as relevant as questions get. With what shall we worship God? Is it burnt offerings that He desires? Rams and oil? Our first-born? Honestly, what can we give to the Lord that He has not already made—and could make more of, if He wanted to? Or, to put the question in more contemporary terms, what do you give to the person who already has everything he or she wants?

The prophet clearly implies that these things, in themselves, are not what honors God. We don't normally think in terms of the rams or oil we could give Him, but we have our sacrificial trinkets as well: our money, the catch-phrases of praise, fish symbols and message bracelets, ministry titles, our cast-offs for the poor, and more. But after we've exhausted all of our lists, Micah presents us with the truth of what God really desires from us: both an act of worship and a demonstration of His character. In being like Him, we honor Him. It's a matter of who we are, not what we can pay Him off with.

In Deed

"He has showed you, O man, what is good. And what does the LORD require of you? To act justly and to love mercy and to walk humbly with your God" (v. 8). Think about that. It's more than a matter of being a decent person. At its core, our worship is realizing who God is and who we are. He acts justly and loves mercy. And He has called fallen, sinful men and women to participate in His character. If you really want to worship, give the gift of highest honor. Demonstrate God to your world.

Worship is the submission of all our nature to God.

—WILLIAM TEMPLE

Undignified

**I will celebrate before the LORD. I will become
even more undignified than this.**
2 SAMUEL 6:21-22

In Word

When the Ark finally made it to Jerusalem after David's lengthy attempts to bring it there, the happy king danced before the Lord. Apparently it was a wild celebration. There was nothing immoral to it, of course, but it certainly defied the social expectations for a monarch. It was, according to Michal, David's wife, much too undignified.

David wasn't very concerned with social expectations. Bringing the Ark to Jerusalem wasn't for show; it was an act of devotion to the God of Israel. David's heart overflowed with joy. His exuberance could not be contained.

That's characteristic of a heart in a true attitude of worship. When a deep passion takes center stage within us, nothing else seems to matter. Young lovers rarely care how nauseating their excessive affection is to those around them. The affection assumes a life of its own. And David didn't care how nauseating his excessive affection was to Michal or to anyone else. He was in love with his God. The affection had assumed a life of its own.

In Deed

Is that too undignified for the modern worshiper? It shouldn't be. God is looking for those who will worship Him in spirit and in truth, according to Jesus (John 4:23), and if the spirit knows the truth, it will jump up and down in wild celebration. It won't care what other eyes observe; it will only care about the internal festival of joy.

That's a foreign thought for many Christians. What's the solution? No, God doesn't expect us to go out and make fools of ourselves simply to demonstrate our love for Him. He does, however, expect that we will demonstrate our love for Him however His Spirit leads. When the Spirit says to dance—literally or figuratively—and the world says dancing is not appropriate, we have to follow the Spirit. The world has no claim on us. God does. He's the One who fills our hearts. When He does, our hearts can dance.

I believe unself-consciousness is characteristic
of the fruit of the Holy Spirit.
—BILLY GRAHAM

A Life-Changing Encounter

I saw the Lord seated on a throne.

ISAIAH 6:1

In Word

The story of Isaiah's call to be a prophet begins with the historical context ("In the year that King Uzziah died . . .") and ends with the heartbreaking message about Judah's coming judgment. The highlight, of course, is the vision of the Lord, His train filling the temple and His angels shouting, "Holy, holy, holy." But the staggering phrase that gets passed over far too quickly is the initial claim: "I saw the Lord seated on a throne."

Think about that. This is no small claim. Many judges and prophets had had encounters with God since the days of Moses, hearing His voice and seeing His angels. But seeing God Himself? Seated on a throne? That's emotional overload for any human being. In that situation, it would be impossible to get deep enough into the floor. The brightness would be blinding and the presence could even prompt a lethal adrenaline rush. Human beings, other than Moses the great prophet, don't see God and live.

What would Isaiah say about his encounter? Would anyone believe him? When you're facedown in the holy Presence, do you even care? Isaiah's thoughts were filled with nothing but God's holiness and his own sinfulness. And anything God asked—anything at all, even Isaiah's life itself—would be well worth the cost for this moment in glory.

In Deed

We need to realize that what Isaiah saw is happening all the time. Right now, seraphs are surrounding God's throne and shouting "Holy, holy, holy" to one another. Right now, blinding light and overwhelming glory are emanating from the Presence. And right now, Isaiah's response is appropriate.

Let that scene fuel your worship today. Know that if you were in His manifest presence to the degree that Isaiah was, you'd offer Him anything—anything!—and it still wouldn't be enough to satisfy your desire to give to Him. Knowing that, give Him everything today. The One on the throne, whether you see Him or not, is worthy of that response.

> The radiance of the divine beauty is wholly inexpressible;
> words cannot describe it, nor the ear grasp it.
>
> —PHILIMON

An Overwhelming Vision

The whole earth is full of his glory.
ISAIAH 6:3

In Word

In the beginning, God created the heavens and the earth. How? He spoke. Words made all of this out of nothing. The voice of God is just that powerful.

When God made this creation, He didn't separate Himself from it. It is full of His glory. In other words, His fingerprints are all over it. His presence is always in it. His attributes have orchestrated it. Though it is horrendously fallen, it is not abandoned. Glory is everywhere.

The question that naturally arises is, "Then why don't we see it?" And the answer is that all who want to—all who really seek God with all their heart—can see it. It's there to be observed. The God who wants to be known did not create a world in which His presence would be tragically hidden. It's obscured from the eyes of those who persist in sin and will not embrace faith, but it is enthusiastically offered to all who crave spiritual sight and ask God for it. The God of intimacy has made His glory visible to all with eyes of faith.

In Deed

Do you see it? He wants you to. He has extended an open invitation for you to see His wonders. While eyes of unbelief see a world of randomness and evil, the heart of God tells you to look at the glory. There's beauty and design, marvels and mysteries, expressions of His wisdom and His love. There's a reason that on each day of creation He called everything good. It's good because it's full of Him.

It's easy to get depressed in our world, but that's only because we have too many options before our eyes. Observing glory requires a choice, and that choice can only be made in faith. Isaiah saw God's glory because He was overwhelmed by it. He couldn't really resist. But what about us? We can point our eyes wherever we want to, never realizing what a serious choice we're making.

Choose glory. Throughout the day today, set your mind on the things above, where Christ is. Realize that "the things above" are right in front of your face—if you're open to seeing the heart of God displayed in this world.

> The world is charged with the grandeur of God.
> —GERARD MANLEY HOPKINS

An Awesome Presence

I am ruined! For I am a man of unclean lips, and
I live among a people of unclean lips, and my
eyes have seen the King, the LORD Almighty.

ISAIAH 6:5

In Word

What does God's glory do to the human heart? It displays the awesome contrast between holiness and . . . well, not. It shows the exhilarating evidence
of what we're missing because of our tragic sin and the Fall. It makes us long
from the very depths of our soul to be reunited with the divine breath that
brought life to the first man. It makes us want to simultaneously run straight
away from and straight into the glory we see.

The dark side of glory is that it shows us how unclean we are. That's painful. It prompts a woeful lament from the deepest part of the heart, the part
that knew all along we were missing out on the blessings of God, the part we
quieted because we wanted to think everything was okay. But the bright side
of glory—and it is unimaginably bright—is that God always offers a recovery
from our woeful lament, if we're willing to accept it on His terms. And when
we really understand the glory, we'll always welcome His terms.

Isaiah did. He cried out in woe, but he was purified and then called
to serve. That, in a nutshell, is what our prayer of salvation was all about.
Granted, Isaiah's call was in a moment of extreme crisis—an encounter with
God is always a crisis of some sort—but the transaction is the same. God is
infinitely, incomprehensibly holy. We aren't. And there's nothing we can do
about it. The remedy has to come from Him.

In Deed

When you see the contrast between your human condition and God's glory,
what does that do to your heart? Some people keep God at arm's length in
an attempt to hang on to their human condition. Others cry out and let God
come to them in their paralyzed state.

Which kind of heart do you think God prefers? Which kind of heart has
been guiding your relationship with Him? What adjustments do you need to
make today?

We should always honor and reverence Him
as if we were in His bodily presence.

—THOMAS À KEMPIS

A Holy Mission

**I heard the voice of the Lord saying, "Whom
shall I send? And who will go for us?"**
ISAIAH 6:8

In Word

The voice of the Lord is looking for a representative. You might think that
the voice that created a massive universe out of nothing would not need a
representative, but such is the nature of the relationship between an invisible
God and His visible creation. The invisible seeks a concrete presence that even
faithless eyes can see.

Isaiah didn't just hear the Lord's voice and move on. God never leaves
us with that option. Hearing the voice means making a decision about what
the voice says. There's no way out. Even indecision is a decision. When God
speaks, the next thing we say or do is our answer.

Many have never thought of God's voice that way. We read the Bible and
take our time considering what we'll do about what we've read. We hear
God speak to us through a sermon or a friend, and we add the word of wisdom to our structure of understanding, like one brick in a wall of many. But
when God speaks, that approach isn't an option. When we hear His voice,
it's a moment of crisis. We can be affected by it or we can put it on the back
burner, but either way, we've made a choice. And the choice has powerful
implications.

In Deed

What you do with God's Word—whether it speaks to you from a Bible, the
voice of another believer, or the loneliness of the night—will determine the
course of your life. There's no way around it. When God speaks, a decision is
inevitable, and the decision makes the difference between living in His manifest presence or not. When a voice comes out of the dazzling glory and says,
"Who will go for me?" it isn't a rhetorical question. There simply must be an
answer, and it must come from everyone who heard the question.

What do you do with God's voice? Have you made the mistake of letting it slip by unheeded? Never let it happen again. A prophet who said "send
me" is part of the eternal Word. The impact of your obedience can be just as
lasting.

> The crowning wonder of God's scheme
> is that He entrusted it to men.
> —HENRY DRUMMOND

A Global Message

As the terebinth and oak leave stumps
when they are cut down, so the holy
seed will be the stump in the land.
ISAIAH 6:13

In Word

Not many people aspire to be a stump in the land, but according to Isaiah, it's a holy calling. Those who have heard the voice of God and responded to it are firmly planted, regardless of the judgments of the age. When God is pouring out His blessing, they are the first to flourish. When He is pouring out discipline, they are the only stumps with green shoots growing out of them. Regardless of what the landscape looks like at any given moment, sensitivity to God's voice preserves us and causes us to thrive. Those rooted in the words of God have deep roots indeed.

You live in a land of shallow roots, you know. That's true of any age, but especially of ours. Absolutes of society have been uprooted, alternative life-styles are now conventional, and transition in all forms is the norm. Never have people been so mobile and unattached. A world searching for some constancy can hardly find it.

We're an exception to that. We may be mobile—upwardly, geographically, or any other way—but we who have heard the voice of God do not follow shifting trends. We are members of a remnant—a growing remnant, a flourishing remnant, a remnant that is changing the course of history. We are stumps of the highest order. We are the greenery on a desolate landscape.

In Deed

We may not have a message as stark as Isaiah's—in fact, as messengers of the gospel of grace, we most often do not—but we may feel as alone and rejected as he sometimes did. If that's the case today, remember the high calling of someone who has heard the voice of God. You are in an honorable position as a stump, a representative of the righteousness of God, a disciple of the true Branch that offers salvation to the world (Isaiah 11:1). In a world needing greenery, you flourish for the sake of Him who called you.

The awareness of a need and the capacity to
meet that need: this constitutes a call.
—JOHN R. MOTT

Unfaithful Friendship

**Anyone who chooses to be a friend of the
world becomes an enemy of God.**
JAMES 4:4

In Word

We'd like to make everyone happy. We'd like to have both popularity in this world and popularity with God. We want to avoid offending God and also to indulge in the frivolous pleasures of this world that contradict His character. We want to have our cake and eat it too. But we can't. We have to choose. The values of the world and the values of God stand in violent opposition to each other. We cannot embrace them both.

But oh, how we try. The church is full of Christians with split allegiances. We aren't intentionally trying to oppose God; we just want Him to allow us to get in bed with the enemy. Is that metaphor too graphic? Not to James. He calls it adultery (v. 4). Friendship with the world is an insult to the Lover of our soul.

Why is God so exclusive? Because "the world," as the Bible often uses the term, represents man-made systems that are inspired by the devil and filled with corruption. We'd like to think that there is a wide tract of neutral territory in which we can stand, making both God and the world happy. In truth, there is a narrow line. We are either wholehearted toward our God, or wholly invested in this passing age. The values of each are so opposed that there can be no happy medium. Just as a coin cannot land on both heads and tails simultaneously, a Christian cannot plant his feet in the present age and the Kingdom of God simultaneously. Even attempting to play both sides is unfaithful flirtation.

In Deed

Heed the words of verse 5: "The spirit he caused to live in us envies intensely." God is a jealous lover. He does not enjoy our flirtations any more than a husband or wife would enjoy the indiscretions of his or her mate.

Be very careful as you walk through this world. It rebelled long ago against its Creator, and it lives in open rebellion today. It slanders His name, defies His values, abuses His character, and strives for its own kingdoms. Forsaking the Lord is not worth the cost. Forsaking the world is.

This world and that to come are two enemies.
We cannot therefore be friends to both.
—CLEMENT OF ROME

Pleading Mercy

We do not make requests of you because we are righteous, but because of your great mercy.

DANIEL 9:18

In Word

Mercy. It's the entire basis of salvation, from Genesis to Revelation. God showed mercy to Adam and Eve by covering their sin and promising a righteous seed. He showed mercy to humanity by preserving Noah's family from the flood of judgment. He showed mercy to Israel by delivering them from Egypt. He showed mercy to David for his sin, to Judah after captivity, and to the world through a Savior. Even when God judges, it's done for a merciful purpose.

That's why those who bring their own righteousness to God in prayer are foolish. They have no idea how insufficient is the basis of their prayers. Human righteousness, according to God, is like filthy rags. It is never enough.

Mercy, however, is enough. When we make requests of God, our requests are based on His righteousness, the righteousness He has mercifully provided as a remedy for our sins. We bring the life and works of Jesus into our prayers, knowing that our own works are completely unpersuasive to our righteous God. But Jesus, the Son He delights in, the One who is worthy to receive glory and honor for eternity, is the foundation of every request. And God, who loves mercy, does not deny the merciful Son.

In Deed

How often do you base your prayers on nothing but God's mercy? Intellectually, most of us are aware that everything we receive from God is of grace. But the motives of the human heart are sometimes subtle and well hidden, and at some level we often want God to answer us because we deserve it. But God looks at us in mercy, and in mercy He answers. The promises of God are always based on grace.

Remind yourself daily of the grace in which you stand. Immerse yourself in it, receive it with joy, and bring it into your prayers. And the God of mercy will hear your requests.

Grace is God Himself, His loving energy at work within His church and within our souls.

—EVELYN UNDERHILL

Living Glory

For your sake, O my God, do not delay, because
your city and your people bear your Name.
DANIEL 9:19

In Word

There's a lot at stake in Daniel's prayer. This isn't simply about Judah getting to go back home. It's about God's own possession, His chosen people, and most of all, His reputation in the world. Daniel knew how to tie the benefit God's children seek with the glory that God can receive.

That's always a powerful prayer. When we can find the intersection between God's glory and our answer—especially when God has already connected them in a previous promise or prophecy—we can know we are praying according to His will. And whenever God's reputation is at stake in the world, God comes through. He doesn't pass up chances to show His glory when people of faith are expecting Him to.

There's plenty of biblical precedent for this kind of prayer. Moses prayed that God would spare rebellious Israel in the wilderness for the sake of His reputation (Exodus 32:9-14). Several psalms request an answer from God for the sake of His name. Ezekiel and Jeremiah contain prophecies and prayers about both judgment and redemption for the sake of God's reputation. The message is clear: the welfare of God's people in the eyes of the world is tied to the world's knowledge of God. When His people are sustained, blessed, comforted, healed, provided for, or forgiven, God is seen as Sustainer, Blesser, Comforter, Healer, Provider, or Forgiver. However God deals with His people, that's how He is seen.

In Deed

What does the world see of God in your life? If a non-Christian is looking for evidence that God changes lives, would he look to you? What about evidence that He is powerful, or merciful, or generous? Let your prayer requests revolve around displaying His glory and enhancing His reputation in a lost world. Wherever His glory and your need intersect, that's where your prayers honor Him. And that's where your world will see Him.

> The chief purpose of prayer is that God
> may be glorified in the answer.
> —R. A. TORREY

Worthy of Suffering

The apostles left the Sanhedrin, rejoicing
because they had been counted worthy
of suffering disgrace for the Name.
ACTS 5:41

In Word

Peter and the other apostles had been healing and teaching, making the authorities jealous and anxious to reassert their dominance. So they were taken to court, flogged, and given orders not to preach in the name of Jesus any more—orders which they, of course, could not obey without disobeying God. As they walked away, they rejoiced. Why? Because they had suffered!

Under what conditions can people rejoice over their sufferings? Only when they know there is a benefit that outweighs the pain. The apostles knew that. They had heard the Beatitudes, when Jesus told them that those who were persecuted would be blessed because of it (Matthew 5:10). They had seen the brutality directed at Jesus, and they had seen the glory of His resurrection. They could rejoice because suffering for the Name is an indication that someone is a lot like Jesus.

There's another reason that people might rejoice when they suffer. We consider suffering minimal when it's for someone we passionately love. Our love songs are filled with desires and promises to "do anything" for the one we love. Suffering isn't painful when the cause for which we suffer is a deep affection in our heart. We'll make any sacrifice for what we greatly prize.

In Deed

That's the level of love the apostles had for Jesus. It's the level of love we are to have for Him too. When it comes to oppression, persecution, and pain, our faith is to rejoice in hardship for the blessing and joy that will eventually result from it, and for the love that makes it bearable and even meaningful.

When you suffer, do you rejoice because God considered you worthy of the honor? It isn't a natural reaction for us unless we happen to be so filled with love for our Savior that any identification with Him—even a painful one—thrills us. Aim for that attitude. Nurture that love.

Persecution is one of the surest signs of
the genuineness of our Christianity.
—BENJAMIN FERNANDO

Encouraging Mercy

**Since through God's mercy we have this
ministry, we do not lose heart.**

2 CORINTHIANS 4:1

In Word

Discouragement is a fact of life. Everyone has faced it, and everyone will face it again. No matter how well things go for us at times, we will have periods when setbacks, distractions, and obstacles will get us down. Everyone who has desires and hopes will sometimes find him or herself frustrated. Discouragement in this life is a given.

How can we overcome it? We can study the promises of God and take them to heart; we can rely on the encouragement of the fellowship of believers; and we can fix our hope on the future God has promised us. But there's more. We can remind ourselves of the mercy that God has already shown us. That's the basis of all encouragement. The God who sent His Son into this world to die an excruciating death for our redemption is not going to let us down now. He has already demonstrated that He is not hard-hearted, fixated on judgment, difficult to please, or lacking in love. When things get tough for us, we can remember: The God of wisdom, power, and love is on our side. That's encouraging.

Paul knew that the ministry he had been given was an act of mercy, and it was also a ministry of mercy. When a life is surrounded by and bathed in mercy, it can never get too discouraging. Such a life is based on the tender side of God. Whenever trouble looms large, grace looms larger.

In Deed

What steps can you take to make sure your life, your mission, your agenda are all based on grace? One thing you can do is remind yourself of the fact daily. Another is to demonstrate to others and to yourself the mercy that God demonstrated in Christ. The more you cultivate an attitude of mercy—toward everyone and about everything, inasmuch as your mercy accurately reflects God's—the more you will be encouraged. It's like bathing in a soothing, restoring balm. The mercy of God is the foundation of our entire lives.

> There is a wideness in God's mercy,
> like the wideness of the sea.
>
> —FREDERICK WILLIAM FABER

Renounce Impurity

We have renounced secret and shameful ways.
2 CORINTHIANS 4:2

In Word

We live in a truth-impaired world. We always have to be careful to read between the lines, to check out the fine print, to see through the smoke-screen, and to ignore the rumors and innuendo. The people we meet will usually put forth the image of themselves and of others they want us to see. Most people have their own spin on the truth with which, even unwittingly, they try to influence others. By the time we wade through slanted news-tellers and cultural spin doctors, we can hardly see straight.

Paul declares that he and his fellow evangelists have renounced the methods of slick, self-interested salesmen. The gospel is not being peddled by power-hungry, wage-seeking manipulators. There is no desire to control the Corinthians or to distort the message. Paul and the others have come with purity—honest speech, an unadulterated message, a clean lifestyle, a holy morality, and a self-sacrificing ambition. All they want is for their fellow human beings to know the truth and mercy of God.

That's not only commendable, it's normative. It's exactly how we are expected to live, now that we are in the Kingdom of God. We are to reject the shameful ways of this world: no dishonesty, no immorality, no secret maneuverings and ulterior motives. We are children of the pure, immaculate, perfect God. And His Spirit makes us like Him.

In Deed

Assess the purity of your life. Is your mind filled with gray areas of reality and shades of truth and untruth? Are your relationships pure and honest? Is your conduct transparently open and godly? If you've lived any time in this world, you've probably been stained by its deceptions. Your salvation mandates a cleansing. Your humble obedience and Jesus' power to save will bring you closer and closer into conformity to His character. And His character is as pure as purity gets.

Whatever it takes to renounce secret and shameful ways, do it. Mercy demands it, and God honors it.

Honesty has a beautiful and refreshing simplicity about it.
—CHARLES SWINDOLL

The God of This Age

**The god of this age has blinded
the minds of unbelievers.**
2 CORINTHIANS 4:4

In Word

You would think that "the light of the gospel of the glory of Christ" (v. 4) would be easy to see. Though God is invisible, Jesus, His image, isn't. His glory is bright; His light is pure. So why is His incarnation in this world so easily rejected by so many? There's an obstacle. Or, to be more accurate, there's an obstacle-maker.

We like to think that faith is a simple matter of belief or unbelief. At one level, it is. But there is a malicious subterfuge going on at a deeper level. There is a rival to our God. He's a pitifully outmatched rival, but he does his work with a vengeance. His hatred for God—and for those whom God loves—is insatiable. And his primary weapon is deception. He deceives people into pride, and pride leads to autonomy, autonomy leads to self-direction, and self-direction results in sin. We've all followed that path because we all live in a world that the god of this age has thoroughly infiltrated. We've fallen under his spell. We've been blinded.

The gospel has shined God's light into our blindness. He has opened our eyes and granted us a vision of His glory. We once were blind, but now we see. But there's still a world out there that, for the most part, does not see God because it cannot see God. Lostness is not just a matter of willful disobedience; it's also a matter of hostile captivity in dark, deep places. We get frustrated with people who will not choose God. What we need to realize is that they can't.

In Deed

That doesn't remove human responsibility. People are lost not only because our world is full of sin, but because we've participated in that world wholeheartedly. But having done that, we became slaves to sin, as Paul wrote often in Romans. We got wrapped up in haze and confusion.

That's the world our friends who do not know Jesus live in. Understand that when you talk to them. Your conversations must be preceded with intense prayer. They don't just need to make a decision. They need a miracle of sight.

All unbelief is the belief of a lie.
—HORATIUS BONAR

Let Him Shine

God . . . made his light shine in our hearts
to give us the light of the knowledge of
the glory of God in the face of Christ.

2 CORINTHIANS 4:6

In Word

The worshipful heart sees glory. The more we praise the God of light, the more we see Him. The more we appreciate the salvation that has shined into our hearts, the more we experience it. The more we bask in the warmth of His glory, the more our hearts burn for it. The heart of worship has much to fill it.

How much time do you spend in gratitude and praise? It isn't a peripheral question or a superfluous issue. It strikes at the heart of our contentment. Those who spend time in worship are filled with joy. They go through difficult times, but they never lose sight of the God who gets them through. Just as Paul writes this verse in the context of hardship, so can any believer break out into praise in any circumstance of life.

That's the marvelous nature of the gospel. Worship in the midst of pain is unexplainable to the world, and for that reason is the greatest testimony to those who are blind in their unbelief. Blind people cannot explain sight, but they hear about it and crave it. Non-Christians cannot comprehend glory, but they see it in a worshiper and begin to want it. The light of the knowledge of the glory of God is an invisible magnet to a salvation-hungry world. And the only way for them to see it is when it consumes a believer who loves it, basks in it, and worships God for it.

In Deed

Try a little exercise: Turn to 2 Corinthians 11:24-28. Read of Paul's hardships as he spells them out. Then ask yourself: How can he write of the glory of God in the face of Christ, when Christ is the reason behind his suffering? We know the answer in our minds. Do you know it in your heart? Have you experienced the ability to worship and praise even in the face of extreme stress and pain? That ability is the clearest evidence that the God of heaven has broken into this world. Worship the Source of your light, and let Him shine.

You awaken us to delight in your praise.

—AUGUSTINE

Clay and Treasure

We have this treasure in jars of clay to show that this all-surpassing power is from God and not from us.

2 CORINTHIANS 4:7

In Word

Jars of clay. That's the Bible's assessment of us—molded mud. That isn't very complimentary, but it's true. And those of us who have embraced the gospel don't mind admitting it. If we had not received mercy, we might want to assert a greater competence for ourselves. We would have something to prove. But what is there to prove in a gospel of grace? The only qualification to receive it is an acknowledgment of sin. Who among us doesn't qualify—easily?

We, like Paul, can actually take some sort of pleasure from our weakness. Knowing our weakness qualifies us to receive the gospel; admitting it removes all pretense and the pressure to be self-sufficient; and continuing in it gives God a platform for His glory.

The fragile nature of human flesh makes us susceptible to all sorts of corruptions and failures. But what better showcase for God? In a blinded world, the best way to display God is in a way that human ingenuity and talent cannot obscure. If we were strong and capable, the power of God would be hard to find. But we are so weak! The power of God in a weakling of a human—a moral, physical, mental, spiritual, emotional, finite little weakling—cannot be mistaken for skill or talent.

In Deed

Never overestimate the "earthenness" of your vessel, and never underestimate the treasure within it. Don't deny your weakness—there's no point in that for people who have accepted a gospel of grace, a gospel that is accessible only to the weak and needy. And don't minimize the treasure within. God's Spirit is there, and it is not prideful to believe so.

Quit striving, and let God be God in you. The weaker you are, the clearer His power. The deeper your need, the clearer His provision. His light shines best in darkness. Your treasure looks richer in clay.

The greatness of a man's power is the
measure of his surrender.

—WILLIAM BOOTH

Never Defeated

We are hard pressed on every side, but not crushed; perplexed, but not in despair; persecuted, but not abandoned; struck down, but not destroyed.

2 CORINTHIANS 4:8-9

In Word

God never promised us a life of ease. We had trouble before we believed, and it is entirely possible that our trouble may increase afterward. The way of the Cross—the way that Jesus told us we must embrace—is not an easy way. The road is steep and rocky, and though it leads to glory, it leads to pain first. The life of Jesus made that obvious; the life of the apostles confirmed it. The Christian's walk isn't casual and comfortable.

You've probably noticed that. It isn't an obscure fact about this world. Trials complicate our lives, and pain touches us all. Sometimes that gets discouraging. When we're muddling through hardship, and then more hardship strikes, we often lose heart. It can get overwhelming. We were not redeemed for a life of comfort. At least not yet.

In Deed

The world and its troubles cannot crush the Spirit within you. It tries, but it can't. It simply isn't possible for the temporal to overcome the eternal, for the finite to eclipse the infinite, or for the darkness to shroud the glory. God lives in these clay jars of ours, and though the clay can be broken and crushed, the treasure within cannot. And this treasure, this Spirit, has wrapped Himself in our identity. When trial strikes, He doesn't leave. He shows Himself stronger and He shines brighter.

The mercy of God, with which Paul began 2 Corinthians 4, will not let us be overcome. Remember that when you're overwhelmed. Hang on to it. Cultivate the hope He has placed within you.

How? Refuse discouragement. It doesn't reflect the truth. The truth is that God has saved, continues to save, and will always save. The Victor, the Savior, the Sovereign Lord is faithful. Your trials are no match for Him.

> To added affliction He addeth His mercy, to multiplied trials, His multiplied peace.
>
> —ANNIE JOHNSON FLINT

Carriers of Death and Life

**We always carry around in our body the
death of Jesus, so that the life of Jesus
may also be revealed in our body.**

2 CORINTHIANS 4:10

In Word

Jesus came into this world, lived, died, was buried, and rose again. That whole
Incarnation story is recorded in Scripture, but it doesn't end in Revelation.
There's also an ongoing revelation of it—us. The church—collectively and
individually—is a constant illustration of death and life. Death works within
our flesh; life works in our spirit. The corruption of this world eats away at us,
but the glory of the light of God still shines through. If the world is ever going
to see the Resurrection before Jesus returns, it will have to see it in us.

Many of us think often about our witness, but we may think of it in terms
of our words or even our lifestyle. Those things are certainly important, even
essential parts of our witness. But there's a dynamic that will do more than
any of our words or good behavior can do. It's the dynamic of visible death
and visible life.

What does that mean? It means that people must see in us a sacrificial
life. They must see self-denial and self-restraint, humility and confession,
deference and peace. They must see that the life of Jesus within us costs us a
lot. They must see the very attitude that took Jesus to the Cross. Then they
must see the power of Jesus working in us. They must see that our life is not
something created by our past psychology or present drive, but is given from
above. They must see a joy that transcends this world and a peace that will
not be bothered by it. They must see the very glory that brought Jesus out of
the grave.

In Deed

Sound intimidating? It is. Everyone wants to skip to resurrection life without ever having to take up their cross. It won't work. And it won't display
Jesus. The only way to make our Savior known is to embody His death and
to embody His life. Live like He lived. Sacrifice like He sacrificed. Enjoy the
glory of His resurrection like He did—and does. That's how He is revealed.

Fellowship with Christ is participation in the divine life
which finds its fullest expression in triumph over death.

—WILLIAM TEMPLE

Worship That Loves

**Anyone who claims to be in the light but
hates his brother is still in the darkness.**
1 JOHN 2:9

In Word

Jesus told a story of God-worshipers who passed by a person in dire need
(Luke 10:30-37). Lying in a ditch, the wounded victim watched the guard-
ians of the faith casually walk past him. Perhaps the disciple John recalled that
now-familiar story when he penned these words in 1 John 2. His message?
You can't love God and not love people.

True worship is a vertical relationship with the One above, but if it's
genuine, it always results in horizontal works. To say that we passionately love
our God while being casual about His beloved creation is an inconsistency of
enormous proportions. If God so loved the world that He gave His only Son,
and we love God, then we're going to have passion for His world. We will have
a deep desire for the welfare of our fellow human beings. There is no such
thing as worship that honors God and ignores His children.

What does that mean in real terms? It means first of all that we are to
avoid hatred and apathy. But it also means that we will pursue love and compassion. We will hate conflict and rejoice in fellowship. We will never rejoice
at the downfall of another. We will fulfill all of those magnificent qualities of
love expressed by Paul in 1 Corinthians 13. When it comes to a lost and sinful
world, our heart will beat with God's.

In Deed

That's what worship is, isn't it? It's a heart that's in sync with its Creator. It's
a soul that loves what He loves and hates what He hates. It's a person who
so admires and enjoys His character that His character takes over. To be in
love with God is to be in love with the things of God. And human beings are
"His thing."

God is intensely focused on the welfare of His children. Are you? God is
in zealous pursuit of His chosen. Are you? God loves with a kind of sacrifice
that defies expectations. Do you? Your answer to these questions will indicate,
to some degree, the quality of your worship. Consider them well. God wants
to shine His light not only on you, but also through you.

Can a man love God while ignoring the need of his brother?
—FRANCES J. ROBERTS

The Illustrated God

Go, take to yourself an adulterous wife and children
of unfaithfulness, because the land is guilty of
the vilest adultery in departing from the LORD.

HOSEA 1:2

In Word

The problem with being a prophet is that prophetic illustrations of judgment are often portrayed in life events. Such was the case with Hosea, who, for the purpose of divine illustration, was told to marry a prostitute. What was the point? God's people had been committing spiritual adultery for generations. They jumped from one idol to another like an adulteress jumps from one man's bed to another. And God's heart was broken.

Hosea probably wished he could just deliver the message verbally. But God speaks louder than that when circumstances are dire. When ears are closed to His words, eyes must be opened to His truth. And Hosea's calling was to live the truth of God's pain. Hosea had the unenviable task of marrying someone who would be repeatedly unfaithful, someone whom he loved dearly, someone who would break his heart again and again.

We often read of people who sacrifice their lives for the sake of the gospel—prophets who were killed for the word they delivered. Hosea sacrificed his life in a different way. Men don't dream of marrying unfaithful women who will rip their heart out. They dream of true love that lasts forever. For the sake of God's people, Hosea had to give up his dreams.

In Deed

What would you give up for the sake of God's people? If He called you to sacrifice your life—or harder yet, to sacrifice your dreams—would you be able to? Only a person whose love for God is great, who sees the big picture of eternity, can do such a thing. But that's exactly what we're called to do: love God greatly and see the big picture. We're to embrace the joy and the pain of being living illustrations of His Kingdom—whatever it costs.

God will be our compensation for every
sacrifice we have made.

—F. B. MEYER

Betrayal

Call him Lo-Ammi, for you are not my people, and I am not your God.
HOSEA 1:9

In Word

Israel's adultery was a stinging insult to the Creator. He had seen Himself as Israel's husband, full of hope for a bright future. Sure, the relationship had always had its ups and downs, but reconciliation was always a possibility. Now the Lord Himself speaks words of divorce. He says, "You are not my people, and I am not your God" (1:9) and "I will no longer show love to the house of Israel" (1:6). Those are more than words of judgment; they are words of deep, deep pain.

Theologically speaking, it's hard to attribute such pain to a God of perfect foresight. Yes, God knew ahead of time of Israel's adultery; He had even predicted it in Deuteronomy 31:16-21. Yes, He wasn't blindsided by unfaithfulness at all. But the picture of the forsaken husband grieving for His beloved as she commits rampant adultery is a picture given by God Himself. He wants His people to know: His foreknowledge doesn't remove His pain.

God was true to His word; the separation was, to a degree, irreconcilable. God didn't restore Israel; instead, He allowed the northern kingdom to be sacked and its citizens to intermarry with outsiders. He preserved a remnant in Judah, whom He later restored and through whom He brought forth the Messiah, but northern Israel gradually lost its identity. By the time of Jesus, the mixed-breed Samaritans were despised as the melting-pot decline of a once holy people. God did not take adultery lightly.

In Deed

Let that picture of the heartbroken husband sink in. It reveals the heart of God in a painful but necessary way. We often see God as an emotionally untouchable fortress, impervious to our betrayal. But God gives us a different picture. Our lack of love can grieve Him. Our "indiscretions" wound Him deeply. As He says often in Scripture, He is a jealous God. Never give Him reason to be jealous for you.

I would hate my own soul if I did not find it loving God.
—AUGUSTINE

Jealousy

Call her Lo-Ruhamah, for I will no longer show love to the house of Israel.

HOSEA 1:6

In Word

If we really understood the jealousy of God—and how pure a jealousy it is—we would avoid sin like the plague. We don't understand it because it's hard to imagine the perfect, pure, radiant God having a burning passion for people like us. But people like us were designed specifically to house His holy presence, to commune with Him in the intimate depths of our hearts. That's the fundamental purpose of being made in the image of God, and it's a purpose we can scarcely grasp.

That's why God gives us such graphic images of His jealous love—so we can grasp it. A woman who doesn't know her suitor's love is apt to violate it. So God gives us ample opportunity to know it. We are to be a bride deeply in love, a bride who so adores her Husband that she cannot get enough of His presence. She clings to the whispers of His love and would never even dream of betraying Him. She is fully satisfied in Him and doesn't even notice His rivals. Idols get none of her attention.

In Deed

If idols get any of our attention, we are not satisfied in God. Those who love completely do not spread their love around. That's the message of Hosea and, in fact, of most of the prophets. That's also the thought of the New Testament apostles, who remind us that God has poured out His love into our hearts. His love, of course, is as pure as it gets. If that's what is in our hearts, idols are completely and permanently irrelevant.

But few of us have that testimony. Most of us can tell of struggles with this or that sin, of how our love sometimes grows cold and sometimes is directed elsewhere. We love God, but our eyes wander. We entertain the thought of other loves far too easily.

The key to overcoming a wandering eye is to know how deeply and how purely we are loved by our God. If we truly know His jealousy, we'll never truly provoke it. Our hearts will burn as passionately as His.

The distinguishing mark of a Christian is his confidence in the love of Christ, and the yielding of his affections to Christ in return.

—CHARLES SPURGEON

Reconciliation

I will save them—not by bow, sword or battle, or by
horses and horsemen, but by the LORD their God.

HOSEA 1:7

In Word

Judah's adultery was never quite as severe and persistent as Israel's, so in this
passage from Hosea, God says He will save the southern kingdom. It won't
be a salvation won by war, but a salvation won by the Lord of love Himself.
The divine Husband has no intention of letting what's left of His beloved fend
for herself. Though He lets her suffer the consequences of her adultery, He
will rescue and forgive. All she has to do is return to Him and lean on His
strength.

Those are always the terms of salvation. God delivered Israel from Egypt
by His own strength, illustrating their helplessness every step of the way. He
defeated enemies from the days of Joshua to the days of Jehoshaphat, always in
the strength He provided. He urges His people to be still and know that He is
God (Psalm 46:10) and to understand that quietness and trust is all they need
for salvation (Isaiah 30:15). He even sent His Son to accomplish what sinful
people could never do for themselves—erase their sin with righteousness.
When God saves, He is the One who does all the saving.

Still, we try to save ourselves. Our repentance shifts from helpless offering to spiritual collateral far too easily. Deep down, we want to be able to say
we deserve the favor of God. All the while, God wants to bestow love simply
because it's His nature. The Husband isn't holding auditions for a bride. He
chooses her, even when she has strayed.

In Deed

Do everything you can to understand the nature of God's love for you. Compare it to a man doting on His beloved and restoring her simply because of His
infinite pleasure in what the relationship can be. Trying to earn such a love,
whether consciously or not, is insulting to the One who has already lavished
it on you. The depths of His delight are not bought by "making it up" to Him.
They are received by those with nothing to give in return but love and gratitude. Live your life as one dearly cherished.

Our salvation, thank God, depends much more
on His love of us than on our love of Him.

—FATHER ANDREW

Restoration

In the place where it was said to them, "You are not my people," they will be called "sons of the living God."
HOSEA 1:10

In Word

God's rejection of Israel came only after Israel's rejection of God. That happens sometimes between spouses, and usually the rejection is permanent. But the forgiving Husband portrayed by Hosea had something better in mind. He would eventually bring His people into a place of intimacy deeper than they had ever experienced. His own Spirit would one day intermingle with their hearts and commune with them in the private places of their souls.

Has there ever been such a dramatic restoration? In our hearts, where once there was adultery and heart-wrenching betrayal, now there's intimacy. Where there were disowned, illegitimate children, now there are sons of the living God. In the place where all seemed lost and hopeless—where irreconcilable differences seemed truly irreconcilable—there's fullness and joy. There's even a promise of living happily ever after.

That's why we can never write off the depravity of our world as unredeemable. No matter how vile and disgraceful a person's actions, that person is never out of the reach of God. Though human husbands will only put up with so much infidelity, the divine Husband will forgive all who turn back to Him. In a world we tend to divide between "us" and "them," we need to remember that "them" always has the potential to be "us."

In Deed

If that's not how you approach your world, change your attitude. No one has ever offended any of us to the degree that Israel offended God, yet God still brought about redemption for a remnant purely out of His mercy and love. Wherever our love falls short of that, we need to bring it into conformity with the heart of a holy Husband who delights in His spotless bride. He doesn't even see her stains anymore. Neither should we. Instead, learn to see the purity of a heart in love with God, and do whatever you can to cultivate it—in yourself, in your church, and in your world.

> Redemption means that Jesus Christ can put into any man the disposition that ruled His own life.
> —OSWALD CHAMBERS

The Mystery of Godliness

Beyond all question, the mystery of godliness is great.
1 TIMOTHY 3:16

In Word

Humanity has no shortage of theories about God. For millennia, religious thinkers have stretched themselves toward the Creator. The problem is that religions reduce God—and godliness—to a matter of the right knowledge, of individual self-improvement, or of withdrawal from a corrupt world. In every form it takes, man-made religion is a tower of Babel—a creative, innovative attempt to reach heavenward.

The mystery of godliness bypasses the need to reach God. Paul sums it up in 1 Timothy 3:16: "He appeared in a body, was vindicated by the Spirit, was seen by angels, was preached among the nations, was believed on in the world, was taken up in glory." In other words, God reached us. Our rebellious planet has been visited. The mystery of godliness is the Incarnation.

What does that mean? It means that anyone who wants to be godly—to have a life that is consistent with the will and the character of God—must embrace the Incarnation. Jesus is the intersection between humanity and divinity, where fallen flesh can apprehend the immortal God, where futile minds and fickle hearts can grasp an eternal Kingdom, and where sin is purged and holiness imparted. The mystery of godliness, says Paul, is to welcome the incarnate God with open arms.

In Deed

Most of us who read devotionals like this one have done that. We've asked Jesus into our hearts by faith and accepted His sacrifice for our sins. Still, we struggle. We are weak and frail, sinful and apathetic. We crave godliness, but we do not find it within ourselves. What can we do?

The answer still lies in the Incarnation. Not only do we accept it for our salvation, we must accept it for our daily lives. The fact that Jesus once visited this planet saves us. The fact that He visits us—here and now, in our day-to-day lives—makes us godly. Ponder the magnificence of the Incarnation! But don't stop there. Let Jesus now incarnate Himself in you.

To be like Christ. That is our goal, plain and simple.
—CHARLES SWINDOLL

Talk about It

I will tell of the kindnesses of the LORD.
ISAIAH 63:7

In Word

It's simple, really. One of the easiest, clearest, most profound ways to worship the God who has saved us is to talk about Him. We who have been redeemed are given a holy task that brings substantial honor to our Redeemer. We are to describe for others how He has been kind to us, the deeds He has done, and the blessings of His compassion that we have experienced.

God did not save us for isolation. Like His Holy City, which, not coincidentally, is located on a hill for all to see, His holy people have been placed in a position of testimony. We have taken the stand in the courtroom of this world and are honor-bound to describe what has happened. Easy, isn't it?

Then why does it seem so complicated? Because we know the implications of our testimony. It will indict a world that does not want to believe it. Perhaps surprisingly—or perhaps not—a fallen race does not want to entertain the kindnesses of God because it will then, by logical implication, have to acknowledge God Himself. And to a rebellious people, that's a problem. So we go through all sorts of intimidating mind games of political correctness and social acceptability that keep us silent about creation's greatest secret. Our own culture, for example, has taught us never to speak of politics and religion among people with whom keeping the peace matters to us. So we heed the advice and opt for good taste. Meanwhile, our Scriptures urge us: Tell of the kindnesses of the Lord.

In Deed

Don't be intimidated. The glory of the Lord is worth more than the approval of men. From beginning to end, the Incarnation didn't exactly fit socially refined expectations. Why should we be diligent to do so? No, there is a greater claim on us than the need to fit seamlessly into our culture. There is the call of the God who wants to be known by those to whom the privilege has been granted. He reveals Himself, sometimes through us. Tell of His kindnesses and the deeds for which He is to be praised.

Never, for fear of feeble man, restrain your witness.
—CHARLES SPURGEON

Victorious God

**When the people of Ashdod rose early the
next day, there was Dagon, fallen on his face
on the ground before the ark of the LORD!**

1 SAMUEL 5:3

In Word

The Philistines and Israelites had gone to battle against each other, and the
unthinkable had happened. The Ark of the Covenant—the sign of God's presence among His chosen, covenant people—was captured! The glory of Israel
had departed; God had allowed Himself to be removed from His own carefully cultivated people.

It was utter catastrophe. If drought, famine, disease, or death struck them,
the covenant between God and Israel could survive. But the symbol of God
Himself in the hands of pagans? The icon of deliverance, the relic of God's
guidance into the Promised Land, in foreign territory? That situation could
not persist for long so early in this nation's religious history without calling
the covenant into question. It could not be allowed to stand.

But God has His reasons for working His way into the midst of people
not yet under covenant with Him. His goal is to demonstrate His primacy
and display His sovereignty. In Ashdod, the exalted god of the Philistines fell
facedown before true Deity—not just once, but twice. The second time, his
head and hands were the casualties of his inferiority. Because of God's excur-
sion among false worshipers, God's superiority was made clear. It always is.

In Deed

Think of how this example flies in the face of our approach to interfaith relationships. Don't we often try to protect God's reputation, withholding Him
from the crucial discussions of our age? In the marketplace of ideas, we are
sometimes reluctant to display the emphatic, narrow claims of our faith. Are
we afraid that God will fall facedown to Dagon? It will never happen. Our
God will always stand.

Be confident in the excellence of God. He can compete anywhere. Honor
Him—worship Him—by bringing your faith into a false-worshiping world.

God is never defeated.

—BROTHER ANDREW

The Right Place

**Faith is being sure of what we hope for
and certain of what we do not see.**
HEBREWS 11:1

In Word

You've asked God to deal with a problem in your life. You pray for His help daily, hoping He will intervene. You are burdened beyond comfort, carrying your stress into your relationships and your work, letting it affect your health and your devotion.

Sound familiar? You may not be going through such a trial at the moment, but nearly everyone has, at one time or another. And when we find ourselves in such a position, we turn to God for His help. It sounds spiritual, and perhaps it is. But it isn't faith.

Faith doesn't hold on to worry and stress. Faith doesn't hope that maybe God might possibly consider that perhaps we've met all the right conditions and prayed for the right things so He can potentially grant us what He wills. No, there's an assurance in real faith that knows God will answer us according to His goodness. Faith doesn't necessarily have all the details in place, but it always has in mind the One who holds all details in His hands. It is supremely confident in the will of God, whatever that will happens to be. Faith allows us to rest.

In Deed

Don't confuse pleading with God and believing God. Both are appropriate, but only one qualifies as faith. Many have pleaded for God to intervene but have had no confidence or even awareness of His power and His goodness. Real faith, on the other hand, is absolutely certain that the invisible God has a visible answer for us.

Make real faith your goal. Consider who God is, and then ask yourself why you might have reason to worry. You'll have a hard time coming up with a legitimate basis for your anxiety. When you get to the point where you can be sure—whether you see it or not—that God is taking care of you and will always take care of you, and that His care is the best there is or ever could be, then you have arrived at a position of faith. Ask God to bring you there, and then sit down and rest in that place. This is where God commends His people.

> Belief is a truth held in the mind. Faith is a fire in the heart.
> —JOSEPH FORT NEWTON

The Best Testimony

Without faith it is impossible to please God.
HEBREWS 11:6

In Word

Why is faith so emphasized in God's Kingdom? From Genesis to Revelation, the Bible makes faith primary. The invisible God could show Himself at any time and in any way, eliminating all the guessing about His nature. He could demonstrate His authority and make the importance of obedience obvious to us. But He doesn't. He remains hidden to everyone who chooses not to see Him, revealing Himself only to those with ears to hear and hearts hungry for Him. Why? Why is faith so important to God?

Perhaps it is because faith is the ultimate vote of confidence in the unseen Spirit. It is a profound statement of His worth by those who cannot prove that He even exists. It focuses on the character of the Almighty more than the authority His visible presence would command. It takes His Word at highest value, even when our own senses deceive us. In short, faith honors God's faithfulness, His power, His love, and His wisdom in a world that has forsaken Him. It gives Him glory.

Perhaps another reason for the primacy of faith is that the very act of trusting God has a purifying power like nothing else. If we persevere in believing God's goodness, we have to see through the lies about Him that once corrupted our souls. Where once we wondered whether He cared or was able to help us, or whether He even existed, faith compels us to decide once and for all that He does care, He is able, and He is still on His throne. A visible God would have lots of superficial followers. The more we grow in faith, the more we have to let go of our inward suspicions, rebellions, and self-deceits.

In Deed

Have you considered that your faith is an act of worship? It does have invaluable benefits for you personally, but it also blesses the heart of your Father. It is a witness to the world that there are unseen realities more real than this temporal world can offer. In this midst of darkness, it points to light. Nothing could please Him more.

> The act of faith is more than a bare statement of belief, it is a turning to the face of the living God.
> —CHRISTOPHER BRYANT

Beyond Logic

**He who had received the promises was
about to sacrifice his one and only son.**
HEBREWS 11:17

In Word

A childless couple had been told by an invisible God that they would be the parents of countless descendants. They had no Scripture or fellowship of believers to encourage their faith on a discouraging day. All they had was a promise and a lot of time to think about it. Too much time, in fact. They passed childbearing age, not just barely, but hopelessly. But against all odds, God fulfilled His promise. The child was born, the invisible God was vindicated, and the couple rejoiced.

Then the unthinkable happened. Against all logic, God told Abraham to sacrifice the couple's one and only son, who was their only link to the millions of descendants they were to have. Was God going to give them another child? Was He going to raise this one from the dead? No outcome seemed reasonable. Still, God's instructions were clear enough that Abraham took a long walk up a mountain and raised his hand against his only son. Obedience was more important than the promise. That kind of obedience, at that kind of cost, required extraordinary faith.

Abraham's obedience is commended as the cornerstone of righteous, biblical faith. The faith that led Abraham up that mountain is unimaginable. Any illusion that the life of faith is a life of comfort and ease is undone by this story. Faith is excruciating, sometimes illogical, and always right.

In Deed

Does your faith sometimes defy logic? If not, it hasn't been stretched as far as God wants to stretch it. Has God ever called you to give up His promise as an act of obedience? If not, your faith has deeper depths to reach.

The God who commends and cultivates our faith will sometimes lead us into painful places, into unreasonable places, and into places that simply do not make sense. Why? Because real faith has to outweigh our emotional comfort, our human logic, and our passion for understanding. When it does, the Object of our faith has become the most important thing in our lives.

Faith is the master, and reason the maidservant.
—MARTIN LUTHER

Beyond Pleasure

**He chose to be mistreated along with the
people of God rather than to enjoy the
pleasures of sin for a short time.**

HEBREWS 11:25

In Word

Who would choose discomfort, ill treatment, injustice, and pain? Certainly
no one who has his eyes focused on this world. This world offers too many
treasures. And Moses could have had them all: pleasure, wealth, ease, prestige,
and honor. But he identified with God's people, even though it cost him his
place of privilege. Why?

Those who cannot see the invisible God and who are not aware of the
eternal Kingdom will never opt for faith. If this world is all there is, hedonism makes sense. There is no reason not to "eat, drink, and be merry," for
tomorrow we will all die. Nothing matters, because nothing lasts. Futility and
frustration are the order of the day, and pleasure becomes the intoxicant that
helps one get through it all—if this world is all there is.

But it isn't. There is a sovereign God behind the scenes. There is a hidden
Kingdom being built. There is a driving purpose behind this creation that will
one day point plainly and gloriously to its Creator. According to the writer of
Hebrews, Moses knew that. And he staked his life on it.

That's what faith is. Faith doesn't waffle between obedience and sinful
indulgence, hoping that in the end the two will be reconcilable. Faith doesn't
look forward to the eternal Kingdom while investing heavily in passing pleasures. Faith enjoys the gifts of God in this world, but never pursues them
above God Himself. The eyes of faith see the big picture and cause us to stake
our life on it.

In Deed

A clear vision of the invisible realities behind this world will ground your
life in what matters and what lasts. A lack of confidence in the truths of the
Kingdom will constantly lead to temptation and sin. It's difficult to forsake the
pleasures of earth when the glories of heaven are only speculative. But "being
sure of what we hope for and certain of what we do not see" (Hebrews 11:1)
will keep us moving away from the false treasures and toward the true ones.
It will help us persevere.

Do not let the false delights of a deceptive world deceive you.

—CLARE OF ASSISI

Cisterns and Springs

They have forsaken me, the spring of living water, and have dug their own cisterns, broken cisterns that cannot hold water.

JEREMIAH 2:13

In Word

Jerusalem was steeped in idolatry. Its religious leaders had the books of Moses, so lack of information wasn't an issue. In fact, many of those religious leaders, as well as the prophets, had preached plenty of sermons about the jealous God who had delivered His beloved people and asked them to love and worship Him exclusively. The problem wasn't lack of awareness or knowledge. The problem was apathy and even rebellion. Something else needed to be said, something that might help the political and religious minds of Jerusalem understand what they were doing to themselves.

God gave Jeremiah a picture to illustrate the devastating implications of idolatry. Forsaking God isn't simply a matter of making a mental mistake and choosing an alternative worship style, or even of being brought up in a non-theistic culture. It's a matter of abandoning a life-giving, ever-flowing spring for dirty, broken pots that can't even hold water.

The graphic nature of God's words is meant to startle ignorant people and give them the understanding they need to embrace truth. It's also meant to rebuke rebellious people and shock them into a sudden awareness of the ridiculous nature of their rebellion. In any case, investing worship and honor in anything other than God is wildly irrational, a choice no one in his or her right mind would make. So God paints a picture to help put people in their right mind.

In Deed

Are there any areas of your life in which you've grown apathetic or even rebellious? If so, God longs for you to be awakened to His loving embrace. He wants all of your honor, all of your worship, all of your praise; and He grieves when someone or something else gets them. He wants His children to be refreshed by the living Spring, not trying to dip water from leaky pots. He wants His beloved to love Him back.

> In his natural state, every man born into the world is a rank idolater.
>
> —JOHN WESLEY

Garbage and Glory

My people have exchanged their
Glory for worthless idols.
JEREMIAH 2:11

In Word

Imagine having the world's most valuable masterpiece, a work of art that would bring thirty or forty million dollars if you auctioned it. Then imagine that instead of taking that masterpiece to the auction, you took it to a pawnshop, pawned it for twenty bucks, and blew the whole wad on crayons and paper so you could decorate your own walls.

Or imagine being offered a lifetime pass to the city's best buffet spread, only to reject it in favor of one meal at a truck stop. Silly? Ludicrous? Absolutely insane? All of that and more. People with even an ounce of sense don't squander glory on garbage. But that's what idolatry is. That's what the people of Judah were doing in Jeremiah's day, and that's what we do with alarming ease today.

Think about how much God is worth. He can create anything, so whatever we have, He has something better. He governs and sustains everything, so every circumstance we encounter must bow to Him. And He has promised lavish blessings for eternity, so all our cravings will be extravagantly exceeded by His good gifts. Logically, there's nothing we would take in exchange for a relationship with this God. Practically, however, that's exactly what we often do.

In Deed

What drives us to such insanity? Ignorance of what will really fulfill us, perhaps. Or maybe it's blindness to the beauty of our Creator. Whatever the case, human sin is always a bad trade, an offering to something worthless at the expense of someone infinitely exquisite and priceless.

What drives God to seek us out regardless of our offenses? Love for a pitifully ignorant people and compassion for children with massive, self-inflicted, potentially fatal wounds. God doesn't enjoy our foolishness any more than we do. He longs to share His glory with those whom He loves.

Let Him do that. Never exchange the invitation of God for a self-drawn plan. The cost never will—never can, in fact—match the worth of our Glory.

> Thus does the world forget You, its Creator, and falls in love with what You have created instead of with You.
>
> —AUGUSTINE

Rights and Responsibilities

Have you not brought this on yourselves by forsaking the LORD your God when he led you in the way?
JEREMIAH 2:17

In Word

We're a society of victims. That's what happens when a culture emphasizes human rights over human responsibilities. Both are important, but one without the other has tragic consequences. Focusing on responsibility to the exclusion of rights ultimately results in slavery. Focusing on rights to the exclusion of responsibility results in . . . well, the society we have. Everything is always someone else's fault.

God won't let us get away with that attitude. He loves us too much to allow us to think our brokenness comes to us in spite of our innocence. No, we live in a fallen world, and all of us have deepened the fall. We don't just bear the effects of sin, we've inflicted them from time to time. We live in a climate of rebellion because we've been rebels ourselves. In one way or another, everyone has forsaken the Lord who would have led us in the way we should go.

We like to point our fingers at those who are worse sinners than we are, and we can find plenty of evidence that some people exhibit more depravity than others. But the Bible never really invites us to do that. It's always reminding us of our part in the Fall, rarely, if ever, lamenting that all those other people have messed up the world for us. That doesn't mean that all suffering is at our own hands. It does, however, mean that all suffering comes from the condition of a fallen world—a condition we've helped create. Finger-pointing is never allowed in God's Kingdom unless we also place ourselves in the path of the pointer.

In Deed

God knows we aren't all blatantly idolatrous rebels. Most of us who believe in the gospel have a heart that longs for Him. Even so, never get to the point of thinking that your heart is beyond rebellion or temptation. And never cease to follow the One who leads the way for you and who is jealous for your love. Live as a citizen of the Kingdom of righteousness, not as a citizen of the society of victims.

Pray for a strong and lively sense of sin. The greater the sense of sin, the less sin.
—SAMUEL RUTHERFORD

Variety and Depth

Why go to Assyria to drink water from the River?
JEREMIAH 2:18

In Word

Human nature is always craving something new and different. That's why clothing styles change every season, TV schedules need constant refreshing, and exotic foods expand our trendy appetites. It's also why many believers leave the faith to try out Buddhism, Islam, or some cult that has gotten their attention. When we've tried something and passed through our initial fascination phase, we're ready to move on. We seek variety over depth.

Not God. He knows that a taste for truth should lead to a voracious appetite for deeper truth, not to experimentation with error. Variety may be the spice of life in cuisine and fashion, but it has tragic consequences in matters of faith. Belief is not a buffet spread to pick and choose from; it's a deep well of real sustenance that should draw us back again and again.

Even within the Christian community, we often jump around from church to church and from teacher to teacher. We skim the surface of the land because we're intrigued with the varieties of wood, hay, and stubble we see there, never realizing that if we dig with a little persistence, we'll find gold and silver underneath. Sometimes the cravings we have can be fulfilled right where we are.

In Deed

That doesn't mean that God never lets us change our focus. There are legitimate seasons in life, and He will guide us through them at appropriate times. But far too often we get restless and impatient, and we jump around because we can't get enough of the feeling we have when we're discovering something new and fresh. That's fine within limits. But when "new and fresh" take us outside the bounds of simple devotion to Jesus, we're missing the depth we desperately need.

Don't go to Assyria to drink from the river. Or, along the same lines, don't go to human-devised philosophy, alternative spirituality, or material acquisition to satisfy your thirst. The Spring of life in your heart is what you really need.

> Many of us are not thirsty for God because we
> have quenched our thirst at other fountains.
>
> —ERWIN LUTZER

Evil and Awe

**Consider then and realize how evil and
bitter it is for you when you forsake the LORD
your God and have no awe of me.**
JEREMIAH 2:19

In Word

God is awe-inspiring. Well, He should be, if we see Him correctly. The problem is blindness. He can't inspire awe when He isn't seen.

But we live in a blind world, don't we? People casually take God's name in vain, defy His moral standards, ridicule those who take Him too seriously, and have a "don't-call-me-I'll-call-you" attitude toward Him. When people are desperate, they'll talk to Him—often with indignation that He let them get in this mess in the first place—but otherwise He's treated as a senile grandfather who smiles with affection at everyone.

Yet God calls a lack of awe "evil and bitter." It may not be intentional evil and bitterness. It's simply the result of choosing not to see Him in His greatness and majesty, of remaining unaware of how overwhelming He really is and how His holiness should make us tremble. If people opened their eyes to His presence, they'd fall down in worship. But instead, they have no awe. And this, according to the words of God through Jeremiah, is a horrible sin.

In Deed

How can we cultivate awe? Contemplate the vastness of His creation, and realize that all that vastness fits in His palm. Consider the invisible intricacies of every substance on the planet—especially the kind found in a human cell—and try to comprehend the wisdom that it took to synchronize the vast array of mechanics required to make complex organisms live and grow and function. Imagine light whiter and brighter than you've ever seen choosing to inhabit an utterly dependent human body from day one in a cold, manure-fragranced manger to the last day in a cold, decay-fragranced tomb, and bow before the humility and sacrificial love of the Almighty.

What does your awe do for the world around you? For starters, it's contagious. It's also teachable. No one will be in awe of a God they can't see. Let them see Him in you.

> The world will never starve for want of
> wonders, but for want of wonder.
> —G. K. CHESTERTON

Out-of-this-World Generosity

In this way they will lay up treasure for themselves
as a firm foundation for the coming age, so that
they may take hold of the life that is truly life.

1 TIMOTHY 6:19

In Word

There are rich Christians and poor Christians, those who live in mansions and those who live in ghettos. Just as some disciples bathed Jesus' body with expensive oils and buried Him on prime real estate, others simply shed tears on His feet. But regardless of status, those who truly believe in Jesus are united under a common Lord and given a common perspective. Their lives are not of this world.

Think about the anomaly. Where else in this world are good deeds done not to gain merit but out of joyful generosity? Where else in this world is there a greater passion to give away money than to earn it? When the church is being the church, it has a mission that no other religion, no other lifestyle can rival. Oh, they imitate it. Instinctively, they know that radical generosity and outlandishly good deeds are admirable. But they don't practice these things from the right perspective and with the right motives. They can't. They don't know the radically generous, wonder-working God.

The church in which Jesus lives—not just as a figurehead Lord or a theological premise, but really, vibrantly lives—is a church on a mission. It is a church that understands the difference between what everyone thinks is life and what really is life. It is a church that sees the gospel, the world's wealth, the blessings of God, the talents of believers, and the goodwill of the Kingdom as public property. It shares. Zealously.

In Deed

Those who believe God is a miser of mercy may seem spiritual to some, but they are not. According to 1 Timothy 6, the generous God has lavished gifts upon us for two essential purposes: so that we might enjoy them (v. 17) and so that we might demonstrate His generosity to others (v. 18). They go hand in hand. A believer who misses one purpose will be deprived of the other. Generosity is the clear indication that we are building a foundation not in this world but in another.

A man there was, though some did count him mad.
The more he cast away, the more he had.

—JOHN BUNYAN

Messiah's People

**The Spirit of the Sovereign LORD is on
me, because the LORD has anointed me
to preach good news to the poor.**
ISAIAH 61:1

In Word

Those who recall the story of Jesus' message at the synagogue of His home-town, Nazareth, will recognize these verses immediately. Jesus read them from the scroll and then identified Himself as their fulfillment (Luke 4:18-19). The implications weren't lost on His audience; most of them knew this passage to be a messianic reference. But the message often gets lost in the aftermath of the story, when the crowd got offended at Jesus' seemingly uppity comments about prophets and Gentiles. The substance of the passage is not about identifying Jesus as the Messiah. It's about identifying the Messiah's mission.

Why was the Spirit of the Sovereign Lord on Jesus? Why had He been anointed? To preach good news—to the poor! To comfort the brokenhearted. To free the captives. To release the prisoners. And to proclaim God's favor, His impending vengeance on the unrepentant, and the joy of His redemption.

It's amazing how many of Jesus' "followers" don't actually follow Him. To many, this description is His mission, His calling, His holy agenda. Our role? To accept His salvation by faith and get on with our lives. Or so we think.

In Deed

Think through the implications of this passage. If Jesus' agenda is to zealously pursue the poor, the brokenhearted, and the captive, shouldn't the agenda of His followers appear somewhat similar? Shouldn't the audience of the Messiah's disciples resemble the audience of the Messiah? Shouldn't our purpose resemble His? Shouldn't our zeal burn with an intensity like His?

The messianic pointers in Isaiah's prophecy do indeed identify Jesus as the anointed Savior. But they do more than that. They identify Jesus' followers as people on a divine mission. They define our purpose in life. They constitute a holy calling that none of us can shrug off as exclusive to the chosen One a couple of millennia ago. No, these words identified Jesus, and they are to identify Jesus' people.

> The Spirit of Christ is the spirit of missions.
> —HENRY MARTYN

A Prayer of Worship

**Answer me, O LORD, answer me, so these
people will know that you, O LORD, are God.**
1 KINGS 18:37

In Word

There are many motives behind our prayers. Sometimes our deep need
prompts our petitions. Sometimes our intense desires are behind them.
Sometimes we pray with a heart for ministry and a vision of the Kingdom.
And every one of these motives, if not born out of selfishness, is valid. But if
we're honest, we'll probably admit that most of our prayers are centered on
ourselves. That isn't necessarily wrong, but it is out of balance.

There is a prayer born of worship that focuses entirely on the mission
of God and His purposes in this world. It is a prayer that sees our needs as
His stage, with a higher goal than our own satisfaction. It is a prayer that
honors Him.

Elijah prayed such a prayer. Israel was filled with priests of Baal under
the patronage of King Ahab and Queen Jezebel. Elijah challenged them to a
spiritual showdown, asking the true God of heaven to set ablaze the true altar
on earth. In his prayer, Elijah surely hoped for his own vindication. But even
more, he hoped for God's validation of His own worth. He prayed that God
would answer in a way that would cause people to praise Him.

In Deed

Is there a desire in your heart for God's name to be honored, His character to
be appreciated, and His mercy to be known? If so, that desire will have a profound effect on your prayer life. Even in your deepest needs, you'll be aware
that your prayers of desperation contain elements not just of deliverance but
also of glory. In your despair, in your lack, and in your ambitions you will
see an opportunity for nonbelievers to see God's glory. You'll have a higher
purpose than your own small circle of influence.

How do you acquire such a desire? Perhaps there are ways to cultivate
it, but the primary source of it is God Himself. Ask Him to fill your heart
with it. Ask to passionately crave His glory. It's a prayer that God will always
answer.

*Some people pray just to pray, and some
people pray to know God.*
—ANDREW MURRAY

A Higher Perspective

**Hallelujah! For our Lord God Almighty reigns.
Let us rejoice and be glad and give him glory!**
REVELATION 19:6-7

In Word

Are you beaten down by circumstances? The best antidote to our depression and anxiety is surprising to many. But those who have put into practice the prescription of Scripture have found an amazing truth: Praising God lifts us above our trials and reminds us of how He overcomes them.

Why does that work? It's a matter of perspective. When we focus on the turmoil of life and the weakness of our flesh, we get discouraged. When we focus on the problems of the day and the people who seem to oppress us, we get intimidated. Our praise reminds us of who God is. As we worship Him, the threats and burdens that weigh us down grow smaller and He grows bigger—at least in our own eyes. The thought of an exalted God who is entirely on our side is an awesome inspiration.

We don't find that perspective very often. We have subtly but persistently trained our minds to think negatively. We don't feel like praising God when the bills are overdue or our loved one is lying sick in the hospital. We don't even feel like praising Him when our lives have gotten mundane and we've become restless. Perhaps we mistakenly think that our praise is based on how much of His power and love we've seen today. It isn't—or shouldn't be, at least. It is based on who He is. And He is who He is all the time. For that, we can praise Him. All the time.

In Deed

That might sound like a platitude, setting us up for insincerity. How robust will our praises be when life has beaten us into the ground? We could end up mouthing the words without ever passing them through our hearts, and we know that's wrong. But we must try. The more we worship, the more we see who He is and the more sincere our worship becomes. And our perspective jumps from one lowly, impossible place to the side of the God who reigns, both now and forever. Our praise opens our eyes to the truth of the situation: God rules.

A sight of His crucifixion crucifies sin.
—CHARLES SPURGEON

Delivered for Delight

I have raised you up for this very purpose,
that I might show you my power and that my
name might be proclaimed in all the earth.
EXODUS 9:16

In Word

If we think that God's ultimate purpose of redeeming a people to praise Him was only revealed at the end of the story, we've missed some clear cues from the beginning. God's purpose is thoroughly proclaimed throughout Scripture. His purpose in this creation is to reveal Himself. His purpose in redemption is to reveal Himself. His purpose in the dramatic story of humanity's fall and God's incarnational dive into the depths of fallenness is to reveal Himself. From before the foundation of the world, God had an overarching goal: He wants to be known, to be enjoyed, and to share His glory.

The book of Exodus gives us a microcosmic picture of salvation. Israel was delivered from Egypt not only because God cared for their suffering, but because He cared for their worship. In nearly every ultimatum given to Pharaoh, there's a "so that." Moses doesn't just relay God's message for Pharaoh to let His people go. He tells Pharaoh to let God's people go "so that they may worship me." The demonstration of mercy—God setting the people free—is to be followed by a joyful acknowledgment of it. The gift of deliverance requires an expression of thanks. And the miraculous means by which it is given are always designed to elicit our most extravagant praise.

In Deed

Always be conscious of your purpose. Are you going through a difficult trial? Are you in bondage in Egypt? Watch for deliverance, and when it comes, know that it is not only because God cares for you—which He clearly does—but also so that you might worship Him. Are you wandering through a wilderness and in need of provision? Know that when providence is shown, it is your cue to erupt in praise. Whatever situation you find yourself in, remind yourself of your sacred mission. You were delivered to declare His power, saved to sing His praise, and called to claim His mercy.

We should dedicate ourselves to becoming in this life the
most perfect worshipers of God we can possibly be.
—BROTHER LAWRENCE

A Culture of Gratitude

Give thanks to the LORD, call on his name.
1 CHRONICLES 16:8

In Word

When was the last time you were so overjoyed with God's work in your life that your praise began flowing spontaneously? If you have a hard time answering that question, ask yourself why. Is it because God has not blessed you enough? Or is it because you have failed to thank Him for His blessings?

Those who praise God for His many blessings will find those blessings abounding more and more. Some of that effect is psychological; we begin to see what was there all along. But there's more to it than what goes on in our own minds. The God who has told us that it will be to us according to our faith (Matthew 9:29) will find us increasingly more "blessable" when we gratefully acknowledge His goodness.

That's one of the reasons that gratitude is essential—it paves the way for God to bless again. There are many other reasons too: It ascribes glory to God by acknowledging His goodness; it testifies to His character in the eyes of the world; it keeps our hearts focused on the glass that's mostly full rather than the glass that's slightly empty. Mostly, gratitude is a statement of truth. It is an accurate reflection of what God has actually done. He has treated us well. It is only right for us to acknowledge that with joy.

In Deed

Does joyful gratitude characterize your life? Does your heart dwell in a culture of thankfulness? It should. Gratitude is an attitude that, if it isn't flowing naturally now, should be cultivated zealously. Practice it often, and it will soon become as natural as breathing.

Try an experiment: Compare the number of times today that you ask the Lord for something with the number of times that you thank Him for something. If you're like most people, the first category will far outweigh the second. That has to change. There's nothing wrong with petitioning God for His help, but there's something tragically wrong with failing to thank Him often. Cultivate in your life a culture of gratitude.

> The Christian is suspended between blessings received and blessings hoped for, so he should always give thanks.
> —M. R. VINCENT

A Culture of Glory

Make known among the nations what he has done.
1 CHRONICLES 16:8

In Word

God is not a private matter. Our culture tells us otherwise, of course, and it does so in a number of ways. We have been socially trained to keep our beliefs to ourselves. Faith is too personal, too individual to be discussed in public, we are told. It is too offensive to those who were raised in another tradition. It comes across as bigoted and narrow when we assume that our absolutes apply to everyone. Who's to say that our version of truth is any more valid than someone else's, anyway? Our world tells us to keep our convictions private. The Word of God tells us not to.

Whom will you obey? The culture of the age of diversity and tolerance, or the culture of the Kingdom of God? From Genesis to Revelation, God is publicly celebrated. If we are people of the Book, as we claim to be, we must be people of the global Savior. We cannot be silent about the goodness of God.

If we publicly make our gratitude known to those around us, including those from other traditions, will we be misinterpreted as naive optimists with simple, unquestioning minds? Probably. Will we sometimes be accused of intolerance and absolutism? It's likely. So be it. When it comes to obeying the eternal Word of God or obeying today's cultural expectations, we have a pretty easy decision. Though in the world, we are citizens of the Kingdom of Heaven. One culture is our home, the other our mission.

In Deed

Our home culture—the Kingdom of Heaven—is a culture in which God's glory is undeniable. His goodness is celebrated, His deeds are praised, His character is admired. In the Kingdom of God, creatures fall on their faces in amazement, blinded by His radiance and comforted by His warmth. It has been granted to us to participate in that culture now.

But we walk in a world that, for the most part, does not know God. What better place to be ambassadors for His Kingdom? Be public about your Savior. Make Him known.

> Be examples in all countries, places, islands,
> nations, wherever you come, that your life
> may preach among all sorts of people.
> —GEORGE FOX

A Culture of Singing

Sing to him, sing praise to him.
1 CHRONICLES 16:9

In Word

Are you aware of how many times the Scriptures urge us to sing? Taken in isolation, we might think of such references as nice suggestions. Taken in bulk, we get the impression that they are imperatives. A spoken voice that praises God is wonderful, but it isn't sufficient. A natural conclusion, from the scriptural emphasis on song, is that music was created to bring our voices closer to an accurate reflection of His beauty.

Have you noticed how powerful music can be? It adds weight to the spoken word in movies, on the radio, and even in commercials. Most important, it adds beauty to our worship and prompts our hearts to praise God more passionately. According to our sages, it soothes savages and calms nerves. And, if you haven't noticed, it's the preferred medium for expressions of love—not just in our day, but in all of history. A singing voice is a passionate voice.

Few sermons are preached on the imperative of singing, but perhaps that's a tragic oversight. The Bible is efficient in its instructions, and it instructs us often to make music to the Lord. And why wouldn't we? If there is anything in this world worth singing about—and billions of people clearly think there is—it's the Lord of glory. He is of highest value in this or any universe. As another psalm so pointedly urges: "Let everything that has breath praise the LORD" (Psalm 150:6). Songs, as every ear has noticed, have breath. They're living testimonies to the Creator.

In Deed

Does your praise reflect the importance of song? Musical expertise isn't the issue, and neither is a good voice. The attitude of the heart is the target of the Bible's instructions. David appointed musicians to praise God in the tabernacle, and Paul urged the church to "sing psalms, hymns and spiritual songs with gratitude in your hearts to God" (Colossians 3:16). We are expected to make melody.

Let your voice produce music for God. Hum. Whistle. Sing—any time. Regardless of your talent, your heart will soar. And God will be glorified.

When your heart is full of Christ, you want to sing.
—CHARLES SPURGEON

A Culture of Rejoicing

Glory in his holy name.
1 CHRONICLES 16:10

In Word

We understand what it means to praise God for His works. We even understand what it means to praise Him for His character. What seems foreign to us is the absolute giddiness one should have just to be called His child—the relish with which one should treasure the inheritance of His nature.

Young girls in love will write, over and over again, the last name of the man of their dreams after their own first name. They'll rehearse their identity as Mrs. So-and-so, simply because they love what their new name will represent. Young men will envision themselves with titles either earned or bestowed, simply because they love the idea of being identified according to their ideals. When the image we desire for ourselves is officially designated by a name that confirms it, we rejoice. Why? Because our identity is precious to us.

When the Lord of glory determines our identity—when we are called by His name—we have ample reason to celebrate. We are sons of the ultimate Father, brides of the ultimate Groom. There is no more precious identity we could have. God has given us His name!

In Deed

Do you glory in His holy name? The sense of this verse implies the delight of a new identity, the exhilaration of a precious calling. We aren't just followers of God, obedient servants, or members of a church. We don't just hold to our beliefs as adherents of a religion. We are family! We are the bride of Christ and children of the King. We are Christians. The name that is above all names is the name by which we are called. That's a profound, holy reason to have a wild, glorious celebration.

What does "the name" mean to you? Spiritually and figuratively speaking, do you wear it on your sleeve? Print it on your business card? Doodle it over and over again in your notebook? If you think of its implications, you will. If you realize what a marvelous thing it is to be identified by the One who made you, you will fulfill this verse. Your heart will exuberantly rejoice.

How sweet the name of Jesus sounds in a believer's ear!
—JOHN NEWTON

A Culture of Dependence

Look to the LORD and his strength.
1 CHRONICLES 16:11

In Word
We forget it often, but our self-sufficiency dishonors God. Just as a toddler who has had to learn to survive on his own reflects poorly on his parents, children of God who will not trust His provision and strength reflect poorly on Him. It isn't that His provision and strength aren't available, but our independent streak overestimates our resourcefulness and underestimates His love.

Many of us have been trained to admire the independent and to strive for self-sufficiency. We've been led to believe that taking care of ourselves is desirable. But have we learned that from the Word of God? No. God tells a military leader like Gideon to reduce his army so that the power from above might be demonstrated more clearly. God inspires little shepherd boys to venture into deep valleys to take on imposing giants. God's chosen people are pressed into a hopeless situation at the edge of the sea and given military victory by marching in circles. His chosen leaders are raised up from floating baskets in the river and humble mangers in the stable. He delights in the humility of mankind and the impossibility of its circumstances.

Why? Because humility and impossibility set the stage for His power. Weakness demonstrates His strength. Human futility is a platform for His capability. When we look to His strength, He enjoys displaying it.

In Deed
When people look at you, do they see self-sufficiency or reliance on a greater sufficiency? Do they know where your strength comes from? If not, ask yourself why God is not more clearly the source of your life.

Create a culture of dependence in your life. How? By acknowledging your need constantly. It may not be natural to do so, but it's an accurate reflection of reality. Those who look to Him are looking to the most potent force in all of existence. And, as another psalm says, "those who look to him are radiant" (Psalm 34:5). No one who calls on His strength is disappointed.

> When a man has not strength, if he leans
> on God, he becomes powerful.
> —D. L. MOODY

A Culture of Memories

Remember the wonders he has done.
1 CHRONICLES 16:12

In Word

Anthropologists lament lost civilizations. Historians lament lost records. Archaeologists lament lost relics of the past. When something considered valuable is forever hidden from the eyes of history, we consider the loss tragic. The meaning of people, events, circumstances, and accomplishments is preserved and validated by our memories. When we forget those things, the meaning is gone.

So it is with the works of God. Who knows how many of His works were buried in the memory of some suddenly mortal saint? Who knows how many of His deeds have gone unrecorded, and are therefore uncelebrated today? The loss of history's miracles is a tragedy indeed, more so than lost civilizations and artifacts. God has often done marvelous things that few eyes have seen.

Sometimes our own memories lose the wonders He has done in our own lives. Given the gift of a personal experience with God, we move on too quickly to the next need, the next prayer request, the next big hurdle to clear. In our haste, we forget His past mercies. In our forgetfulness, we cultivate a tragic vacuum of evidence when we need a boost for our faith.

In Deed

It's natural to be preoccupied with future concerns, but we undermine our own faith by our preoccupation. Why? Because the best way to cultivate faith is to remember His faithfulness. And the best way to remember His faithfulness is to rehearse its evidence. When we create for ourselves a culture of remembering, we grow in knowledge of God and we build an impressive file on His providence.

The worshipful heart celebrates God. It celebrates His renown (v. 8), it celebrates His acts (v. 9), it celebrates His name (v. 10), it celebrates His strength (v. 11), and it celebrates His past mercies (v. 12). If it helps you, write down His answers to prayer, His deliverance from your troubles, His provision in your need. Worship Him better by remembering why He is worthy of your worship.

Gratitude is not only the memory but the homage of the heart—rendered to God for His goodness.

—NATHANIEL PARKER WILLIS

The Big Picture

Lift up your eyes to the heavens, look at the earth beneath; the heavens will vanish like smoke, the earth will wear out like a garment.
ISAIAH 51:6

In Word

Isaiah begins chapter 51 by comparing his readers to rock and pointing them back to the quarry from which they came. They didn't know what kind of stone they were made of, having forgotten the legacy of faith passed down to them by Abraham. Having reminded them of the past, Isaiah now points them ahead toward what is to come. Their situation will look a lot better from the proper perspective.

The right perspective, of course, is a matter of focusing on the eternal plan of God rather than on the here and now. When God's people see the temporary nature of suffering, persecution, and discipline from God's hand, and see beyond all that to the joy that lasts forever, they can bear a lot more than they could when they saw from the old perspective. When people get a glimpse of who God is, their preoccupation with where they are tends to fade away. When God is magnified in the eyes of His people, everything else gets smaller. Perspective changes a lot of things.

Isaiah had a personal encounter with God and then wrote prophecies that spanned the rest of time, all the way to the end of the age. That's not a coincidence. Big visions come from a big God. But when people don't encounter God, their vision gets blurry. They become nearsighted and develop tunnel vision, and all they see is the bad stuff. To someone without an eternal perspective, the glass is always half empty. To someone who has seen God, the glass is always overflowing.

In Deed

When you look at your life, what do you see? Is your glass half empty, or is it overflowing? Have you focused your gaze on one little sliver of time riddled with problems and pain? Or have you put down the magnifying glass, broadened your vision, and seen the big picture? It's important to do that because the big picture looks fantastic from afar, especially when you're able to take in the dazzling glow that comes from behind the clouds. Whatever trial you're going through, it will pass. The salvation of God, however, will never fade away.

The created world is but a small parenthesis in eternity.
—THOMAS BROWNE

A Big God

Do not fear the reproach of men or be terrified by their insults.
ISAIAH 51:7

In Word

Skeptics scoff at our faith. Some of them are downright mean about it, and they can be very intimidating. While some believers seem to be able to shake off the contempt with ease, others of us hide our faith in the comfort of our homes and churches. We treat our commitment to Jesus like we treat our most personal garments. When we're out in public, it's all under wraps.

God has a clear word for those who are intimidated by a non-Christian culture: Don't be afraid. People who live in fear have a small God and a big Satan. That's slander against the Almighty, and none of us really wants to make that statement. No, those who have a big God have no fear. We can see the end result, and we can have pity on those who have empty hearts and no hope. With a sharp focus on the eternal Kingdom of God—and, for that matter, the eternal King—no amount of contempt can bring us down.

That's easy to say. Even back in childhood days, everyone knew that the kids who said, "Sticks and stones may break my bones, but words will never hurt me," were big liars. Words can hurt. Those who look down on us for our faith can wound us. Anyone with a sensitive heart will feel the sting of contempt unless he or she can adopt a radically new perspective.

In Deed

That's God's answer: a radically new perspective. Isaiah is writing to people who can't see past the next few years, which look pretty depressing. They need a new view. They need to set their hearts on the vision of God's plan, not the smoke and mirrors of present probabilities.

That's God's answer for you too. You have a choice about which voice is louder in your ears—the voice of those who don't know God or the voice of God Himself. The right perspective will lead you to the right choice every time.

We fear men so much because we fear God so little.
—WILLIAM GURNALL

Priceless Salvation

**The grace of God that brings salvation
has appeared to all men.**
TITUS 2:11

In Word

What a comfort that it's the grace of God that brings salvation. Not the judgment of God, not the holiness of God, not even the love of God, in itself. Though our God is a holy judge, and though He is love itself, holiness and love were in tension over the rebel race on planet Earth. The holiness of God could not compromise His need to distance Himself from sin. The love of God could not remain distant. The attributes of God, from what we can tell, had never competed so intractably. Would He compromise His holiness by loving us? Or compromise His love by judging us? A case could be made for either. Yet the wisdom of God made a case for both.

Yes, the wisdom of God affirmed love and holiness on the Cross of the incarnate God-man. Humanity was judged in the One who fulfilled its righteous obligations. And with judgment out of the way, love could flourish. Holiness and divine affection were satisfied without either being compromised. What a plan.

We don't consider the divine dilemma as often as we should. It wasn't as if God were in a bind and had to figure a way out of it. He has much more foresight than that. But He created a race that would eventually fall, and He redeemed a race that would eventually be glorified with His own Son. Love, holiness, judgment, affection, righteousness, grace, and mercy—they're all wrapped up in Jesus, and we're now all wrapped up in Him.

In Deed

Don't let many days go by without remembering the awesome truth of redemption. It was the grace of God that reconciled His competing attributes. If another attribute had dominated, we would be lost, pitiful creatures indeed. But grace has taken crawling insects and made them butterflies. Grace has taken scrawled graffiti and turned it into a masterpiece. Grace has snatched us from certain condemnation and clothed us in royal robes. Be ever thankful for this priceless salvation.

Man needs, above all else, salvation.
—NORMAN GOODACRE

Transforming Grace

**It teaches us to say "No" to ungodliness
and worldly passions.**
TITUS 2:12

In Word

There are two typical responses to the priceless grace of God. One is to use it as carte blanche in the world of temporal pursuits. After all, if God has forgiven us for all past and future sins, as Paul and other biblical writers certainly imply, then why not sin all the more? Live in both the world and the Kingdom, and let God's ever-increasing grace cover our indiscretions. So say the lawless—those who assume grace is a license to defy the order of God's creation.

The other response is actually to appreciate the magnitude of the gift. Those who are aware of the enormity of the debt that has been paid for sin are reluctant to increase the debt. Those who have narrowly escaped death know better than to flirt with it again. Those who really understand mercy can never take it for granted.

There's a reason that Paul follows a sentence about grace (v. 11) with a sentence about godly purity (vv. 12-14). The latter is to flow out of the former. As Paul said in Romans 6, grace should never be used as a license to sin. That's a slap in the face of the Forgiver and a slander of the Redeemer. No, God has better things for us. Grace is a teacher. It lets us know where we once stood and where we now stand. And seeing the difference, we are to bow in humble gratitude at the greatness of our salvation. It was radical. It was enormous. It was a holy foundation on which to build the rest of our lives.

In Deed

All true Christians know that salvation comes by grace. Many forget that salvation leads us into godliness. Jesus would be a halfway Savior if He spared us from judgment but did not cleanse us of the things that require it. The fact that He saved us from the effects of sin should make it obvious that He wants to save us from sin itself. Salvation from sin didn't just happen when we prayed a prayer. It happens now, every day, as grace teaches us to live godly lives. That's the kind of grace that glorifies the Father. It shapes His children to be like Him.

*A baptism of holiness, a demonstration of
godly living is the crying need of our day.*
—DUNCAN CAMPBELL

Blessed Hope

. . . while we wait for the blessed hope—the glorious appearing of our great God and Savior, Jesus Christ.
TITUS 2:13

In Word

"While we wait." We who live in a microwave society don't like the implications, but the Kingdom of God requires waiting. It isn't a passive waiting, and it isn't boring, either. Still, there is an interim between our calling and our kingdom, at least as we perceive them both. We aren't ushered into final glory the day we accept Christ. Peter speaks of "the salvation that is ready to be revealed" (1 Peter 1:5), and he isn't speaking to the unsaved. There is something more glorious coming, something that we know we want but that we cannot exactly envision. We are waiting for fulfillment.

Paul has already given us our instructions for the interim. We are to say no to ungodliness and worldliness, and we are to say yes to self-control and uprightness (v. 12). But the grace that taught us to do that wasn't given for that purpose alone. There is an end result we haven't yet realized, and we are given free license in Scripture to go ahead and place our hopes fully in that end result. We can look forward to a blessed hope and a glorious appearing. We can start listening to the wedding bells that announce the coming union of the Groom and His bride. We can go ahead and dress for the occasion. In fact, that is what Paul has just instructed. The godliness to which we are urged is the wedding garment with which we prepare ourselves for the blessed event.

In Deed

It's okay to celebrate the glorious appearing. It doesn't matter that it hasn't happened yet—it will. Like a bride who practices writing her new last name before it is actually hers, we can practice writing the character of our Savior on our hearts, before we have actually seen Him face-to-face. We can picture the vows, practice saying "I do," envision the reception, and dream about the consummation. The Scriptures tell us to avoid futile speculations—but it never discourages the real ones. Go ahead. Fantasize about that day. Let it shape you every way it can.

He who lives in hope dances without music.
—GEORGE HERBERT

Chosen Desire

. . . to purify for himself a people that are his very own.
TITUS 2:14

In Word

It may be hard for us to understand, but this salvation for which we thank God isn't entirely about ourselves. True, we were bought with a price and shown the magnitude of God's mercy. We were redeemed because we needed redemption and saved because we needed saving. We were cleansed of sin because we were dirty and pardoned because we were treasonous. But the rhyme and reason of creation isn't humanity. It's God. Humans, like all things, were created by Him and for Him (Romans 11:36; Colossians 1:16).

Think of what that means! It means that when teams were being selected, you were chosen by the One who will win. When you were the lonely wall-flower, Jesus asked you to dance. When partners were being chosen for the firm, the founder handpicked you. When the town's best catch was ready to marry, He proposed to you. And more than that, He didn't just choose you because He thought you needed it; He chose you because He wanted to.

Let that sink in. We are the chosen bride, the esteemed friend, the host's invited guest, the desired catch. People all over this world crave to be wanted, and those whom God has drawn to Himself are not just wanted, but intensely desired. Our salvation is not a random, happy accident. It is a divine appointment with a holy Suitor. We have a calling we have not even begun to grasp.

In Deed

Meditate today on your chosenness. Let it have its many fruitful effects. Let it make you feel highly esteemed and wanted. Let it give you the desire to preserve yourself in all purity for your coming Bridegroom. Let it drive your life with a passion to fulfill the high calling you have been given.

Did you think today was going to be a routine day at home or at work? No, it is a holy day. It is a day of communion with the Lover of your soul. Be pure. Be passionate. Be His.

> I knew nothing; I was nothing. For this reason, God picked me out.
> —CATHERINE LABOURE

Holy Reverence

The LORD's anger burned against Uzzah
because of his irreverent act.
2 SAMUEL 6:7

In Word

It's easy to sympathize with Uzzah. After all, he was only being careful about the Ark of God, making sure it didn't topple over and hit the ground. What could be wrong with that? What's wrong with trying to protect the presence of God?

God doesn't need our defense. He is the ultimate defender. He's sovereign over every atom in this universe, and He created the physical laws by which the Ark almost fell. Furthermore, God had made it clear that the Ark was untouchable. Uzzah had even observed the great lengths to which the Ark's carriers had gone—inserting poles under it and placing it on the cart without human hands having touched it. Yet somehow in Uzzah's thinking, he replaced reverence with practicality. He got casual with the holy presence.

We can imagine ourselves making such a mistake, and for that we can sympathize with Uzzah. But it was still a mistake. Many places in Scripture stress the evil in being casual about holiness. Uzzah did that. So do we.

In Deed

How relevant is Uzzah to us? Consider this: The Ark was where God said His presence dwelt—first in the Tabernacle, then in the Temple. In the New Testament, the Holy of Holies, where the high priest met with God, was opened when Jesus paid the final sacrifice. The veil was torn to show that the presence of God no longer dwelt in a temple. There's a living temple now—the individual bodies of the saints and the collective body of the church, according to 1 Corinthians 6:19. In a sense, the holy Ark of God is holding these words in hand and reading them right now.

How casual are you with your own body? Do you consider yourself a fallen human being or a vessel of the most high God? You were once the latter, and the vestiges of fallenness remain. But just as the Ark was made with common wood, the temple of God is made with common flesh. Even so, don't treat it commonly. Live in reverence for what you have become.

The indwelling of God is this—to hold God ever
in memory, His shrine established within us.
—BASIL THE GREAT

Deepest Fears

I am the Living One; I was dead, and
behold I am alive for ever and ever! And I
hold the keys of death and Hades.

REVELATION 1:18

In Word

If someone asked you about your deepest fear, you might come up with a
number of possible answers. Is it fear of failure? a fear of abandonment? a fear
of betrayal or loneliness? Perhaps those affect your emotional life, but we
have a deeper fear than these. It's the fear of death. We know that our lives are
coming to an end, and much of our lives are spent figuring out how to handle
that. Some people ignore their mortality, others wallow in it. Existentialists
conclude that it's a sign of meaninglessness, and cults conclude that it is only a
rite of passage into a better world. Every religion tries to deal with it, because
every person wrestles with it. Deep down, we know we're going to die. And
it scares us to death.

Those who believe that the Christian faith is superficial and naive have
neglected its claims. Jesus came to heal and to save, to bless and to build a
different kind of kingdom. But He addressed first and foremost our deepest
fear: He overcame death. And not only that, He dealt with its awful source—
sin. Death came into this world because of our sin, and we leave this world in
absolute dread of its further results. When Jesus told a paralytic that His sins
were forgiven—he had come to the Healer only for a cure—Jesus was dealing
with his deepest need. He was preparing His child for judgment.

In Deed

Believe it or not, many believers have accepted Christ but still fear their death.
They're pretty sure that they've been forgiven and that Jesus has conquered
death, but they wonder if perhaps they've sinned too much or missed some
critical step toward God. Jesus comes to them in the same way He comes to
John as recorded in Revelation: "Do not be afraid" (v. 17). Your fears—your
very deepest anxieties—are the reason He came. He did not offer you a superficial salvation. He goes to your depths and He casts out your fear.

God incarnate is the end of fear. The heart that realizes that
He is in the midst . . . will be quiet in the midst of alarm.

—F. B. MEYER

Countercultural Worship

**About that time there arose a great
disturbance about the Way.**
ACTS 19:23

In Word

The goddess Artemis, great patroness of the city of Ephesus, was annoyed. Actually, it wasn't Artemis herself, but the people who worshiped her—and profited from her worship—who were bothered. Paul and the Christians, by preaching the worship of Jesus, were depriving them of their normal Artemis-income. So they started a riot.

That's what happens when worship turns utilitarian. It's a phenomenon in every religion: Those who worship their gods and goddesses often do so only for the practical benefit they will receive. In Ephesus, the Artemis cult was big business. In many world religions today, worship is also big business. Sometimes, as you've probably noticed, worship can be big business even in Christianity. When that happens, worship has turned away from God and back to self. When we worship only for our own benefits, we worship ourselves.

The temptation to do that is subtle, but it's widespread and profound. Any time we attend a church primarily for networking purposes, any time we honor God mainly for His fringe benefits, any time we read the Bible with "fortune-telling" motives, we've adulterated our worship. We've tainted the very thing in which God has asked for purity and sincerity. We've opted for idolatry over life in the Spirit.

In Deed

We may be able to recognize utilitarian worship by how little it contrasts with our culture. Real worship may create a riot, just as it did in Ephesus. Short of that extreme, it will almost always challenge the traditions of our society and even some of our churches. Blending in with "Ephesus" is always a red flag. We can never just "fit in."

How can we avoid utilitarian worship? Test yourself. If a more beneficial religion came along—not truer, just more advantageous—would you jump on board? If your culture changed religions, would you? In other words, when you have to, can you stand alone for God?

For the Christian, this world is an arena, not an armchair.
—ANONYMOUS

Legally Insane

Listen to what the LORD says: "Stand up,
plead your case before the mountains; let
the hills hear what you have to say."

MICAH 6:1

In Word

The prosecutor paced in front of the jury, carefully stating his case. "Ladies and gentlemen of the jury, I'd like you to listen carefully to what this defendant says when he's on the stand," he said. "His excuses will be completely irrational. Try not to laugh. He will plead ignorance, but he knew exactly what he was getting into when he broke his word and betrayed me. He will try to convince you that his choice was rational—that he was being mistreated or ignored—but everyone who knows me understands how ludicrous that is. Let's hear what he has to say, but realize that he's in an absurd position. If you decide he's insane, I certainly won't argue with you."

That's the picture in Micah 6. The world is a courtroom, and the prosecutor is God. Before a jury of mountains, hills, and solid ground, He brings an accusation of blatant idolatry against His people. As the evidence unfolds, the reader will wonder how this trial ever even got to court. It's an open-and-shut case. The accused traded in all the blessings of the King of the universe, whose riches are unfathomable and unsurpassed, in exchange for the opportunity to bow before roughly chiseled chunks of rock. The infinite God has been casually, carelessly betrayed by the very people on whom He lavished His affection. Their rejection of Him makes no sense. Once the prosecutor is done with His case, the accused will be utterly ashamed at having made history's most embarrassing, foolish choice. They scrapped everything worthwhile to get nothing.

In Deed

God never asks of us anything unreasonable. Everywhere He leads us makes perfect sense in the grand scheme of things. We may not see how at the moment, but walking in another direction is the epitome of foolishness. In the courtroom of God, the judgments are obvious. Never let your choices put you across the table from Him.

Sin is the dare of God's justice . . . and
the contempt of His love.

—JOHN BUNYAN

Understandably Hurt

My people, what have I done to you? How have I burdened you? Answer me.
MICAH 6:3

In Word

Imagine a husband with devastatingly good looks, a charming personality, and enormous confidence and competence in all he does. Imagine that he selflessly dotes on his wife at every opportunity, lavishes expensive gifts on her, takes her on exotic vacations, dresses her in regal, stylish fashions, and cooks for her every night. His affection is demonstrated at considerable sacrifice, but it doesn't seem sacrificial to him because he adores her so much. He is the perfect husband, and she is the delight of his eyes.

Now imagine this privileged woman demanding more of her husband, complaining when his gourmet cuisine was steak instead of fish—or fish instead of steak, depending on her mood—and, out of boredom, sleeping with other men in the neighborhood. In other words, imagine her forgetting how blessed she is and trading her riches for refuse.

The absurdity of such apathy and ignorance is hard to comprehend, isn't it? Most women wouldn't choose to leave a palace to go live in a slum or to divorce a good-hearted, compassionate husband in favor of an abusive slob. But, according to an inspired prophet, that's exactly what Israel did. And the pressing questions weighing on the heart of the betrayed are, "Why? What did I ever do to you? Haven't I given you everything you could ever possibly want?"

In Deed

Only people under great deception can make such tragic choices, but there are a lot of people in the world who are deceived. (We came out from among them, but once shared their folly.) And the heart cry of the Lord of all creation is, "Do you realize what you've lost? Don't you know what I would have done for you? I'd lay down my life for you!"

Only an amazing love could maintain that kind of sympathy in the face of such insulting betrayal. But God has an amazing kind of love. Count His blessings and treasure them. Never take them for granted. Let Him lavish you with His love. And return it with a passion.

> We have a God who loves. That means that we have a God who suffers.
> —J. B. PHILLIPS

Enthusiastically Generous

With what shall I come before the LORD and bow down before the exalted God?
MICAH 6:6

In Word

A heart that loves is a heart that loves to give. That certainly applies to God; He's got the greatest, deepest love, and He gives the most extravagant, sacrificial gifts—with joy. But what do we long to give? From what passions do our sacrifices flow? Do they flow toward God?

It's a penetrating series of questions, isn't it? Our treasures will always flow naturally in the direction of our loves. We might be able to divert them sometimes in the direction of our "supposed to's," but whatever discretionary valuables we hold will go toward what we're most passionate about. When Micah wonders what he'll bring to God, he's expressing a natural desire to give in light of God's tremendous favor. The past deliverances and compassions of our Lord should captivate our hearts and leave us wishing we could give Him more.

When we find ourselves completely captivated by an interest, a relationship, a project, or a possession, and simultaneously find ourselves reluctantly giving to God—not just money, but time and talents and energy—we're making a major statement about our love. Our heart is betraying the confidence of our mouth, acting as a true barometer of our deepest feelings. If our energy and resources flow naturally in the direction of something other than God and His Kingdom, we're in a disappointing relationship with our Father. He wants so much more than lip service and tithes. He wants our love for Him to flow freely and genuinely.

In Deed

In what direction do your choices point? Are you looking for more that you can offer to God, or are you merely fulfilling an obligation toward Him so you can enthusiastically pursue your real interests? Every human being wrestles with authenticity toward God. Few recognize the counterfeits.

If you just diagnosed a cold heart toward the warmth of His love, dwell on His extravagance. Let it soften you. Let yourself be captivated by your God.

> You can give without loving, but you cannot love without giving.
>
> —AMY CARMICHAEL

Clearly Instructed

He has showed you, O man, what is good.
MICAH 6:8

In Word

When God's people don't do His will, it isn't because the information isn't out there. God gave us His holy Word, He sent His Son into this world, His Son has been preached and taught all over this planet, and millions of Christians are quite vocal about their faith. He even sent His Spirit to put wind in the sails of every believer and get the good news out with power. No, ignorance isn't a legitimate problem among the people of God.

The real problem is rebellion. Stubbornness. Hardness of heart. Apathy. Whatever you want to call it, we can never claim that we just didn't know. No one can say, "I wanted to love and obey God, but I just didn't have enough information." God is very clear on that point: "He has showed you, O man, what is good."

When there's a disconnect between God's will and our lives, it can be traced to a moment of decision. Willingness is the key. James warned about people who heard the Word of God and then forgot what to do about it (James 1:22-24). So did Jesus, who told His disciples that much seed is sown in places where it will not bear any fruit (Matthew 13:18-22). In neither case was ignorance the issue. When we arrive at that great day of accounting at the end of the age, and God asks us why we didn't do His will, we won't be able to say, "I didn't know what it was." Anyone who really wants to know can ask Him and seek diligently. He always directs believers who are open to being directed.

In Deed

Do you want to follow God? He has shown the way. There's no need to abandon the quest, to resign yourself to the idea that you'll never hear His voice. Much of it is already evident in the pages of Scripture. Any of the finer points of His will about your specific circumstances are yours for the asking (James 1:5). Our God is a God of revelation; He even created us for the simple reason of being known. If you ever feel aimless in life, remember: He has shown you what is good.

In doing God's will we find our peace.
—DANTE

Formally Commissioned

**What does the LORD require of you? To act justly and
to love mercy and to walk humbly with your God.**

MICAH 6:8

In Word

God gave His people ten commandments, out of which flowed hundreds
more. He was rather specific about many of them: moral behavior in relationships, rules for forgiveness and restoration, specifications for worship, and
more. At first glance, it could look like a highly complex legal system. Seemingly, any defendant on the stand would be justified in saying, "I just didn't
understand the law."

But the Judge makes it simple for us. In effect, He says: "It all boils down
to this. Do justice, be zealously merciful, and have a humble heart toward Me.
Those three things will put you in a position of being guided into all truth and
goodness. I always keep loving, fair, and humble hearts on track."

The key to life in our world isn't simply to follow all of God's rules. It's
to live by God's character. One is formulaic and will drain the life out of you.
The other is personal and will infuse you with the life of the One you love.
It's not a complicated choice. It may be hard sometimes, but there's nothing
complex about it. If you know who God is, you know how you're to be: righteous, merciful, and humble—just like Jesus.

In Deed

The world can be a complicated place to live, but often the complexity is an
illusion. People make things more difficult than they really are. Some Christians come up with behavioral codes that rival the excitement and joy of the
fine print of a legal contract or an accounting sheet. And behind all of the specifics is a God who tells us that if we're like Him, following the rules will come
naturally, and if we're not like Him, following the rules will be impossible.

In God's courtroom, the rules aren't hard to remember. Whenever we
look at the Judge, they sink deeper into us. His character begins to define our
walk—our just, compassionate, humble walk.

The pearl of justice is found in the heart of mercy.

—CATHERINE OF SIENA

The Hub of a Prayer

**This, then, is how you should pray: "Our Father
in heaven, hallowed be your name."**
MATTHEW 6:9

In Word

Have you noticed that the first line of the prayer Jesus modeled for us is an expression of praise? We might pass over it easily, regarding it as an obligatory introduction, a cursory acknowledgment of the basis of our prayers. But though Jesus' words are certainly economical, there is nothing cursory about this statement. Jesus is efficient with His words, not careless. These are stated first for a reason: Our prayers are to begin with praise.

Does that seem too much like buttering God up? It shouldn't. There's a more profound purpose in it than getting God on our side. It's a declaration of the truest truth there is—that this world is all about Him. If we want our prayers to align with His will—if we want Him even to hear them—they must acknowledge truth at every turn. And the first step in acknowledging truth is declaring His primacy and His worth. We pray to our intimate Father because He is hallowed and holy, the Name above all names. We might as well set that straight in our own hearts before we bombard Him with petitions. So Jesus tells us how to set it straight.

In Deed

Consider how you begin your prayers. Do they first and foremost acknowledge the glory of the One to whom you pray? Do they admit up front that everything to follow will fit under this overarching principle of the universe, that God's name is above all? Does praise become the centerpiece of your prayer, the hub around which the rest of it will revolve?

That's Jesus' purpose in making a declaration of worship primary in the model prayer. The disciples had probably heard many similar statements of praise in the prayers of the religious leaders. But did those prayers really revolve around the holiness and glory of God? If not, they weren't the kind of prayers Jesus commends. He shows His disciples, and us, a better way. Acknowledge straight off the top that the Name is hallowed, holy, glorious, and true. And your prayers will be blessed.

Adoration is the highest form of prayer.
—LOUIS CASSELS

The Sum of All Prayers

**Yours is the kingdom and the power
and the glory forever. Amen.**
MATTHEW 6:13

In Word

Many translations of the Bible have this verse as a footnote because it appears only in some manuscripts, not all. But isn't it an appropriate conclusion that confirms the way the prayer started? Not only are our prayers to begin with praise and center around it, they are also to conclude with it. At the beginning we acknowledge that the whole point of prayer is God; at the end, we affirm it. The whole point of prayer is still God. It may be intensely focused on our own needs, but underlying our expectations must be this awareness: Our prayers—as well as the entire universe—are about God's Kingdom, His will, His character, His purposes, His plan, His ways. His attributes and deeds are front and center. His glory is the highest value. As Romans 11:36 and Colossians 1:16 tell us, everything comes from Him, everything goes to Him, everything is about Him.

There's a reason Jesus emphasizes praise from beginning to end in the model prayer. We turn prayer into a self-absorbed activity much of the time. What starts out as a petition for God to be glorified turns into a petition for us to be saved from some discomfort, or to be vindicated, or to be victorious. Though our purposes and God's may often overlap, given our choice of one or the other, deep down inside we would often choose our own. That's why Jesus reminds us: Prayer, the Kingdom, even our very lives—they're all about God.

In Deed

The heart that does not realize that, not only in principle but also in practice, will never be content. Why? Because it has an agenda that is swimming against the flow of the universe. When all is said and done, everything will point to God. If our prayers don't go ahead and point to Him, they are futile activities and illusions.

No one wants a futile prayer life. How do we avoid it? The model prayer is to be our model. We should begin with hallowing the Name and end with seeking the Kingdom. A God-centered prayer is glory from beginning to end.

The pulse of prayer is praise.
—WILLIAM ARTHUR WARD

Pure Truth

It is impossible for God to lie.
HEBREWS 6:18

In Word

On the surface, this declaration does not startle us. Of course God doesn't lie. He is the truth. He defines what truth is and He is the standard by which all things are measured. He is the only truly absolute being in this or any universe. Whatever He says is, by definition, true.

Furthermore, we're well trained in the idea that God is honest. He does not deceive. He who tells us to be faithful and trustworthy is Himself faithful and trustworthy. He who has no corruption in Him cannot utter corrupt words. No, of course God doesn't lie. So we quickly move on to other, more theologically intriguing verses.

But stop and consider this assertion, spelled out both in Titus and Hebrews and implied in other places throughout the Bible. God can't lie. It's impossible for Him to do so. Forget the contradictory riddles posed by pseudo-theologians, idle speculations such as whether God can create a rock so large that He cannot move it. And forget also, when it comes to God's character, the oft-repeated biblical truth that "nothing is impossible with God." Certainly no event, no problem, no catastrophe is too great for Him. But when it comes to His character, there are impossibilities. There are things He cannot do. He cannot contradict His own nature, and He cannot cease to be the holy, loving, infinite, immortal, all-wise, all-powerful God. He cannot cease to be Himself.

Think of the implications! Every word that God has ever uttered to you—by any means of revelation—every word is inviolable. When God says He delivers His people from all their troubles (Psalm 34:17), He does. Why? He cannot lie. When God says that those who delight in Him will be given the desires of their heart (Psalm 37:4), they will. Why? Because God cannot lie.

In Deed

Every promise ever uttered by our God is unbreakable. There is no fine print, because God does not deceive. He does not bait and switch. He does not equivocate. He does not renege. His words to you are surer than the sun coming up tomorrow. He does not, cannot lie.

God is the God of promise. He keeps His word, even when that seems impossible.
—COLIN URQUHART

A Singing God

He will rejoice over you with singing.
ZEPHANIAH 3:17

In Word

Did you know that God is a singer? Why would that be a surprise? He created us to sing; one would expect that He has some experience at it Himself. Yes, the Lord of all creation sings. That defies our image of the frozen-faced, always-disappointed God of high expectations. Sure, we have failed Him and our love is far too cold for such a lovely Lord. But that's not what the Lord of glory focuses on. When judgment is spent, when He looks at a redeemed soul conforming to the image of Christ, God sings. And not just because He has to. His heart is in it.

That boggles our minds, doesn't it? The God who loves us sings over us. We often think of His love as obligatory; He has to love us because He made us and redeemed us, but He doesn't really enjoy it because of how we've failed Him. As we imagine Him, He has a purposeful love but not a passionate one. But that's not the biblical picture of God. Scripture paints Him as highly emotional, deeply grieving over our sin and dancing in celebration over our repentance. In the Bible, God weeps, rejoices, grieves, dances, laughs, gets angry, and celebrates. And He sings.

Imagine the voice! In Revelation, His voice sounds like a trumpet (1:10) and a waterfall (1:15). Can you imagine a voice that exceeds all human instruments and the forces of nature? The volume, the tonality, the quality, the range! And the creativity of the song must be amazing. God-produced music must be astoundingly beautiful. And what's most humbling and amazing is that He sings it over us.

In Deed

Today, imagine the Lord Himself standing over you and singing with a huge smile on His face. No, it doesn't matter what sin you've committed or what part of your character remains woefully underdeveloped. Not at this moment, anyway. Picture the singing Lord who can see into your heart, knowing what it will become. Picture the Savior who knows what you will finally look like one day when redemption is complete. Hear Him sing.

> When I hear this singing I stand dumbfounded,
> staggered, speechless that He is singing over me.
> —JOHN PIPER

Open Arms

Come, Lord Jesus.
REVELATION 22:20

In Word

When the return of Jesus is mentioned, how do you react? Does your inner voice say, "No, not yet"? Or does it say, "Yes, Lord, come"? The Christian's hope is always focused on His return. But it isn't always focused on His quick return.

The church is filled with folks who see the return of Jesus as a one-day-in-the-future kind of event. It's so far ahead that it seems to have no practical impact. Perhaps it's natural for us to want to delay His return. If He's coming later, we can settle into the life we plan to lead right now. But if He's coming soon, we fear the uncertainty and chaos that will likely precede Him. We worry about the loose ends we haven't tied up yet. We're not quite ready.

The consistent plea of Scripture is to get ready. Jesus told His disciples to be ready—not only the ones who followed Him in Galilee and Judea but also the ones who follow Him today. In all ages and all times, we are urged to be ready. God doesn't tell us the day and the hour because those who live long before it would live without anticipation of His appearance. And the prospect of His appearance can have a dramatic, positive influence on how we live our lives.

That's why it's imperative that Christians not assume His return is too far in the future. It may be centuries or even millennia from now, but we must expect it today. When we do, we will live as a bride getting ready for her wedding day—with excitement, expectation, purity, and purpose. Our lives will be shaped not by our past, as the psychologists insist, but by our future, as our God insists. We will grow into the image He has given us.

In Deed

If we really think about it, that day comes soon enough for all of us. We may not be standing on this earth when Jesus breaks forth into it, but every day we live, there's a chance that our next one will be in His presence. Are you ready? When John wrote, he welcomed Jesus with open arms. Can you? When He says He is coming soon, does it thrill your soul?

> Christ has told us He will come, but not when, that we might never put off our clothes, or put out the candle.
>
> —WILLIAM GURNALL

Supremacy of the Son

**The Son is the radiance of God's glory
and the exact representation of his being,
sustaining all things by his powerful word.**
HEBREWS 1:3

In Word

The world wonders what God is like. Some religions see Him as a hard, harsh taskmaster who favors violent judgment every time He doesn't get His way. Others see Him as an abstract force, more of a principle than a deity. Even some secularists embrace a shadow of God, though they end up with a very generic picture. Perhaps the favorite concept of God in our generation is the idea that "God is love." After all, that's biblical, isn't it? But a disobedient culture defines love on its own terms and demands that God be nothing more and nothing less than its description of love. And that god simply doesn't exist.

No, the idea that we can actually know God is elusive. We live in a confused society that makes up religion as it goes along. Meanwhile, Scripture tells us plainly that Jesus is the exact representation of the Father. It is He, in fact, who sustains all there is.

For a culture that thinks of Jesus as a nice teacher and a brave martyr, the idea of His representing God doesn't make too many waves. But the Jesus of the Bible? The One who talked a lot about sin and hell, who spoke harshly to the Jewish elite, who said He didn't come to bring peace on earth but to establish a dividing line? That Jesus isn't very popular. He bruises egos and insists on being Lord. He not only carries His cross, He gives one to His followers. That Jesus doesn't go over very well.

In Deed

So be it. Those who really want to worship God in spirit and in truth, who really want to adore Him for who He is, must look first at Jesus. The Son said that if we've seen Him, we've seen the Father (John 14:9). Disciples worshiped Him, and He let them. Sinners asked God's forgiveness, and Jesus gave it. The Word really did become flesh. And the Word was God (John 1:1). Worship the radiance of God's glory by worshiping Jesus.

Christ, by highest heaven adored, Christ, the everlasting Lord.
—CHARLES WESLEY

Incarnations

**God . . . was pleased to reveal his Son in me so
that I might preach him among the Gentiles.**
GALATIANS 1:15-16

In Word

Paul's mission to preach to the Gentiles is well known. We have stories of
his proclamation of the gospel in cities all across the Mediterranean, boldly
asserting the supremacy of Christ, the forgiveness of sins, and the resurrection
of the dead. What we sometimes don't realize is the comprehensive nature of
his proclamation. It wasn't just a matter of words; it was a matter of life.

That comprehensive sense of calling often comes through in Paul's letters.
Here in Galatians, he could have told the congregation that God was pleased
to reveal His Son to Paul, but he chose another way to say it. God revealed
His Son in Paul. The wording is subtle, but the difference is enormous. Paul's
mission was more than just information about the gospel. It was an incarnation of the Son of God.

Paul said that we "carry around in our body the death of Jesus, so that the
life of Jesus may also be revealed in our body" (2 Corinthians 4:10). He said
that God's glory will be revealed in us, and that "the creation waits in eager
expectation" for that revelation (Romans 8:18-19). And, perhaps the boldest
of all statements, he believed that he himself no longer lived, but rather, Christ
lived in him (Galatians 2:20). The ministry of Paul was not the words he said,
but what he carried around within him all the time.

In Deed

Most of us deeply desire for God to reveal Himself to us so we can worship
Him more clearly and profoundly. And God wants to do that. But He wants
more. After revealing Himself to us, He wants to reveal Himself in us so
others can worship Him more clearly and profoundly. Just as Jesus was the
incarnation of God, so are we to be incarnations of Jesus. The Spirit lives in us
specifically so that the world might see, in the flesh, a power worth worshiping. Make that your heart's desire—not just to see a revelation of God's grace,
but to be a revelation of God's grace.

The incarnation is the pattern for all evangelism.
—EVERETT L. CATTELL

God's Goodness

**How great is your goodness, which you
have stored up for those who fear you.**
PSALM 31:19

In Word

It's a strange enigma: The goodness of God is almost universally recognized
and yet rarely trusted. At an intellectual level, we know that God is good.
After all, He says He is, and we have plenty of evidence that He has been good
to us. At the same time, when we think about our future and the dreams we
have, we suspect God might not really give them to us. We have our preferences for career directions, mates, children, friendships, interests, and more.
And deep down, we wonder: Will God bless me with these things, or will I
have to strive for them myself? We seem certain that obedience will always
result in pain.

It's true that obedience is sometimes painful. But the life that is surrendered to God will experience blessing, and the blessing will be good. Will it
be hard? Maybe. But not without ample benefit. The mistrust we have about
how God will treat us is a lie. It comes from the hard truth of the cost of discipleship, but it leaves out the amazing promises of a God who is good by His
very nature. When He tells us that His plans for us are good, we forget that
He might actually know how we define "good."

Think of this: The God who designed you, interests and passions
included—the God who wove you together in your mother's womb and has
sovereignly shaped your personality ever since—is the God who has promised
you goodness. Whatever He has planned for you, you will like it. Cast aside
your assumptions that He always defines goodness as something terribly hard
and painful. His goodness may involve hardship, but it doesn't center on it.
He knows what you need, and He promises it will be good.

In Deed

Is that hard to grasp? For those of us who have long envisioned a hard-to-
please, down-to-business God, it is. But God doesn't portray Himself that
way. He knows our definition of good, and He has promised to satisfy us with
good things.

> God is all that is good, in my sight, and the
> goodness that everything has is His.
> —JULIAN OF NORWICH

God's Holiness

Who among the gods is like you, O LORD?
Who is like you—majestic in holiness,
awesome in glory, working wonders?
EXODUS 15:11

In Word

Few people get excited about the holiness of God. For most, it's a dreadful thought, because the God of holiness is a God we can't relate to. We've heard of His righteous judgments against Sodom and Gomorrah, against Jericho, and against all who have sinned and fallen short of His glory. Holiness makes us think of thunderbolts and hell. Why? Because we know, deep down, that we're unholy.

It's true that holiness implies sinless perfection, that unimaginable quality of righteous purity that only God possesses. By its very definition, that convicts us and makes us feel unworthy. But holiness is so much more than righteousness. It's the idea that God is completely different, completely transcendent, completely other than who we are and what we can conceive. In other words, He's beyond our wildest imaginations.

That certainly has scary elements to it, but it has exciting elements too. This God who is "other" satisfies our longing for something beyond this fallen world. The attribute of holiness tells us that when we're trapped in sin, captivity, and pain, there's a bigger and better entity beyond the confines of this planet. Need a biblical illustration? Just look at the context of today's verse. It is taken from a song of celebration on the safe side of the Red Sea. Who delivered Israel from Egypt? The God who is "majestic in holiness." Only a God like that could.

In Deed

If God's holiness awes you, that's good. If His holiness paralyzes you with fear, adjust your thinking. Yes, His holiness makes Him naturally unapproachable by sinful humans, but His sacrificial offering of His Son took care of that. His holiness is, for us, not a condemnation but an invitation—to share the Spirit of the majestic, pure, completely "other" God. It is our constant reminder that there is always Someone infinitely greater to guide us.

> A true love of God must begin with a delight in His holiness
> . . . ; for no other attribute is truly lovely without this.
> —JONATHAN EDWARDS

Reflecting Holiness

**Just as he who called you is holy,
so be holy in all you do.**
1 PETER 1:15

In Word

Something within us interprets the call to holiness very rigidly. We almost always associate it with becoming pure and sinless. And our attempts to do so almost always default to a futile method: We assume we must do a better job of following the rules.

But reflecting God's holiness is not simply a matter of keeping the rules and being better people. Human motivation and self-discipline are horribly inadequate to get us close to God's holiness. We cannot accomplish the fruit of the Spirit by the works of the flesh.

To reflect God's holiness, we first need to have a better understanding of what it is. God's "otherness" requires a challenging response from us: It is a call to be set apart for His specific use. Does that mean purity? Yes, but more. It also means distinctiveness. We can no longer fit into the fallen cultures of this world. There is to be a quality in the believer's life that distinguishes him or her from the society at large. As Peter goes on to say in his first letter, we are to submit when most people would resist; we're to endure when most people would cave in; we are to suffer when most people avoid it at all costs. Just as God's holiness makes Him radically distinct from anything we can conceive of, our reflection of His holiness should make us radically distinct from the world. Christian faith is the ultimate countercultural experience.

In Deed

Have you ever thought of holiness that way? It has never been a matter of hairstyle, fashion, or any other sort of legalism. It will certainly involve the externals in our lives, but it isn't defined by them. Far from being a matter of strict behavior simply for behavior's sake, it is more a matter of a radically changed heart. Holiness will always separate a believer from his surroundings—not physically, but in his emotional attachments, his perceptions of reality, and then, as a result, his behavior. As a work of the Holy Spirit, holiness begins within.

A holy life will produce the deepest impression.
Lighthouses blow no horns; they only shine.
—D. L. MOODY

God's Sovereignty

"To whom will you compare me? Or who is my equal?" says the Holy One.

ISAIAH 40:25

In Word

God is in control. We've all heard it before, probably hundreds of times. We know it doesn't mean that He handles us like puppets, but we also know it doesn't mean that this world is a random free-for-all. Somewhere in between those two extremes is an existence that is under the sovereign hand of our Creator.

What does God's sovereignty entail? According to Isaiah, it means that "people are like grasshoppers" (v. 22). It means that the rulers of this world are pitifully small in God's eyes (v. 23). It means that all the stars our eyes can see are under the watchful eye of the One who created them with just His voice (v. 26). It means that God has no equal.

That's great news, but it doesn't make us feel any better if we don't learn to count on it in the hard times. We see injustice in this world, we feel pain, and we suffer from our sin as well as the sin of others. It sometimes looks as if the world is under the sovereign hand of no one—that it is spinning recklessly out of control. And when it spins hard, it takes a lot of faith to confirm in our hearts what we know in our minds: God is in control.

How does it help to know that? If we know He is in control, we can follow the instructions of Scripture. We can be meek and humble because we know He is our defender. We can suffer unjustly because we know He will bring about justice in the end. We can shun futile hedonism because we're in this life for eternity, not for the short run. We can count on the promises He has made, because only a sovereign God could work them out. We can know beyond the shadow of a doubt that He will work all things together for the good of those who love Him (Romans 8:28). Why? Because He's sovereign.

In Deed

God's sovereignty is a hard pill to swallow sometimes, but it's infinitely more comforting than the alternative—a random, reckless world. We can be sure, as this world spins wildly, that a sovereign God is working all things out for His good purposes—even our own lives.

> No one can dissuade God from His purposes; nothing can turn Him aside from His plans.
>
> —A. W. TOZER

Reflecting Sovereignty

You intended to harm me, but
God intended it for good.
GENESIS 50:20

In Word

We aren't sovereign. As much as we try to control our environment—and
we really try hard sometimes—all it takes is one little catastrophe to prove
to us that we can't. So if our calling is to reflect God's attributes, and God is
sovereign, how can we fulfill our calling? Should we try all the harder to exert
control over our world?

Of course we can't do that. It's true that God gave us authority over
aspects of His creation (Genesis 1:26), and He also sent us out into the world
with His authority to make disciples (Matthew 28:18-20). But our responsibilities are always under His authority. We may be stewards of His sovereignty
in some limited ways, but we can never really exercise it. Sovereignty implies
ultimate authority, and when it comes to that, God stands alone. He is the
only Being who is entirely free to exercise His own will.

So how do we reflect His sovereignty? We live like we believe in it. We
refuse to worry, even when worry seems like the natural thing to do. We
refuse to let our fears and anxieties rule us. When circumstances are confusing, when life isn't fair, when someone has treated us badly, we can trust that
there's a sovereign God. We do that by not working things out on our own or
manipulating our circumstances for our shortsighted purposes. We can take
the promises of God for the certainty that they are. He can live up to them
because He is sovereign.

In Deed

Joseph is the classic example of someone who reflects an understanding of
God's sovereignty. His brothers' treachery that landed him in Egypt was inex-
cusable, and the deceit of Potiphar's wife that landed him in jail was heinous.
But Joseph saw the bigger picture—a God who was working things out for
His own good purposes.

Can you do that? If you're going through a difficult time, it's hard to see
the big picture. But it's there, and it's good. The sovereign God is in control.

The great Maker of the will is alive to
carry out His own intentions.
—CHARLES SPURGEON

God's Wisdom

Oh, the depth of the riches of the wisdom and knowledge of God!
ROMANS 11:33

In Word

The characteristics of our God aren't very comforting if they aren't backed by this one, are they? How would we feel about a sovereign but unwise God? He'd scare us to death. What would we think of a God who was good but not very careful in how He applied His goodness? He'd have our sympathies, but not our confidence. No, without wisdom, the rest of God doesn't make us feel very safe.

But His wisdom! It means that He always knows what to do in every situation. It means His sovereignty can work out every detail of this life to result in something good and ultimately worthwhile. It means that as confused as we get as we walk through this life, there's always Someone perfectly wise to turn to. We can have confidence in our God because our God knows everything. Not only that, He knows what everything means.

God's wisdom is an often-invisible thread running throughout human history. All our provocative questions about the ancients, all our ideas about where history ends, and every mystery in between—these are simple matters to the all-wise God. And the best part of His wisdom is that He makes it accessible to us. The all-wise God chose us as His children.

In Deed

Have you ever thought of that? You were born into this world, suffered in a sinful condition, were redeemed by His mercy, and are called His child all because these things were right! He was not surprised; in fact, He knew all about you, your problems, and your plans before the foundation of this world. Before dinosaurs roamed, before horses were drawn on cave walls, before pyramids were built, you were seen. God knew every aspect of your current circumstances and put you into them anyway. Why? Because somehow He's using them for good.

Are you frustrated? tired? confused? Acknowledge the wisdom of God. Trust in it. Ask for it. Realize that it stretches deeper and further than you can see.

As a blind man has no idea of colors, so have we no idea [how] the all-wise God perceives and understands all things.
—ISAAC NEWTON

Reflecting Wisdom

If any of you lacks wisdom, he should ask
God, who gives generously to all without
finding fault, and it will be given to him.

JAMES 1:5

In Word

In an unwise world, wisdom speaks volumes. Rarely does someone do the
right thing simply because it's the right thing to do. Our relativistic culture
doesn't understand why we point to absolutes like we do, but it still takes
notice. At some level, probably deep within their hearts, people see wisdom
as a sign of the One who is wise.

How do we become wise? We're born into a confusing world just as surely
as anyone else. We have no special insight in our natural intuition or intellect.
We all begin at the same starting line: as an unwritten slate bursting into a
delivery room and taking in all we can see and hear. So how can we possibly
claim any particular advantage over the wisdom of this world?

We have a God who shares His wisdom. He has written His revelation,
and it is at our fingertips as often as we are willing to reach for it. He has
birthed us with His Spirit, the interpreter of the inner workings of the holy,
sacred mind of God. He has placed us into a community of believers, His own
body to which He speaks and through which He moves. Yes, by all means, we
have an advantage. The mind of Christ is available and accessible.

In Deed

How can you reflect God's wisdom in this unwise world? Base your life on
eternity. Invest your money and your talents in things that are ultimately
meaningful. Use your time for everlasting purposes. Leverage your sorrows
and your pains as glorious demonstrations of His mercies and His comfort.
Invite Him into your circumstances to do His will. Accept His invitation into
His global agenda to make His name known and loved. In other words, in all
these things, base your life on reality.

That's what the world needs to see. Reality shows on TV are no reflection of reality. You, however, can be. In a strange, confused world, ask for His
wisdom and then show it.

Knowledgeable people are found everywhere,
but we are cruelly short of wise people.

—MICHEL QUOIST

God's Love

Greater love has no one than this, that he lay down his life for his friends.

JOHN 15:13

In Word

"God is love." Not only is this a profound declaration from the apostle John, it's also the mantra of a culture that has made God in its own image. We can rest assured that the biblical and the cultural definitions of love do not match up very well. But when it comes to understanding the love of God, not even the biblical language has the full meaning. It's something we simply cannot understand.

Still, the Bible gives us pictures. One of them is of God hanging on a wooden torture stake in the Middle East a couple of millennia ago. To outsiders, it's a sad story of martyrdom, but to those within the faith, it's the ultimate expression of love. Why? Because Jesus didn't have to go there. He chose to. He volunteered for that torturous execution because it somehow covered our own rebellion. The mutiny was paid for by the very captain against whom it was committed. That's a kind of grace—a kind of love—the world doesn't understand. Frankly, neither do we.

Survivors of a violent attack don't normally pursue the criminal who committed it with only his restoration in mind. Companies don't often care only for the welfare of the embezzler who bilked them of millions. Victims of slander don't usually put their own reputation aside in order to preserve the reputation of the slanderer. But that kind of grace is what God demonstrated on the Cross. That's the kind of love that defines Him.

In Deed

Think of the implications for you. When you sin, God doesn't discipline you to make you pay for the trouble you've caused Him. He does it because He cares only for your restoration. When you go through difficult times, God hasn't allowed them because you somehow deserved them—though as sinners, we always do. No, because of His love, everything He does for His people is redemptive. Everything—even difficulty—is a sign of His favor. He wants the best for us, all because of His love.

> Amazing love! How can it be, that Thou,
> my God, should die for me?
>
> —CHARLES WESLEY

Reflecting Love

We ought to lay down our lives for our brothers.

1 JOHN 3:16

In Word

Though we don't fully understand God's love, we can accept it. Even though its depth is beyond our imaginations, we can assume that because He is God—infinite, perfect, and completely "other"—He is capable of it. We, however, know how short we fall. We are not capable of that kind of love, because self-sacrifice is only part of our nature within a few special family relationships.

Nevertheless, that's exactly the kind of love to which God calls us. We are to lay down our lives for our brothers and sisters. He came into this world to lay down His life for us, and He never said that's the end of the story. We are to lay down our lives in exactly the same way. If we want to have God's kind of love, we have to realize its depths. And its depths call for the ultimate sacrifice.

That's hard to obey. In fact, this commandment to love each other in the same way that Jesus loved us is perhaps the most neglected in all of Scripture. It isn't that we can't love each other. It's that we can't love each other like that. We usually don't mind going out of our way for our friends, being generous with our money, even forgiving our enemies from time to time. But to die for them? Even if we take that figuratively, it's beyond us. We can sacrifice to a point, but there's a line we won't cross. We don't pay ultimate sacrifices easily. The flesh cannot do such a spiritual thing.

That's why it's a certain sign of God at work in a person. Sacrificial love, in its purest sense, can only be birthed in us from above. Only the Spirit of the sacrificial God can produce sacrificial children. Only a supernatural being can do something so . . . well, supernatural.

In Deed

Ask the hard questions about your love life. Who do you love? How much? Are you willing not just to go out of your way occasionally, but to radically sacrifice for the sake of reflecting God's love?

He alone loves the Creator perfectly who
manifests a pure love for his neighbor.

—VENERABLE BEDE

God's Justice

He did it to demonstrate his justice at the present time, so as to be just and the one who justifies those who have faith in Jesus.

ROMANS 3:26

In Word

The justice of God is unyielding. We would like it to be selective, applying to those who slight us and softly bending when it comes to our own offenses. But the character of God does not bend. Just as surely as God's love is constant, so are His judgments. He is utterly reliable in every area, even the painful ones.

That's good to know when the wicked prosper and bad things happen to good people. Where is the God of justice then? Waiting. When all is said and done, no injustice will be left. Everything will be perfectly fair.

That's a comfort when we see people getting away with evil deeds; they won't get away with them forever. But there's a flip side to God's justice that is frightening. We know we deserve penalties for our sins. Regardless of the size of the sin, when we consider the size of the One against whom we've sinned, we tremble. Sins against an infinite being require an infinite penalty. Justice gives us nightmares.

We easily see the Cross as an expression of God's love, but it's also an expression of His justice. The bloody body of our sinless Jesus is what justice looks like in front of a backdrop of love. If God were all justice, we would be on that cross. If He were all love, He would have compromised His character for our sake long ago, and we'd want little to do with Him. But on the Cross, love and justice stand together.

In Deed

The Judge of the earth is at work. Sins will be paid for—all of them. Nothing is left unpunished. But the wisdom of God means that the love of God and the justice of God are perfectly integrated on the Cross. God is both the judge and the justifier. In the ongoing work to make all things right, God has given us a chance to put our sins under the covering of His payment. It's an amazing plan: Justice prevails without prevailing over us.

> [The Cross] means the verdict which God will pronounce over us on the day of judgment has been brought into the present.
>
> —ANTHONY HOECKEMA

Reflecting Justice

Be careful to do what is right in the eyes of everybody.
ROMANS 12:17

In Word

We might think that the best way to reflect God's justice is to implement it, but it isn't. We are certainly required to treat people honestly and fairly. But we are specifically told in Romans 12 not to seek our own form of judgment. Vengeance is God's. We are to leave room for His wrath.

How does this reflect God's justice? It acknowledges Him as judge over all the earth because it refuses to take justice into our own hands. Our governments must provide order, of course, and must execute justice fairly. But the individual Christian? We have a higher authority. Anything done to us unfairly will be dealt with by a zealously fair God. We are to seek fairness; we are never to seek revenge.

Jesus made it clear in the Sermon on the Mount. The eye-for-an-eye mentality laid out in the Mosaic law was an expression of God's standards of righteousness. But righteousness has been fulfilled on the Cross, and our sin has been paid for. We have been treated with extreme grace, and we are to treat others with similar grace. Mercy saved us, and it is to shape our lives. "Eye for an eye" just doesn't apply in the individual believer's life anymore. We had to choose between a grace life or a justice life, and when we accepted Christ, we chose grace. Unless we want to submit to a system of justice and suffer the consequences of our sin, we'd best apply grace broadly.

In Deed

Justice is so sweet when it puts others in their place, yet so frightening when it threatens to do the same to us. But when we realized our sin and the impending judgment, we chose mercy. When we see the sin of others, we have to continue to choose it.

Just as with God and the Cross, love and justice are to meet in the heart of the believer. We may know what's right, but we also know His grace. He turned justice on Himself and absorbed the cost of sin so others wouldn't have to. We can reflect justice in exactly the same way—absorbing the cost of others' sins and forgiving them in grace.

Do you wish to receive mercy? Show mercy to your neighbor.
—JOHN CHRYSOSTOM

God's Faithfulness

His compassions never fail.
LAMENTATIONS 3:22

In Word

It was a devastating scene. Jerusalem—the city of God, the seat of His Temple, the center of the world's priestly nation—had been sacked. It was totally destroyed. Walls had fallen, thousands had been killed or taken captive, and the Temple had been toppled. The chosen people had been chosen for catastrophe. The world's link between heaven and earth had been broken.

The book of Lamentations is just what its name implies—a lament. It is an outpouring of grief by the prophet Jeremiah over the destruction of Jerusalem and its temple. It is a cry of anguish rising up from the rubble. And yet right in the middle of it is this astounding declaration: "Because of the LORD's great love we are not consumed, for his compassions never fail. They are new every morning; great is your faithfulness" (vv. 22-23).

Despite circumstantial evidence to the contrary, God was faithful to Israel. Despite the fact that this devastating destruction would cause the ultimate crisis of faith—a chosen people questioning their chosenness—Jeremiah saw something greater than the circumstances of despair. He saw the faithfulness of God. That just doesn't compare to anything our eyes can see, no matter how bleak life appears.

In Deed

Jeremiah's understanding of God's faithfulness is the understanding God longs for each of us to have. When life is falling apart—when a marriage fails, when a loved one suffers with a fatal disease, when bankruptcy is imminent, when the valley of the shadow of death is before us—God is faithful. We may not be able to figure out exactly how He will be faithful to us, but we know He will. Why? Because He said so. And the faithful always keep their promises.

God's faithfulness is hard to grasp because God is vastly different than we can imagine. He isn't fickle like even the best people we know. He doesn't change His mind in the same sense human beings do. He doesn't ride the waves of cultural trends and popularity polls. He is faithful—ever constant, utterly devoted, and always true. Rely on Him.

> God's investment in us is so great He
> could not possibly abandon us.
> —ERWIN LUTZER

Reflecting Faithfulness

Be faithful, even to the point of death.
REVELATION 2:10

In Word

Faithfulness comes in many forms. Jesus told His disciples to be faithful by letting "yes" mean "yes" and "no" mean "no." Paul told his churches to be faithful in their behavior and their giving. Here in Revelation, Jesus tells the church at Smyrna to be faithful in the midst of persecution. In every case, the stakes are high. In Smyrna's case, they're extremely high.

Faithfulness is relative in our society. Many people define their faithfulness in a relationship as a temporary burden to bear until the relationship fizzles out. In our culture, "yes" has lots of meanings. So does "no." Simple agreements necessitate long contracts because we've nuanced our language in alarmingly deceptive ways. And, in our age, faithfulness to a cause or to a person is admirable, but certainly never expected. Death is too much to ask of anyone, so we just don't ask. We always define faithfulness to a point.

God doesn't. His faithfulness is eternal, and He calls us to be like Him. Our faithfulness should reflect the constancy of His. Our integrity should go to the very depths of our being and to the farthest reaches of our relationships. Our character, like God's, should be inviolable and incorruptible.

It isn't, of course. We're fallen sinners, and we're as fickle as a political poll. Though Jesus tells His disciples to be faithful even in the small things, it's especially the small things that we can be so casual with. When it comes to God's constancy and reliability, we just don't fit very well.

In Deed

God knows that. Nearly every biblical reference to faithfulness is about Him, not about us. We're certainly called to be like Him, but we're never held up in Scripture as the ideal. Only God is.

That's why faithfulness simply must be a fruit of the Spirit. Galatians 5:22 confirms it; we can only be faithful because of a work that God does in us, not because of ourselves. The measure of our faithfulness will be defined by the measure of our relationship to Him.

> Only by fidelity in little things can a true and constant love of God be distinguished from a passing fervor of spirit.
> —FRANÇOIS FÉNELON

Released

See, I have taken away your sin, and I will put rich garments on you.
ZECHARIAH 3:4

In Word

How do you feel before God? That's not a question you hear very often—rational, Western Christians like to take the focus off of feelings—but it's a valid one, because your emotions flow out of what you really believe. (You don't want to base your salvation on emotions, but you can't help but have them. God gave them to us for a reason.) So when you stand before Him, which feelings fill your heart?

A prisoner who has been set free after a lengthy prison term may not know how to act at first. The truth of his status may take some time to sink in. Freedom is a strange feeling for those who aren't used to it, and many long-term prisoners suffer anxiety from all the decisions they have to make on their own after they're released. Some look over their shoulders for months to come with a nagging feeling that their freedom will be revoked. The deep claws of guilt are very reluctant to let go.

In Zechariah 3, God declared the captives free. The sins of Joshua and his countrymen had been absolved, their penalty fully satisfied. And not only had their sin been taken away, it was being replaced with luxurious garments of royalty. From filthy rags to extravagant riches, God's people were being transformed. They had permission to enjoy all the security and privileges of freedom before Him.

In Deed

That's not just the story of Joshua and the freed captives. In fact, their story points to ours, the good news of redemption for all who believe in Jesus. The prison term is over. Freedom is to be experienced and savored.

If you don't feel a deep sense of joy in God's presence, even after you have confessed your sins and accepted His forgiveness, perhaps you haven't fully embraced the truth of your cleansing. God has taken away your sin; it's not yours anymore. Ignore the evidence to the contrary. Faith banks on what He says, not on a guilty conscience. Give yourself permission to feel absolutely free. God already has.

> Clean is the one who is righteous, if not in the sight of men, yet in the sight of God.
> —AUGUSTINE

Celebrate Cleansing

**In that day each of you will invite his neighbor
to sit under his vine and fig tree.**
ZECHARIAH 3:10

In Word

The Judge told Joshua that He would remove the sin of the land in a single day (v. 9). In immediate terms, that judgment was effected for the captives upon their return to the Promised Land. In ultimate terms, however, it wasn't applied until a sinless man acting as an offering for the human race was sacrificed on a Roman cross. The decree of the court was swiftly and officially implemented with the execution of an innocent man.

But God's removal of sin wasn't the final step of His judgment. Those who are freed are to share their freedom with the community. The Judge's decision is universally applied to those who will accept it. Liberty isn't much fun unless it's a shared experience.

The picture Zechariah gives us is of a group of released, guilt-free people celebrating their freedom with those around them. They invite their neighbors to sit under their vines and fig trees. They eat and drink together, laugh together, and tell stories of the merciful Judge who exonerated them. Captivity had twisted their thinking, suppressed their desires, and shamed their souls. Now everything has been set right.

In Deed

How do you celebrate your freedom? Don't worry; this passage is not a command to go plant a vine and a fig tree in your yard so you can invite the neighbors to sit under them. It is, however, a snapshot of what salvation is supposed to look like. Our cleansing is supposed to be celebrated among many.

Those who have been released from a huge sense of oppression from sin are more likely to express their exuberance, but the release is just as dramatic for all of us, whether or not we feel it. If we really saw the whole truth of what the Judge has decreed and how emphatically He cut off the accuser's testimony, we would feel like throwing a party. And we would invite all the neighbors.

All our life is a celebration for us . . .
God is always everywhere.
—CLEMENT OF ALEXANDRIA

On Mission with God

May he work in us what is pleasing to him.
HEBREWS 13:21

In Word

Are you on a mission with God? It's an important question to ask, isn't it? Our God looked upon this rebellious race and saw a world festering with need. He saw brokenness and pain, despair and disease, and sin and rebellion. He saw a lost race. How did He respond? He met the need. It was His nature to do so—He's driven by love and mercy.

That's not all. He has given us His nature. Not only did He meet our deepest needs, He has drawn us into His redemptive work. We aren't just recipients of His grace, we are ministers of it. We labor together with Him.

The eyes of the biblical God search His creation, and when He finds brokenness, He points it out. All around us are hurting people and sinful lifestyles. The God who sent Jesus into this world to save us sends us into this world to further His mission. Why? Because He wants to work through us to meet the needs. The God of compassion, mercy, peace, and hope wants to use us as instruments of compassion, mercy, peace, and hope. He doesn't often reveal Himself out of context. Instead, He reveals Himself through His people.

That's the picture of the New Testament church. God has drawn us into partnership with Him to demonstrate that our salvation is complete. Redemption wasn't just about getting us right with Him, it's about getting us completely in sync with Him. We are to reflect Him in every way that He has revealed Himself, and part of our reflection is to have a zealous compassion for those who need Him. He works in us to accomplish His will, because by being like Him, we glorify Him.

In Deed

So the question remains. God has revealed Himself to you in some degree, but the issue now is whether He is revealing Himself through you. And for a world in desperate, screaming need of a God who cares, your answer to the question is critical: Are you on a mission with God?

> We do the works, but God works in us the doing of the works.
> —AUGUSTINE

High Places

Destroy all their carved images and their cast
idols, and demolish all their high places.
NUMBERS 33:52

In Word

There were times in Israel's history when worship at the "high places" was appropriate. Usually, however, the high places pointed to one forbidden, nauseating activity: idolatry. They were shrines and altars on hills and mountaintops designed exclusively for worship of a Canaanite god like the Baals and the Asherim. Chemosh, Molech, Rimmon, Tartak—the pantheon of ancient biblical civilizations was diverse and vast. But regardless of the name, the idolatry was detestable. God always forbade it.

The high places in Scripture are usually written about with contempt, because they were something God had forbidden. They were the temptation of many rebellious kings and the target of many good ones. A good king of Israel or Judah would search them out and destroy them. A bad king would build more and more. But whether the high places were destroyed or built, flourishing or faltering, there was one arena that kings could not reform: the human heart.

We build high places in our hearts. You can probably identify right away which ones are some of your most persistent. When Jesus is on the throne of your heart, those high places have little effect. When you're going through a spiritually dry time, those high places are easily restored. The altars we build are diverse and vast, just like the ancient Near Eastern pantheon. But there is a King who can deal with them effectively, if we will let Him. The landscape of our souls can be cleansed of worthless altars.

In Deed

What are your high places? False religion? It abounds in our day, though it is often subtle. But most Christians can avoid those. We fall for the seduction of other altars: careers, income, relationships, misused sexuality, highly adored possessions, a purpose and a plan that are not of God's prompting. Our opportunities for high places on which to kneel are nearly limitless. Learn to recognize them. As God instructs, demolish them and turn to Him alone.

*Whenever we take what God has done and put it
in the place of Himself, we become idolaters.*
—OSWALD CHAMBERS

Solomon's Folly

As Solomon grew old, his wives turned his heart after other gods, and his heart was not fully devoted to the LORD his God.
1 KINGS 11:4

In Word

He is known as the wisest man in history. Rulers came from distant countries to hear him speak. He wrote proverbs and poems for posterity, inspired by God to pen substantial portions of Scripture. And still, in spite of all his wisdom, he made the unwisest decision of all. He went after other gods.

Why would Solomon do such a thing? Early in his reign he had asked God for wisdom, and God answered with that and more. And after years of faithful service as king and sage, Solomon did the unthinkable. He built "high places" for his wives. He aided and abetted the worship of Chemosh and Molech. Why?

Surely Solomon's unfaithfulness was not planned. Neither was it an abrupt break with "the God of Israel, who had appeared to him twice" (v. 9). It was apparently gradual, the result of being married to so many women from different countries. The text implies a slow turn—"as [he] grew old"—where the black line between obedience and disobedience grew wider and grayer. Little by little, he let his devotion to his God slip and his devotion to his wives take God's place. Though he may never have worshiped other gods wholeheartedly, he let his wives become his idols. They became more important to him than God's clear instructions.

In Deed

We can relate. There are things in our lives that gradually turn our hearts. At first they seem innocent, but over time they insidiously steal our worship. They redirect us from a pure heart toward God to a mixed heart toward whatever makes us feel good. We, like Solomon, become idolaters.

Solomon's apostasy is scary. If the wisest man in the Bible could fall, how are we immune? We're not. That's why we have to avoid Solomon's error. We have to abruptly stop the gradual turning of our hearts, and focus them where they belong—on the will of the only true God.

That to which your heart clings is your god.
—MARTIN LUTHER

An Unholy Exchange

They exchanged the truth of God for a lie.

ROMANS 1:25

In Word

That's what idolatry is: the exchange of a truth for a lie. Whatever takes God's place in our hearts is a travesty of unspeakable proportions. In any kind of worship other than the God-exalting, Christ-honoring kind of passion, we have substituted the profane for the holy, the cheap for the priceless, the finite for the infinite, a curse for a blessing, and like Esau of old, our birthright for a bowl of soup. It's a foolish exchange, but we do it all the time. It's our nature.

Sixteenth-century reformer John Calvin said we were, even from the moment we were born, "master craftsmen of idols." He was right. We seek things to make us whole and then pursue them with a passion. Some people seek sex or food, others seek profits or possessions. Some people feed themselves with status and accolades, others with interests and knowledge. And while nothing is wrong with any of these things in themselves, we use them wrongly. We put them on the throne of our hearts, where God belongs. We fall in love with unlovely things. We exchange truth for a lie.

That's a painful assessment, but it's entirely biblical. The history of humanity, according to Scripture, is a fall followed by a desperate search for meaning. We crave fulfillment because our sin has left us unfulfilled. We thirst for self-esteem because the esteem of being God's special child of creation, made in His image, was forsaken. We exchange the truth for a lie because we had a falling out with the truth, and lies are the only options left. Until we come face-to-face with the truth again—in the person of Jesus, who declared Himself to be the truth—we are getting the raw end of a bad, self-inflicted deal.

In Deed

Know your heart. Understand its tendencies. Learn to recognize when you are enthroning unworthy substitutes in place of your Lord. His rule is not as easy as theirs, but it is infinitely more worthwhile. So choose what's worthwhile. Daily exchange your lies for the truth.

Man's mind is like a store of idolatry and superstition.

—JOHN CALVIN

Low Priorities

The high places, however, were not
removed; the people continued to offer
sacrifices and burn incense there.

2 KINGS 12:3

In Word

Joash was a decent king—for a while. The verdict on his reign is split: While under the guidance of Jehoiada the priest, he did well. He restored and maintained the Temple, and he did "what was right in the eyes of the LORD" (v. 2). But after Jehoiada had died, Joash was a different king. He killed a priest and bought off the Syrian army with the Temple's sacred objects.

God's assessment of Joash's reign is two brief chapters: 2 Kings 12 and 2 Chronicles 24. He was neither Judah's finest king nor its worst. He was good part of the time and bad part of the time. And one reason for the shift may have been the problem in verse 3: He never dealt with the high places.

Why not? Perhaps he was somehow attached to them. Or perhaps it was simply a problem of neglect. Either way, his reign demonstrated the condition of his heart. In a time of peace, he tolerated the high places. In a time of war, he violated the Temple. The sacred objects were apparently more expendable than the places of false worship.

That's easy for us to judge, but we can be just as double-minded. We often find time for a favorite hobby but say we just don't have time to serve in our church's ministries. We find ways to pay for that vacation or new gadget, but we cut back our missions giving when things are tight. In other words, we tolerate the high places, even while selling off the sacred parts of our lives. We act like Joash.

In Deed

There's nothing wrong with hobbies and vacations, of course. The problem is in making them a higher priority than the Kingdom. The high places in our hearts are often not what we zealously pursue but what we passively tolerate. We avoid dealing with idols and are then forced to make painful compromises to our true worship. We fall into the sin of Joash, and we pay the price.

Avoid double-minded worship. Flee from compromise. Get rid of the high places in your life.

> The dearest idol I have known, whate'er that idol be; help
> me to tear it from Thy throne, and worship only Thee.
>
> —WILLIAM COWPER

Serious Devotion

This is what the Sovereign LORD says to
the mountains and hills, to the ravines and
valleys: I am about to bring a sword against
you, and I will destroy your high places.

EZEKIEL 6:3

In Word

It's a harsh judgment. The description of the devastation God will bring against
the high places—and the people who cultivate them—is ominous and frightening. It is an indictment of idolatry that should be enough to make its prac-
titioners repent. It's a clear sign that God is serious about worship.

There's a purity of worship to which God calls us repeatedly throughout
Scripture. He's rather emphatic about it. It isn't just a suggestion or a request.
It's a life-or-death command that we are told to follow. And because most of
us are fickle followers, we're given a promise of divine assistance through the
power of the Holy Spirit. Our true, pure worship is a holy preoccupation of
the Father. Whenever we take it casually, we can simply read this passage for
a wake-up call. God's desire for our wholehearted, single-minded worship
is intense.

Most of us grow up wondering what career we will have or who we will
marry. We envision our life and fill our dreams with hopes and adventures.
We make plans and pursue them as though these issues will define our lives.
But they won't. The most important issue we need to clear up is less about
what we do and more about who we worship. A wholehearted devotion to
the One who created and redeemed us is paramount. It's the most important
thing we can ever decide.

In Deed

Try a little exercise: Compare the amount of time you spend thinking about
how to accomplish your career and relationship goals with the time you spend
thinking about how to purify your worship. If you're like most people, the
most important issue loses that contest.

Turn that tide. Make what's most important to God also most important
to you. Get in line with His holy agenda for your life, and judge your high
places before He has to. Be as serious about your worship as He is.

No one has ever lost out by excessive devotion to Christ.

—H. A. IRONSIDE

The Highest Place

They brought Jesus to the place called Golgotha.
MARK 15:22

In Word

God followed through on His promise of judgment, and He concentrated it all on one high place in particular—a place called Golgotha. It was a crude altar, to be sure, but the sacrifice that was lifted up there was the purest and costliest ever. Now it stands as the only legitimate place of worship on the planet.

No, our worship isn't based on a physical place. But the hilltop called Golgotha represents a spiritual crisis that any true worshiper must come to. It's the spiritual place where the ultimate payment for sins was made, and no one worships the true God with a true heart unless his or her sins are dealt with there. And we don't bring the sacrificial offering with us when we come; it's provided. The place of real devotion, of real sacrifice, and of real worship is the Cross of Christ.

It isn't coincidental that Jesus laid down His life on a hilltop. Neither is it a coincidence that God inspired a temple on another hilltop centuries before. There is something about the high places of our terrain that makes us think we can get closer to God there, and men have tried for centuries. From the Tower of Babel to the mountaintops of Tibet, people yearn to reach upward. The miracle is that in one place, at one point in time, God reached down. He met us on a mountaintop that stands at the centerpiece of all history. The sacrificial offering on that hill is the focal point of the entire universe.

In Deed

Our idolatries drive us to the high places, where we have built our altars and cultivated false worship. While we were doing that, the incarnate God walked up one high place and paid the price for all the others. His is the least attractive to our fallen human nature, and not a pleasant place to worship at all—who enjoys being reminded that sinfulness requires blood? But it's central, it's unique, and it's required. It's the only right place to worship.

God's wrath has judged idolatry on the high places. But His wrath was directed to His Son on the highest place of all. That's where we are to bring our idolatry. That's where we purify our hearts. That's where real worship takes place.

God gives the Cross, and the Cross gives us God.
—JEANNE GUYON

The Worst Exchange

"My people have exchanged their Glory for
worthless idols. Be appalled at this, O heavens, and
shudder with great horror," declares the LORD.

JEREMIAH 2:11-12

In Word

It's perhaps the strangest of ironies. The nations who worship false gods
wouldn't think of adopting another nation's god (v. 11). But Israel, the only
nation in that era worshiping the true God, did. God had brought them out
of Egypt through the Red Sea, sustained them in the wilderness, made them
victorious in the Promised Land, sent them prophet after prophet, and did
amazing miracles all along the way. And yet at some point in its history, Israel
essentially said, "Never mind. We'll just worship these stone idols instead."

What a trade. The infinite, almighty, loving, compassionate, all-wise God
was removed from their hearts, and small statues of metal, stone, and wood
were put in His place. The God who crafted life and this universe in intricate,
awesome detail was taken out of the picture; common materials made by His
own hand were brought in to replace Him. If ever there was a miscarriage
of justice, this was it. If ever there was a travesty of mind-boggling proportions, this qualifies. Israel exchanged the awesome for the pitiful, the holy for
the defiled, the majesty for the misery. We've heard about some of history's
bad deals—state-sized tracts of land sold for a few beads, millions of dollars
paid for soon to be worthless stock, Babe Ruth sold to the Yankees for some
cash—but this was the worst. This was metal and rocks in exchange for the
eternal God.

In Deed

We do the same. We worship gadgets, cars, sports, styles, clothes, entertainment, and other worthless junk. We're not sure why. We just know that in the
absence of God, we need something else. The problem is that we've miscal-
culated. God isn't absent.

That was Israel's problem too. They thought He wasn't available, but He
was—just not on their terms. And He's the same with us: always available,
always on His terms. Forsake foolish exchanges. Embrace your Glory.

A man's god is that for which he lives.

—MARTYN LLOYD-JONES

Costly Gifts

**I will not sacrifice to the LORD my God
burnt offerings that cost me nothing.**
2 SAMUEL 24:24

In Word

David could have simply taken Araunah's threshing floor. After all, the offering was for royal purposes, a sacrifice to end a plague on the kingdom. And Araunah offered his property willingly. There was no reason for David to pay for the site other than one overriding fact: This was an act of sacrifice!

David understood the central significance of sacrifice. It has to cost something. Worship that is easy to give is neither deep nor meaningful. It may contain the right words and the right actions, but it doesn't indicate anything about the heart of the worshiper.

We have no trouble understanding this principle in our social lives. When we receive a gift that cost the giver a lot, we are deeply grateful. When we receive a gift that was cheaply obtained, we are more casual about our gratitude. Costly gifts mean something to us because they tell us something about the feelings and generosity of the giver. They give us a glimpse into the depth of the giver's love. They reflect the true meaning of giving.

Sacrificial worship reflects the true meaning of giving too. God receives gifts like we do: with an understanding that the sacrifice involved usually correlates directly with the love behind it. An act of worship that costs us nothing isn't much of an act of worship. No love is required to give cheap gifts. The God who sees into our hearts knows that better than anyone.

In Deed

Does your worship cost you anything? Or, more pointedly, does it cost you anything other than a couple of hours on Sunday morning and a small percentage of your paycheck? Those are important gifts to give, but God is looking deeper. He is looking for worship that flows from the heart every day of the week. He is looking for the love behind the gift.

Learn to say with David, "I won't make cheap sacrifices for God." After all, He didn't make cheap sacrifices for us.

The sign of our professed love for the gospel
is the measure of sacrifice we are prepared
to make in order to help its progress.
—RALPH MARTIN

Noisy Praise

If they keep quiet, the stones will cry out.
LUKE 19:40

In Word

Our mission toward global worship is going to happen, whether or not we participate in it. If we don't cry out in praise of the Savior, God will get the rocks to do it. All creation will point to Him in one way or another, and we're usually the last ones to get in on the plan. At the centerpiece of this universe is a Savior with a Cross, and yet segments of humanity reject that centerpiece while other segments don't even know it exists. That's what our mission is about.

But it's going to happen. That's a promise. Philippians says that every knee will bow and every tongue will confess that Jesus is Lord (2:10-11). We can gather from other verses that this is far from a universal salvation; it's only a universal acknowledgment of ultimate reality. In the end, everyone will see Jesus for who He is. And in the end, no one will be able to rationalize Him away.

But if universal worship is going to happen anyway, why should we worry about it? Why should we get bent out of shape about getting the gospel to the ends of the earth, if the ends of the earth are eventually going to worship Him regardless of what we do? First and foremost, because Jesus told us to. The mission is every Christian's mandate.

But there's another reason. We should be zealous for the glory of God's name because we can't swim against history's tide. If the direction of the universe—even its rocks—points to Christ, it would be shameful if His most precious creatures, specifically made in the image of God, do not. It would also be active rebellion against the sovereign God who made us agents of His mission. The ultimate authority has told us: Love Him, worship Him, tell of His goodness, and sing His praises. The noisy disciples irked the Pharisees, but God had ordained their noise.

In Deed

Do you have it in you to irk a Pharisee? Exuberance is ordained. Noisy praise is part of the plan. Declaring His goodness is the mission to which we're called.

> Men in general praise God in such a manner that He scarcely obtains the tenth part of His due.
> —JOHN CALVIN

Beyond Desolation

**The hand of the LORD was upon me, and he
brought me out by the Spirit of the LORD and set
me in the middle of a valley; it was full of bones.**
EZEKIEL 37:1

In Word

God's chosen people were in crisis. Generations before, the twelve tribes of
Israel were one nation, and all of them were in the Promised Land. Now, after
the succession of evil king after evil king, the northern kingdom of Israel had
been sacked by the Assyrians, and the southern kingdom of Judah had been
carried off into exile by the Babylonians. From all outward appearances, the
salvation experiment seemed dead.

Where God is concerned, though, "dead" doesn't mean very much. So
what if the chosen people were scattered all over ancient civilizations? So
what if the situation was so hopeless that all of Isaiah's promises made years
before now seemed wildly unrealistic? So what if the bones had been dead so
long that they were now dry?

God specializes in resurrection. He demonstrated that through Elijah and
Elisha, and He had promised it through earlier prophets. And, as we now
know, He would demonstrate it centuries later through Jairus's daughter,
Lazarus, and the Savior of the world. No matter how hopeless a situation
seems, even as hopeless as death and decay, God is a God of hope. Nothing's
impossible for Him.

In Deed

We know that intellectually, but we don't practice it. We let our impossibilities convince us that God isn't on our side, or that He is a God of miracles
only on rare occasions, or some other discouraging thought along those lines.
When we find ourselves in an impossible situation, we usually assume our
desire for better circumstances simply wasn't God's will to begin with. What
we don't realize is that, as He did with Ezekiel, He brings us to the valley of
dry bones not to discourage us, but to show us something amazing. It was the
Spirit of God who took Ezekiel to the place of despair, and it was to show him
that despair wasn't true. He'll do the same for you. When you see dead, dry
bones, trust the One who showed them to you.

It is impossible for that man to despair who
remembers that his Helper is omnipotent.
—JEREMY TAYLOR

Toward Resurrection

This is what the Sovereign LORD says to these bones:
I will make breath enter you, and you will come to life.

EZEKIEL 37:5

In Word

God is the source of all life. He breathed life into Adam on day six of creation, and He sustains life every minute of every day. Whatever God touches flourishes. The Living One is never the author of death.

Sin is the source of all death. It isn't that God decides to kill those who have sinned; sin cuts off the supply line of life by severing communion with the Living One. By its very nature, rebellion against the source of life results in death.

So when God says He will breathe life into dry bones scattered over a desolate valley, He's giving a dramatic picture of the new creation, or regenesis. He is pointing back to day six of creation, and He is pointing ahead to the resurrection of Jesus and the flourishing Kingdom of God. He is demonstrating that He has a heart for redemption that overshadows His need to judge sin. In the midst of one of Israel's most desperate situations in history, He promises restoration. He is a God who loves to breathe life.

In Deed

Think of all the situations in your life that seem hopeless or even dead. If you're honest, you'll realize that you have plenty of them: broken dreams, disappointing relationships, thwarted plans, devastating regrets. Realize that they aren't hopeless to God. In fact, He loves breathing life into impossibilities.

Maybe that's why inspired Scripture tells us that the sovereign Lord says He will breathe into the dry bones and make them alive again. He has authority over every situation in our lives, even the tragedies we've tried to put behind us. If He wants to resurrect them, He's fully capable. He's sovereign.

Never give up on a situation by looking at the circumstances surrounding it. Look at the sovereign God who exudes life. His will is all that matters; visible circumstances are no obstacle. The heart of the One who breathes life wants to fill your circumstances with His breath.

Resurrection is . . . the crucial quality of life.

—WILLIAM TEMPLE

Through Faith

I will put breath in you, and you will come to life. Then you will know that I am the LORD.
EZEKIEL 37:6

In Word

Every desperate situation in your life implies a critical moment of decision. There comes a point when you either believe that God has promised what He has promised, or you believe that His promises for you aren't understandable, applicable, or true. Those who are able to believe in the life-breathing God will know that He is the Lord. They will see the evidence of His wisdom, power, and love. Those who are not able to believe in the life-breathing God will not know that He is the Lord. They may accept His lordship at an intellectual level, but they will not see it or experience it. They will not receive faith's reward for faith they did not have.

That's a consistent principle of the Kingdom of God. Witnessing God's power results in greater faith, and missing His power results in weaker faith. Those who see dry bones get up and dance have fewer struggles with doubt in the next crisis situation. Ezekiel believed—he didn't dare say no when God asked him if dry bones could live (v. 3)—and he saw a miracle unfold. The vision God gave him would be dramatically fulfilled when God restored the chosen people to the Promised Land. Ezekiel's faith in the prophetic word would lead to Israel and Judah's knowledge of the Living One.

In Deed

What has God spoken about your life? The answer may be obvious to you, or it may be obscure. You may have never considered that He has a specific plan and purpose for you, though you've probably sought His will on a number of issues. What you need to remember, however much knowledge of His will you have, is that God's plan for you is to discover His purposes; to believe His promises, no matter how unlikely they seem; and to know Him as a result of the process. Your heart is designed to connect with His and to experience His loving agenda for the rest of your days.

Faith tells us of things we have never seen and cannot come to know by our natural senses.
—JOHN OF THE CROSS

After Life

I will put my Spirit in you and you will live.
EZEKIEL 37:14

In Word

The world is full of death. Despite the fact that billions of people live on this planet, few of them really *live* on this planet. Spiritually severed from the God who loves them—from the Living One—people live transient lives in painfully mortal flesh. We walk among human graveyards waiting to happen.

That sounds pretty stark, doesn't it? It certainly doesn't fit the mood of our generation, which believes that all people are basically good and everything's okay. It does, however, fit the biblical assessment of human fallenness. Paul wrote that we, in our natural condition, are "dead in [our] transgressions and sins" (Ephesians 2:1), and Ezekiel's vision of dry bones does nothing to contradict that truth. God had even spelled it out long ago in the Garden: "When you eat of it [the forbidden tree] you will surely die" (Genesis 2:17). In a fallen world, death reigns.

Christians should appear dramatically different from the world around us. We should seem strangely "alive" compared to the walking dead of creation. When nonbelievers observe Christian believers, they should see a spark of life, evidence of a new creation that comes from beyond fallen flesh. The evidence of joy, purpose, and gratitude among people who have those blessings should speak volumes to those who don't have them. In a desolate world, Christians should flourish.

In Deed

Are you flourishing? Does life overflow from your heart? If not, there's some sort of disconnect or obstacle between you and the Living One. That doesn't mean that Christians should put on happy masks for the world around us; we must be authentic. It does, however, mean that a chronic lack of joy and peace and life indicates a problem. If that's the case, ask God to breathe new life into you daily. Invite His Spirit to be as alive in you as He was in the bones of Ezekiel's vision. Let Him restore and resurrect you with the kind of life a dead world needs to see.

One filled with joy preaches without preaching.
—MOTHER TERESA

A New Satisfaction

Listen, listen to me, and eat what is good, and your soul will delight in the richest of fare.
ISAIAH 55:2

In Word

Deuteronomy 8:3 says that we don't live by bread alone. Jesus quoted that verse during His temptation and later told His disciples that His food was to do the will of the Father. The Word of God affirms that the voice of God is the key to a satisfying life.

That should be no surprise. It stands to reason that the God who created the world for His own pleasure would know exactly what it takes to live life to its fullest. The infinite, omniscient God knows what we should eat—spiritually, emotionally, and physically—to nourish us well. There's no reason ever to ignore His voice.

That's why the first temptation in the Garden targeted the voice of God. "Did God really say . . . ?" the serpent mused (Genesis 3:1). If a slithering liar really wanted to profane the sacred image of God, that was his logical first step: slander the voice that spoke this good creation into being. In Satan's view, the voice that breathes life into human beings, that speaks forth life-giving truth, that leads us into all blessing and abundance, is a voice that must be interrupted. The hater of God and humanity knew exactly how to attack the source of a soul's richest fare.

In Deed

If God says the key to your soul's abundance is in His voice, and the enemy chose as his first temptation to attack that voice, what does that tell you about your response to God's voice? Isaiah prophesied words that express God's heart to us: "Listen, listen." God is always pointing us in the right direction, guiding us in His ways, and showing us what to "eat." Is it because He loves being a dictator? Or could it be that He seeks our abundance, our pleasure, our delight?

The answer is spelled out pretty clearly in Scripture. God wants us to have "the richest of fare." He isn't a cosmic killjoy who wants to stamp out our pleasure. He wants us to delight in Him and His work. He wants our souls to be fully satisfied. And His voice will always tell us how.

God is not silent. It is the nature of God to speak.
—A. W. TOZER

A New Direction

Seek the LORD while he may be found;
call on him while he is near.
ISAIAH 55:6

In Word

"He has endowed you with splendor." That's how God spoke of the salvation of His people and the Kingdom life to which they were called (v. 5). When God delivers, He doesn't just deliver; He conquers and crowns, exalts and bestows honor. He doesn't just save us by the skin of our teeth and tell us to hang on tight. He's extravagant with His blessings. He saves "to the uttermost" (Hebrews 7:25, NKJV). Nothing God does is "barely enough."

We sometimes don't act as if we believe that. Somehow we got the impression that God gives us only enough to barely get by. We forget how extravagant He is with His blessings, how deep and fulfilling are the joy and peace and love He offers us. For some reason, we assume that the God who tells us to give generously is Himself a spiritual miser, withholding His graces from those who haven't yet lived up to their end of the bargain. In other words, we forget the definition of grace. And our relationship with God falls into a rut.

Isaiah tells his readers to seek the Lord while He may be found. If the God of extreme deliverance is offering you the blessings of His Kingdom, don't walk into His presence. Run. Pursue His nearness zealously. At every whisper of His voice and every nuance of His work, turn and give Him your full attention. Don't wait for His thunderous commands to move you; jump on His gentle suggestions. Like a beggar who lives for a glimpse of the king, let your heart treasure anything He offers.

In Deed

You can tell a lot about the condition of your heart by how hard it beats when God speaks. Those who crave His generosity will seek Him diligently. Like a plant that grows toward the sunlight, your soul will lean into the splendor of His Kingdom. His voice will be your life, and His salvation will be savored. You will consider your deliverance a privilege of the highest order.

It is essential that we acquire the habit of
hearkening to His voice . . . listening so as to
lose nothing of what He says to us.

—FRANÇOIS FÉNELON

A New Victory

You will go out in joy and be led forth in peace; the
mountains and hills will burst into song before you,
and all the trees of the field will clap their hands.

ISAIAH 55:12

In Word

Imagine creation celebrating the path God has put before you. Imagine mountains singing and trees clapping. Imagine streams babbling your name and
birds praising their Creator when they see you. Imagine having the kind of
journey that makes the universe quiver with joy.

That's the picture God gives of Israel's return from captivity and of the
redeemed coming out of sin's bondage. It's a portrait of the Kingdom, as all
creation rejoices at the fulfillment of God's Word. His victory sends shouts of
joy around the world, and the heavens ring with glorious singing. When God
delivers, it's a party.

For Christians who trudge through life with heavy burdens, this picture
doesn't make sense. That's good; the incongruity between our lives and God's
picture should bother us. Our pessimism and apathy are often symptoms of
a lifestyle and attitudes completely contrary to the Kingdom God promised,
and those symptoms should be extremely alarming. Despite the captivities
and burdens of this world, we have a God who is a conquering Warrior and
a mighty King. At some level of our thinking, life should be a dance. But for
many of us, it's a dirge.

That's because we live according to something other than God's promises.
We let the visual circumstances around us speak louder than the Kingdom He
describes. We walk in defeat because we don't have enough faith to walk in
victory or in joy. We don't believe the picture God has given us.

In Deed

If you want to experience victory in your life, believe what God has said.
Nowhere in the Bible does He give His people victories without prior faith.
The prerequisite to seeing God's power is believing that He has it—and that
He'll use it on your behalf. Walk in faith. Look past the falsehood of your
circumstances and see what God sees: mountains that sing for you and trees
that clap their hands.

God wants us to be victors, not victims . . .
to overcome, not to be overwhelmed.

—WILLIAM ARTHUR WARD

A New Purpose

**This will be for the LORD's renown, for an
everlasting sign, which will not be destroyed.**
ISAIAH 55:13

In Word

God is on your side. Nice words for a greeting card, but are they biblical?
After all, this is the God who cast us from His garden, gave us a bunch of laws
that go against our nature, and disciplines us when we break them. Life can
be brutally hard and painfully frustrating. Sometimes it doesn't seem that God
is on our side, does it?

But consider what God says through Isaiah: Our deliverance is for His
renown. It's an everlasting sign that will point to His glory. He delivers us
because He loves us, but He also delivers us for the sake of His name. God has
a lot at stake in how well we live. We are evidence of His kingdom; He wants
us to display it accurately.

God has sworn to us that His Word will not return to Him empty (v. 11).
Like a refreshing rain, it makes things flourish. His promises will be fulfilled,
His plans will be accomplished, and His character will be proven to all humanity. He will zealously pursue His own passions until His Word is completely
satisfied at end of the age. And since the redeemed are at the center of His
plan for our world, we can be absolutely sure: He is on our side.

In Deed

Our tendency is to interpret everything in God's Word through the lens of
what it means to us. We see ourselves as individuals in a relationship with our
Creator. We focus on His love and His wonderful plan for our life, and we are
exactly right on all counts. God is on our side because of His love.

But God is also on our side because of His glory. He created this world to
praise Him, and His reputation matters. When the world sees His wonders in
the people He has redeemed, many turn to praise. When His wonders aren't
evident in us, praise wanes. The worship of His name directly correlates to
the witness of those who bear it. You can live as though God is on your side.
He always is.

> The great end of God's work . . . is most properly
> and comprehensively called, the glory of God.
> —JONATHAN EDWARDS

In the Darkness

Stay here and keep watch with me.
MATTHEW 26:38

In Word

His soul was overwhelmed to the point of death. And even though He felt pretty lonely, He was by no means alone. He had the fellowship of the Father and, as much as they could give Him, the fellowship of the disciples. In the most pivotal, excruciating moment of His mission, Jesus invited others into it.

Just as Jesus was, we've been called on a mission that will take us to some pretty dark places. We are promised a banquet in the end, with feasting and fellowship and all the bright, warm things we human beings enjoy. It will be a great celebration with our God when the Son has returned in glory. But there are dark, lonely gardens first—struggles in the dead of night and anxieties over the cup of suffering. In our mission to take the gospel to the ends of the earth and to see the glory of God shine everywhere on this planet, we will have hard times. Jesus even promised His disciples that they would have tribulation. He told them He would always be with them; but would they always stay with Him? Going out with Him on His victorious mission is one thing; staying with Him at midnight in the garden of Gethsemane is another. That's where faith is truly tested.

Mentally put yourself where those disciples were. After all, Jesus' mission still has pivotal moments, and it can still be excruciating. If you were with Him in a dark, lonely garden, and He turned to you and said, "Stay here and keep watch with me," would you? Could you? Do you have any desire to abide with Him in this painful, costly program of redemption?

In Deed

Of course you do. We all do. He has put His Spirit into us and made us His co-laborers. He has called us to carry this heavy cross and to die daily. He has told us that we must lose our lives for His sake or else lose them altogether. And, amazingly, He has promised an enormous victory celebration for those who will stay with Him in the darkest moments of the mission. For better and for worse, we and the Savior are in this mission together—even in the dark of Gethsemane.

> By suffering the Father would lead us to enter
> more deeply into the love of Christ.
> —ANDREW MURRAY

Great and Precious Promises

He has given us his very great and precious promises.
2 PETER 1:4

In Word

Imagine how you would feel if Jesus walked up to you and said, "I am sending you on a mission to live a godly life and to represent Me to your world. This won't be an easy mission, but I will give you everything you need. I will be there with you the whole time, but you won't be able to see Me. Nevertheless, I will walk with you everywhere you go, and whenever you need anything for this mission—anything at all—I will give it to you. It's a promise."

Would you accept this mission? It isn't hypothetical, of course. You have already been chosen for this mission, and, if you're reading this, you have probably already accepted it. More than that, whether you realize it or not, you have accepted it on these very terms. The promises of God Himself—very great and precious promises, we are assured—are part of the contract. Everything you need for life and godliness—in other words, everything period—is available to you. The only catch is this: You have to know the promises, and you have to ask Him in faith to fulfill them. Other than that, there are no overriding restrictions.

Do you believe that? Do you realize that everything for life and godliness has been promised? Do you understand that every time we say we couldn't help our sin, we didn't have enough resources for the mission, or we couldn't get along with someone we're required to relate to, we're deceiving ourselves and contradicting His Word? The great and precious promises are rock-solid guarantees. Everything we need is available.

In Deed

God's great and precious promises are like a forgotten storehouse containing priceless goods. The treasures within it are mind-boggling. The ignorance about them is mind-boggling too. There's a gap between the fact of the promises and our willingness to believe them. And Peter's words are an emphatic encouragement to bridge that gap. The promises are everywhere—and God invites us to count on them completely.

> There is a living God . . . He means what He says and will do all He has promised.
>
> —HUDSON TAYLOR

Promised Deliverance

**Whoever believes in him shall not
perish but have eternal life.**

JOHN 3:16

In Word

Perhaps we've heard this verse so often that it has lost its impact. Familiarity breeds contempt, they say, and while we may not have contempt for this greatest and most precious of all promises, it does tend to go in one ear and out the other sometimes. It's such a standard verse that we don't stop and think about it, and that's a shame. Today, stop and think about it.

Think about the sweeping scope of the promise: It applies to "whoever." Think about the amazing simplicity: It requires only genuine belief. Think about the astounding implications: It's the difference between eternal death and eternal life. And think about its unfathomable time frame: Eternity is a really, really long time.

Most of all, think about the high price of the promise. Consider the excruciating condescension of a God who would clothe Himself in human flesh, be tempted by all its fallenness, suffer all its pains, die one of the worst of its deaths, and do it with the kind of humility a lowly human being ought to have. We can scarcely imagine the king of a vast kingdom dying for the least of his citizens, but that's what we're asked to believe about our God. It doesn't seem typical, and in fact it isn't. It doesn't even seem practical, and perhaps it's not. But passion isn't always typical or practical. It's extravagant, persistent, and sometimes even absurd—at least on the surface. And yet, we are told, this absurd extravagance is lavished on us. Why? Because God so loved the world.

In Deed

That's a lot of love. It's hard for us to understand, because our love is usually limited or tainted with self-serving motives. But not God's. His love results in promises that deliver us from utter catastrophe. And His promises are backed up with painful sacrifice.

If you ever doubt that God is serious about keeping His promises, consider this one. He promised salvation and He bled to keep that promise. There's no greater guarantee than a promise written in divine blood.

See from His head, His hands, His feet,
sorrow and love flow mingled down.

—ISAAC WATTS

Promised Forgiveness

**If we confess our sins, he is faithful and
just and will forgive us our sins and
purify us from all unrighteousness.**

1 JOHN 1:9

In Word

We often take far too passive an approach to the continuing promise of forgiveness. The bountiful nature of God's pardon frequently raises our comfort
level with our sin. Despite Paul's warning that the blessing of grace must not
expand our capacity for disobedience (Romans 6:1), it often does. It's one
of the many annoying vagaries of fallen human nature; whatever we have in
abundance, we treat casually.

That's why we need to read a lot into the word *confess*. It means agreeing
with God about our sin, and we would do well to take it a step further. Not
only must we agree with Him about the fact of our sinfulness, we should
agree with Him emotionally about the grief of our sinfulness. If He is angered
and grieved over the defacing of creation's beauty, we should be angered and
grieved over our role in it. When sexuality is distorted and abused, it should
bother us profoundly. When greed puts mere things in the place of God in our
hearts, it should stagger us. When deceitfulness—even in the small things—
slanders the pure and true character of our God, it should knock the spiritual
wind out of us. Whatever God thinks about our sin should be what we think
about our sin. Whatever grieves Him should grieve us. Whatever vandalizes
His purposes should make us outraged. That's what it means to "confess."

In Deed

That kind of confession can never be casual about the offer of forgiveness.
The trauma of confession should prompt a traumatic acceptance of mercy.
The promise of never-ending grace should prompt never-ending grati-
tude. The promise should never be taken for granted.

Is 1 John 1:9 a "great and precious promise" to you? If not, consider the
sacrifice that made it possible. Consider the Savior who granted it. And consider the God whose grace is never exhausted. Never forget how precious
that grace can be.

> God has cast our confessed sins into the depths of the
> sea, and He's even put a No Fishing sign over the spot.
>
> —D. L. MOODY

Promised Escape

**He will not let you be tempted
beyond what you can bear.**
1 CORINTHIANS 10:13

In Word

In promising us everything related to life and godliness—in other words, everything—God has first taken care of the three biggest issues: salvation, sin, and temptation. All humans experience them in reverse order, first being tempted, then sinning, then accepting salvation. But God deals with them by saving us, forgiving our sin, and giving us a way out of temptation. His mercies undo the trouble we got ourselves into.

But while we are quick to embrace the benefits of salvation, and almost as quick to accept the ongoing forgiveness He offers, we are less diligent about addressing temptation. After all, if God has forgiven us and is going to continue to forgive us for everything we have ever done or ever will do, why should we get hung up on temptation? Whether we commit the sin or not, we're forgiven, right?

We are, but that's not the point. God has redeemed us for a new life, and temptation wars against that new life. When we give in to it, it threatens the blessings God wants to bestow on us, it undermines our process of conforming to Jesus, and it slanders the One who says He saved us and cleansed us of all unrighteousness. Giving in to temptation makes a statement about the power of the God we serve. It calls into question His ability to keep His people.

God's power is not insufficient, of course. The fault lies entirely with us. He has given us a way out of temptation every single time. He will never allow us to be tempted beyond what we can bear.

In Deed

Most of us will have a dual reaction to this promise. We will be comforted that we never have to be overwhelmed by temptation. We will also be exposed every time we claim we were overwhelmed by it. God's promise gives us a way out, and it also holds us accountable. That's both encouraging and convicting. In either case, it's a call to a purer, more godly life—with a promise to help us in it.

> When Satan finds the good man asleep,
> then he finds our good God awake.
>
> —WILLIAM GURNALL

Promised Prompting

It is God who works in you to will and to act according to his good purpose.
PHILIPPIANS 2:13

In Word

Perhaps the most relaxing of all of God's promises is that He is at work in us. He does not tell us to conform to the image of Jesus and then leave us alone to do it. He does not send us out on a mission and then cross His fingers for our success. He does not urge us to live godly lives and then blow up when we fail. No, every step of the way He is there. And, as this verse indicates, He is not just working on our behavior from the outside, He is transforming us from within.

That's what it means for God to work in us to will and to act according to His good purpose. His values shape our will, our inner drives, our ambitions and dreams. And then His Spirit helps us with the follow-through, acting on those inner impulses that He has placed within us. Far from being handed a religion that tells us to shape up, we are handed a Savior who gets inside to shape us. The promise of transformation is that God is busy gutting our temple and renovating it from within. He's a master Craftsman at work.

The comforting part of this promise is that when we have deep internal desires to do something entirely consistent with the stated purpose and plan of God, those desires are probably God-given. And when we are driven to act on those desires with a strategy and a worthwhile agenda, we are likely driven by God Himself. The fact that He is at work in us both to will (desires) and to work (behavior) for His good purpose is a tremendously relaxing fact. Once our prayers have determined that we're motivated by the Spirit and not by the flesh, we can trust that our work is not just our agenda, but also His.

In Deed

That means, of course, that He will see it through. The sovereign God who sees the future doesn't abandon projects midway through. If He started His work in you, He's committed to it. Rest in that truth, and trust what He is doing in your heart. There is a holy agenda shaping your life.

A man's heart is right when he wills what God wills.
—THOMAS AQUINAS

Promised Guidance

**In all your ways acknowledge him, and
he will make your paths straight.**

PROVERBS 3:6

In Word

The shortest distance between two points is a straight line. And usually when it comes to our lives, we want the shortest path. We don't want to waste time on peripherals; we want to get to where we're going as soon as we can.

God promises that we can. If we trust in Him with all our heart and refuse to rely on our own understanding—the conditions for this promise—then He will direct us, making our paths straight and getting us where we need to go. The believer who seeks His will in prayer, trusts His wisdom, and is obedient to His instructions will end up on exactly the right path. It's guaranteed.

The problem with our understanding of this promise is that we and God often have different definitions of "the right path." We are often diverted from our preferred route by a God who has other purposes for us. We find ourselves taking a roundabout way to where we want to go. It isn't actually roundabout, as God has a purpose in it; but it seems that way to us. We get impatient.

God ignores our impatience. He is directing our steps whether or not we realize it. If we trust Him, ask His help, seek His wisdom, and acknowledge His authority over our lives, His direction is certain. We may feel awfully lost; God assures us we are not.

In Deed

Do you feel like you've gotten off course? You may have gotten off of your course, but that doesn't mean you've gotten off of God's. You may be like Joseph, wasting away in a pointless prison, not realizing that in the end it will have a point. You may be like David, fleeing from a rabid king, not realizing that faith is being built in you in remarkable ways.

Make sure you are being faithful to God and are trusting His direction. If you are, do not fear. The course you are on, regardless of what it looks like, is the straight path He has designed specifically for you.

> Thy way, not mine, O Lord, however dark it be! Lead
> me by Thine own hand, choose out the path for me.
>
> —HORATIUS BONAR

Promised Protection

If you make the Most High your dwelling—even the
LORD, who is my refuge—then no harm will befall you.
PSALM 91:9-10

In Word

The sheltering protection of God is a glorious promise, if we can accept it.
The problem is that we know people who have presumably been faithful and
then have suffered disaster. Following God, from our observation, doesn't
necessarily lead to a pain-free life.

But a pain-free life isn't the subject of this psalm. Safety is. And our hang-
ups with it come with the difficulty of defining safety. On the one hand, we
know it doesn't mean that we will never have difficulties, even painful ones.
On the other hand, this promise must mean something. Surely it's not just a
spiritual promise that does our bodies no earthly good. God wouldn't pull a
bait and switch on us like that, would He?

No, He wouldn't. He is faithful and true to His Word. He means what He
says, and He says it clearly enough for us to understand. What God promises
here is that we can walk through this life with a guarantee. If we will trust Him
as our Refuge, we can know that we will never experience any catastrophe
that is devoid of redemptive purpose. If we have believed in His salvation and
trusted in His provision, we will never know the ultimate disaster of eternal
death. And in our short lives on this earth, we will never see a trial or difficulty
that is not under His sovereign, permissive hand that specifically ordains our
steps and redeems our problems. If "harm" falls, we can rest assured: It isn't
ultimately disastrous, and it didn't slip in under God's radar. He has a plan.

In Deed

That may be of little comfort to those who are struggling with life's difficulties
right now, but in the grand scheme of things, it's a huge relief. Like Paul's, our
path may be rocky, but it still leads us where we need to go. Like the prophets,
our days may be painful, but we are still being conformed to the character
of God. Our enemies may threaten, but they have no power over us. Why?
Because we have been bought by God. Nothing—not one single thing—can
threaten our security within His plan.

We sleep in peace in the arms of God, when
we yield ourselves up to His providence.
—FRANÇOIS FÉNELON

Promised Provision

Seek first his kingdom and his righteousness, and
all these things will be given to you as well.
MATTHEW 6:33

In Word

Jesus assured us: God takes care of flowers and birds. By comparison, human beings—we who are made in the very image of God—are much more significant. Why would He not take care of us as well?

The problem is what our eyes see. We know there are starving people in impoverished countries who are not receiving "all these things" as Jesus promised. There are millions of people lacking in the basic sustenance that life requires. What does that make of Jesus' promise? Is He wrong?

Of course not. Scripture is emphatic that God satisfies the needs—even the desires—of every living thing (Psalm 145:16, among others). God is not short on supply. The problem must be elsewhere. The problem must be in the conditions Jesus laid out. In a world gone wrong, there are billions of people who are not seeking first His Kingdom and His righteousness. And many of them are starving.

That's not to lay the blame for hunger entirely at the feet of the hungry. Though God is able to sustain them, His provision is often thwarted by corruption and misuse. The hearts of those who need Him are often deceived and exploited by those who hate Him. And so we have a needy world, and a call to help meet its needs. The Giver has made us part of the solution. Part of seeking His Kingdom and His righteousness is acting it out in this world.

In Deed

Do you worry about your life? God commands us not to. Why? Because He is the Provider. He withholds no good thing from us, He opens His hand and satisfies, and He clothes us and feeds us better than the lilies and the birds. Though we live in a world infected with sin, we have a God who has promised sustenance in the midst of it. And He has called us to be His ministers of sustenance to those who don't know Him. Seek first His Kingdom, and you—and others—will be filled.

Providence is the care God takes of all existing things.
—JOHN OF DAMASCUS

Promised Goodness

**No good thing does he withhold from
those whose walk is blameless.**

PSALM 84:11

In Word

What a comforting promise! God longs to be good to us. Regardless of our impression that He is often waiting to discipline us for our mistakes and purposeful disobedience, the truth is that He is waiting on high to have compassion on us (Isaiah 30:18). Think of that! The God we rightly fear is the God who thoroughly enjoys every opportunity to give us something good.

But what a discouraging condition. The promise in Psalm 84:11 is for those whose walk is "blameless." We may do our best, but we know we don't qualify for "blameless." If this promise is for those who never make mistakes, it's a meaningless promise—a nice idea, but never to be applied.

But God doesn't make meaningless promises. "Blameless" can't mean "perfect." Perhaps a better way to understand it would be "those whose walk is in God's direction," or "those whose walk is inspired by Him and inclined toward Him." On our best days, we could qualify for that kind of condition. We could reap the benefits of this promise.

There's still another way to look at it, though. Consider this: Jesus' walk was, in fact, blameless. It was perfect, completely without sin and error. And here's the clincher: Jesus lives in us! The One who is most qualified to receive this promise is the One who has become our life. If He dwells within, and if we are resting in Him by faith, by His righteousness we qualify to receive the promise of all good things. If we abide in Him, God delights in us.

In Deed

Do you see God as the cosmic school officer, meting out discipline at every opportunity? He does discipline us, of course, but His good hand is behind it. And His good hand has lots of other things in it—everything pertaining to life and godliness, every blessing His bounty has to offer, everything our heart truly desires. There is absolutely no good thing that He will withhold from those who are inclined toward Him and are trusting their lives to His Son.

God is not merely good, but goodness.

—C. S. LEWIS

Promised Satisfaction

**Delight yourself in the LORD and he will
give you the desires of your heart.**

PSALM 37:4

In Word

It's such an easy verse to abuse, isn't it? On one hand, we could take it to
mean that anything our heart fancies becomes ours, as long as we're worshiping God. On the other hand, we could define the condition of "delight" so
restrictively that the promise doesn't really mean anything. Yet at some level,
we know what the Spirit is getting at here: If our relationship with God is in
order, we will somehow be satisfied.

Consider the thrill of this promise. Think of how you would feel if every
one of your desires were fulfilled. What would it be like to have no more
unfulfilled longings? No more pipe dreams? No more fantasies that are just
too fantastic to come true? That would be amazing, wouldn't it?

Yes, it would. And, in a sense, that's what God promises. Whether we take
this verse to mean that He will give us what our heart desires or that He will
actually put the right desires in there to begin with, the result is the same:
satisfaction. A direct correlation between the things we crave and the things
God gives us. No more misplaced longings. No more unrequited loves.

There's a lot to the condition here—delighting in the Lord—and there's
also a lot to the delivery—the desires of your heart. But at the very least, true
love of God and a passionate submission to Him will result in the cravings and
the blessings matching up. He will work in us the desires He wants us to have,
and He will fulfill them.

In Deed

Sounds nice, doesn't it? And it's true. God doesn't guarantee us a pain-free
life, and He doesn't promise us the whims of our heart. He doesn't say we can
name our price and He'll pay it, and He doesn't tell us we'll have no more
troubles. He does, however, tell us that the key to being satisfied is in Him—
our utter delight in who He is. If that's in place, He becomes our greatest
desire. And that desire will always be fulfilled.

> Do not give your heart to that which
> does not satisfy your heart.
>
> —ABBA POEMEN

Promised Purpose

**In all things God works for the good of those who love
him, who have been called according to his purpose.**
ROMANS 8:28

In Word

It's a remarkable guarantee from a sovereign God. It would be impossible for
Him to back it up if He were not who He says He is. But our God is in charge
of history, and He works all things out for His purposes. And one of His purposes is to make all things work out for the people who love Him.

That's good to know when life looks like it has gone haywire. There's
precious little comfort in the midst of chaotic circumstances. When a loved
one lies dying, when unemployment hits home, when children are rebelling,
when cancer is diagnosed—all of the things that attack our sense of well-being
are on a divine leash. When everything is falling apart and our peace is being
threatened, we can know one rock-solid fact: There's a purpose.

The purpose isn't always discernible. Sometimes it isn't even clear until
decades later. But it is there. The God who promised to work all things
together for our good has proven that He does. His track record is perfect. A
look at Joseph in prison, Israel in Egypt, battles against the Philistines, David's
affair with Bathsheba—or ultimately the Cross—confirms that some pretty
ugly circumstances can be woven seamlessly into His divine plan. Joseph said
it best in Genesis 50:20: What is intended for evil by some can be intended for
good by God. The ugliness of the circumstances is never to be our guide.

In Deed

If you are going through a trial, you need to know that. The trial doesn't define
for you who God is, and it doesn't define His plan for you. Somewhere behind
it, or even in it, He is working out His purposes, and His purposes are very,
very good. The things that threaten your peace now are the things He will use
to establish it. You may not see it for a long time, but one day—even if only
in eternity—you will see it clearly. All things—every one of them—work
together for the good of those who love Him.

*Judge not the Lord by feeble sense, but trust Him for His
grace; behind a frowning providence, He hides a smiling face.*
—WILLIAM COWPER

Promised Destiny

> "I know the plans I have for you," declares the
> LORD, "plans to prosper you and not to harm
> you, plans to give you hope and a future."
> JEREMIAH 29:11

In Word

We look into our future and we fear. We are afraid of catastrophe, of heart-ache, of trouble and distress. We are afraid of crises in our finances, our families, and whatever else makes us feel secure. The problem is that we don't know the future, and we imagine all the bad things that can happen in it. Our fear springs from a lack of knowledge. When we look ahead, we look with ignorance.

God sees our entire future and tells us to relax. No, it may not be easy and pain free. It may not stroke us in all the places we like to be stroked by fulfilling all of our fantasies and dreams. But it will be good. It will fulfill all of God's plans for us, and His plans are never bad. He offers us hope and a future.

Those who say that God never promised us prosperity have missed this verse. What they mean is that God has not promised us prosperity as we often define it. That's true, but He has promised us prosperity as He defines it. Whether we've been held in captivity, as Jeremiah's audience had, or just gone through the school of hard knocks, we are under the watchful eye of God. He is directing and planning, restoring and forgiving, laying out a destiny that is full of His peace and purpose. The future is bright with the glory of God's grace.

In Deed

Why would anyone read a horoscope when they could take this promise to heart? No, it doesn't give specifics, but when the One who promises is God Himself, who needs specifics? We know the details will be good because the One who is ordaining them is good. Instead of clairvoyance, we need clear thinking. We need faith and rest in the character of God.

We have been given a destiny by the hand of God, the Giver of all good things. It is a plan for real prosperity and peace. It includes all His fullness and mercy. Cling to it. The only condition for it is turning and looking to Him.

Never be afraid to trust an unknown future to a known God.
—CORRIE TEN BOOM

Promised Answers

Ask and it will be given to you; seek and you will
find; knock and the door will be opened to you.

LUKE 11:9

In Word

God clothed Himself in human flesh and visited our planet. He was here all
along, of course, but not like this. Jesus was seen and heard, not in a mystical
sense, but visibly and audibly. And what did God incarnate say to us? "Ask Me,
and I will give to you."

We fail to realize the magnitude of this promise because we often don't
see its results. Oh, we pray. But perhaps not in the spirit Jesus intended, or
perhaps with selfish motives, or any number of other conditions that weaken
our prayers. Still, the promise is there. Those who persistently, faithfully,
humbly come to the Father with a petition are given a guarantee: It will be
answered.

We know all the standard ways to place conditions on this promise. He
may answer "no," He may answer "wait," He may answer "yes, but not in the
way you hoped," or He may actually answer "yes." When He does, He may not
answer right away. After all, this promise has no deadline; prayers we uttered
years ago may be answered years from now. But still, the promise is certain.
God will answer. Not to do so would make Him a negligent Father. And God
has proven throughout history that He is never negligent toward those who
seek Him and are called by His name.

In Deed

There's a temptation to water down this promise to the point where it means
very little. All of those conditions—those varying responses we speculate
that He might give, and those disqualifying attitudes with which we come
to Him—are legitimate aspects of this promise. The abuses are real. But this
promise is more real. Don't let the conditions and the qualifications water it
down to the point that it becomes unreal to you. The God who calls Himself
our Father is responsive, and He will never drop your prayers unless you
drop them first. Be persistent. Be bold. And be ready. God will honor your
request.

Pleading the promises of God is the whole secret of prayer.

—MARTYN LLOYD-JONES

Promised Fruit

**If you remain in me and my words remain in you,
ask whatever you wish, and it will be given you.**
JOHN 15:7

In Word

Taken by itself, it's a sweeping promise. "Whatever you wish," Jesus tells the disciples. He could have told them to say, "Not My will but yours," but He didn't. That was for other times and other contexts. Here He asks, "What's your will? If you could ask Me anything your heart desires, what would it be?" In this promise, the heart of the disciple matters.

Jesus could have restricted this promise with a few conditions in His following words, if He had wanted to. But we're given no hint of any backtracking. In fact, He emphasizes the promise again: "whatever you ask" (15:16; 16:23), and "ask and you will receive" (16:24). In His last instructions to His disciples before the Crucifixion, Jesus tells His disciples over and over again: Ask, ask, ask.

There's a heartwarming context to all of these instructions about prayer. It is the result of an intimate relationship with Him. We are to ask "so that the Son may bring glory to the Father" (14:13). We are to ask in order to "bear much fruit" and thereby glorify the Father (15:8). We are to ask so that our "joy will be complete" (16:24). In the context of a relationship with Jesus in which His words fill us and His personality has mixed and melded with ours, we are given perhaps the world's most extravagant promise outside of the promise of our salvation. We can ask anything in His name, for bearing fruit and glory, and expect Him to answer it.

In Deed

If a Fortune 500 company trained you to think and act in its best interests, and then handed you a pile of signed blank checks, what would you do with them? File them away? No, the temptation to use them would be too great. The CEO of the Kingdom of God has signed His name to a stack of checks and handed them to us—to use for advancing His interests. What will you do with them?

I would rather teach one man to pray than ten men to preach.
—JOHN HENRY JOWETT

Promised Presence

Surely I am with you always, to the very end of the age.
MATTHEW 28:20

In Word

We forget that our purpose in this world, after we have accepted Christ, is to make Him known. That is essential, secondary only to our grateful worship. It doesn't mean that we all become full-time evangelists, though we all have a responsibility to evangelize. It doesn't mean that we all must evangelize by means of public proclamation, though we have a responsibility to use words. It does mean, however, that we all are given the mandate to glorify the King of glory by somehow, someway, making our lives point to Him. And the purpose of all our pointing should be to make disciples.

How do we do that? In our weakness, we let Him be seen as our Strength. In our trials, we let Him be seen as our Refuge. In our victories, we let Him be seen as our Victor. In our humility, we let Him be seen as our Lord. In every circumstance we find ourselves in, no matter how glorious or how painful, there is a way to point to Him. It is our ultimate purpose. In fact, it's the ultimate purpose of all creation.

On this mission, we are given a great and precious promise: the King of glory is right there with us. We can't see Him, but we can talk to Him. Others can't see Him, but they can see that we're affected by Him. When we feel alone, we aren't. When we're in pain, so is He. When we're joyful, so is He. When we're tempted to sin, He is right there pointing to a way out. Our problem, despite all His presence, is in not looking for Him. Though the King is right there with us, we often ignore Him.

In Deed

Why would we do that? Perhaps we're just forgetful. Perhaps we want His eyes to turn away sometimes. Perhaps we've decided His presence isn't all that real or very relevant. But Jesus tells all of His disciples, including us, to focus on Him. Be aware of His presence. Remind yourself daily, hourly, or second by second that His Spirit is with you and in you. Never let yourself feel distant or independent. It will make all the difference in your discipleship. His promise is meant to draw you closer to Him.

God is always near you and with you; leave Him not alone.
—BROTHER LAWRENCE

Promised Transformation

**We, who with unveiled faces all reflect the
Lord's glory, are being transformed into his
likeness with ever-increasing glory.**
2 CORINTHIANS 3:18

In Word

Maybe you had your heart set on a promising career or a certain spouse.
Maybe you had planned out your education or your retirement. Maybe those
things became your preoccupation. Maybe you've lost sight of God's plan.

Your purposes for your life are not necessarily wrong, but unless you've
set your heart on being like Jesus, those purposes aren't the priority. God's
plan for you—for every one of us—is to make us look like Jesus. We were not
made to generate light; we were made to reflect it. And to the degree that we
are gazing at God and reflecting His glory to the world, we are fulfilling His
ultimate purpose for us.

It's an incredible purpose with an amazing promise. First we are approached
by the King of all creation, the ultimate authority in the entire universe, and
given the highest possible role in the Kingdom—to point to Him. Then we
are told that our purpose will inevitably be fulfilled. We may be slow learners,
and we may miss out on a lot of meaningful reflection in this world, but in the
end, we will be the spitting image of our Savior.

That was God's plan for us from before the foundation of the world. We
thought we were to build a career, start a family, and have a nice life of treating others well and loving God. But that was just a start. There's a greater
point to this life than living a nice life. We will be a demonstration of the
glory of God.

In Deed

Think of that. When all is said and done, we will be even more than shiny
trophies on God's mantel. We will be children who look like Him, apples who
fell very close to the tree. As He is radiant, so will we be. As He is merciful
and compassionate, so will we be. As He is glorified, so are we. The reflection will deepen and brighten for all eternity. Our lives could have no greater
purpose.

> Fire transforms all things it touches into its own nature. . . . In
> the same way, we are transformed into [the likeness of] God.
> —MEISTER ECKHART

Promised Heaven

We know that if the earthly tent we live
in is destroyed, we have a building from
God, an eternal house in heaven.

2 CORINTHIANS 5:1

In Word

There is an infinitely holy Spirit within this fallen flesh, and He makes us groan
with longing. It's a holy longing that feels the burdens of this world and craves
heavenly clothing. Under the weight of the world, heaven calls. We know we
were not born to be clothed in fallen flesh forever.

Eternity is in our hearts. We were crafted for it, and deep down, the heart
knows it. And when the Spirit fills our lives, we can taste it. The yearning
becomes conscious and the desire grows more intense. Our deep needs have
been confronted with a promise: Heaven waits for us.

Unless you are in peak form and full of vigor, you have already experienced frustration with this earthly tent. If you haven't yet, you will. It grows
old and weary eventually, and then it dies. The great and precious promises of
God have not forgotten that. The provision has been made. When hope in this
life proves futile, when bodies ache and souls cry out, we can count on the
glorious promise of resurrection. There is an eternal house fitted just for us.

In Deed

We often forget to live in this world with an eye on eternity, but tragedy and
hopelessness remind us to look ahead. One of the greatest gifts God has given
us in His Son is an incorruptible eternity with Him. In eternity, bodies will
not ache and tears will be wiped away. Trials will be forgotten and joy will be
made full. When that time comes, the groaning will stop.

Does the thought of the heavenly Kingdom influence your life today? It
should. Your life should be anchored in a future hope. That doesn't mean you
avoid living the Kingdom life right now; it only means that the Kingdom life
will be assaulted by trials and tribulations for a time. Unless you have your
heart set on heaven, the trials and tribulations will become unbearable. That's
why the Spirit has guaranteed what is to come. Eternity changes everything.

Earth has no sorrow that heaven cannot heal.

—THOMAS V. MOORE

Jealous Pursuit

**The LORD will be jealous for his land
and take pity on his people.**
JOEL 2:18

In Word

When parents warn their children of impending danger, it's never out of spite. We generally don't voice our concerns for the sake of criticizing. We have a much greater purpose: We want to avert potential harm. We don't want our kids to get hurt.

God's warnings of judgment usually come from similar motives. They never come without opportunity for repentance and promises of restoration, at least not when first sounded. They are designed to get His people to snap out of their delusions, to come to grips with His ways, to turn from their self-destructive behavior. When God sees His children swimming against powerful tides, He warns them of their futility. He takes pity on those He loves.

God's ultimate goal for Joel's audience, for the entire human race, and for each of us individually, is to pour out His blessings. Judgment is not, and never has been, His overriding purpose. It is only a tool of correction for humble hearts and a punishment for pridefully, stubbornly unrepentant hearts. The God of judgment has a greater concern than judgment: He wants His kingdom to bear fruit and flourish, blessing all who will come into it. God loves to demonstrate love.

In Deed

A lot of people don't know that. God's righteous judgment is often seen as the core of His character. Even Christians, who should be well informed about the love of God, sometimes live with a deep sense of guilt and an unsettling feeling that God is not on their side. But the jealousy of God is a solid scriptural teaching. And He isn't jealous because He's petty; He's jealous because His love is deep and intense.

God doesn't forgive halfway. He pursues His people and never gives up on them. When He chooses to bless, He doesn't relent. Not even His discipline gets in the way for long. He will satisfy His love by satisfying His beloved. Expect blessing. God certainly does.

The goal of God's discipline is restoration—
never condemnation.
—ANONYMOUS

Gracious Opportunity

**Return to the LORD your God, for he is
gracious and compassionate.**

JOEL 2:13

In Word

God has made it clear from the beginning what He desires from us. He wants humble hearts that love Him, that take pleasure in submitting to Him, and that welcome His will for their lives. Seems like that ought to be simple enough, but we have a way of complicating things—especially when we want to justify a certain level of independence from our Creator. Then we develop shades of truth and shadows of sin, relating to God in complex terms He never desired or authorized. We are masters of subtle rebellion.

But God's desire hasn't changed. He loves simplicity of devotion. He enjoys those who enjoy Him without compromising Him. He created us for the kind of intimate relationship with Him where we can rejoice together, weep together, work together, and love implicitly. And since we don't start out that way in life, there's no way to develop that kind of relationship without moving from where we are.

The good news is that God moved first. He did everything necessary for us to boldly approach His throne of grace and to enjoy His presence. Now it's our turn. We repent—or "return," as Joel says—by changing our minds about who He is and letting Him change our hearts to truly experience Him. The result of that turn is a God who is "abounding in love" and wild about showing you His mercies.

In Deed

If you want to experience the God who is on your side, who will defend you, lavish His love on you, provide for you, and bathe you in His favor, try the simple approach He prescribes. Turn toward Him, live in deep humility, believe His promises, and thank Him constantly for His mercies. You will begin to see—and enjoy—His presence more and more. A repentant, humble heart is like a God-magnet. He enthusiastically attaches to those who love Him. His tenderness surrounds them and His favor pours out on them. He never lets them down.

Repentance is the golden key that
opens the palace of eternity.

—JOHN MILTON

Happy Hearts

Be glad, O people of Zion, rejoice
in the Lord your God.
JOEL 2:23

In Word

There are a lot of hard commands in the Bible. This isn't one of them. Well, it shouldn't be one of them. The instruction to be glad and rejoice should be the most enjoyable command of all. If we ever needed permission to be happy people, this is it. God's own Word tells us to.

Why, then, don't we rejoice? Perhaps we don't know why we should, forgetting that God wouldn't tell us to be glad unless we had a really good reason to do so. Or maybe we obsess about what we don't yet have, focusing on the half-empty part of our glass rather than the half-full—or the 99 percent full, as it most likely is. Or perhaps we worry about the future, not realizing that negativity is nowhere mentioned as a characteristic of godliness. Regardless of the reason, the command to rejoice—reiterated many times over in the Bible—seems unrealistic.

But it's only unrealistic to those who ignore who God is and what He has promised. When we refuse to rejoice, we are refusing to acknowledge His deliverance, His provision, His favor, His power, His presence, and everything else He tells us is ours by faith. In a sense, it's slander. We impugn His character by focusing our attention on the negatives of the world rather than on the positives of His Kingdom. We forget that the negatives are temporary and the positives are eternal. When it comes to our moods, we have grossly misplaced priorities.

In Deed

Psalm 103:2 tells us not to forget any of God's benefits (a gentle rebuke, by the way, to those who don't think we should focus any attention on what God does for us). Remembering His benefits not only encourages us, but in many cases, it can be a safeguard against anxiety disorders and depression. The fact is that the Bible is very persistent in its instruction for us to "be glad." Nowhere in Scripture is negativity rewarded. Only those who look to God in hope and faith are honored. Spend some time today listing God's benefits. Let yourself be glad.

God cannot give us a happiness apart from
Himself because there is no such thing.
—C. S. LEWIS

Extravagant Gifts

I will pour out my Spirit on all people.
JOEL 2:28

In Word

Joel foresaw a day in which God would inhabit human flesh rather than a holy building. For those of us on this side of the day of Pentecost, it's hard to imagine the staggering implications for someone first hearing this prophetic prediction. Moses had spoken with God face-to-face, and prophets had heard His voice and seen His glory. But His Spirit on all flesh? That's mind-boggling.

It makes sense, though, doesn't it? Those like Isaiah and Ezekiel who saw visions of God saw Him surrounded by living creatures—angels to cover Him; awesome creatures with multiple faces, wings, and eyes who would move the appearance of His throne from place to place; and loud voices shouting His glory. There's nothing inanimate about the presence of God. A temple made from rocks and trees could never be a permanent residence. It was only a shadow of the flesh God would one day inhabit. God not only entered this world through a baby in a manger, He now enters it daily through those of us who live and breathe His presence.

If you think about it, that's the only way a desolate world can receive life. What God once created as a garden became a wasteland. There's no way for a wasteland to flourish unless the source of life is showered on it again. God's promise through Joel is to shower His life on this dark, dismal planet through those who know and believe that the Kingdom of God is in them. As people inhabited by the holy Presence, fragile clay vessels like us can become lights in the world.

In Deed

You may not feel like a light in the world today. You may not sense the Holy Spirit who was poured out on your flesh. One reason for your doubt may be that you've focused your attention on what you see rather than on what the Word has spoken to you. If so, the Presence will always be elusive to you, even though He is most certainly there. Believe that He's there, rest in the fact, ask for His power and purpose, and watch what God does. The desolate wilderness around your living temple will begin to thrive.

All of the Holy Spirit's influences are heaven begun, glory in the seed and bud.

—MATTHEW HENRY

The Glory of Wisdom

**The king said to Daniel, "Surely your God is
the God of gods and the Lord of kings."**

DANIEL 2:47

In Word

God's wisdom is noticeably different than the world's. Psalmists and kings craved it. The queen of Sheba even came an enormous distance to witness its fruits. It is "inside information" from the throne room of God, and it always has an impact on those privileged to be around it.

When wisdom is missing, the results can be tragic. The impact of a believer or church is practically nullified by a lack of wisdom. When God's people act in ignorance—which usually happens because of rash decisions, personal agendas, and not having an open mind when seeking God—the power of a testimony is lost. It's virtually impossible to witness to the power and purposes of God while living in futility.

That wasn't the case with Daniel, of course. The opposite was true: Daniel's ability to hear God's voice and accept His guidance had a powerful impact on the kings of Babylon and their pagan empire. It also had a powerful impact on God's own people, at times assuring their preservation and deliverance. When God's wisdom is made manifest, He receives glory.

In Deed

We live in a foolish world, and it's sad when Christians blend in. But we're just as capable of making reckless decisions as anyone, at least when we are not in the practice of listening to the voice of God and obeying His Word. A carefully cultivated relationship with Him rarely results in tragic missteps, but a person or church that functions in human wisdom without truly, diligently seeking God is destined for failure. The best we can do on our own is to establish respectable families and effective organizations. That's fine as far as it goes—but no one glorifies God over that.

No, praise results when the Revealer of mysteries leads us where no one could go without "inside information." God makes paths straight and fills us with purpose. When we live with His wisdom, people who do not know Him—even hardened ones like King Nebuchadnezzar—are introduced to His glory.

His wisdom's vast, and knows no bounds, a
deep where all our thoughts are drowned.

—ISAAC WATTS

Trust Uncompromised

This day is a day of distress and rebuke and
disgrace, as when children come to the point
of birth and there is no strength to deliver them.
ISAIAH 37:3

In Word

God had invested a lot in Israel. The nation had been through seasons of exuberant celebration over God's mercies and power, and it had been through seasons of open rebellion and dreadful consequences. Through it all, God had been faithful, upholding His covenant even while disciplining His children. But now the situation looked bleak. The Assyrians were surrounding Jerusalem and had the power to destroy it. King Hezekiah was in a jam.

The questions God had addressed through Isaiah in the first thirty-five chapters of the book all led up to this point: Is our God unique, or is He one of many gods among the nations? Does salvation come through political alliances or through God's power? When circumstances look impossible, can compromise make the best of a bad situation?

We know the answers to these questions, especially having read Israel's history and Isaiah's prophecy. We know the end of the story. But if we were within the walls of a surrounded city listening to the taunts of a God-mocking general who had already destroyed all the cities he'd previously attacked, we might waver between faith and compromise as Hezekiah did. We might see our nation, church, or family as a project God had started but was now aborting. We might feel the shame of bringing a baby to term and not having the strength to deliver it.

In Deed

As uncomfortable as it is, that's a great situation to be in if—and only if—it prompts us to put down our strategies and trust in God. Those who compromise their worship of God by bowing to the dictates of circumstances will never find rest. But biblical faith looks beyond walls, surrounding armies, and excruciating labor pains. It sees the God above them all, and it believes.

Never doubt in the dark what God told you in the light.
—VICTOR RAYMOND EDMAN

Fear Undone

I am going to put a spirit in him so that when he hears
a certain report, he will return to his own country,
and there I will have him cut down with the sword.
ISAIAH 37:7

In Word

In the midst of a desperate situation, Isaiah gave Hezekiah the reassurance he needed: "Do not be afraid of what you have heard—those words with which the underlings of the king of Assyria have blasphemed me" (v. 6). In other words, Hezekiah was to ignore the fact that a powerful army was surrounding him. He was to look instead to the character of the God who made a commitment to the kingdom long, long ago. He was reminded to focus on who was really in charge.

That advice is easy to hear and to accept as God's voice. For many of us, however, it's nearly impossible to follow. We want to believe it. We say we believe it. We just have a hard time keeping our minds off of the threats. We worry about what will happen next and how we'll manage to deal with it. We play out scenarios in our minds about all the possibilities before us, calculating our responses to almost endless variations. We become downright obsessive.

The words of God in verse 7 ought to remind us how silly our obsessions can be. God can put a spirit of any kind into an enemy or a situation. He doesn't manipulate the human race like a puppeteer, but He certainly knows how to use our moods, decisions, and circumstances for His purposes. And when those who oppose His Kingdom have made a stand for their own agenda, He can harden a heart (like Pharaoh's) or instill fear (as He did with the king of Assyria) to thwart them. God's desire is to establish His own plan. If we're in line with it, we have nothing to fear.

In Deed

Ask God today how His heart perceives your circumstances. Draw near to Him in intimacy and let Him whisper His plans in your ear. You'll be encouraged by what you hear. He's sovereign, and nothing can thwart His purposes for you. Lay down your obsessive fears and be fascinated with His goodness instead.

It is only the fear of God that can deliver
us from the fear of man.
—JOHN WITHERSPOON

Worship Unrestrained

O LORD Almighty, God of Israel, enthroned
between the cherubim, you alone are God
over all the kingdoms of the earth.

ISAIAH 37:16

In Word

When Hezekiah received the message from Isaiah that the God-mocking
Assyrian would be thwarted, he had a couple of options: He could continue
in his anxiety, or he could worship God. There was no other alternative. He
had been given no allies to persuade and no plan to execute—only a promise that God would save. Worship would be a statement of faith. Continuing
anxiety would be the opposite.

Hezekiah chose to worship. His heart was compliant enough to know
God's voice when he heard it. If God said He would deliver, He would deliver.
The living God, the faithful and true, does not lie. Why should He? He has
nothing to hide and lacks no power to accomplish His purposes—so none of
the reasons we lie apply to Him. He has absolutely no lack of integrity. Hezekiah believed God's promise to save.

But Hezekiah did more than believe. He prayed. He could have worshiped
God in advance for the victory and waited for it to happen. He knew, however,
that there's a difference between the promise of God and the execution of
the promise. The promise was given to provoke faith. Prayer—the kind that
banks on the promise, not just hopes that it might come true—was the natural
response. God tells us what He is going to do so that we will ask Him to do
it. Hezekiah, unlike many of us, seemed to understand that.

In Deed

That dynamic of promise, then prayer, then fulfillment is a running theme
throughout Scripture. God affirmed it to Hezekiah a few verses later, telling
him that the word would be fulfilled "because you have prayed to me con-
cerning Sennacherib" (v. 21). It's a dynamic we need to learn and relearn. The
promises of God are not fatalistic guarantees; they are a call to prayer. They are
intended to dispel our fears, stir up faith, and put us on our knees. We won't
see them simply by sitting on a couch and letting them happen. Accept your
call to arms. Get stirred up. Pray the promises of the faithful and true God.

The Word of God represents all the possibilities
of God as at the disposal of true prayer.

—A. T. PIERSON

Faith Unpersuaded

It is true, O Lᴏʀᴅ, that the Assyrian kings have
laid waste all these peoples and their lands.

ISAIAH 37:18

In Word

God had promised to deliver Hezekiah from Sennacherib, the vicious king of
Assyria. Hezekiah had believed the promise and prayed for it to come to pass.
According to popular theology, that should be the end of the story. It's a rock-
solid formula: promise plus faith equals the powerful intervention of God.

But our God is not a formula God, and popular theology isn't always true.
We can't live the Christian life assuming that faith in a promise is a simple
formula. It's true that God makes promises, and it's just as true that we receive
their fulfillment by faith, but there's a lot that happens between the faith and
the fulfillment. Threats grow larger and promises get tested. And God allows
it; that's how faith is stretched to be more God-sized than we've ever known
it to be.

Hezekiah knew the dynamic well. While his faith was being severely
tested, he acknowledged how devastating Assyria's army had been. The invading kingdom's territory was massive; Jerusalem was a lonely holdout in a
vast empire. The odds were enormous that Sennacherib would complete his
conquests by sacking the city of God's people. That's why his taunts were so
boastful (vv. 10-13). But Hezekiah knew that God doesn't give in to the odds.
He understood that the enormity of a threat is always minuscule compared to
the enormity of God. He insisted on believing.

In Deed

That's the posture of a Christian life: insisting on believing. We can't afford
to live by formulas. The Holy Spirit is always on the move, stretching our
faith this way and that way. It's never predictable and always challenging.
Those who live by faith have to expect the unexpected. And we have to persist through all obstacles to stake a claim on what we know is true: that God
always comes through.

> You never know how much you really believe anything until its
> truth or falsehood becomes a matter of life and death to you.
>
> —C. S. LEWIS

Blessing Unhindered

Now, O LORD our God, deliver us from his
hand, so that all kingdoms on earth may
know that you alone, O LORD, are God.
ISAIAH 37:20

In Word

There's no better testimony than a story of supernatural intervention.
When an unwavering pattern is broken by an unexplainable force, people
take notice. Natural laws build into us certain expectations: gravity pulls us
down, incurable diseases take lives, and might makes right in politics and
war. So when natural laws are made to bow before a greater power, it's a
remarkable event.

Hezekiah understood that there was a greater purpose in his prayer than
saving his skin. There's no doubt that he desired personal safety for himself,
his city, and his people, but he saw a bigger picture. He knew that if an invading king who had never been stopped was suddenly stopped, the world would
take notice. The God of the people who stopped him would be glorified. A
weak city spared from a strong army would be shown to be unexplainably
blessed.

That dynamic has been repeated often in Israel's history and in the history
of Christian communities in oppressive countries. God is the defender of the
underdog when the underdog happens to be someone close to His heart. Any
power can prevail against human beings alone; no power can prevail against
human beings backed by God.

In Deed

How can your life, your family, and your church impact the world? They
have to be supernatural and unexplainable, provocatively over and above all
rationalizations. Only then does a status-quo world take notice of a peculiar
people. Natural laws are noticeable only when they're broken.

Live a supernatural life. Let God put His dreams into your heart, dreams
that are so impossible that only He can fulfill them. Then live by faith in His
might—visibly and powerfully. Ask God to make your life and your church
unexplainable forces in your world.

Attempt something so great for God it's
doomed to failure unless God be in it.
—JOHN HAGGAI

A Prayer to Shine

You have taken off your old self with its practices
and have put on the new self, which is being
renewed in knowledge in the image of its Creator.
COLOSSIANS 3:9-10

In Word

Long, long ago, we were made in the image of God. Sin corrupted that image, and it became hardly recognizable. The new creation, though, has not abandoned that image. God is re-creating it in us, day by day and bit by bit. Romans 8:29 tells us that we are being conformed to the image of Christ, and Colossians 1:15 tells us that Christ is the image of God. Through the divine Mediator, the image is being restored.

That's a process. Today's verse tells us that we have exchanged selves, the old for the new. It was a once-for-all transaction, but the verb tense changes noticeably halfway through the sentence. We have exchanged selves; we are being renewed. The image of God in us is being restored as painstakingly as a Michelangelo masterpiece. In the meantime, we often lose sight of the goal.

Remind yourself frequently. The ultimate purpose for your life is to be a worshiper, but the only way to be a true worshiper is to reflect the glory and the image of Jesus. We are told that we are being transformed into His likeness with ever-increasing glory. We are reflectors of the image of Christ, who is the image of God. Our primary purpose in this world (and the next) is to reflect Him well.

In Deed

That's a profound thought. This transformation touches every area of our lives, from our skin and bones to the deepest corners of our psyche. It should affect the words we speak, the endeavors we pursue, the relationships we cultivate, and the moral purity we embrace. And there's a requirement for it: It can only come through prayer.

The image of God is clearly given from above; it is not a matter of willpower and self-improvement. And all things from above come through prayer. Today, pray that the light of Jesus would reflect from you in ever-increasing intensity.

The rule of life for a perfect person is to be
in the image and likeness of God.
—CLEMENT OF ALEXANDRIA

More of Christ?

God has chosen to make known among the
Gentiles the glorious riches of this mystery,
which is Christ in you, the hope of glory.
COLOSSIANS 1:27

In Word

How many Christians struggle to receive more of Christ, more of His Spirit, more of His presence? It's a common misperception, commendable for its right assessment of human sin and the gospel's promises. But it is a misperception. How can we, who have Christ living within us, get more of Christ? He's already there. We already have the One we so desperately need.

The desire to grow in our relationship to Jesus is right; perhaps our methodology is not. What we need to realize is that Jesus really, truly indwells the person who believes in Him. The problem isn't that we need more of Jesus in the equation; it's that we need less of ourselves so our perception of Him will be more accurate.

Envision a candle enveloped by a stained-glass shade. If the glass is encrusted with dirt, the candle will hardly shine through. It isn't the flame's fault—it's burning brightly enough already. The problem lies in the shade. Erode the layers of grime, and the flame will be visible. Tolerate the dirt, and it won't. It's that simple.

When we feel a need to have more of Jesus' Spirit, what we really crave is a clearer experience of Him. A persistent prayer life that appropriates His cleansing power, along with a cooperative willingness to do the work of self-denial and attitude adjustments, will make Him more real, both to us and to those who observe us. Lights shine brilliantly and beautifully through clear glass. Our Light seeks clarity in us.

In Deed

Quit striving for more of God. You have Him already, if you have believed in the resurrection power of His Son. The living, breathing Spirit of Jesus dwells within the heart of faith. Let Him remove your outer shell of hindrances—pride, discouragement, misplaced desires, and the deceptions the enemy has lodged in your heart. The need is not for Him to increase, but for the barriers to Him to decrease.

God reigns in the hearts of His servants; there is His kingdom.
—JEREMY TAYLOR

Search and Find

**You will seek me and find me when
you seek me with all your heart.**
JEREMIAH 29:13

In Word

Most Christians would say they have found God. And it's true; those who have accepted Jesus as their Savior have in fact found the Father and His will for their lives. But often our knowledge of God goes no further than our minds. In many ways, we're still looking.

In some respects, we're not much different than the Jews of Jeremiah's day. They too had found God. Actually, God had found them—first by choosing their father Abraham, then by prying them out of slavery in Egypt, then by descending on Sinai with a covenant. Jeremiah's listeners and readers had the Torah and all the laws revealed through Moses. They had a miraculous history of God's dealings with them. If you asked any of Jeremiah's contemporaries if they had found God, they would have said yes. Just like us.

Was that enough? No, of course not. If it had been, Jeremiah would not have penned verse 13. God would not have inspired him to prophesy to these people how they would one day seek Him with all their heart. He would have said, "You've already found me. So live like you have." As we know, that wasn't God's message to them—or to us.

In Deed

There's a seeking after God that goes beyond the ink on the paper of your Bible, that goes further than His past dealings with you, and that goes deeper than you are right now. Even David—a man after God's own heart, as we're often reminded—hungered and thirsted for God with desperate desire (Psalm 63:1, for example). David wasn't content to say he had found God. There was always more of God to be found.

Is your heart content? When we see Him face-to-face, we'll marvel at how much of Him there is to discover. Like a tourist satisfied with a glimpse of the spray from Niagara Falls, we'll be ashamed at our ignorance when we see what we missed by not pressing in for a fuller view. Seek God with all your heart—every bit of it—and you won't be disappointed.

Thou hast made us for Thyself, and the heart of
man is restless until it finds its rest in Thee.
—AUGUSTINE

Hide and Seek

**"I will be found by you," declares the LORD,
"and will bring you back from captivity."**
JEREMIAH 29:14

In Word

In the Garden of Eden, Adam and Eve hid from God. In the Song of Songs, the bridegroom was hidden from the bride. Much of Scripture, it seems, is hide-and-seek between God and His people. Sometimes they seek Him with all their heart, and other times they hide. Sometimes He surprises them with His presence, and other times He maintains His distance to keep them coming closer. In Scripture, God isn't always easily found, and we aren't always looking. But when God and His people are in each other's presence, things happen. The relationship deepens and activity increases. We bestow gifts on Him—our lives and offerings—and He bestows gifts on His beloved.

God promised the captive Jews that if they sought Him, they would find Him, and if they found Him, they would be brought back from their exile. He fully intended that the hide-and-seek would have a satisfying outcome. He wanted to be sought, and He promised to be found.

Our relationship with God is like that too. We get frustrated sometimes because we think it ought to be a cause-and-effect formula: When we follow certain steps, there God is. When He isn't, we get confused.

The Bible doesn't give us a formula, though. It calls us into a relationship. Like a courtship in which each member sometimes pursues and sometimes plays hard-to-get, love is cultivated in the dynamics of attraction. The pursuit is eventually rewarded. The one who plays hard-to-get is eventually gotten. There comes a time when both are satisfied—much more so than if the relationship were an instant event.

In Deed

Look at your relationship with God like a courtship and expect a satisfying result. Things will happen when you seek Him. You will find each other's presence, and He will bestow gifts on His beloved. He wants to. And He knows that deep down inside, so do you.

Seeking with faith, hope, and love pleases our Lord;
and finding Him pleases the soul, filling it full of joy.
—JULIAN OF NORWICH

Promise and Paradise

I will gather you from all the nations and
places where I have banished you.
JEREMIAH 29:14

In Word

The Jews in captivity would be restored back to what they had lost—the Land of Promise. That's always the way of God for those who seek Him. Job, after all his troubles, was given double what he'd lost because he clung to God and never let go. Joseph was made doubly fruitful in the land of his affliction because he never lost sight of the God who was always with him, even in Egypt. When God's people lose what they were promised—whether through their own sin or someone else's—and continue to seek Him where He may be found, the result is always better than at first. God's abundance never decreases the second time around.

So it is with the world at large. Adam and Eve fell and were exiled from the Garden, and it's a long, long exile. But God makes a promise to all those in this world who will seek Him with all their heart: They will find Him, and in finding Him they will be restored to what was lost. And from what we know about God's restoration, the next paradise will be much better than the first. The Garden of Eden was only the beginning. The best is yet to come.

That's how we are to live in this world: as citizens of what's yet to come. There is no grief, no sin, no problem, no frustration, no captivity, no abuse that cannot be redeemed, and the redemption will be more than worthwhile. Paul assured us that the glory to be revealed will far outweigh anything in our present circumstances; that no eye has seen or ear heard what God has in store for those who love Him (1 Corinthians 2:9). We're to live like we know that.

In Deed

If we live like we know what's coming—with a smile of anticipation we can hardly suppress—people will ask us to explain the hope we have within us. We can then tell them of the restoration God promises and how to get in on the plan. We can introduce them to the God who wants to be found. We can end the captivity of many.

There is only one real inevitability: it is
necessary that the Scripture be fulfilled.

—CARL F. H. HENRY

Delightful Fear

He will delight in the fear of the LORD.
ISAIAH 11:3

In Word

Delight and fear. To the human mind, they seem utterly contradictory. We're well familiar with fear, and it's anything but delightful. It ties our stomach in knots, raises the hairs on our neck, and keeps us awake at night. We spend long hours turning over every future possibility in our mind so we can avoid the most dreadful ones. We position ourselves as far away from fear as we can. And yet the Messiah, we are told, will delight in the fear of the Lord.

We find this concept so difficult to comprehend that we redefine what Scripture means by "fear." It's awe or reverence, we assure ourselves, confident that God would never want us to be afraid of Him. We see from a single writer in Hebrews that we are to boldly approach the throne of grace (4:16) and that it's a terrifying thing to fall into the hands of the living God (10:31). We see from a single disciple that it's okay to lean on Jesus' chest in intimate repose (John 13:23), that perfect love casts out fear (1 John 4:18), and that it's paralyzing to see Jesus in His glory (Revelation 1:17). The people who saw God most clearly in Scripture were the people who were simultaneously most comfortable and most terrified in His presence. We don't know how to reconcile that.

Jesus shows us how. He delighted in the fact that God is awesome and transcendent. He knew that the reality of God would cause a holy terror of His majesty. We can get glimpses of this paradox when we stand at the edge of the Grand Canyon or Niagara Falls. They are both beautiful and frightening, yet they are only extremely tiny fractions of the magnitude of God. It is a delightful kind of fear, and Jesus had it.

In Deed

Imagine being assured by the Almighty that you will safely walk a tightrope over a three-thousand-foot gorge. Even with no chance of falling, your heart would race from fear and exhilaration. That's a small picture of our attitude in God's presence: thrilling, terrifying, awesome, and very safe. It's a strange place to be.

Let your times of intimacy with God get you to that place of awe. It will change your life from the inside out.

> Men who fear God face life fearlessly. Men who
> do not fear God end up fearing everything.
> —RICHARD HALVERSON

True Righteousness

**With righteousness he will judge the needy, with
justice he will give decisions for the poor of the earth.**
ISAIAH 11:4

In Word

According to Isaiah, the Messiah would not judge by what He saw and heard
(v. 3). Instead, He would judge the needy with righteousness, bring justice on
behalf of the poor, speak truth to the earth, and rebuke the wicked. In other
words, He would make things right.

We admire that about our Savior. He defended the defenseless, went out
of His way to lift up those who were beaten down, fed those who were hungry,
healed those who were sick, touched those who were dirty and offensive, and
suffered for those who didn't deserve it. We praise Jesus for His compassion
precisely because He demonstrated it in these ways. And yet, though we say
we want to be conformed to His image, we don't do much to demonstrate
compassionate love like He did.

Think about that: Many churches are concerned for the poor and needy,
but usually not in heavily sacrificial ways. When we come to Christ, we define
righteousness in terms of morality and purity, not realizing that God defines it
more fully. The righteousness of Jesus goes out of its way to take care of those
who do not deserve His mercy, and it does so in visible, practical ways. If we
have His righteousness, we'll do the same.

In Deed

In all of our conforming to His image, it's easy to forget this side of it. Jesus
is self-sacrificing, deeply concerned for the poor and downtrodden, willing
to go out of His way for the rough and ragged. We define "righteousness" as
honesty and moral purity. Jesus defines it much more broadly. His is the kind
of righteousness that zealously goes after everything that isn't right in the
world in order to make it reflect God's Kingdom.

As you pray to be made in the image of Christ, remember what that
image looks like. It has practical, tangible fruit. If you have His image, you
will too.

Christ came to reveal what righteousness really is.
—MATTHEW ARNOLD

The Power of a Life

**The earth will be full of the knowledge of
the LORD as the waters cover the sea.**
ISAIAH 11:9

In Word

One man came into the world empowered by the Spirit of God, full of faith
and obedience, passionate about the will of God, and zealous about making
right the things that are wrong—that's how the Branch is described in Isaiah
11—and the world has never been the same. Nor will it ever be the same.

We tend to think that the Messiah's reign is simply the result of His
being the Messiah, a natural outgrowth of His identity. But it's more than
that; it's the supernatural result of a life wholly committed to God. The reason the earth will be full of the knowledge of the Lord is that someone holy
and pure came and demonstrated the knowledge of the Lord. As we follow
Him and are being made in His likeness, that knowledge spreads. Eventually,
it will be as extensive and complete as the water that covers the sea.

The Messiah's reign is still expanding, and we have the awesome privilege of participating in its growth. To the extent that we, like Jesus, live out
our knowledge of God, the world gets a glimpse of that knowledge. To the
extent that we, like Jesus, are empowered by the Spirit, full of faith and
obedience, passionate about God's will, and zealous about righting wrongs,
we'll cover the earth with His glory. We can bear the image of the Messiah
just like He did.

In Deed

Does that sound like too bold a claim? Jesus told His disciples they would be
like Him, be filled with His Spirit, be sent on His mission, and do His works.
If we think it's too bold to claim His image, we're choosing to ignore His
words. The knowledge of God will cover the earth because Jesus' disciples
will cover the earth.

Live as an image-bearer. That's how we were created in the Garden, and
that's what Jesus redeemed us for. The world needs people who will be like
Jesus in every way, full of faith and truth. The power of God changes lives
through lives that have been changed to be like Him.

> Be much with the solid teachings of God's word.
> . . . They shall produce in you a Christ-likeness
> at which the world shall stand astonished.
> —CHARLES SPURGEON

Fellowship with God

**If I have found favor in your eyes, my
lord, do not pass your servant by.**
GENESIS 18:3

In Word

Abraham received a special visit. One day, out of the blue, three "men" showed up—God and two angels, it seems by the time the rest of the story is told. After doing what was culturally appropriate for highly honored guests—providing shade and water and arranging a lavish meal—Abraham stood by and watched them eat. His hospitality was rewarded; God didn't eat and run. In fact, God stayed, talked, reiterated an old promise, and divulged new secrets. Apparently, that's what happens when God is welcomed with open arms.

Think of the implications! When God shows up in our lives—and He always does, although we are sometimes slow to recognize Him—we are to honor Him with our hospitality. Having done that, we can expect the same gift Abraham got: the God who lingers and speaks.

Does that seem like a stretch? After all, we never received the personal promises Abraham received. That covenant was unique to him, wasn't it? But as Scripture goes on to say, we are heirs of the very same covenant (Romans 4:16). The special attention Abraham received is part of the inheritance. God may not deal with us in exactly the same way, but He deals with us with exactly the same character. His love and holiness aren't exclusive to Abraham. His promise clearly extends beyond Abraham to many descendants and many nations (Genesis 12:3). The God who approached Abraham approaches us.

In Deed

Are you hospitable toward God? When He comes to you in the heat of the day, do you bow before Him, offer Him the refreshment of your hospitality, and give of your possessions? Do you aim to serve? Then don't be surprised if God lingers. Don't be surprised if He communicates with you as with a privileged friend. Show Him honor, and He'll spend the day. That's what Abraham did, and the blessings of fellowship with God were extended and intensified.

Hospitality is one form of worship.
—ANONYMOUS

Love the Lord

**Love the Lord your God with all your heart
and with all your soul and with all your
mind and with all your strength.**

MARK 12:30

In Word

Is the Christian life primarily about loving or doing? It's a tricky question, isn't it? On the one hand, if we say that love is the priority, we risk blending in with the rest of the world. After all, everyone loves. The objects of love may differ, but the presence of love is nearly universal. If our faith is about love—at least the human type—we're not very distinguishable from the corrupt world we live in.

On the other hand, if action is the priority, we're only one step away from becoming card-carrying Pharisees. Nearly every religion is filled with long "to do" lists. There is no end to the activities that spiritually hungry minds can come up with in an effort to get closer to God. The problem is, as we know, that good behavior never made any sinner acceptable to a holy God. It's never enough.

So how can we love God in an authentically Christian way? When Jesus tells His listeners to love God with everything in them, what does He mean? What does that look like in the life of an ordinary believer? Is it a feeling? an action? an unsolvable mystery?

In Deed

The love we are to have for God is unique among loves. It is comprehensive. It is a radical reorientation of life around what we consider to be ultimately, overwhelmingly valuable. Is it a feeling? It certainly involves our emotions. Is it an action? It certainly involves our behavior. But it is more.

Loving God means doing God's will because we treasure and value His plans. It means feeling passion for Him because He is worthy of our passions. It means expending all our emotional, spiritual, mental, and physical energy for His sake and not our own. Though we still relate to others and have activities in this world, everything is now in reference to His central role in our lives. As our greatest love, He takes His place at the core of our being.

> A man's spiritual health is exactly
> proportional to his love for God.
>
> —C. S. LEWIS

With All Your Heart

If you love me, you will obey what I command.
JOHN 14:15

In Word

Why is the Christian life so hard sometimes? There are probably lots of legitimate reasons; after all, Jesus never promised that it would be easy. But one troubling reason shows up in our lives frequently: We find it hard to obey God because we don't want to obey Him. And when we don't want to obey Him, it's usually because stronger desires compete against Him.

Think about that. If God were truly the deepest passion in our hearts, anything that could interrupt our relationship with Him would be horrifying to us. And yet we entertain such interruptions frequently. The reason must be some deficiency in our love. We human beings have never had much trouble following our passions. If we have trouble following God, should we conclude that God is not our passion?

It seems logical. We always lean in the direction of the heart's desires. We often have to subdue those longings and discipline ourselves against them. But suppose those desires always pointed in God's direction. Our leanings would naturally take us where we need to go. Righteousness would be our instinct, not our obligation. Obedience would be our desire, not our hard discipline. God would have His way with us because His way would be the one we crave.

In Deed

Does that oversimplify our struggles? Maybe. But they often, if not always, can be traced to a lack of love. We need to be reminded of our duties only when our hearts are not naturally following them. The reason we need self-discipline is because of competing desires.

That's why the greatest commandment is to love God. Not only is this the reason for which we were created—and therefore the only means by which we can be fulfilled—it is also the key to discipleship, spiritual formation, evangelism, community, and more. A heart that loves God thoroughly is a heart that adoringly falls in line with His will and His ways. It's a heart that naturally grows spiritually mature—and enjoys it.

> Obedience to God is the most infallible evidence
> of sincere and supreme love for Him.
> —NATHANAEL EMMONS

Worshipful Affection

God has poured out his love into our hearts
by the Holy Spirit, whom he has given us.

ROMANS 5:5

In Word

There's a huge difference between knowing God as an obligation and loving Him as a companion. Though He is Lord, He doesn't mean to "lord" it over us, demanding obsessive obedience. He much prefers the kind of obedience that comes from affection and trust. As children who are enamored of their father, we are to love Him not with compulsion but with joy. Not to do so hardly fulfills the command to love Him.

But for many of us, that's a problem. We love God with a sterile sense of duty rather than with an overflowing passion. Our minds know the right thing to do, and in our best moments, we do them. But if our hearts are not in it? Well, we can love Him anyway, and we should. But it isn't the best kind of love. He offers us a better way. Duty doesn't connect us with His heart nearly as much as affectionate trust that what He has told us to do is good.

How can fickle hearts like ours love Him that way? How can our apathetic condition be transformed into an intimate, joyful love? There's only one way. God offers to pour His love into our hearts. As Paul testifies, we rejoice in the hope of the glory of God because God has granted us the pleasure of doing so. Whatever hope we have in God, even when it comes through suffering and perseverance (vv. 3-4), does not disappoint. Why? Because it comes from God. He's the source of our love.

In Deed

If you've ever been frustrated at your level of love, welcome to the human race. Our hearts are hard and are not softened easily. But there's hope: We aren't called to generate more love. We're told that love comes from the Spirit at work in us. The fact that love for God doesn't come naturally doesn't matter. We have a supernatural source.

If you want to love God more, try this: Ask Him to pour out His love in your heart. Test Him and see. Such prayers never remain unanswered for long.

The Spirit of God first imparts love.

—D. L. MOODY

With All Your Soul

O God, you are my God, earnestly
I seek you; my soul thirsts for you.
PSALM 63:1

In Word

When the Bible refers to your soul, what does it mean? It isn't simply the spiritual life, as modern culture has defined it. It involves everything about you: your personality, your will, your thoughts, your inner life. In the Law and the historical books of the Old Testament, the soul is almost always linked with the heart. In Job, it is almost always the place of bitterness. Anywhere in Scripture, it can be the site of grief, anguish, boasting, or great delight. "Soul" is the most comprehensive term for your life in the Bible, other than "life" itself.

So what does God mean when He tells us to worship Him with all our soul? It means that deep in the core of our being, where we can hardly discern between good and bad motives or right and wrong desires, that's where God must reign. It means that there can be no corner of our true selves that God does not touch. It means being laid completely bare before Him and letting the integrity of our love for Him—not to mention His love for us—shine brighter than any rival. It means that we love Him like our life depends on it.

Why is that so hard to do? Because it has to be real. It's all or nothing. No one loves God with all his or her soul at about a 90 percent success rate. The soul cannot be compartmentalized into one area of life that loves God while other areas are withheld. If we've pledged our souls to Him, we've pledged ourselves. We're His. There's nothing left to hold on to.

In Deed

The soul is hard to define, but God doesn't really ask us to define it. He asks us to love Him with it. He tells us that our life is all about Him. That affects our commitments, our passions, our drives, our motives, our thoughts, our feelings, our will, and our ways. Our whole personality is to revolve around Him as the earth revolves around the sun. Our soul is the center of our lives, and He is to be the center of our soul. When we dive deep down inside, we should find Him there. That's what it means to love Him with our soul.

Lord, You are my lover, my longing, my flowing
stream, my sun, and I am Your reflection.
—MECHTILDE OF MAGDEBURG

Worshipful Will

To you, O LORD, I lift up my soul.
PSALM 25:1

In Word

When God tells us to love Him with all of our soul, how do we actually do that? How is it possible to submit such a vague concept of ourselves to such a concrete command? The soul involves so much of us, isn't it a massive undertaking to surrender it to God?

That depends. Over the course of one's life, it's a massive undertaking. Today, it isn't. Think about that: God never asks us to love Him completely and consummately forever. He wants that, of course, but He doesn't approach us that way. He approaches us right now. He wants us to love Him with everything in us at the moment. He wants that for this moment, and then when the next moment comes, He'll want that again. But our whole lives all at once? He doesn't give our lives to us that way; we can't offer them back to Him that way.

That makes loving God a whole lot easier, doesn't it? Whatever decision is facing us today is the decision in which God wants us to demonstrate our love for Him. Whatever struggle we're having, or whatever depression we're feeling, He only asks us to turn it over to Him minute by minute. We struggle with our eternal commitment to our Creator, but the struggle of the moment, while difficult, is a lot easier. Our strategy for loving God is a matter of the here and now, not of the one day and forever.

In Deed

Why is that important to know? Because if we look at the big picture, we'll get depressed quickly. We can see our failures in the context of our whole lives and assume that we've done a miserable job of loving God. Just like a married couple that always lives in the past, we'll be doomed to repeat it—we'll question our devotion because our devotion has a spotted track record. Or like a couple that hopes for the future but ignores the present road to get there, we'll question our devotion because it always seems unattainable. God helps us not to play those mind games. He wants our love in the immediate decision, the current workload, and the present mood. Give Him your life and your love, one manageable minute at a time.

There is only one time that is important—now!
—LEO TOLSTOY

With All Your Mind

We have not received the spirit of the world
but the Spirit who is from God, that we may
understand what God has freely given us.

1 CORINTHIANS 2:12

In Word

Your mind has been highly trained. Maybe you didn't know that, but it's true. From the day you were born, you have been taught how to live. Your family, your culture, and your own exploration have given you plenty of ideas about who you are, how your world works, and what your God is like. The problem is that you've grown up with a finite mind in a corrupt world.

According to the Bible, we all begin with a darkened understanding. Despite the best intentions of our families and friends, our culture, and our own senses, we have distorted perspectives. Our understanding is only as good as the influences that have shaped it. And, in most cases, that's not good enough. What's the solution? Paul says to "be transformed by the renewing of your mind" (Romans 12:2). That means that once we've embraced God's truth in Christ, we're to embrace His truth about everything. We are to reject our old perspectives and live by the Spirit of truth.

Living the gospel, of course, is not simply a matter of the intellect. If it were, brilliant people would have it made, and the mentally handicapped would be far from God's blessing. But we know that isn't the case. We know that when God talks about obtaining wisdom from Him, it's about perspective and wise living. It's about knowing what to do with the circumstances, the gifts, and the relationships He has given us.

In Deed

Do you know what to do with God's resources? Do you know how to spend your life? Knowing such things requires a lot of time in His presence, His Word, and the community He has established. The only way to retrain a mind is by immersion. Old thought patterns are simply too deep; they can't be redirected without considerable trauma. Let the Spirit of God, the Word of God, and the people of God immerse you in His grace. Let your mind love Him in every way.

To possess a Spirit-indwelt mind is the
Christian's privilege under grace.

—A. W. TOZER

Worshipful Wisdom

The mind of sinful man is death, but the mind
controlled by the Spirit is life and peace.
ROMANS 8:6

In Word

Life and peace. Every human being craves such blessings. Every human being
strives for them too. The striving can take many forms. Some seek their life
and peace in work, others in relationships. Some focus on their sexuality, others on intellectual inquiry. Some even reduce life and peace to such things as
eating and drinking, or spending and acquiring. Pleasure, passions, and people
become the objects of our desire, as we try to construct our life and peace
from the things around us. And though we seek the blessing of life and peace
in such things, we are really accomplishing death for ourselves. Nothing will
satisfy apart from the Spirit of God. Nothing.

The mind is a miraculous thing. It's also corrupt. It doesn't know how to
worship God until it is told. Even then, it must be empowered. Fallen flesh
does not worship God naturally, so our only hope is beyond the natural. If
we really want life and peace, we have to realize that the mind will not find it
with its own intuition or inquiry. It has to embrace an outside Guide. It needs
the Spirit of God.

Contrary to the tradition of many Christians, the mind is a critical locus
of worship. The heart has its passions, and God loves it when those passions
are directed toward Him. But God is worshiped logically and reasonably as
well. The Logos who designed all of creation with unfathomable brilliance
and precision is worthy of our worship, and our worship of Him is not to be a
worship from ignorance. The Creator gave us our own minds so that we might
begin to understand His.

In Deed

Use your brain. That's the encouragement of all the Scriptures that urge wisdom and intelligent worship. But submit your brain to the guidance of the
Spirit. Make this your prayer: Lord, fill my mind with Your thoughts; give
me insight into Your ways; help me to appreciate Your wisdom. Let my mind
behold Your glory. Grant me life and peace through Your Spirit.

Sanctification is the mind coming more and
more under the Holy Spirit's control.
—DAVID JACKMAN

With All Your Strength

It is God who arms me with strength.
PSALM 18:32

In Word

In the Bible, strength is very physical. It was the subject of psalms and songs whenever Israel defeated its enemies. It was the genius of Joshua, the blessing of Samson, and the provision of David. It secured Israel's borders and over-came its obstacles. And it always came from God.

In the Bible, strength is also often internal. It was the intestinal fortitude of those who engaged enormous Philistines or corrupt kings. It was seen in the zeal of Elijah, the boldness of Daniel, and the perseverance of Jeremiah. It was a sure sign of confidence in the power and glory of God, and it was the intended result of the Bible's frequent command not to be afraid. It was the courage that grows from knowing the Almighty. It, too, always came from God.

When God tells His people to love Him with all their strength, He means that we are to love Him physically and with courage. Every ounce of energy we have is to be directed in one way or another toward Him, His Kingdom, and His ways. Just as a halfhearted love toward a spouse or a child is hardly love in the first place, so is halfhearted love toward God a shadow of reality. To sort of love God, to love Him a little, is not to love Him very much at all. Devotion doesn't come in portions. It is either there or it isn't. And God urges us to make sure that it is there.

In Deed

Assess your love for God. If you're honest, you'll come to the conclusion that many saints of old were forced to admit: Our love is usually lukewarm. Martin Luther became so frustrated with the holiness of God vis-à-vis his own unholi-ness that he confessed, "Love God? Sometimes I hate Him." Many Christians, though not nearly so blunt, have felt the same way. It takes an eye-opening experience with the grace of God to begin to love Him truly.

If your love for God is cold or distant, remedy the situation. No, of course you can't manufacture love. But you can ask for the zeal of the Holy Spirit to kindle it in you. You can ask for the kind of love that consumes your whole being and is as deep as God desires—with all your strength.

When God is our strength, it is strength indeed; when our strength is our own, it is only weakness.
—AUGUSTINE

Worshipful Energy

I have labored and toiled and have often gone without
sleep; I have known hunger and thirst and have often
gone without food; I have been cold and naked.

2 CORINTHIANS 11:27

In Word

If ever someone loved God with all his strength, it was Paul. The energy that he expended for the sake of his King was not only admirable, it was supernatural. Though confessing genuine weakness (v. 29), he also claimed God's strength (12:9-10). Toward the end of his ministry, Paul could tell Timothy that he was being "poured out" (2 Timothy 4:6). Like all of us, he was being spent on his work and his relationships. Unlike many of us, all his work and relationships revolved around Christ.

Paul demonstrated what it means to love God with the kind of boldness, courage, and physical endurance that the great commandment back in Deuteronomy 6:5 (and repeated by Jesus in Mark 12:30) urged. And we can see such love in an even greater example. Jesus endured the Cross—boldly in His body and His willful courage—for the sake of the Father and for the sake of His Father's chosen children. Love was poured out from the Cross in the form of divine blood. That's what it means to love God with all one's strength.

In Deed

It's a hard act to follow, isn't it? But we've been called to follow it anyway. To love God with all our strength, we are to spend our energy for Him, suffer discomfort for Him, and endure resistance for Him. It's a high and holy calling, and we're often afraid of it.

That's where the supernatural strength of God comes in. Our fear makes us weak, keeping us from loving God with all of our strength. God, who knows our frailties, tells us to follow the example of Paul: to rejoice in our weaknesses and rely on God's strength.

Don't be afraid to hunger or thirst for God. Don't shy away from labor and fatigue. Such gifts honor the God you serve. They are a form of worship. They are an act of love.

Love for God is ecstatic, making us go out from
ourselves. It does not allow the lover to belong
any more to himself, but only to the Beloved.

—DIONYSIOS THE AREOPAGITE

All for Glory

Whatever you do, do it all for the glory of God.
1 CORINTHIANS 10:31

In Word

God doesn't give us any impossible commands. That would be cruel. He may give us commands that require us to depend on His Spirit to fulfill them, but they aren't impossible. A wise and loving God would hold no one accountable for completely unavoidable transgressions.

So it follows that if God tells us to do everything for His glory, it must also be true that anything we do—if done in the right way, for the right reasons—can glorify Him. That applies even to eating and drinking, as in this passage. In other words, anything can become an act of worship.

In theory, we have no trouble believing that, but in practice it's hard to grasp. For example, how does it glorify God for someone to keep doing the same menial task in a dead-end job? How can we go shopping to the glory of God or study history to the glory of God? How do we eat for His glory or dress for His glory? Is glorifying God just for ministers and missionaries, or can the daily grind of average people be honoring to Him?

Intellectually, we know the answer. If the Bible tells us that anything we do can be an act of worship, then we can approach anything with that attitude. The same menial task may demonstrate to others that we have an otherworldly source of fulfillment. The stewardship of shopping and the dignity of dressing may demonstrate otherworldly values. Our studies, our habits, our interests, and our relationships are all able to reflect some aspect of His character. And reflecting Him is critical; making the invisible God visible in this world is what glorifying Him is all about.

In Deed

The most important question to ask yourself in any decision, no matter how small, is whether it will reflect God's glory or deflect it. Is your lifestyle a distraction that obscures a clear view of Him? Then take Paul's words to heart. Learn to live them. Remind yourself of them daily until they become part of the fabric of your life. Whatever you do, do it for His glory.

A concern for the glory of God is the
ultimate motive for Christian living.

—ANONYMOUS

When God Shows Up

When they heard that the LORD was concerned
about them and had seen their misery,
they bowed down and worshiped.

EXODUS 4:31

In Word

For years they had groaned under the weight of captivity. Slaves in Egypt, the Israelites were used ruthlessly (Exodus 1:14). Joseph's leadership had long been forgotten by the pharaohs. The Egyptians had made the lives of the Israelites bitter with hard labor and oppressive social policies. It was, according to today's verse, "misery."

It's no wonder, then, that they worshiped when they learned of God's concern for them. Oppressed people often believe that God has abandoned them under the crushing weight of some unspecified judgment. They don't know what caused His disfavor, but they interpret every burden as a sign of it. And when God demonstrates that He is, in fact, on their side, it's a cause of great rejoicing. The thought that God might intervene renders Him immediately worthy of worship.

That's a shallow sort of worship, but it's still legitimate. We can hardly blame the Israelites for celebrating the favor of God when we do exactly the same thing. We, too, often interpret our burdens as signs of the judgment—or at least absence—of God. When He demonstrates that He is on our side, we rejoice. It had been true all along, but we weren't perceptive enough to realize it. We worship our Redeemer, our Rescuer, and our Deliverer for no other reason than the fact that He has come to redeem, rescue, and deliver.

In Deed

That's a good place to start. For anyone who has known the burden of captivity—to sin, to difficult circumstances, to oppressive relationships, to the heavy agendas of our own personal ambition or that of petty rivals—when God shows up, it's time to celebrate. And when we really think about it, that's the position of every believer. We once were lost, but now we are found. We once were blind, but now we see. We once were captive, but now we are running around freely as children of God. It's a divine drama, and the Redeemer is the star. Let your worship always begin there.

*My chains fell off, my heart was free. I rose,
went forth, and followed Thee.*

—CHARLES WESLEY

Love Gone Cold

May the LORD look upon you and judge you! You have made us a stench to Pharaoh and his officials.

EXODUS 5:21

In Word

Only a few days before, God's people were praising Him for His favor. Now they were cursing His handpicked deliverer. Instead of instant freedom, they got a heavier workload. So they complained. It's alarming how quickly worshipful hearts can turn fickle. When love rides the waves of circumstances and hangs its hopes on the situation of the day, it can grow cold awfully fast. When we worship God only as long as He fuels our desires, we have a brief and shallow worship. Israel couldn't see past the troubles of the day, so they quit trusting the God of eternity. Instead, they cursed His servant.

Human beings have always had fickle hearts. A few pages later in Exodus, a celebration at the edge of the Red Sea is followed by complaints about the drinking water. In the book of Judges, every deliverance is followed by idolatry and its tragic consequences. In Matthew 16, Peter's declaration of Jesus as the Messiah quickly gives way to a blind indictment of God's plan. And today, we repeat the cycle: worship one day, complaints the next. White-hot passion can quickly freeze.

That's terribly shortsighted. Think about this: What if Pharaoh had let Israel go at Moses' first request? There would have been no drama of deliverance, no sense of salvation history, no celebration of miraculous victory. The nation that was destined to be a priest between the world and its redeemer God would have understood little of its redeemer God. There would be no Passover, no Red Sea, no manna from heaven—just an easy deliverance. But that's not how redeemers are revealed.

In Deed

Next time you find yourself in hardship, look for the big picture. God is revealing Himself in your personal history. Complaining about today's headaches won't help the process. By faith, see that He is doing something much larger, much more dramatic than today's troubles. And be assured that regardless of what you see, His plan is always, always good.

> There is a strange perversity in men concerning their trials in life, and only grace can cure it.
>
> —WILLIAM PLUMMER

Disappointment with God

Ever since I went to Pharaoh to speak in your
name, he has brought trouble upon this people,
and you have not rescued your people at all.

EXODUS 5:23

In Word

Israel's cursing led to Moses' accusations. The reluctant deliverer's fears were proving true. He had told God that asking Pharaoh for freedom was a fantasy, a long shot that could backfire. God still sent him, and now the consequences were dreadfully predictable. The omniscient God of burning bushes and ancient covenants must not have foreseen the crisis. Asking for freedom leads to more oppression. That's the way oppressors have always treated their victims.

Moses was learning the lesson that generations since have had to learn: Often the way to deliverance is through a deeper captivity. Sinners have to hit rock bottom before being in the frame of mind to accept salvation; bad relationships have to go through painful crises before healing begins; diseases often require difficult treatments before the cure comes; and oppressed slaves have to pay an even heavier price while their redemption is being worked out. That's just the way it works.

Like we do, Moses judged God by the beginning of the process, not by the big picture or a vision of the final outcome. That's a dangerous thing to do when speaking with the eternal, omniscient God. We have so little information, and we still complain and accuse. We're sure we're getting the raw end of the deal. The Sovereign of the universe must not know what He is doing. We feel obliged to point that out.

In Deed

Christians simply must be big-picture kind of people. We need that perspective, and so does the world. Complaints at the beginning of the redemptive process aren't helpful. Our enemy, like Pharaoh, resents our redemption with a passion, and God tolerates the oppressor's vengeance for a time. Those with their eyes on the end result won't mind that, and in fact will rejoice in the glory of the process. The deeper the oppression, the greater the deliverance. Keep your focus on the celebration, and today's trials won't seem nearly as intense.

God is to be trusted when His providences
seem to run contrary to His promises.

—THOMAS WATSON

Managing God

They have been quick to turn away from what
I commanded them and have made themselves
an idol cast in the shape of a calf.
EXODUS 32:8

In Word

While Moses was on Mount Sinai receiving the law—which began with commandments against worshiping false gods—the recently redeemed people of the covenant were at the bottom of the mountain making a false god. Despite an overwhelming body of evidence that the transcendent God of the universe had powerfully delivered them from Egypt and promised them a land of their own, they decided that a few days with an absent leader nullified their salvation history. The God who had redeemed them couldn't be found; they would just have to make another one.

That's the tendency of the human heart. We want a God who is accessible, a God we can see and touch and taste. And when the true God offers us Himself, "accessible" turns to "intrusive." What we really wanted was a god we could manage. That's more comfortable. We don't really want God to lead us through the wilderness on His terms; we want a god we can drive through the wilderness on our terms. We're content to live with the illusion of faith. It's a small price to pay for our autonomy.

But it always turns out to be a huge price, much more devastating than we'd thought. No matter where we choose to put our faith, and no matter who we credit with our deliverance, it turns out that there's only one truth and only one Deliverer. Truth is not a personal choice. Truth is true, whether we follow it or not.

In Deed

We live in an age of relativism. If the true God is too absent—or too present—for us, we'll just make one that "works" for us. That way, our god can command us only what we want him to command us. And we can follow him only when it makes sense for us to follow him.

That's the antithesis of worship. That's self-worship, the worst form of pride, and the worst form of self-deceit. Know the human tendency to make our own idols, and resist it every day. Never try to "manage" God.

When we invent our own ideas of God, we
simply create Him in our own image.
—KENNETH F. W. PRIOR

Grieving Impurity

Moses saw that the people were running wild . . .
and so become a laughingstock to their enemies.
EXODUS 32:25

In Word

Why do we turn worship into a self-oriented event? There are books, CDs, and sermons in circulation that encourage worship because of the benefits it brings to a believer—peace of mind, power over circumstances, victorious living, and more. These benefits are certainly legitimate, but when they become the reason we worship, we are worshiping ourselves.

Worship, by definition, is about God. It pulls us outside of our own orbit and puts us into the orbit of an infinitely brighter star. The moment it becomes designed for us, it has become self-worship. And that is a tragedy of massive proportions.

When that happens, there is nothing left for God to do but purify His people. Though we are not called to take up swords as the Levites did—God is not in the early stages of establishing a physical, priestly nation with us—He calls us to continue the work of being "set apart" (v. 29). That's what being a living sacrifice is all about: It's setting ourselves apart for His purposes and not our own (Romans 12:1).

What does God think when His worshipers "run wild" in disobedience and devotion to materialism, greed, religiosity, lust, status, and prestige? If worship is first and foremost about His reputation, and we fall away from it so easily—allowing all sorts of rivals to compete with His reputation in our lives—do not His enemies have a right to laugh? When people expressly devoted to God devote themselves to other things, what have we contributed to His reputation in this world?

In Deed

God is serious about purity—not because He wants to spoil our fun, but because He wants to enhance it. His desire is for His people, called by His name, to bask in a relationship that celebrates exclusive devotion, commitment, and the deepest forms of love. When His people shun His love for a dance with golden calves, He grieves. Our hearts will beat with His when we've begun to grieve too.

Idolatry is an attempt to use God for man's purposes,
rather than to give oneself to God's service.
—C. F. D. MOULE

Worship in Pain

I am feeble and utterly crushed;
I groan in anguish of heart.
PSALM 38:8

In Word

We never feel so alone as when we're hurting. Broken hearts are usually lonely hearts, and they rarely bask in the presence of God. In fact, loneliness and brokenness often produce shame, which makes us want to run from our Maker. And running makes the pain worse.

God understands. He pursues us in our pain not because He wants us to explain it, or even because He wants to take it away. He wants to be with us in it. He wants to say, "Yes, I know what it means to suffer, and I'm with you." In this psalm, David did something fairly unnatural when he didn't hide his pain from God. As with all his passions, he put them before the Lord. He didn't necessarily know how God would help, just that He would. He worshiped God with his pain.

In Deed

Can you do that? Worship and pain don't seem to go together, but when we bring our anguish to God, we actually honor Him. Isolating ourselves from the One who cares, perhaps because we're convinced He doesn't, is actually a refusal to accept the comfort He offers. It is an assumption that He can't help, or won't help, or doesn't have the answer for us. But presenting our suffering to Him demonstrates an expectation that He is somehow critical to our well-being. It acknowledges a hope that He might care, that He might be able to help, and that if there's an answer, He might know it.

How you handle your pain says a lot about what you think of God. It indicates whether you trust Him or not, even in your deepest despair. It says that you may not understand your circumstances, but you know who governs them. It is a difficult expression of faith when faith is hard to come by.

When life hurts, give it to God. Trust Him with it. When you're crushed, your faith honors Him in ways that your faith at other times cannot.

Regret looks back. Worry looks around. Faith looks up.
—JOHN MASON

Bare Longings

All my longings lie open before you, O Lord.
PSALM 38:9

In Word

What does a heart in pain do with an unfulfilled longing? Wallow in self-pity? Cry itself to sleep? There just aren't many options. An unfulfilled desire is one of the deepest pains we can know. It can challenge our identity and destroy our hope.

Do Christians struggle with unfulfilled longings? Of course we do. We like to think that God is truly the center of our lives at all times, and all desires pale in comparison to Him. But passionate hearts aren't so easily tamed. In our best moments, perhaps God reigns supreme and all other desires pale. But we didn't lose our humanity when we were redeemed. And our humanity still often longs for what it can't have.

We can rebuke ourselves, of course, and tell ourselves that we've gotten our focus off of God. We may be entirely right, but a rebuke doesn't usually satisfy us. If our dreams are still unfulfilled and our cravings are intense, right answers won't help. Even when they're wrong cravings—and they often are—we can take them to God. There's no need to flee. He understands how the human heart longs.

In Deed

All our longings lie open before God, even when we don't want them to. But it's best to let them lie honestly before Him, regardless of whether they are good or bad, right or wrong, godly or painfully human. The God who created our hearts understands them. He knows how they hurt. And He wants us to open them up before Him.

Do you long for the right spouse, a precious child, a meaningful career, a healed relationship, a different situation than you now find yourself in? Welcome to life as a human being. God may or may not fulfill that specific desire, although you can rest assured that He fully intends to fulfill the needs behind it. In the meantime, lay yourself bare before Him. Don't hide your sighs. Trust that the God who made you for Himself plans to fill you with Himself, with blessings beside. His timing isn't yours, but His love is. Open yourself to it, even when it hurts.

Dry wells send us to the fountain.
—SAMUEL RUTHERFORD

Contemplate Eternity

You destroy all who are unfaithful to you. But
as for me, it is good to be near God.
PSALM 73:27-28

In Word

The world is a confusing place. Sometimes the wicked prosper and the righteous don't. On the surface, that runs contrary to God's promises, but we can't afford to look for God on the surface. Eventually we learn that the prosperity of the wicked and the misfortune of the righteous are temporary conditions. From the perspective of eternity, the wicked never prosper and the righteous never lack. It's a promise of God.

The psalmist, Asaph, struggled with perspective. His feet had almost slipped and he had almost fallen. While he was struggling, he noticed that the arrogant weren't. They were healthy and strong, free from burdens, wealthy, and bold in their sin. In spite of all God's promises to bless obedience and curse disobedience, the obedient psalmist was in pain and the sinners were doing fine. It didn't make sense.

We can relate. The godless of our age are often the most carefree and prosperous. They drive flashy cars, take wildly extravagant vacations, build gaudy houses, change spouses regularly, avoid responsibilities, and never seem to suffer from their prodigal ways. Meanwhile, we struggle—to make ends meet, to get relationships right, or just to be faithful to our God. Why are we having a hard time and those who don't care about God at all are having the time of their lives?

In Deed

The answer for Asaph was getting the right perspective. It didn't make sense until he "entered the sanctuary of God" (v. 17). When he sat for a while in God's presence, he got a glimpse of eternity. He understood the destiny of the wicked and their slippery ground. Seeing God does that; it makes the illusions of this world fade and the reality of eternity come into clear focus. It sets things right.

If you've struggled with this problem, sit in God's presence for a while. Contemplate eternity. You'll come away with perspective, and you'll be grateful for the way God is carefully cultivating you, even in hardship.

God's promises are like the stars; the darker
the night, the brighter they shine.
—DAVID NICHOLAS

Insignificant Toys

What good is it for a man to gain the whole world, yet forfeit his soul?
MARK 8:36

In Word

A bumper sticker says, "Whoever dies with the most toys wins." While the statement is a humorous look at the shallow pursuits of mankind, it is also the implicit principle beneath many actual lifestyles. Though we acknowledge the superficiality of a life built on possessions, we have the tendency to build our lives on possessions anyway. We embrace the superficial with alarming ease. We forget the truth behind the joke: Whoever dies with the most toys is dead—just like the person who dies with nothing.

Jesus' comment on discipleship pierces the lie. What good is it to have a lot of things—even the whole world—yet have a fallen life that cannot even see heaven without a rebirth? In other words, it's not what you have, it's who you are. Or, more accurately, it's who you relate to. And if you don't relate to the eternal God, then your life is a disappearing vapor. Whoever dies without the life of God within him or her is simply dead. Painfully empty, unfulfilled, and spiritually dead. Forever.

Why is it so hard for us to grasp the essentials of the Kingdom? In spite of Jesus' stark warnings, we spend an awful lot of time worrying about what we have, insuring it well, and striving to earn more so we can buy more. The minimum standard of living keeps rising, and we find ourselves unwilling to do without the things most people on the globe consider luxuries. Meanwhile, the true life that we've been entrusted with is neglected. We stock up on materials while depleting ourselves of character. We invest in the wrong things.

In Deed

Is that too harsh? Perhaps so, but Jesus was not afraid to say harsh things to His disciples. His judgment on materialism has been watered down over the years. Perhaps He wouldn't condemn how much we have; He would only condemn how much we've valued it. To Him, the soul matters. So does the Kingdom. So do the hearts of His disciples. Give Him a heart purified of possessions. Whoever dies with nothing but a love for God is really the one who wins.

> Nobody can fight properly and boldly for the faith if he clings to fear of being stripped of earthly possessions.
>
> —PETER DAMIAN

Building Towers

Come, let us build ourselves a city.
GENESIS 11:4

In Word

God placed human beings in the Garden to be stewards. Man and woman were to exercise God's dominion over the earth—in His name, for His purposes, under His authority. As we all know by now, that didn't work out. The rebellion against God's order has been passed down through every generation since creation. But in the beginning, we were to be stewards. That was our role.

In the story of Babel, we see human beings not as stewards but as spiritual entrepreneurs. There is no submission in this story, just an agenda. Mankind has a plan. They will "make a name" for themselves by reaching into the heavens with a handmade city. Rather than building a tower for God, they were building a tower for themselves. Somehow they got from the Garden of Eden to the City of Pride. It was an utter contradiction to their created purpose.

There's nothing wrong with building towers, of course. God has nothing against them, in themselves. It's what they represent that's the problem. The evil is in the motive. And the motive at Babel was self-sufficiency—an unhealthy faith in the human community and a drastic independence from God. The only worship at Babel was in the ability of humanity to take care of itself. It had to be undone.

In Deed

Think about the towers you build. Perhaps your independence isn't as blatant as that of the citizens of Shinar, but every human being has a streak of it. We tend to trust man-made creations for our security. We build monuments that will make a name for ourselves. We lose sight of what it means to be a steward and take ownership of our domain. All the while, God plans to undo our work—not out of spite but out of mercy. He simply cannot let us have our way. We have to relearn stewardship and dependence.

Consider your approach to your possessions and your work. Are you an owner or a steward? Are you working for your name or for His? Are you a spiritual entrepreneur or a servant of God? Weigh your motives carefully. After all, God does.

> Pride not only withdraws the heart from God, but lifts it up against God.
> —THOMAS MANTON

Misplaced Glory

I will not give my glory to another or my praise to idols.
ISAIAH 42:8

In Word

The mission of God is to make Himself known, displaying His glory in a dark, imprisoned world. The light of the Kingdom is meant to pierce the blindness of fallen humanity, and God's people are the primary means by which He shows Himself. That's true for the Messiah, who is the subject of the first part of Isaiah 42; that's true for Israel, to whom God speaks throughout the chapter; and that's true for the church, those who have trusted the Messiah and His mission. When God steps into the world, glory is to become clear.

That's why idolatry is such a tragedy. It gives God's glory to some unworthy object made by human hands or craved by human hearts. But idols of wood and stone are not the only glory robbers in this world. We who worship God in our hearts often obscure Him in our actions or our speech. Though God has done marvelous things in our lives, we know that pointing to the light is not always welcome in the darkness. The glory of God is not always a socially acceptable topic. The light of day hurts eyes that have adjusted well to the night. Rather than offend blind eyes, we accommodate the blindness.

How do we do that? Subtly, imperceptibly, unconsciously. When healing comes, we praise the wisdom of doctors and the marvels of modern medicine more easily than we praise the Healer. When relationships are repaired, we praise the humility of the parties or the wisdom of the compromise more easily than we praise the God of reconciliation. When our depression clears up, we honor the things or people or subjects that have captured our interest and drawn us out. The Hope of all creation is often left out of the celebration.

In Deed

God doesn't share His glory, not with idols of material substance nor with idols of internal affections. He paid a high price to shine into this world, and blessed are those who do not hide the light of His honor. Vow to live in uncompromising recognition of the God who saves, restores, heals, comforts, encourages, exalts, and blesses. The glory is all His.

Praise, my soul, the King of heaven;
to His feet thy tribute bring.
—HENRY FRANCIS LYTE

Slow Faith

**If God will be with me . . . then
the LORD will be my God.**
GENESIS 28:20-21

In Word

You'd think the vision would have been enough. Jacob was fleeing for his life
from Esau—stealing blessings can make a brother angry enough to kill—and
when he spent the night on a rock, he had a dream. It was a powerful dream,
with angels ascending to and descending from heaven. With the vision came
a promise: the promise given to Abraham for blessing throughout all generations to come. The implications weren't lost on Jacob; he named the place
"house of God" and built a monument.

His vow, however, indicates the level of his spiritual maturity. He was still
undecided about the greatness and worthiness of God. Lordship was still an
issue. Jacob's faith, even after an amazing night, was going to be conditional.
"If God will be with me . . . then the LORD will be my God." The reality of
God's presence had been made clear. The value of following Him hadn't. As a
result, Jacob placed conditions on his allegiance.

That's how we operate too. God understands; He had chosen Jacob
unconditionally, and this wavering spirituality later turned into patriarchal
substance. But it shouldn't have been so long in coming. Jacob, like us, had all
the upbringing and evidence he should have needed for a strong and vibrant
faith. Instead, his patriarchal qualities only showed up after years in the school
of hard knocks and a mysterious wrestling match (Genesis 32:22-32). The
faith of fallen human beings takes time to develop.

In Deed

Have you been overwhelmed with God's awesome presence, built monuments to His glory, and then gone on to act with all the steadfastness of an
agnostic? If you're like Jacob—if you're a human being in need of significant
grace—you probably have. The self-will is often so stubborn. The remedy?
Remember God's past graces, but go ahead and count on His future blessings
as well. Looking ahead to the promises He has given is a form of worship.
Jacob's "if" prayer was completely unfounded. God is with us. Know that, and
live confidently under His lordship.

> Ask God to work faith in you, or you will remain forever
> without faith, no matter what you wish, say, or can do.
>
> —MARTIN LUTHER

Desire God

Earth has nothing I desire besides you.
PSALM 73:25

In Word

Asaph's psalm is filled with disillusionment until he gets into God's presence and comes to his senses. Perhaps he was basing his happiness on his own success or status compared to others. We know he was not seeing life from an eternal perspective; he tells us as much. But even more than that, he was looking at the spiritual life from a physical point of view. And that never brings a happy result.

We do that. We get frustrated at our lack of contentment, not realizing that if we are basing our happiness on material things or temporal standards, we will always be discontent. Any life that is consistently disappointed is a life that was hoping in something other than God. How do we know? Because God never disappoints, not in the long run.

Hope in the trappings of this life ends in despair. We tend to pin our hopes on the places we live, the people who love us, the things we can achieve, or the legacy we can leave. We base our contentment on income, feelings, people, location—in other words, on a lot of things that fluctuate. We've based our happiness on shifting sand.

But hope in God is unending—satisfaction after satisfaction. It isn't constant perfection; even redeemed and sanctified lives are prone to occasional discouragement and frustration. But hope reigns if it's based on God. Why? Because God reigns. He never shifts like the sand.

In Deed

Learn Asaph's lesson: desire God above all else. He's the only desire that can ultimately be satisfied. Our flesh and our heart may fail (v. 26), but if we've learned not to rest our heart on failing foundations, we've found the key to inner peace. The heart that knows its only fulfillment is found in God—that desires nothing else above Him—will find the kind of contentment that is completely alien to this world. Why? Because this is a restless world with constantly changing standards. And God, the object of our desire, is changeless.

Desire only God, and your heart will be satisfied.
—AUGUSTINE

Relinquishing Dreams

**Bring joy to your servant, for to you,
O Lord, I lift up my soul.**
PSALM 86:4

In Word

If we had windows on our hearts, we'd notice a common condition in everyone: We all have a dream of fulfillment. We also have some pretty specific
ideas about how that fulfillment should come. Perhaps it's through a career, a
certain income level, a person to be with, a house to own, or some other thing
that just has to happen before we can be truly content. The specific dream may
differ, but its presence is almost universal.

Our prayers are often filled with these dreams, even obsessed with them.
We want to be fulfilled, and we know God wants us to be fulfilled too. And
since we think we know what would make us feel happy and complete—or,
if we spin it more spiritually, what we would consider the greatest blessing—
we pray for our dreams to come true. After all, Jesus told us to ask what we
will and it would be done for us (John 15:7). We don't hesitate to tell God
what our will is.

But if we come back down to earth and think a little more realistically,
we have to realize that God knows what will fulfill us better than we do. He
knows the dreams we have—He probably even put some of them there—
but He knows what form and timing their fulfillment should take. He knows
the true desires that lie beneath the dreams, the motives under the scenarios
we've envisioned. He knows how to say no to our specifics and yes to our
hearts, both at the same time.

In Deed

One of the greatest ways to honor God—to demonstrate your trust in who
He is and how He works—is to relinquish your dreams to Him. Instead of asking Him to fulfill you according to your hopes and dreams, ask Him to fulfill
you according to His hopes and dreams. It's a pretty sure bet that His plan for
your life exceeds yours, and in the end it will be more satisfying than you ever
dreamed. Trust Him with your heart. He knows exactly what it needs.

God is most glorified in us when we are most satisfied in Him.
—JOHN PIPER

Desperation

**In the day of my trouble I will call to
you, for you will answer me.**
PSALM 86:7

In Word

Have you ever noticed how often the Bible urges us to cry out to God in our
distress? It never tells us that we annoy Him with our petitions, or that we've
gotten ourselves into trouble far too often for Him to be bothered anymore.
It never implies that we're on our own now, and it never even hints that God
helps those who help themselves. No, the Bible is emphatic that when we get
into trouble, we are to call to Him.

Why is that? Because there's a holy dynamic in our relationship with Him.
A people of great need are a necessary condition for God to reveal Himself as
a God of great mercy and great provision. If we had no need, no one would
ever know of God's supply. If we had no hurt, no one would know of His comfort. If we had no disease, no one would know of His healing. He is revealed as
a Redeemer and Rescuer only when we need redemption and rescuing. Our
need highlights who He is.

That's why the Bible urges us to call on Him in the day of trouble. That's
why it never implies—not even once—that He will not respond to His children. That's why millions throughout history have called to Him and found
Him faithful. The God of mercy demonstrates it—often.

In Deed

For whatever reason, we're hesitant to bare our souls before Him. We let Him
know of some of our needs, but we're afraid to be desperate in His presence.
But desperation is the key. Desperation puts us in perfect position to see the
merciful God who saves and restores.

You will have days of trouble. You know that. When you do, go ahead and
come to Him empty-handed. Like David, tell Him that all your hopes are
hanging on Him, and that if He doesn't respond, you'll be devastated. Then
watch Him respond. Experience His restoration, His providence, and His
love. Know that the God of mercy is looking for people who will accept it. It
shows us—and the world—who He is.

Groanings which cannot be uttered are often
prayers which cannot be refused.
—CHARLES SPURGEON

Undivided

Give me an undivided heart, that I may fear your name.
PSALM 86:11

In Word

A divided heart. It's a Christian's greatest enemy, and it should be our greatest fear. It wreaks havoc on our contentment and undermines our devotion. It corrupts our worship because one side of our heart competes with the other. The competition causes us to tell God we want to love and honor Him, while simultaneously telling ourselves we can pursue our own agenda at will. A divided heart has multiple loves, and multiple loves are always weak.

That's what Jesus said too. He told His disciples they couldn't serve two masters because they would end up loving one and hating the other (Matthew 6:24). That's what divided hearts do; they are eventually compelled to choose one of their loves over the other. They have too many choices to start with, so they compromise.

David prays in this psalm that God might give him an undivided heart so that he might fear God's name. He knows that when a person tolerates other loves, it's because that person has grown casual with God. An undivided heart solves the problem; single-mindedness toward God makes a person free to serve and love Him with everything at his or her disposal. It reintroduces respect and awe. It puts things in the proper perspective.

In Deed

Pursue an undivided heart. Ask God for it. A divided heart will ruin your spiritual life, introducing apathy, removing godly fear, and tempting you with other loves. Worship cannot exist under such conditions. A divided love is hardly love at all.

David's remedy isn't within himself. He knows that his heart is God's domain, and only God can change it. He resolves to praise God with all his heart and glorify God's name forever (v. 12), but pure resolve isn't the answer. So David asked God for His resources, His strength, and His work within him. We can too. We can trust Him with the greatest enemy to our worship and ask Him to give us a single, focused love.

> Blessed are the single-hearted; for
> they shall enjoy much peace.
> —THOMAS À KEMPIS

A Radical Result

**We hear them declaring the wonders
of God in our own tongues!**
ACTS 2:11

In Word

They were gathered together "in one place," these early followers of the resurrected Jesus. He had told them to wait in Jerusalem, so they did. Frequently, they waited together. It only made sense on this Day of Pentecost to be united in their expectation of His promise. So the fellowship gathered, presumably to worship.

It's hard to imagine the spectacle that followed, but whatever that rushing wind felt like and those tongues of fire looked like, it was dramatic and overwhelming. We might assume from the description that chaos ensued, except for one remarkable indicator to the contrary: All the believers were declaring the same message. Different languages, one truth. They declared the wonders of God—a single, solitary theme through wildly diverse words. When the Spirit of God came down, people worshiped. That's not a coincidence.

In our examination of what worship really is, we would do well to look to the early church. After all, Scripture indicates that this Day of Pentecost is the inauguration of a new age and the fulfillment of the Messiah's purpose for His people in a fallen world. Sometimes we fall into the egotistic trap of thinking that the early church was primitive and that we've learned so much since then. But this church was pristine and pure in its primitiveness. It's our prototype. This is our supreme example of what happens when the Spirit falls on human beings.

In Deed

As we look at the early church today and in the next few days, consider this question: Is my worship consistent with the work of the Holy Spirit in the book of Acts? Don't assume that your worship or your church must necessarily follow the same forms and phenomena. The essential parallel for us to consider is not a matter of particular gifts but of a particular attitude and outcome: declaring the wonders of God. That's what true worship is about—a radical God-focus that reorients our entire lives. Does your God-focus have that result?

Fill Thou my life, O Lord my God, in every part with praise;
that my whole being may proclaim Thy being and Thy ways.

—HORATIUS BONAR

Overflowing

**They devoted themselves to the apostles'
teaching and to the fellowship, to the
breaking of bread and to prayer.**
ACTS 2:42

In Word

The worship of the first church didn't stop with praise. There were other implications. All of a sudden, these Spirit-led people were intensely interested in truth, zealous about each other, and always communicating with God. The work of God was overwhelming.

This picture of the early church doesn't always fit well with fellowships in the free West. There's no hint of individualism—a hallmark of our culture—in their worship. In fact, this church was perhaps the first community ever to practice a radical redistribution of wealth (v. 45), not because a government imposed it but because a Spirit prompted it. They called each other "brother" and "sister." They ate together, worked together, and practically lived together, because something larger than their own agendas had taken over. They were filled with awe, and awe-filled people do amazingly sacrificial things. Full fountains always overflow.

That's the challenge for every believer: maintaining the awe and over-flowing with joy and praise. We learn from our romantic relationships that newness and excitement wear off, coming and going in waves; but even if our relationship with God has that dynamic, there are things we can do to keep from growing stale. These early disciples devoted themselves to the things of God. They craved the Word and the fellowship. Their possessions meant little to them in light of their new Possession. When God came powerfully into their lives, everything else paled.

In Deed

To what degree does God overwhelm you? Does His presence drive you into His Word? Do you live in selfless unity with your brothers and sisters? Do you regard your possessions as the property of God to distribute as He wills? Worship—true, Spirit-filled worship—leads to such things. You can't muster up awe, but you can ask for it. It's a gift from God, and He gives to all who look to Him for it.

Spirit-filled souls are ablaze for God.
—SAMUEL CHADWICK

Worship in Adversity

Lord, consider their threats and enable your
servants to speak your word with great boldness.

ACTS 4:29

In Word

Peter and John had proclaimed healing for a cripple at the Temple gate, and
the man's celebration created quite a stir. Peter seized the opportunity to
preach, but his unreasonable insistence that Jesus had been raised from the
dead irked the officials. The Sadducees—who didn't believe in anyone's resurrection, much less the heretical Nazarene's—had Peter and John arrested.
After another sermon from Peter, some wise words from calmer heads among
the officials, and threats against future preaching and miracles, the bold disciples were released. What was the church's response? Praise and worship.
And more power.

Real worship does not bow to adversity. In fact, adversity magnifies the
faith and the adoration of a believer. If Peter and John had won the admiration
of all the crowds and officials, they would have had reason enough to praise
God. But it might have been a circumstantial praise, born of human exhilaration over visible victory. Instead, their praises came in the midst of threats and
persecution. Such worship magnifies the Father's reputation because it can't
be false. It can't be based on circumstances or pride. It can only come from
real joy in hearts that are really redeemed.

Days later, Peter and company would be arrested and released again.
They would leave the court of the Sanhedrin "rejoicing because they had been
counted worthy of suffering disgrace for the Name" (Acts 5:41). The glory in
that kind of joy doesn't point to fallen humanity. It points only to God.

In Deed

Does your adversity point only to God? If not, you are missing a golden
opportunity to magnify your worship. You may be accustomed to praising
God when life is easy, and you wonder where His favor has gone when life is
difficult. Learn from the apostles; worship in the midst of trials, and see His
glory shine. Adversity can bring out the best or the worst in a redeemed heart.
The choice is yours, and the reputation is God's.

> The greatness of our God must be tested by the
> desire we have of suffering for His sake.
>
> —PHILIP NERI

Inspired Unity

All the believers were one in heart and mind.
ACTS 4:32

In Word

The early church was utopian, the kind of community that everyone craves and no one believes is even possible. Christian movements (and many other religious or secular ones as well) always begin with a sense of unity. The excitement and newness of a fresh work of God seems to subvert everyone's petty agendas, while awe forces observers to realize that something greater than their individual selves is taking center stage. It was like that with numerous monastic orders, the movements of the Reformation, the denominations of later centuries, and here in the earliest church. The power of God gently and thoroughly overcomes the selfish individuality of men and women. When God does wonders, people live in wonder. And living in wonder puts us in the audience rather than on stage. Wonder and unity work well together.

Sadly, the newness of the Spirit's movement fades, the excitement wears off, and eventually individual interests crawl back on the stage. Spirit-filled fellowships turn into institutions, with all the baggage institutions seem to require. Personal agendas and concerns begin to rival one another, and eventually fellowship is corrupted or even broken. The body of Christ becomes a collection of churchgoers, and instead of one heart and mind, there are many.

What can break this trend? How can we get back to the awe and wonder that recognizes that God is on stage and we are not? Worship. A wholehearted passion for God. A desire for the holy. A sacrifice of the mind, will, and emotions to something—to Someone—who is and shall evermore be greater than we are.

In Deed

If you want this kind of church—and deep down inside, everyone does—drop the personal agenda. Fill your days and nights with overflowing praise, letting the character and work of God become your obsession. Encourage others to do the same. Churches unite when they can focus on a single goal. And for Christians, there is always only one legitimate Goal on whom to focus.

> Form one choir, so that . . . having all taken the tone of God, you may sing with one voice to the Father.
> —IGNATIUS OF ANTIOCH

Restoring Love

**Restore me, and I will return, because
you are the LORD my God.**
JEREMIAH 31:18

In Word

We live in the tension between two obvious facts. First, the world is full
of corruption and sin. Second, it was made to be so much better. People
can ignore those facts if they want to—in fact, many have tried to portray
our world as a product of random natural processes—but deep down inside
everyone knows that we live in a place of perfection gone wrong. We make our
longings for Eden obvious by our constant attempts to insulate ourselves from
trouble and craft for ourselves a paradise of success, prosperity, and pleasure.
Ask anyone you meet on the street what he or she wants out of life, and you'll
get some pretty specific answers. No one is completely content.

The good news is that our Father is a restorer. For all the judgment and
captivity declared in the prophetic books, all of them contain a ray of hope,
a promise that God will bring back and restore the blessings once forsaken.
In the prophets, the restoration applies to Israel and Judah. In the Bible as a
whole, it applies to all of us who believe. We can take those truths and count
on the promises for ourselves because the restoration isn't an isolated incident. God doesn't just tell a particular people and a particular time that He
will restore. He tells them He's a restorer. It's His nature.

In Deed

Your craving for restoration may be nothing more than a deep desire for life
to work out and be fruitful. Or, if you're like most of us, you lament mistakes
that have shaped the course of your life and wish you could do a particular
year or two over again. In either case, whether looking forward to what you
wish could be, or looking back to what you wish wasn't, you can count on this
fact: your Father is a restorer. He gives back what you've lost.

That's the message of the Bible from Genesis to Revelation, the high point
being the incarnation of Jesus. The Savior came to save, the Redeemer to
redeem, the Healer to heal—your world, your life, and your heart. Praise
Him for that. Whatever your loss, return to the Father who restores and
worship Him.

> If I find in myself a desire which no experience in this
> world can satisfy, . . . I was made for another world.
> —C. S. LEWIS

Wildest Dreams

There is hope for your future.
JEREMIAH 31:17

In Word

What does a father dream for his child? Exciting adventures and great exploits, wise decisions and complete success, exemplary behavior and fruitful activity, and much, much more. Most of all, he wants his child to be deeply, wonderfully happy and full of joy.

What does a mother dream for her child? Safety and peace, encouragement and nurture, security and prosperity. Most of all, she wants her child to be deeply, wonderfully happy and full of joy.

Put all of that together and you have a picture that may begin to capture God's heart for you. You also have a picture of God's heart for everyone around you. Our Father wills nothing but blessing on His people, and He desires that everyone fall under that category of "His people." In a world full of people who are suspicious of God—and many Christians fit that description too—we need to know that the Father always wants the best for everyone. That's what His kind of love is. He wants us to be deeply, wonderfully happy and full of joy and gratitude.

In Deed

That means that every time He blesses you, every time He disciplines you, every time He speaks to you, every time He comforts you, every time He catches your tears, and every time He shares a laugh, it is all toward that end. The Father put Israel through some pretty difficult times, but it was toward this end. He gave some pretty hard commands, but it was toward this end. And He made an excruciatingly precious sacrifice, and it too was toward this end.

What should we do with this knowledge? First, apply His dreams to your life. Is He watching you with folded arms, wondering how you'll mess up next? Does He plan to withhold a gift from you? Does He enjoy watching you stumble? No, God delights in your progress and excitedly anticipates your fulfillment. Never forget that.

Second, apply His dreams to the people around you. He delights in their progress too, and He anticipates their fulfillment just as zealously. Knowing that He will satisfy His dreams for you, ask Him how you can help Him satisfy His dreams for them. Live like a child who has extraordinary hope and a radically loving Father.

> However devoted you are to God, you may be sure
> that He is immeasurably more devoted to you.
> —MEISTER ECKHART

A Humble Victory

See, your king comes to you, righteous
and having salvation, gentle and riding on
a donkey, on a colt, the foal of a donkey.
ZECHARIAH 9:9

In Word

Looking back on this prophecy, we know it refers to the triumphal entry of
Jesus into Jerusalem. But prophecy is always a lot clearer in retrospect. At the
time, it had to sound pretty strange. The great deliverer, the king Israel had
long hoped for, the general who would raise defenses and lead armies against
intimidating nations like Persia and Greece, would come to His people on a
donkey.

That's a less than inspiring picture for a perpetually oppressed people.
When you've been beaten up by the nations around you, a donkey-riding
warrior-king is not the savior you're looking for. All someone like that would
do is make the oppressors laugh and deepen your inferiority complex. Don-
keys don't win many battles.

But God frequently fulfills His promises in unexpected ways. A great
deliverer like Moses spent his first eighty years in futility and obscurity. A
great king like David was the last, smallest son in the family, who hid in the
desert for years before assuming the throne. Or, as in this prophecy, the Messiah was born in a stable, raised in the country, and executed on a stake just a
week after riding into town as king—on a donkey. God's deliverance always
defies expectations and gives glory to Him.

In Deed

Expect God to fulfill His promises, but don't make the mistake of forming
expectations for exactly how He'll do it. Whatever your need is, His deliverance will come—that's a certainty. But we don't get to define deliverance for
Him. He does that, and it's always better than we could have dreamed—even
if it doesn't look that way at first. When God foretells a victory, don't be surprised if victory comes riding in on a donkey. After all, that's exactly how the
greatest victory in world history came to us.

The greatness of God was not cast off, but the
slightness of human nature was put on.
—THOMAS AQUINAS

Unwavering Words

**Because of the blood of my covenant with you,
I will free your prisoners from the waterless pit.**
ZECHARIAH 9:11

In Word

God is a God of covenant. He makes promises and will not violate them. If we think He might renege because circumstances change or because we don't deserve His fulfillment, we've forgotten who He is. He has perfect foreknowledge and He has perfect character. He makes His promises in full view of the future, and His integrity never bends. No, when God promises something, it will be done.

So when God makes a covenant of blood, we know it cannot fail. We may not be as faithful as we want to be, but His faithfulness never wavers. If He has promised freedom for prisoners, we will be free. If He has promised to take us from waterless pits and place us in flourishing oases, we will be there. If He has promised to give us the desires of our heart, answer our prayers, or make a way through the wilderness into our Promised Land, it will happen. We can fully invest our heart in His promises because His promises are certainties. We should be the most secure people on the planet.

In Deed

What level of confidence do you live with? If you struggle with insecurity—and face it, all of us do at some level—then you've forgotten the integrity of God. He has assured you of His unconditional love with a covenant of blood; there's no need to wonder whether it applies to you. He has given you great and precious promises pertaining to everything in life and godliness (2 Peter 1:4); there's no reason to think He's holding out. Whatever emotional need you have, God has already made provision for it. He has already met it. The only question remaining is whether you actually believe He has.

We forget that our doubts about His promises really amount to slander against His character. Our souls question whether His words are true for us, even though His integrity has never failed once. He has invested love and blood in each of us. Believe that His covenant means exactly what He wants it to mean.

> The bond of the covenant is able to bear the
> weight of the believer's heaviest burden.
>
> —WILLIAM PLUMMER

Prisoners of Hope

Return to your fortress, O prisoners of hope; even now
I announce that I will restore twice as much to you.

ZECHARIAH 9:12

In Word

Zechariah prophesies to people who are stressed about their battles. The Lord speaks through him to His people: they won't need horses and weapons because He's their warrior (v. 10). In fact, their great king will come on a donkey, trusting in God's strength alone. The people can come in from the battlefield and become "prisoners of hope." The warrior has stirred Himself to rise up in victory.

It takes faith to see that victory, because it doesn't come through massive armies with the latest in devastating weaponry. To be a prisoner of hope, one must make a decision about where hope is to be found. The eyes of faith can take God at His Word and return to the fortress in peace, knowing He will fight His battles well. The eyes of fear and anxiety cannot.

How can we become prisoners of hope? By seeing who God really is. By letting go of our sense of control—it's only an illusion anyway—and trusting Him to accomplish His purposes. By praying in faith and then knowing He will respond. By resting instead of striving, by believing instead of fearing, by praising Him for what He will do rather than taking a wait-and-see attitude. Prisoners of hope have abandoned all their devices and have risked everything on the Warrior's ability to come through. That kind of faith sees victories.

In Deed

Prisoners of hope reap bountiful rewards: "twice as much" as they had to begin with. It doesn't matter how much the enemy has stolen or how many years seem to be wasted. With an infinite God of infinite wealth, hope never ends in disappointment (Romans 5:5). It never regrets the decision to let Him fight the battles. It never says, "I thought God was going to come through, but He didn't." It sees victory and restoration from a position of rest. It rejoices in the strength of the Warrior.

The future belongs to those who belong to God. This is hope.

—W. T. PURKISER

Costly Testimony

**I see heaven open and the Son of Man
standing at the right hand of God.**
ACTS 7:56

In Word

The heart that is in tune with God will tell what it knows, even when the costs are high. That's what Stephen did, as he preached a scathing (but God-honoring) sermon to the religious leaders. Surely he knew that such words—words that accused his captors of killing prophets and defying God, words that ascribed divinity to the executed Nazarene—would get him killed. It didn't matter. The words were more important than life. That's the conclusion that every God-filled heart comes to.

That's also the testimony of martyrs throughout history. The words, or at least the beliefs those words express, are more important than anything. Truth reigns; self-preservation does not. A living sacrifice will ultimately have to decide either to follow that principle or to forfeit the high calling of being a living sacrifice. The life of worship—one that goes far beyond words—will eventually be confronted with that decision. Living sacrifices have to be willing to die.

Most of all, living sacrifices have to be willing to testify to the truth. The cost of the testimony is never to be a factor for the speaker. It is, however, almost always a factor for the hearer. Witnesses who sacrifice a lot to take the stand are always more credible than those whose testimony costs them nothing. Christians who claim Christ at all costs are a living demonstration that their testimony is true, or, at the very least, truly believed. As early Christian leader Tertullian said, "The blood of the martyrs is the seed of the church." Why? Because the witness is believed when the witness sacrifices everything to tell his story.

In Deed

Stephen's martyrdom carries a profound challenge to us. Are we willing to stand boldly before our culture and claim a vision of the divine Son of God? Even if it costs us a job, a relationship, or our very lives? A testimony that so honors God is always honored by God. It is always taken more seriously than casual conversations about faith. It is one of the highest forms of worship because it declares the glory of God in a sacrificial offering.

The blood of the martyrs is the seed of the church.
—TERTULLIAN

Living in Awe

[The church] was strengthened; and
encouraged by the Holy Spirit, it grew in
numbers, living in the fear of the Lord.

ACTS 9:31

In Word

It's not often that we hear of strength, encouragement, and fear complementing one another in the same context. But when God is doing His work, all
three dispositions result. When God is involved, there is strength, because God
is incomprehensibly powerful; there is encouragement, because His works are
validation that He is interested in our lives and acting on our behalf; and there
is fear, because the transcendent nature of His work makes it painfully obvious
that we are very, very small and He is very, very big. When God's awesome
power is unleashed, we feel the urge both to jump up and down with joy and
to tremble in our shoes with fear.

The story of the early church makes for inspiring reading, but we have to
wonder how it applies to us. After all, no matter how many miracles Peter,
John, Philip, and the other early disciples saw, these are not commonplace
in most of our churches. We don't always share all things in common with
other church members; we don't lay all our possessions at the apostles' feet;
we don't see bold confrontations and power encounters between our leaders
and institutional hierarchs; and we don't usually see three thousand people
come to the Lord in one day. We have hints of the power of God in the modern
church, but we have two millennia's worth of corruption and stagnation as
well. Awe is hard to come by.

In Deed

We struggle to have regular prayer times and daily Bible readings, we endure
church politics, and we are fairly busy earning a living and bearing up under
the daily grind. We don't really have time for awe. But if God worked that
powerfully and dramatically in our lives—and He is working—our fear and
awe would drive us in different directions than we are now taking.

Ask yourself this question: How would my life be different if I were overwhelmed with awe of God? Then ask Him to make His majesty visible in your
life. Watch it change.

> More spiritual progress can be made in one short
> moment of speechless silence in the awesome
> presence of God than in years of mere study.
>
> —A. W. TOZER

The Openness of Worship

When they heard this, they had no further objections and praised God.

ACTS 11:18

In Word

Religious people are often accused of being narrow-minded. And it's right that we cling persistently to absolutes that our Lord has given us. But we can hardly resist defining our standards as formulas, and we turn things that are relative into law. All the while, we're missing an encounter with Him that would blow our minds.

Peter's mind was blown. He had been directed to go into the house of a Gentile—taboo for a Jew. He was nudged into the life of a Roman just as Philip had been nudged into the life of an Ethiopian (Acts 8:26-40). But Peter's words to Cornelius were revealing: "God has shown me that I should not call any man impure or unclean" (Acts 10:28). God confronted Peter about his false absolutes, and Peter had to repent of them. He then had to convince the rest of the church that God was interested in saving Gentiles.

A true encounter with God will challenge our assumptions about the world we live in and about the plan God has for that world. It will confront our insecurities and stretch our boundaries. It will prove to us that God cannot be tied down to our systems of understanding.

In Deed

You may have noticed that a true encounter with God can transform your entire way of thinking. The worship that brings us into His presence may be affected; we may become entirely different worshipers, seeing His redemption plan in entirely different ways. We may be called to do things we thought we'd never do, or to praise Him in ways we never thought we'd enjoy. We may be thrust into relationships with people we've never had anything in common with—that is, until we had Christ in common with them. Spiritual awe and obedience will stretch us in unpredictable directions. We become surprisingly, remarkably open to what God is doing in our lives—whatever that happens to be.

Accept surprises that upset your plans. . . . Leave the Father free Himself to weave the pattern of your days.

—DOM HELDER CÂMARA

Point to Glory

**Because Herod did not give praise to God,
an angel of the Lord struck him down.**
ACTS 12:23

In Word

The Judean king made a public appearance bedecked in all his splendor—
including a shining silver robe, according to first-century historian Josephus.
When the audience praised Herod Agrippa as a god, he kept quiet. He could
have corrected them, of course, but why would he? Praise and affirmation
are music to a human being's ears—especially the ears of a public official. So
Herod let the praises continue. He willingly accepted what he knew belonged
only to God.

We do that. We aren't quite as depraved about it as Herod was, boldly
allowing blasphemies to go uncontested. But we do often attribute God's
work to the human agents who do it. We give credit to human inventions
far more easily than to the God who supplied the wisdom and materials. We
find it much easier to honor visible glory than the invisible. And though our
mouths rarely slander God, our silence does so far too often. We don't give
Him His due.

The story of Herod's death is a microcosmic hint of the coming judgment
on humanity. There in a small capsule is a statement of eternal truth: What
glorifies God will continue "to increase and spread" (v. 24), and what glorifies
corrupt people will be eaten by worms and die. That's clear throughout Acts;
converts, seekers, onlookers, healed cripples, and bold preachers gave glory
to God, while corrupt leaders, rulers, pagan cultures, and temple cults did
not. We see two strands of worship in the book, and they lead in two different directions. One leads to life and peace and the blessing of the Spirit; the
other leads to death.

In Deed

We aren't as blatant as Herod in our self-glorifying silence, but we usually
aren't as vocal about God's glory as we should be. We need to remind ourselves: There are two directions in this world, and we must constantly choose
between them. Herod chose the wrong one, and he died. God offers us the
right one with a promise of life. Let your whole being point to His glory.

> Men think that glory lies in being exalted over
> others—Christ . . . . stooped when He conquered.
> —CHARLES SPURGEON

The Mission of Worship

**What you worship as something unknown
I am going to proclaim to you.**
ACTS 17:23

In Word

The mission trip began in a prayer meeting. The church at Antioch had been worshiping—"ministering to the Lord" (Acts 13:2, NASB). And whenever people truly worship, the desire, even the compulsion, to make known the God they know takes over. So Paul and Barnabas were set apart for the work of proclaiming the gospel in distant territories. It was the beginning of a lifetime of Greco-Roman evangelism.

Paul's second journey led him to Athens, where philosophers and spiritual speculators mined the marketplace of ideas for nuggets of truth. Paul noticed their tribute to an unknown god—a safeguard against inadvertently neglecting a real deity—and made a landmark statement for Christians: "What you worship as something unknown I am going to proclaim to you." That, in a nutshell, is the call of children of light in a dark world.

That's where our worship should lead us. Worship means that we know who God is and we love Him for it. But simply knowing Him creates a holy discontent if multitudes do not. How can Someone so lovely, so knowable, remain a private matter? Treasures like God are not to be hoarded. They are public domain, a shared commodity that is not diminished by the sharing. Those who really know God will want Him to be known.

In Deed

Believers need to realize that our secular culture pays tribute to an unknown god. Religion is everywhere, while the gospel often remains obscured. Religion may satisfy the philosophers and spiritual speculators of the marketplace, but among them are people hungry to know the truth. They aren't content to worship an unknown god, because unknown gods can't satisfy known needs.

We live in a world that knows it's in desperate need. We know the God who promises in the gospel to meet that need at its deepest levels. Worship will always make a connection between those two propositions. It will compel us to proclaim who we know.

If a person is filled with the Holy Spirit, his witness will
not be optional or mandatory. It will be inevitable.
—RICHARD HALVERSON

At All Costs

**I consider my life worth nothing to me, if
only I may finish the race and complete the
task the Lord Jesus has given me.**
ACTS 20:24

In Word

The Holy Spirit had spoken to Paul. The message was not a dream of great accomplishments or a vision for new types of ministry. It was a warning that he would face "prison and hardships" in the coming weeks in every city in which he ministered. He had long made a practice of claiming God's promises, but this one probably wasn't on his list of favorites. Still, Paul remained focused.

Did Paul look back to that first worship session in which he and Barnabas were set apart for this kind of ministry? If so, did he struggle with whether God was still worthy of worship? We have no indication of wavering. Paul was bold in his perseverance: "I consider my life worth nothing to me, if only . . ." To Paul, there were things more important than life: Jesus. Fulfilling the mission. Completing the task. Honoring the God who had redeemed him by His grace. A heart inclined toward God realizes that worship, whether the true or false variety, is actually a statement of our highest priority. And Paul's was certainly a heart inclined toward God.

What would you do if the Holy Spirit told you your future would be full of prison and hardships? Perhaps you'd turn and run. Plenty of believers have done that, at least internally, if not visibly for all to see. Or maybe you'd be like Paul and say, "Hey, if that's what it takes to glorify God in my life, I'm all for it." That's a harder response, but it's the only appropriate one for a heart that loves God more than self.

In Deed

Consider your worship. Does it lead you to ultimate sacrifices? Would you lay down your life for your Lord one day? Or, for an even more difficult question, would you sacrifice your self-will in the small decisions of today? The heart of worship has abandoned its own life for the glory of the Lord. There is only One who matters, and it's worth losing everything—everything!—for His sake.

A religion that costs nothing is worth nothing.
—J. C. RYLE

Thrilled

**As a bridegroom rejoices over his bride,
so will your God rejoice over you.**
ISAIAH 62:5

In Word

Imagine a young man in love with a young woman. She is the delight of his heart, and he adores her with the deepest, purest love a person can feel. He makes sacrifices for her, and they don't even seem like sacrifices because of his great love. He treasures every moment with her because he knows she was created specifically for him. He can't imagine anyone else complementing him so perfectly. He is fulfilled in the intimacy of a partner made in his image.

That describes the romantic dreams of nearly every human being. It also describes the romantic dreams of the God who calls His people His bride. God created us for the kind of love that is exhilarating and pure, delightful and deep. He designed us specifically for Himself—we were made in His image, we're told—for the kind of intimacy we instinctively crave. And God, though we can hardly believe it, feels the joyful ecstasy of that relationship.

That hasn't always been the case; God has expressed His frustration with His beloved throughout Scripture. But He purified His bride through Christ's sacrifice, and He continues to purify her today. In the day of Jesus' coming, the bride will have made herself ready. In His eyes, she is breathtakingly beautiful, regardless of her past. When He sees her, He feels only delight.

In Deed

If you're like most believers, your response to that is something like, "Yeah, right. Maybe for His people as a whole, but not for me." That's because we don't understand the heart of our God, or what the blood of His Son did for us, or how His Spirit within us fellowships with the Father and the Son. It's also because we wonder if we were a mistake, as if God set creation in motion but wasn't watching when we were conceived. But Scripture tells us otherwise, and it's far more reliable than our sight, our circumstances, or our feelings. This is one time when the truth doesn't hurt; it thrills. God looks at you and His heart beats faster. Go into your world today knowing how much you are loved.

Joy is the experience of knowing you
are unconditionally loved.
—HENRI NOUWEN

What Love Treasures

**You will be a crown of splendor in the LORD's
hand, a royal diadem in the hand of your God.**

ISAIAH 62:3

In Word

God made sweeping promises to the remnant of Judah that would return from Babylon. He would rejoice over them as a bridegroom rejoices over his bride, He told them. They would be a crown of splendor and a royal diadem in His hand. The God of the universe gives no indication that He has other interests elsewhere, and if this experiment with Israel doesn't work out, He'll get over it. No, He uses the all-or-nothing language of love, and He accepts all-or-nothing perils for the sake of His beloved. He even spills the blood of His Son violently for the redemption of His people worldwide as a fulfillment of His promises to Israel. This King is deeply in love, and He stakes His Kingdom on it.

One of the saddest things in the universe is the weakness of the love of those for whom God gave everything. Repeatedly in Scripture He portrays Himself as an enraptured bridegroom, while His bride is often portrayed as lukewarm at best, and as a prostitute at worst. The most lavish, persistent, intense love in the universe is often accepted casually by the redeemed. If this were a movie, we'd cry for the King in love.

It's not a movie, and we usually don't cry about it. That's because we don't realize how deeply, passionately, and thoroughly we are loved. We assume that since God is a big God, He can take us or leave us without much of an emotional investment on His part. According to Scripture, we are devastatingly wrong. God treasures us as a crown of splendor.

In Deed

If that doesn't give purpose to your day, nothing will. Your heart should race a little faster today, knowing that the greatest power in the universe is completely in love with you. How will you return that love? Will you spend time in His presence, silently enjoying His company? Will you give the gifts of love, like time and attention? Will you make sacrifices for Him that don't even seem like sacrifices? You can. You should. Because He does.

God's love is like the Amazon River
flowing down to water one daisy.

—ANONYMOUS

A New Identity

**You will be called by a new name that
the mouth of the LORD will bestow.**
ISAIAH 62:2

In Word

A name in the Bible is more than just a name. It's an identity. It describes the person who bears it, and it shapes his or her actions and attitudes. It is often a prophetic declaration of who that person is and what he or she will become. A biblical name is a destiny.

When God redeems, He often gives His people a new name. He did that with Abram, who became Abraham; with Jacob, who became Israel; and with Saul, who became Paul. He does that because He knows the destiny of those whom He has called. And when the God of the universe speaks a prophecy over someone He loves, no power in heaven, hell, or anywhere in between can thwart it.

God has given us a new name. "The mouth of the Lord" has bestowed it on us. Whatever it is, we can be sure that it's accurate and that it's good. We know much of what it implies, as anyone called into His Kingdom goes through the person of Jesus. We are in Him, and He is our identity. Our name will therefore be related to Jesus Himself. But beyond that, we can only imagine. And we should.

In Deed

You have a sense of identity, whether you want to or not. And unless you have perfect understanding of heavenly realities, your sense of identity is somewhat off the mark. You may have shaped your self-perception around Jesus and you may be known as one who follows Him, but none of us knows our destiny as He does. He who created us and redeemed us has the privilege of defining us. And according to the Word, His definition is remarkable.

There should be a wild celebration in your heart today. You are not defined by your past, as the psychologists say; neither are you defined by your culture, as the sociologists say. You are defined by your future, and God knows exactly what that is. And it's very, very good.

Your celebration of your destiny should also include stepping toward it. God will give you glimpses of it, and faith will move you into it. Ask Him to do that today, and take bold steps of faith that are worthy of your name.

Don't let the past determine your destiny.
—ANONYMOUS

Glorious

**The nations will see your righteousness,
and all kings your glory.**
ISAIAH 62:2

In Word

Earlier in Isaiah, God reminded His people that He does not share His glory with another (48:11). That was in the context of their idolatry, which actually led them to give glory to false gods. But now the story is different. When Judah is restored from Babylon, and when we are redeemed from sin, the kings of the earth will see our glory. Our glory. The very thought of it is foreign to us. All glory is His, and yet He has promised that we will have some. That's astounding.

There will come a time when all nations and all kings will see the glory of God's people. Some already have, but not fully. One day when Jesus comes again, it will be undeniably obvious. This world that has defined glory in strange, fleeting ways will get a glimpse of the real thing. Those who have craved it and spent their lives striving for it will see something much different than they sought and far better than they imagined.

And what about us? Many of us are painfully aware of how the world looks down on those who profess the gospel of Jesus. We are seen as simple-minded, narrow-minded, uptight, intolerant, culturally oppressive, deceived, or deceivers. Sometimes those perceptions are right, but usually they are not. We bear the consequences of them anyway. We who believe in the true gospel—the gospel that claims Jesus as the only Lord and Savior and expectantly looks for His coming again—are not society's favorite people.

In Deed

If that was your ambition—to be one of society's favorites—abandon it now. It won't happen. But something far greater will. The glory of the Lord on and in His people will be revealed, and the world that looked down on the gospel will then be amazed by it. Jesus was clear that the last would be first, and this is part of that prediction. What is passed over as foolish now will appear glorious then. As much as you can, let your world see your righteousness and the Lord's glory now. One day, it certainly will.

*All [trials] are nothing when compared with the glory
which shall hereafter be revealed in, and for, us.*
—DAVID LIVINGSTONE

The Art of Serving

Live as servants of God.
1 PETER 2:16

In Word

A fine dinner at an expensive, upscale restaurant yields a rich illustration of the meaning of service. Off to the side of the table, a waiter stands, observing every move of every member of the dinner party. When a glass is half empty, he is there to fill it. When the last bite is taken off a plate, he removes the plate. When a diner gives even a slight, highly nuanced expression of need, the waiter discerns the sign and meets the need. He is highly trained to notice, and he notices everything.

That is the posture of a Christian who is called to be a living sacrifice for the Lord. We are to be "noticers." We are to be highly trained in interpreting the signs of the Spirit's work, and we are to step into the picture at every slight prompting. Like the waiter, we are content to stand in the background, completely and intentionally unnoticed, blending in so that we will not interrupt the evening's natural course. But when our service is required, we are to step momentarily into the picture—unobtrusively and only for a specific purpose. We are assigned to only one table for the entire evening. We exist for its pleasure.

That's a far cry from the lives of most Christians. We want to serve the Lord, but we have our own agendas too. Some of us don't stand in the shadows very easily, and others of us don't know when to step out of them. We can discern and react to the subtle signals of a spouse, a child's health, a boss's expectations, a rough-running car engine, or an aging appliance, but we're clueless when it comes to the subtle working of God. We just haven't learned to serve.

In Deed

Like the waiter in the restaurant, we need to be highly trained. We need to enjoy the art of service—and it is an art, beautifully and delicately performed. We need to derive our pleasure not from seeing the items of our own personal agendas checked off, but from our quick, decisive, yet unobtrusive role as one who meets needs. It's our calling, and according to Jesus, it's the way to greatness (Matthew 20:26). We live to serve.

> In the Kingdom of God, service is not a stepping-stone to nobility. It is nobility.
> —T. W. MANSON

From Self to God

**The world and its desires pass away, but the
man who does the will of God lives forever.**
1 JOHN 2:17

In Word

A consistent theme of the New Testament is that we have been bought. Paul
tells it to the Corinthians twice, in two different contexts (1 Corinthians 6:20
and 7:23). Paul calls himself a servant, a bondservant, or a slave of Christ in
nearly every epistle that he wrote. Both Peter and Paul tell us that the church
and individual believers are a possession of God (Titus 2:14 and 1 Peter 2:9).
Regardless of whether the context is personal freedom, sexual morality, life in
the fellowship of believers, or anything else, we are not our own. We belong
to Another.

When that really sinks into a believer's heart, it is a profound revelation.
A living sacrifice—in other words, a true worshiper—does not claim his own
rights. He does not complain about slights and grievances, because he knows
that his Master has ordained them and may even be using them for marvelous
purposes. He bypasses the world and its desires. He throws his own personal
agenda in the trash, no matter how many goals and dreams and preferences
are on it. He does not make out his own schedule, he does not consider any
possession his own, he does not make decisions from human reasoning, and
he does not maintain any self-interest in his relationships with other people.
He disregards the cultural warnings that too much selflessness is unhealthy,
because his health is not the issue. God alone is the issue. His will, His character, His plans, and His providence are paramount.

In Deed

We know better than to assume any of us have lived up to that ideal. But it's
still the goal, isn't it? A heart that truly worships another is a heart that has
completely abandoned itself.

Most of the stresses of life come from threats to our self-interest. But if
we have no self-interest, where is the stress? The heart that has abandoned
itself to God is at rest. It has learned to love the eternal over the world. It
lives in peace forever.

Self is the opaque veil that hides the face of God from us.
—A. W. TOZER

Just Jesus

The Lord be with your spirit.
2 TIMOTHY 4:22

In Word

We pray for a lot of things: success in work or relationships, salvation for family and friends, comfort in times of trouble, deliverance from our trials, and much more. They are appropriate prayers, legitimate requests of the One who provides for all of our needs. But our prayers often reflect a scattered focus—a little bit of this grace and a touch of that one. We're often asking for a few more ingredients to round out our lives.

There's a simpler prayer, and it really should come before all others. We need Jesus. We have Him, of course, as our Savior and our Lord. He is always with us, and He lives in us. It isn't that we need more of Him—He's given all of Himself already. But we do need more of a sense of His presence in our lives. We need His character and His will to be made manifest in our thinking and our behavior. We need a palpable, reliable sense that He is there and that we are operating in His Spirit. We simply need Jesus.

That really is the gist of many of our prayers. If Jesus were profoundly present in our lives, and we knew it in the very depths of our hearts, a lot of our other prayers would be superfluous. Instead of praying that a lost loved one would be convicted of sin, moved to repentance, filled with faith, and steady in discipleship—it's a multifaceted process, as we're well aware—we can simply pray that Jesus would be very present in that person's life. Instead of praying for more love, patience, joy, or any other fruit of the Spirit for ourselves, we can simply pray that the Spirit of Jesus would overflow in our lives. If He is powerfully there, surely His gifts will be present as well. He is what most of our needs boil down to. We don't need more of this or that; we need more of Him.

In Deed

He's there already, you know. You don't really need more of Him, you only need to experience more of Him. Make that your prayer for the next few days: Jesus, let Your presence dwell powerfully in me, in my family, and in my work. Manifest Yourself in every area of my life. Your other requests will be answered powerfully in that one prayer.

All His glory and beauty comes from within,
and there He delights to dwell.
—THOMAS À KEMPIS

A Sufficient Salvation

[He] has blessed us in the heavenly realms
with every spiritual blessing in Christ.
EPHESIANS 1:3

In Word

A profound change occurs in a believer when he or she stops seeking the gifts of God as something to be gained and starts seeing them as something already obtained. It isn't very biblical to ask God for blessings in Christ; it's much more consistent with Scripture to thank Him that those blessings have been given. When we do that, we notice a shift in our thinking; we begin to act on those gifts. Those gifts then become more concrete to us—and more useful.

It may feel presumptuous to claim the gifts of Christ, but it isn't. It's simply a matter of accepting the reality that we don't yet see very clearly. Whenever Paul speaks of the blessings of salvation, they are generally past tense. This passage in Ephesians is a prime example. God has blessed us in Christ; He has already redeemed us, forgiven us, and lavished His grace on us. We have already been sealed with the Holy Spirit (v. 13). We have already been raised up and seated with Christ in heavenly places (2:6). Paul validates the well-known saying that where other religions say "do," Christianity says "done." All that we need in Christ is ours—right now, already, forever. We are in Him, and He is in us.

That should radically change our prayers. We can pray from a position of triumph and authority, not from a position of defeat and lack. We can apply the victory Jesus has already won, not having to ask that He win it again in our particular situations. We can pray to understand what we have rather than to acquire what we need. We can stop seeking treasure in other fields, because the treasure is within our borders already. We need only to see it.

In Deed

The Christian truly lives where Christ is, in heavenly places at the right hand of God. It doesn't always seem like it because we're too used to seeing with our eyes and not with our spirit. Ask God to open your eyes to the reality of your position in Christ. Ask Him to give you a vision of His power in you. Then pray from where you sit.

In the spiritual world, there is nothing but
Christ, since He is God's everything.
—WATCHMAN NEE

Loving Jesus

**Whatever you did for one of the least of
these brothers of mine, you did for me.**
MATTHEW 25:40

In Word

It's a familiar, frightening parable. Like all visions of judgment, this one has a
sense of impending shame and destruction. It seems so hard, so horrifying,
so final. When the Son of Man comes in His glory, He will have only a right
hand and a left hand. No in-betweens. No economy plans for those who went
halfway with Him. No extra options for those who don't fit into either one
of these categories. There are simply those who loved Jesus by loving His
unfortunate brothers, and those who didn't.

It's easy to make this parable into a salvation of good works. Out of the
context of the rest of the New Testament, we might conclude that those who
have humanitarian concerns are saved, and those who don't, aren't. Leaders
of social programs love this parable because it seems to define spirituality
as human compassion. Such a reading leaves out an important point: The
humanitarian concern in this passage is only relevant as an outcome of loving
Jesus. It is an act of worship. It is a compassion that links Jesus with His people
and His people with Him. It isn't compassion for its own sake, or good works
as a means to good merit. It is a blessing not on those who see the world's
needs, but on those who see their relationship with Jesus as an imperative to
meet the world's needs. Those who love Jesus will meet needs, whether or
not they see Him in the needy.

In Deed

Have you ever considered your acts of charity as acts of worship? Jesus' identification with His "brothers" who are hurting establishes a link between love
for Him and love for the outcast. Whether this parable is about His brothers in Jewish faith and ethnicity, His brothers in the church, or His brothers in general humanity—many commentators unfortunately argue for such
distinctions—is not the point. The point is that if you love Jesus, human need
will compel you. To love the Creator is to minister to the creation. Does your
love lead you there?

> To go to people and say "Jesus loves you!"
> and yet do nothing to help change their
> circumstances is not a complete message.
> —JOHN WIMBER

The Worth of Your Worship

"All this I will give you," he said, "if you
will bow down and worship me."
MATTHEW 4:9

In Word

For only one life in history was it ever appropriate to worship and to be worshiped simultaneously. Have you ever considered that? Jesus as the incarnate God is worthy of our worship, yet at the same time He demonstrated true worship for us in the flesh. The worshiped became the worshiper for a brief moment in time. He's our key to how worship ought to work.

His lesson in human worship begins for us in His temptation. Satan, the enemy of anything and anyone who honors God instead of him, waved his withered hand toward all the kingdoms of the world and promised them to Jesus in exchange for the Son's worship. It was a monumental request for Jesus to flip the switch of our universe so that all worship would flow in the opposite direction from its true course. If the Son had worshiped the rebel, the tide would have turned. God would have given up His place as rightful Lord. In effect, Jesus would have lied about who was worthy of true worship. All the kingdoms of the world weren't worth that.

But that's a temptation we're faced with daily. Our sinful flesh and our number one adversary try to distract us, to distort our motives and our vision, and to get us to tell a monumental lie. A corrupted world, still firmly gripped by the chief rebel, still waves its kingdoms in front of us and tells us we can have them—at least intriguing and provocative pieces of them. A little misplaced ambition here, a little greed and lust there, and suddenly we're lying about the worthiness of God. We're worshiping the unworthy. We've tried to flip the switch ourselves because we want the current of the universe to run in the direction of our cravings.

In Deed

It won't work. Jesus is our model. He knew up front that the kingdoms of the world were a pitiful reward for forsaking the true God. That thought has to permeate our thinking so that our response in temptation is always an automatic reflection of verse 10: "Worship the Lord your God, and serve him only."

He who with his whole heart draws near to God must
of necessity be proved by temptation and trial.

—ALBERT THE GREAT

God in a Box

They worship me in vain; their teachings
are but rules taught by men.

MARK 7:7

In Word

It's a tragic tendency of the human heart. We take our redeemed spiritual
passions, inspired by the Holy Spirit of God, and try to regulate them. For
some reason, we crave order and manageability. And when we're honoring
an infinite Father of unlimited mercies, order and manageability are hard to
come by. So instead of modifying our boundaries, we modify our worship.
What's worse, we often try to modify our God.

That can't happen. God won't fit into our boxes and He won't settle for
finite, understandable worship. If He wanted our love to be manageable, He
wouldn't have filled us with the wind and the fire of His Spirit. If we really
want to honor the God who is, rather than the God we want to control, we
need to be content with wind and fire. We need to let the passions—the right
and divinely inspired ones—rage. In other words, we need to get past legalism and celebrate life.

That doesn't mean God dispenses with holiness, of course. The Pharisees
were right about one thing: God is righteous, and people who relate to Him
must be righteous. Their problem wasn't in knowing that God is holy, it was
in not knowing how humans can relate to Him. They thought their laws would
do it. But you can fit laws into a box. Not God.

In Deed

The point of Jesus' criticism is that relating to God isn't about living up to the
minutiae of human standards for righteous behavior. In fact, our hearts have
even failed in the major points of God's law. Our only hope now is in being
filled with the Spirit of the law, who will guide us into right behavior. And
that behavior will be an expression of true worship. It will be passionate—
untamed and unrestrained. It will defy our expectations, but it will be true.
No hypocrisy and no vanity. And the God of truth will love it.

I'm a man in need of a box, serving a God who
constantly proves that He doesn't fit in one.

—TIM WALKER

Zeal on a Mission

I will be zealous for my holy name.
EZEKIEL 39:25

In Word

A reputation is a valuable commodity. People spend their lives trying to earn and keep a good one. When a reputation is tarnished, it's hard to rebuild. Friends, positions, and plans can be lost and never recovered. A good name is worth protecting.

God Himself understands the need for a good reputation. We sometimes think He's beyond such concerns, but the One who is worthy of worship and who, in fact, designed creation to declare His praises is zealous about His name. A slithering serpent lied about Him long ago in the Garden and every day since, and the human race buys the lies far too often. The King who loves His bride has to put up with her misconceptions daily, suffering the consequences of His love being slandered and His intentions being misrepresented. Yes, God has every reason to be zealous about His name.

The prophets are clear that God's fame is enhanced by His judgments and His mercies: His judgments because He is seen as righteous, and His mercies because He is seen as compassionate. When God's dealings with His people become visible, His name is honored. He draws people from the nations through His relationship with us.

In Deed

If God is zealous for His holy name, it only follows that we should be too. Our words, behavior, and relationships can reflect who He is. When they don't, He often distances Himself from our sins by chastising us for them. That teaches us to conform to His character, but it also displays what His character is like for those who know we claim Him as our Lord.

If you are under God's discipline, understand that He is teaching you and protecting His own reputation. If you are not, understand that your life can enhance His reputation by the words you say, the actions you take, and the relationships you have. You are in a remarkable position to satisfy God's zeal by honoring His holy name. Guard His reputation like you would guard your own.

> The glory of God . . . is the real business of life.
> —C. S. LEWIS

Selective Memory

They will forget their shame and all the unfaithfulness they showed toward me.
EZEKIEL 39:26

In Word

The Bible commands us to remember. "Remember well what the LORD your God did to Pharaoh and to all Egypt" (Deuteronomy 7:18). "These stones are to be a memorial" (Joshua 4:7). "Remember the former things, those of long ago" (Isaiah 46:9). The references could go on and on because God and the writers He inspired speak often of the importance of memory. If we don't remember what God has already done, we won't be able to believe what He will do now and in the future. Memory builds faith.

But we are also called to a holy forgetfulness about some things. The same prophet through whom God told us to remember the former things also wrote, "Forget the former things; do not dwell on the past" (Isaiah 43:18). Paul boldly wrote that he forgets what is behind and strains toward what is ahead (Philippians 3:13). God doesn't want us to dwell on the past because the things of the past—sin, mistakes, shame, guilt—don't define us anymore. His forgiveness has rewritten our history. Even God chooses not to remember what happened (Jeremiah 31:34).

In Deed

Most of the spiritual warfare a Christian does is on the battlefield of the mind. And nothing can sabotage that battlefield more thoroughly than the inability to let go of the shame of sin. While remembering God's acts brings faith, remembering ours brings despair. And most believers who feel defeated all the time are choosing to remember their former deeds, not God's.

Yes, it's a choice. It may not feel like a choice, but it is. The restoration of God's people is not complete until they are able to let go of the shame of their past. Those who focus on the sins of the past are writing a dreadful future for themselves. Those who rejoice in God's wisdom, power, and love find that their history has been rewritten and their future is being written brightly. The only difference is where the mind chooses to dwell.

Do not grieve about a sin that is past and gone.
—ANTONY OF EGYPT

A Gift for All

I will no longer hide my face from them, for I will
pour out my Spirit on the house of Israel.

EZEKIEL 39:29

In Word

Throughout Israel's history, God had sent His Spirit selectively. He inspired the artisans of the Ark of the Covenant to craft that place of His presence. His Spirit had come upon Moses and kings, as well as occasional prophets. But for God to "pour out" His Spirit on a nation? His presence touching an entire population? That was unheard of.

But God makes it clear that this was His plan all along—not to measure His Spirit sparingly upon those He needed for the moment, but to lavish it on everyone He calls His own. What was once the privilege of those specially anointed with sacred oil would now be given to all. Every man, woman, and child would be treated as God's royalty and His special servant. The house of Israel would indeed be blessed.

God's word through the prophet Joel carried His intentions even further: He would pour out His Spirit on all people (Joel 2:28), a phenomenon Peter identified on the day of Pentecost. The domain of a nation of priests would become a global domain, available to everyone who believes. The Holy Spirit, so mysterious and hidden for all of human history, would manifest Himself on any human being who asked. The face of the Almighty would never be hidden again.

In Deed

We are privileged to live in the day of which the prophets spoke. The problem is that we don't invite His presence as openly and persistently as we could, and we lose sight of the gift. Oblivious to much of what He does, we lose the ability to recognize Him. Then the Spirit becomes mysterious and hidden once again, a subject of theological debate and a casualty of cold hearts.

Make this your most persistent prayer request: Holy Spirit, show Yourself in my life. Let me breathe Your breath, see with Your eyes, feel Your feelings, think Your thoughts, speak Your words, and hear Your voice. You'll be amazed at how lavishly He pours Himself out for you.

The Holy Spirit is not a blessing from God. He is God.

—COLIN URQUHART

Alone with Him

Jesus often withdrew to lonely places and prayed.
LUKE 5:16

In Word

You're busy. It's a fact of life, especially in our culture. All of our modern time-saving technology hasn't solved our busyness for us. We're spread as thin as ever.

At the same time, we're called to be Christlike. The image of Jesus is being imprinted in our spirits so that we will one day be like Him. In some respects, if we have any level of discipleship at all, we already are like Him. And we know, when we read His Word, that we are to take our cues from Him. That means that when the Word tells us He would withdraw to lonely places to pray, we know we are to do the same. Christlikeness means, of course, being like Christ.

What are we to do when our culture, our work, even our families dictate against an attribute of Jesus? Are we to follow our culture or follow Christ? On the surface, it's an easy question. When we try to apply the answer, it isn't. Getting away to pray is next to impossible, especially getting away often. The demands of life compete against the demands of Jesus, and we far too often choose the former. It's easier.

But it won't get us where God wants us to be. The bulk of discipleship is to be learned in community, but there are some aspects of it that we can only get when we and God are alone together. Sometimes that can happen in a brief morning devotional, but there are other times when the Spirit wants to teach us a deeper lesson or perhaps simply to have a longer time of fellowship with us. That can't happen unless, from time to time—as often as possible, in fact—we get alone with God.

In Deed

If getting away with God in a secluded place is not part of your regular discipleship, start thinking today how you might be able to change that. Plan a potential time to do it. If it seems impossible because of work or family demands, ask God to help you see when it could happen and to help arrange the details of it—who will cover for you, where it might be, and so forth. Remember that He is even more interested in your rendezvous than you are. In Jesus, He gave us that truth: Worship involves solitude with Him.

The more a man loves Christ, the more he delights to be with Christ alone. Lovers love to be alone.
—THOMAS BENTON BROOKS

United in Glory

Glorify your Son, that your Son may glorify you.
JOHN 17:1

In Word

All of our life is a struggle between self-centeredness and God-centeredness. We know our lives are supposed to revolve around Him and His will, yet we have so many personal dreams and goals. We'd like to think our agenda and His always overlap, but deep down we know they don't. We want Him to be satisfied at the same time we are.

The beauty of God's plan is that our worship of Him—our God-centered existence, if we'll only live that way—is ultimately satisfying to Him and to us. When Jesus prayed to God that the Son be glorified in order to glorify the Father, He expressed a truth that applies to us as well. God, for some amazingly mysterious reason, has tied His glory in this world to the glory of His children (John 17:22). We glorify Him when He glorifies us; He glorifies us when we glorify Him. It's two sides of the same coin. The blessings on God's children reflect something about the Blesser. He has wrapped up His reputation in us.

That means that when we sacrifice our lives entirely for His sake and for the glory of His name, we ultimately are not making a sacrifice. Oh, there are short-term sacrifices, to be sure, and we don't always define "glory" as He does. Sometimes glory hurts. But in the grand scheme of things, the Father glorifies Himself by glorifying His children. His expressions of grace, of beauty, of truth, of power, of love, and so much more are invisible unless expressed toward a visible object. That just happens to be us. The splendor of the Father is seen in His children.

In Deed

It's not arrogant to pray, like Jesus did, that God would glorify us so that we might glorify Him. We need to understand that sometimes glory involves a cross, but it is glory nonetheless. We aren't out of line to ask for it. Pray it today, in fact: Lord, glorify me that I might glorify You. Understand that your welfare is wrapped up in worship of Him; you and He will be satisfied together.

God's greatest glory is His grace.
—DONALD GREY BARNHOUSE

Beyond the Rebellion

**They are not of the world any more
than I am of the world.**
JOHN 17:14

In Word

We are not of the world. That's what our Savior tells us. We are in it, of course—that's all too clear—but we are not of it. It is not our natural habitat anymore. We have a higher citizenship.

That's good to know because the Bible is clear that this world is in rebellion against God. To the degree that we fit right into it, we're in rebellion against Him too. John tells us that anyone who loves the world (its systems and ways) does not love the Father (1 John 2:15); and James tells us that friends of the world are enemies of God (James 4:4).

For those of us who live here in the midst of this rebellion, that presents a problem. We want things to go well for us. No sane sports fan wears the visiting team's colors in the home team's cheering section, and no soldier of the King wants to raise the Kingdom flag in the midst of the rebel camp. It's a precarious position to support the Sovereign among those who reject Him. We're not on friendly ground.

So what are we to do? We are to rise up against the uprising. We are to embrace the Father's character in a world that doesn't understand Him. We are to quash the rebellion in every area of our influence. Sounds scary, doesn't it?

In Deed

It's easier when you understand the weapons we're to use. We quash the rebellion by refusing to participate in it. The anti-rebellion attitudes are selflessness and humility, love and peace, joy and contentment. Every time we love someone in spite of his or her hatred for us, we are undermining the rebellion against God. Every time we humble ourselves and consider the needs of others above our own, we are subversive counter-rebels defusing the enemy's weapons. Every time we live Kingdom values in an unholy territory, we are taking back the King's ground.

That's how we live in the world while not participating in its evil. We infiltrate and undermine, under the King's authority. It's what Jesus did, and He asked God that we might do the same.

If you keep in step with God, you'll be
out of step with the world.
—ANONYMOUS

Hearts Divided

**I . . . am about to come and gather
all nations and tongues.**
ISAIAH 66:18

In Word

Ever since the disaster in Eden, false worship has plagued the earth. Cut off from the Creator who made them, people have sought out the supernatural in man-made idols, magical rituals, mysterious shrines, and dark arts of the occult. We've created empty philosophies and rote religions, all in a vain search for the union we once had with the One who made us. We've craved what we forfeited long ago.

As the book of Isaiah closes, the prophecy gives us a picture of this culture of idolatry. It also gives us a contrasting picture of true worship of the Most High God. On one hand, there's the pervasive darkness of ignorant hearts; on the other, the shining light of the redeemed who love the Lord. It's a stark division, a clear distinction between the fall of humanity and the Kingdom of God.

Everyone who believes in Jesus has experienced both sides of that divide. We've all taken sips or even gulps of the poison of false worship, and when brought to our senses, we've drunk the wine of the new covenant. And in spite of the fact that we constantly seek to live in the light of that covenant, we're still painfully aware that we inhabit a planet of darkness. Our light has risen, but we see murky chaos wherever we go. We press into true worship while continually being tempted with the false.

In Deed

Every Christian has a moment-by-moment choice of which kingdom to stand in, which cup to drink from, which worship to embrace. Nearly everything we do, even in the mundane decisions of this day, has the potential to reflect either the glory of our Creator or the shroud of a dying rebellion. The message of Isaiah is that this now-mysterious choice, this life of faith in invisible realities, is going to become visibly obvious to everyone. So the question you have to ask yourself is this: When God puts an end to false worship, as Isaiah prophesies that He will, how painful will it be to you? How much of your heart will you lose when vain idols die?

*Those cannot worship God aright who
do not worship Him alone.*
—MATTHEW HENRY

Grateful Love

They will come and see my glory.
ISAIAH 66:18

In Word

Every good love story has a moment in which love is revealed, a moment when the secrets of the heart, once whispered in private, are suddenly confessed and made plain. The love story of our Savior is no different in that respect; there will come a day when His heart will be visible and all the earth will see it. False worship will be exposed for the foolishness that it is, and true worship will be vindicated as the deepest of loves. When Jesus is visible to the nations, the nations will come to see His glory.

Isn't that the dream of every romantic—that the heart be exposed for its love and that this love be accepted and reciprocated? Yes, every passion of every heart deeply wants to be seen and appreciated. Real love wants to explode in expression, to spill out to the object of its affection. It can't remain silent forever, not without inflicting devastating wounds on the one holding it in. Real love wants the one adored to come and adore.

That's the nature of our God. He created us with love's longings so we could relate to Him on His heart's own terms. His longings, His affection, cannot be contained. That's why creation has a chosen people, a holy priesthood, a redemptive story, and a cross. God's love spills itself out, and He waits for His beloved to come and see His glory. He wants to have a celebration of who He is.

In Deed

God could have chosen to satisfy His love only within His triune nature, or with angels, or with another created order of beings. But He chose us—those made in His image, crafted with affection and intricate loving detail. Interestingly, Paul identifies those who choose not to love God as those who refuse to give thanks. There is something about pure love that provokes gratitude. And there is something about gratitude that glorifies the one who loves.

This is a week of gratitude. The One who loves has poured His heart out. He looks for those who will one day come and see His glory. Thanksgiving is a way of saying you already have.

Gratitude is heaven itself.
—WILLIAM BLAKE

How Worship Flows

**The LORD is coming with fire, and his
chariots are like a whirlwind.**

ISAIAH 66:15

In Word

Why is it so hard for us to worship the one true God? Why is it so difficult to remember to thank Him for what He has done? It should be the easiest, most natural thing in the world for us to praise and honor Him. But the natural ways of the world have been twisted and confused, and praise and honor have been pointed in too many other directions. The God who was manifest in the Garden became the God who is mysterious and invisible in the chaos. When sin entered the picture, it was as if all compasses lost their ability to identify due north, or as if gravity suddenly lost its power and all matter floated wherever it would go. The connection between the Spirit of life and the human heart was severed, and we became worship devices gone haywire. We've invested our praise in unworthy things.

But Jesus is already coming with fire—the Spirit's flames have already descended upon true worshipers—and when He comes in fullness again at the end of the age, His flames will burn up all worthless objects of praise. The fire and the whirlwind will reset the specifications on this race of worshipers, and every idol will incinerate while every true word of praise will be refined and made pure. The Second Coming will be about more than just taking God's people to heaven; it will recalibrate the universe to worship Him alone.

In Deed

It's much better to go through that process now than later. Every day should see more of our idols incinerated and more of our authentic worship established. Our lives should be a constant process of purging and confirming, as our worship compasses turn back toward due north and gravity anchors us again to our rightful place. Our tragic devotion to unworthy aspects of life—status, possessions, achievements, and whatever else we invest our emotions in apart from God—must give way to a constant flow of thanks and praise to our Lord. In the end, it will have to. But there's no reason to wait till the end.

The great thing, and the only thing, is
to adore and praise God.

—THOMAS MERTON

Enduring Choices

**"As the new heavens and the new earth that I
make will endure before me," declares the LORD,
"so will your name and descendants endure."**
ISAIAH 66:22

In Word

We know what will last. The prophecy of Isaiah—and of many others—makes it clear. The Kingdom of God, permanently anchored in eternity and brilliantly lit by His radiance, will never fade away. Anyone who wants to leave a legacy in this world must know that. Anyone who leaves a legacy not based on that truth is passing down a worthless inheritance.

Imagine being in a position to make only one large investment but having two options. The first option is to invest in real estate on a small, sandy island that changes shape every few years from the effects of the wind and the waves. The other is to invest in a massive tract of fruitful land in a fertile valley. Which would yield real dividends? Which would you choose?

That's the choice Scripture sets before us. Nothing will be able to endure the fire and the whirlwind God sends on this earth at the end of the age. Nothing, that is, except the plans and purposes His Spirit breathes into His people. The new heavens and new earth, created incorruptible, will have no unworthy elements left after the refining process. It will be pure and permanent, and no fire can destroy or reshape it. This new earth will bear luscious, life-giving fruit for eternity. And the old one will melt in the searing heat of judgment. When you think today about where to invest your time, energy, and resources—both material and spiritual—you will have to make choices between the transient and the eternal. And if you have any sanity at all, you will choose to leave a legacy that lasts.

In Deed

As you give thanks, let your heart be filled and overflowing with thoughts of the Kingdom that lasts. Anchor your soul in eternity, and let the investments brokered by your choices flow from the treasury of God's Kingdom. Make sure you leave a legacy that endures.

*Thanksgiving is the end of all human conduct,
whether observed in words or works.*
—J. B. LIGHTFOOT

Inevitable Honor

All mankind will come and bow down before me.

ISAIAH 66:23

In Word

Every knee will bow. Most of us have heard that a thousand times or more, and we have some kind of picture of what this global acknowledgment will look like. The Son who returns will be visible and glorious, and everything about Him will command the worship of once-darkened hearts. When we see Him for who He is, bowing won't be optional.

Have you considered the implications of that picture? It means that every person who ever behaved arrogantly toward you will bow to Jesus. So will every person who lied about you, or stepped on you on the way to the top, or left you at the altar, told you that you were worthless, or stole your dreams from you. It also means that every corner of your own heart that has been refusing the lordship of Jesus will be compelled to give up the fight and acknowledge His victory. Every inch of your being will make an obvious confession about who He is. Every atom of the universe will fall in line with His purposes.

That should make us feel good about how history will end. But there's a dramatic difference between bowing then and confessing now in the days of faith, before that day of sight appears. Acknowledging the Lord when all is visible misses out completely on the statement made by faith—that the invisible God is worthy of praise and adoration regardless of our outward perceptions of Him. And only faith can save.

It's true. Although everyone will bow before Him, only some will bow before Him in faith rather than in sight. Only some will experience the blessing of the invisible God invading the visible world while they walk in bold assurance of who He is. And only some will bow on that final day knowing that their praise is a voluntary delight rather than a forced surrender.

In Deed

Praise God today in delight. Depend on Him in faith. Your love will honor Him more today than your surrender will when He returns.

Where God is truly known, He is necessarily adored.

—A. W. PINK

Truly Grateful

While they were eating, Jesus took bread, gave
thanks and broke it, and gave it to his disciples.
MATTHEW 26:26

In Word

Nearly every time the Gospels mention Jesus eating, they mention that He
gave thanks. That's the case when He fed multitudes with only a handful of
food to start with, and it's the case here at His last supper. Knowing He was
about to die, He gave thanks for the sustenance of life. Nutrition that would
never build muscles or strengthen bones was still worthy of the Savior's gratitude. Even moments after dismissing His betrayer, He thanked His Provider.
Yes, the giving of thanks was part of the ritual, but Jesus never did rituals
without maintaining their integrity in His heart. When God provided the
basics of life, He was grateful.

It's a simple act, but it has profound implications. A heart that is truly
grateful for the basics of life is a heart at peace with its Creator. Even when
chaos and danger swirl around us, as they did that night with Jesus, gratitude is
appropriate. Even when we're about to go into a garden and desperately plead
with God to change His plan, as Jesus was about to do, gratitude is appropriate. Regardless of whatever is going on in our lives at any given moment, this
fact is clear: We have been given life by a generous Giver, and His providence
surrounds us daily. If we don't think so, we haven't opened our eyes.

In Deed

You will take your next breath only if God provides it. You will eat your next
meal only if God gives it. You will see your next sunset, cherish your closest
loved one, drink in a beautiful landscape, and feel the coolness of the breeze
only if God lets you. While human hearts take His goodness for granted, He
remains good. He often lavishes His blessings on those who will never see
them, yet He lavishes anyway. That's the kind of Giver He is.

Give thanks today, not just for your bread, but for everything. Look out
a window and thank Him for light. Look at yourself and thank Him for life.
Most of all, look at Jesus and thank Him for the body and the blood for which
He Himself gave thanks.

Gratitude makes even a temporal blessing a taste of heaven.
— WILLIAM ROMAINE

New Songs

Sing to the LORD a new song, his praise
from the ends of the earth.

ISAIAH 42:10

In Word

When we're happy, we sing—or whistle, or hum, or do something else that
displays our joy. That's because true joy can't be easily contained. Neither can
our other emotions. Whatever's in us will eventually come out unless we make
a huge effort to keep it in.

The ministry of God's Messiah will make us extremely joyful if we really
understand it. It satisfies those deep desires we have, and it promises eternal
pleasure and peace. We scarcely realize now what it means never to have
another worry again and to live in abundance forever and ever, but that's the
truth of salvation. Though we were once destined for eternal futility, despair,
and pain, we have been adopted into the King's family and share in the inheritance of the favored Son. It's the ultimate rags-to-riches story. That's worth
celebrating.

Isaiah tells us to sing about it. In fact, we can hardly find any mention of
praise in the Bible that does not involve some kind of sound or action. It's
almost never a quiet, internal experience. It's done with shouts, cymbals,
harps, trumpet blasts, dancing, palm branches, lots of food and drink, and
much more. Our happiness should ooze from our being so irrepressibly that
others can't help but notice. Our lives should be saturated with song.

If our discouragement and depression are anything more than temporary
setbacks, we don't understand how thorough salvation is. We don't see the big
picture. People who have been rescued from a pit of despair and been given
the run of the palace don't generally wrestle with moodiness. They celebrate
because they understand. They have been extravagantly blessed for eternity.

In Deed

Practice gratitude and praise. It takes some deliberateness to do that, espe-
cially if you're used to discouragement. But it can be done; the more you give
God thanks and praise for what He's done, the more real it becomes to you.
And the more you'll find yourself singing.

The water of saints' praises is drawn out
of a deep spring, the heart.

—GEORGE SWINNOCK

Becoming "Blessable"

Humble yourselves, therefore, under God's mighty hand, that he may lift you up in due time.
1 PETER 5:6

In Word

We know that we worship a God who is generous with His blessings. He lavishes on us goodness upon goodness, promising to all those who trust Him an infinite supply of kindness. There is nothing stingy about Him; He gives us all good things.

We also know from experience that the blessings we receive are measured. They come to us in increments, sometimes in waves, sometimes in a steady supply. And, if we're honest, we have to admit that they sometimes fall short of our expectations. That may mean that our expectations are not aligned with the will of the God of blessings, but it may mean something entirely different. It may mean that we have not made ourselves "blessable."

We don't earn God's blessings, of course. They come from His grace, which, by definition, cannot be earned. But there are attitudes that hinder us from receiving the life God has planned for us in all its fullness. How can He lavish His blessings on the proud, for example, without ruining them? How can He pour out His grace on the faithless, who will not recognize it when they see it? How can He lavish gifts on the stingy, who will demonstrate nothing of His generosity when they receive them? How can He spoil the immature, who will lose their shaky footing under the weight of His generosity? God's blessings bring with them a fair amount of responsibility. If we want them, we must prove to be responsible.

In Deed

Worshiping the God of generosity in humility, gratitude, and faith will make us eminently blessable by His standards. Only those who recognize their own insufficiency and their own unworthiness can handle the weight of grace with ease. Others will turn it into unbridled self-interest, which runs at odds with God's purposes. The blessings of God come to those who are ready for them. And readiness comes to those who love Him in humility, gratitude, and faith.

To bless God for mercies is the way to increase them.
—WILLIAM DYER

Praise Revolution: Sacrifice

Let us continually offer to God a sacrifice of praise
. . . for with such sacrifices God is pleased.
HEBREWS 13:15-16

In Word

Do you want to please God? As a believer, of course you do. Not only has He put His Spirit into you to prompt such desires, it was your created purpose from the beginning. We often get it backwards, thinking that God exists for our pleasure; but when we read the Bible, we get a different picture: We exist for His. As created beings who exist for His pleasure, redeemed by His blood and filled with His Spirit, a desire to satisfy Him comes naturally. Of course we want to please Him.

Many Christians at this point get caught on an endless merry-go-round—lots of movement with no real progress. We stress and strain, desperately seeking His will that we might do it and please Him. We may feel like we're jumping through hoops just to try to get His attention, doing all sorts of gymnastics to hit the perfect landing and make Him applaud. All the while, He is pleased with His Son, who happens to reside in us; and He is pleased with believers who can fulfill the instructions of this simple passage.

The writer of Hebrews tells us clearly how to please God. Earlier, he told us that it is impossible to please Him without faith (11:6). Now he gives us some more specifics. For instance, God is pleased with a sacrifice of praise. The verse even spells that out for us: It's the fruit of lips that confess His name (13:15). And—a significant "and," to be sure—"do not forget to do good and to share with others" (13:16). These are the things that please God.

In Deed

If you've been stressing about making your Father happy, stop the gymnastics. Jesus pleased Him, and Jesus is our life. God is satisfied by our faith in Him. But if you want your behavior to thrill His heart, start here. This will revolutionize your life. Let your lips praise Him, confessing His name with joy. And do good to others. God is pleased with such sacrifices. Do this, and He'll be pleased with yours.

There is nothing that pleases the Lord so much as praise.
—ANONYMOUS

Praise Revolution: Read

May my lips overflow with praise, for
you teach me your decrees.
PSALM 119:171

In Word

Praise will revolutionize your life. There's no doubt about it. It will reorient your thinking, taking your mind off of yourself and placing it firmly on God, where it belongs. Rehearsing His mercies will open your eyes to them, and confessing His name as the source behind all your blessings will magnify your blessings enormously. Praise is a radical step in a life-changing direction.

The problem many believers have with that is where to start. How do you praise Him? Where do you begin? What if you're discouraged and depressed, and your eyes can hardly see the blessings He's given, much less prompt your mouth to praise Him for them? What if you hardly know who He is and can barely come up with the words to say? The psalmist gives us the answer: Begin in His Word.

Very practically, here's a good way to learn to praise the Lord. Begin reading. Open your Bible to any page in any section—it doesn't matter where, although Psalms or the New Testament are good places to start. Begin reading a passage. When you get to a verse that speaks of God's faithfulness, praise Him for His faithfulness. Think of ways He's been faithful to you. When the Word speaks of His sacrifice or His love or His promises, praise Him for His sacrifice, love, or promises. As often as His Word reveals some aspect of His character or His works, thank Him for that character and those works. Voice your gratitude for the way He is and the things He does. Before long, you will be an endless fountain of praise.

In Deed

Can you think of a better use for your life than being an endless fountain of praise? God uses such fountains mightily. He changes hearts and redeems souls for just such purposes. You might have always thought that He is focused on your behavior—and certainly He cares about it—but behavior begins in the heart. Praise reorients the heart. Focus there, and let your fountain flow.

Man's chief work is the praise of God.
—AUGUSTINE

Praise Revolution: Ask

Show me your glory.
EXODUS 33:18

In Word

There's a key to becoming a fountain of praise. It's simple, really, although we often have a hard time remembering it. We come up with formulas and techniques, strategies that we think will get us closer to the heart of God. Perhaps we want some special insight that will be the key to understanding His nature and praising Him more deeply. If only we had that missing piece of information, we imagine we would be the spiritual giant we intend to be. It all must be amusing to God. But if we look into His Word, we'll realize the simple key to knowing Him: Ask.

Think about that. Is there anyone in the Bible who ever asked with a sincere heart to know God deeply and was turned down? No. We can see it here with Moses—"Show me your glory"—and we can see it repeatedly throughout Scripture. David was a man after God's own heart, and according to the Word, he found it. Jeremiah and others promised that whoever seeks Him will find Him. People came looking for Jesus, and He obliged them. An Ethiopian came looking for God in Jerusalem, and God sent Philip. A Roman was looking for God in Joppa, and God sent Peter. Those who look for God—with an open, sincere heart, of course—find Him. If we want to praise Him for who He is, all we need to do is ask: "Lord, who are You?"

That will transform a life. It isn't a strategy or a secret, just a request. It's a request that God honors—always. And it's a whole lot simpler than some of the tricks we try when we want to see God. If we really want to see Him for the purpose of praising Him, He's there for the asking.

In Deed

Even a small glimpse of glory will utterly transform a life. Moses came down from the mountain so radiant that it scared his friends. Nothing will change a perspective so much as a vision of the eternal God. And nothing can achieve that glimpse other than a sincere request. So ask. Make that your prayer today, and many days to come. "Lord, show me Your glory."

> God alone knows the depth and riches of His Godhead,
> and divine wisdom alone can declare His secrets.
> —THOMAS AQUINAS

Praise Revolution: Suffer

**Do not be surprised at the painful
trial you are suffering.**
1 PETER 4:12

In Word

Perhaps you thought that yesterday's prayer would lead you to unimaginable ecstasy in the presence of God. Maybe it will. But until it does, don't be surprised by trials in the interim. A fundamental truth of the getting-to-know-God process is that some aspects of Him can only be revealed in pain.

The Christians to whom Peter wrote were suffering for their faith, being persecuted simply for the claim that Jesus was their Savior. We may not have that kind of persecution in some of our semi-Christian cultures today—although we can't rule out the possibility—but we do understand a little about trials. And one thing we will learn eventually is this: God shows up in our suffering in ways that He otherwise would not.

Doesn't it make sense that if we are to know the mercy of God, we are going to have to come face-to-face with our sin first? Or that if we are going to know God as our Healer, there must first be some sickness? Or that if He is to be our Rescuer, we must be in some sort of trouble from which we need rescuing? Or that if we are to understand His compassionate comfort, we must have some kind of hardship that makes His comfort understandable? There are quite a few attributes of God that we simply cannot see unless we're in trouble or hurting or desperate. So don't be surprised if, when He shows you His glory, He shows it to you in a difficult context. That's where glory is best viewed.

In Deed

Don't worry; it's worth the price. Moses may have seen God's glory in a pleasant but overwhelming experience on Sinai's peak, but he also saw it at the frightening edge of the Red Sea, in the howling winds of a barren wilderness, and in response to the rebellion of a complaining people. God's glory was both pleasant and uncomfortable to behold—but it was always worth it.

Don't be surprised at the trial you are suffering. It may be the answer to yesterday's prayer to see God's glory. Praise Him anyway. Painful praise is often the most profound kind of praise there is.

Afflictions are but the shadow of God's wings.
—GEORGE MACDONALD

Praise Revolution: Daily

**Every day I will praise you and extol
your name for ever and ever.**
PSALM 145:2

In Word

You want to see a dramatic change in your life. Perhaps you've gotten into a rut, or maybe you've never really been out of one. Perhaps it seems that life keeps going downhill, or maybe that it has been in a valley for a long, frustrating time. Your hope has dwindled and your vision has dimmed. There's only one way to get out of that rut or that valley: Establish genuine praise of the Father, the Son, and the Spirit as a daily experience.

Psalm 145 is a good place to start. It mentions the urge to worship daily, and it was often read in Judaism as a daily prayer. In some circles, it still is. And it is glorious in its sweeping praise of the Lord, so there's no shortage of material in it by which your mouth can honor Him, if for some reason praise is hard to come by. Read it daily—slowly, thoughtfully, worshipfully. Don't let it become a stale routine, only a treasured habit. The exaltation of the King is always to be enjoyed.

That's really what you want for your life, isn't it? A satisfying purpose and a wellspring of joy are everyone's craving. Praising God daily will satisfy those cravings. You want purpose? You were created to overflow with worship of your King. You want joy? There's no greater joy than fulfilling your purpose for the Father in the power of the Spirit and under the mercy of the Son. The wellspring of life may have been hard to discern in your valley, but large valleys have more room for God's presence. You are in the right place. Your trials are a platform for His mercies. Your pain has made you ready for a revelation of His comfort. Your praise is all that's lacking.

In Deed

If you don't have a daily time of praise, make one. Put it even higher on your list of priorities than making prayerful requests of God. Let your praise be the springboard into your requests and your study of the Word. Stop now, if you can, and praise Him for at least one of His benefits. If you've ever needed a dramatic change, daily, heartfelt praise will bring it about.

> You don't learn to praise in a day. But you can begin today,
> and practice tomorrow . . . until it becomes part of you.
> —ERWIN LUTZER

A God of Peace

**First go and be reconciled to your brother;
then come and offer your gift.**

MATTHEW 5:24

In Word

God loves our worship. He tells us repeatedly that He is worthy of it and, in fact, that we were created to give it. It isn't an ego trip on the part of the Creator, just an appropriate celebration of who He is and why He made us. When we worship, all is right.

But worship that is given when all is not right in our relationships does not honor Him. He loves our worship, but only under the right conditions. He doesn't love the worship of someone who unrepentantly embraces his or her fallenness. And that's what broken relationships signify: fallenness. When we are content to be divided among ourselves, we are not ready to be united to God in worship. We deny the greatness of His love and the unity found in His Spirit when we don't mind going without them in our relationships. If we are fractured in our love, we aren't ready for an encounter with the God of perfect love.

Does that seem harsh? Perhaps, but Jesus spent a lot of time talking about the imperative of loving one another. He said it would signal to the world that His disciples were in fact His (John 13:35); He commanded it as the centerpiece of His teaching (John 13:34 and 15:12, 17); He identified it as the key to joy (John 15:11); and He asked the Father to fill His disciples with His love (John 17:26). Jesus implied that if we don't have love for each other, we don't have love for Him.

In Deed

That's why human relationships are a necessary condition for our relationship with God. The kind of love that God lavishes on us can't be withheld from others. If He has reconciled us to Himself, we have no business living unreconciled with each other—if we can help it.

We can't have a perfectly smooth relationship with everyone, of course. But we can try. We can take the initiative to seek reconciliation, and in fact, we must. The nature of God compels us to be like Him, and He is the ultimate reconciler. When we come to worship the God of peace, we must first have demonstrated peace to others.

Lord, make me an instrument of Your peace.

—FRANCIS OF ASSISI

Worthy

Great is the LORD and most worthy of praise.
1 CHRONICLES 16:25

In Word

God is not just worthy of praise, He is most worthy of praise. In other words, whatever praise we can give Him, He deserves it. We cannot overestimate His worth because He is worth more than anything.

Think of how that applies to our lives. We might wonder if it's worth giving up a possession or a habit for Him, but if He's worth more than anything, the answer is clear. We might consider giving up our careers or our ambitions for Him, and we wonder if it will be a worthwhile gift. But if He's worth more than we can imagine, it is. We may wonder if our praise, worship, and sacrifice will be worth the payoff to us, but we're asking the wrong question. Whether it's worth it to us is not the point; He's worthy of it. That's all that matters.

There is no greater investment than God. Whatever we can give to Him, pour out of our hearts to Him, lay down before Him, and do for Him, it's a profoundly worthwhile offering because it is directed toward a profoundly worthy God. No gift is lost on Him. No sacrifice for Him is ever considered unimportant in His eyes.

In Deed

Consider what you have to offer Him. Your obedience? It is never about earning His favor; it's about offering Him your best. Your purity? It isn't because He's a killjoy but because He wants you for Himself—and He deserves you. Your possessions? They are meaningless trinkets in His eyes, and He wishes you could loosen your grip on them. Your time? You have an eternity before you; there's no need to spend time on yourself. Your talents? He gave them to you so that you could worship Him in ways no one else can. Your relationships? The God of relationships wants to demonstrate His peace and His love in them.

What are you holding on to? Lay it down. Give it to Him. It's right to do so. He's worthy of whatever you have.

When all Thy mercies, O my God, my rising soul surveys;
transported with the view, I'm lost in wonder, love, and praise.

—JOSEPH ADDISON

Living to Please

We instructed you how to live in order to please God.
1 THESSALONIANS 4:1

In Word

We know we aren't saved by our ability to please God. We understand that God is satisfied by our faith, not our works. But Paul, the great apostle of grace through faith, also spoke a lot about obedience. In 1 Thessalonians, he actually spoke of ways to please God through behavior.

We want to please God, of course, and we know our obedience falls short. Coming to God on the basis of works makes for a frustrating relationship; it's never perfect. Even so, God is intensely concerned with what we do, and how we live has everything to do with what we offer Him. It's not about earning His favor but about giving Him our best. Our worship is shaped not only by what we feel or what we say, but by how we behave. Our works can honor God.

That's important to know in a culture that doesn't give much attention to obedience. Rules, in our day, are considered relative, always subject to interpretation. Even in the church, we emphasize faith more than obedience, and we're right to do so. But nowhere does the Bible tell us that our obedience becomes irrelevant. James is emphatic that faith without works is dead—not even faith at all. That makes a lot of sense. If we say we believe that Jesus is Lord and then fail to act as if He is, we have made a significant statement. We have demonstrated that our words don't mean very much.

In Deed

Is obedience a part of your worship? Do your beliefs have implications for your behavior? More pointedly, when your desires and your Lord contradict each other, which do you obey? Your behavior is the final word on what you really believe. No matter how strongly you feel a love for God, and no matter how deeply held you think your faith is, if it doesn't result in action, it's an illusion.

Jesus said the same thing: "If you love me, you will obey what I command" (John 14:15). In other words, if you love Him, you will also love His words, and His words will guide your life. And that is immensely pleasing to God.

> The best measure of a spiritual life is not
> its ecstasies but its obedience.
> —OSWALD CHAMBERS

Altars of Gratitude

**[Abram] built an altar there to the Lord,
who had appeared to him.**
GENESIS 12:7

In Word

Abram built an altar to God. What made him want to worship? God had taken a seventy-five-year-old man out of his homeland and led him to a new country, making extravagant promises to him for his faith and obedience. There was no written revelation at the time, no covenant history, no people of God. Just a man and his faith and a land of promise.

In a sense, this father of our faith is the prototype. We, too, have been called out of our homeland (this fallen world) and led to a new country (the Kingdom of God). We, too, have been given extravagant promises for our faith and obedience. And though we have a written revelation to learn from and a history of God's people to inherit, it's all new for us. We enter into the Kingdom with nothing but a call and a promise. We have to proceed by faith.

So whenever God gives us, figuratively, a piece of land—in other words, any victory at any stage of our pilgrimage—we need to build an altar there. We need to worship each step of the way, for whatever He has given and whenever He has appeared. The privilege of the call and the guidance along the way are reason enough for an enormous amount of gratitude. God has called us not only to go to a new country, but to be His. An altar of thanks is only appropriate.

In Deed

Our lives should be filled with such altars, monuments to the goodness of God for how He has called and where He has led. For every step toward the promise of the Kingdom, we owe Him thanks. For every piece of the promised land we're allowed to stand on, we should be grateful. None of it is earned; all of it is grace. And we are allowed to participate in this plan by nothing but faith.

Abraham's faith opened the way to magnificent blessing. So does ours. Give thanks not just today, but every day. Build altars whenever you can. Worship God for the privilege of hearing His call.

No duty is more urgent than that of returning thanks.

—AMBROSE

Single-Minded

**On that day there will be one LORD,
and his name the only name.**
ZECHARIAH 14:9

In Word

Scattered allegiances, divided loyalties. The commitments of this world are fragmented beyond comprehension. Every nation, even within itself, has conflicting alliances and competing agendas. Every person has ties to several obligations. Even within our own hearts, we are a mixture of loyalties.

When we accept Christ, our allegiances are supposed to become clear. We are first and foremost loyal to our Savior; everything else is a distant second. Even so, we still sometimes have difficulty discerning His will and knowing what commitments to allow into our hearts. But one day, there will be no split devotion, not even among those who served other gods their entire lives. There will be one Lord, and His name will be the only name.

This was God's design way back in the Garden. The first man and woman heard one voice and had one commitment. Life was simple then and would have remained so if they had not tuned their ears to another voice. The first sin confused all loyalties, and apart from God's revelation, we've never come out of our confusion. His design was thwarted when our hearts tried to lean in two directions. On that great and terrible day of which Zechariah speaks, the design will be restored. Life will be simple again. There will only be one Lord, one voice, one name.

In Deed

When believers read end-time prophecies and realize what life will be like when God sets all things right, we can have two possible responses. We can marvel at how things will be one day; or we can, by faith, bring eternity's truths into present experience. We can go ahead and live simply, devoted to one voice and one name.

That's our calling. Nearly every description of eternity has implications for the present time. God's people are to be a picture of the new creation, messengers of the end result. Ask yourself today: to what degree does your life represent one Lord, one voice, and one name?

> I need nothing but God, and to lose
> myself in the heart of Jesus.
> —MARGARET MARY ALACOQUE

Nothing Ordinary

On that day HOLY TO THE LORD will be inscribed on the bells of the horses, and the cooking pots in the LORD's house will be like the sacred bowls in front of the altar.

ZECHARIAH 14:20

In Word

Life in a fallen world is often divided into the sacred and the secular. For those who are redeemed, all of life becomes sacred, but it wasn't always that way. From the earliest pages of God's Word this distinction between holy and profane is present. God Himself spends a lot of time telling Israel how to be "holy"—set apart for His special use. Not only must His people be cleansed from the corruption of this world, so must the articles of their worship and sacrifice. Any earthly thing that is to be used for God must be drawn out of the context of fallenness and prepared specifically for His presence.

When the Lord returns, this separation process will be so thorough and final that even the trivial instruments of life—like bells on horses and daily cookware—will have been cleansed and prepared for His presence. Corruption will be so rooted out of creation that common articles in His Kingdom will be considered holy. The religious tendency to isolate oneself from the fallenness of the world will never be necessary again.

This is yet another day-of-the-Lord truth that believers are meant to bring into the present. We have the privilege of bringing common vessels—ourselves, our jobs, our families, our possessions, our finances, everything—under the lordship of Jesus, turning ordinary things into sacred offerings. We already know this is the direction of history. We should be inspired to go ahead and move in that direction.

In Deed

What common vessels have you submitted to God for sacred use? Which ones remain under your own lordship? Do not rest until every area of your life, no matter how trivial, is inscribed with His name. Above all, let the common vessel of your soul be completely, sacredly His.

God wills that you sanctify the world and your everyday life.

—VINCENT PALLOTTI

A Confident Stand

**The survivors from all the nations that
have attacked Jerusalem will go up year
after year to worship the King.**
ZECHARIAH 14:16

In Word

God will establish Himself visibly as King over all the earth (v. 9). In that day, even His enemies will worship Him. It may not be an enthusiastic worship, but it will be consistent. Those who once attacked Jerusalem will flock to it to do homage to the universal, undisputed King.

Think about that. Every atheist who has mocked faith as superstition will recognize the King for who He is. Every adherent of every anti-Jesus philosophy will bow before the Lord. Every nation that shunned God's truth, every persecutor who sought to extinguish God's people, every rebel who ignored God's righteousness—all will come into His presence in humble obedience. One way or another, in heaven or in hell, in this age or in the age to come, everyone will acknowledge the supremacy of Christ. As Philippians 2:11 says, every tongue will confess that Jesus is Lord.

Isn't that encouraging? It means that whatever flak a believer takes in this world is temporary. Every offense, every slight, every insult, every injustice will bow to the vindication of our Lord. When He makes all things right, not only will He correct and restore us from the wrongs we've committed, He will prove to others that we put our faith, flawed as it may be, into the right Kingdom. We laid up true treasures that can never lose their luster.

In Deed

For that reason, never go through this world intimidated. There's no need to. We can wait—calmly, patiently, and without malice or vengeance—for the vindication of our God. Believers who lash out at those who scoff at our faith have forgotten the end of the story. They are like trash-talkers before the big game, wasting energy on a battle of words that means nothing. Don't do that. Live instead in the calm assurance that all enemies of the gospel will one day bow to our Lord. Stand confidently in this world.

> In the first advent, God veiled His divinity to
> prove the faithful; in the second advent, He will
> manifest His glory to reward their faith.
> —JOHN CHRYSOSTOM

Distress Answered

I call on the LORD in my distress, and he answers me.

PSALM 120:1

In Word

Worship is all about approaching God. So are Psalms 120 through 134, the psalms of ascent. Perhaps they were written by captives who had returned to Jerusalem and to a destroyed Temple they had long grieved and now rebuilt. Or perhaps they were simply written and sung by pilgrims on their way to the Holy City. Regardless, they begin with the cry of every human being who ever wanted to know God and draw closer to Him: "I call on the Lord in my distress."

That's where worship really begins, isn't it? We didn't start out with a song in our heart or a confidence in His presence. We didn't even start out knowing He existed, at least not consciously. He was taught to us, and He probably only became real at some distressing point when we felt—even knew—we needed Him. Faith, for most of us, was born in a crisis.

That's okay. There's nothing wrong with coming to God through a crisis. He has ordained many a catastrophe for just such an outcome. He lets His people be traumatized because trauma is often the only thing that will incline our hearts toward Him. But it doesn't end there. The verse doesn't conclude with distress; it concludes with an answer. God doesn't let us go through our crisis so our hearts will be turned toward Him, only later to wonder whether or not He was really there. The plan is for Him to show Himself. Crisis leads to faith, and faith leads to revelation. That's where worship can begin.

In Deed

You've undoubtedly gone through crises in your past, and you'll go through them again. This is a wonderful verse to remember in such cases. But you may even be going through a crisis today. If so, this is a wonderful verse not just to remind you of God, but to hang on to with all your heart. You are given explicit permission through this explicit example to trust that when your world wars against you, you can call on God and He will answer. That's a rock-solid guarantee from the Author of the inspired Word. At some point in your life, you need to know it. You may even need it today.

The great tragedy of life is not unanswered prayer but unoffered prayer.

—F. B. MEYER

Infinite Care

**He will not let your foot slip—he who
watches over you will not slumber.**
PSALM 121:3

In Word

We need to know who's watching over us. This isn't some local deity limited
in power. This isn't some cosmic force that may pay attention to us if we
scream loudly enough. This is "the Maker of heaven and earth" (v. 2). This is
"he who watches over Israel" (v. 4). This is the almightiest of almighties, the
wisest of the wise, the most loving of lovers. Those of us who ascend to His
throne—through obedient faith, through believing prayer, through passionate worship—are approaching the most benevolent, powerful Being in all
creation. Actually, beyond all creation.

We forget that. We know He's up there, but we forget that He's right
here. We know He can help us, but we struggle to believe that He will. We
know He counts all of our hairs, but we're afraid He might have moved on to
other heads. After all, there are so many. It's a big world with lots of problems.
Maybe He's too busy for ours.

But an infinite deity never gets overextended. A being with unlimited
resources can't get overcommitted. He doesn't stress about fitting it all in,
because He's beyond time. He doesn't wonder how your life will play out,
because He knows every possibility, including the one that will actually happen. He laments your lack of confidence in Him, but He never loses His love
for you, because His love is boundless and always overflowing. And it flows to
you, even while you sleep.

In Deed

Yes, the deep-down desire of all civilizations in all ages has a single eye on
you—right now, while you work, while you play, while you stress and strain,
while you try to resolve painful conflict, while you party, while you cry your
eyes out, and while you sleep. He's your shade at your right hand, He promises
to keep you from all harm—absolutely everything that might ultimately do
you in—and He's your constant, unseen companion, whether you're coming
or going (vv. 5-8). You can count on that forever. Sleep well.

God loves you as though you are the only person in the
world, and He loves everyone the way He loves you.
—AUGUSTINE

Jesus, House of God

I rejoiced with those who said to me, "Let
us go to the house of the LORD."

PSALM 122:1

In Word

Pilgrims to Jerusalem, at whatever point in Israel's history, looked forward to
the trip. Regardless of the particular feast involved, it was always a reminder
of national identity—of the God who had brought them out of Egypt, of
the cost of their collective redemption, or of the coming fulfillment of the
prophecies. It was a time for God's people to be God's people together—to
celebrate together, to repent and be forgiven together, to worship together.
Most of all, it was a visitation to the Temple of the One who held the entire
past, present, and future in His hand. It was where God lived.

We don't have anything like that in our collective identity. Our churches
aren't where God dwells, at least not the buildings themselves. Our country
isn't where God dwells, certainly not beyond the extent that He dwells in
many other countries. Christianity has no holy city on which we focus our
devotion as an integral, necessary part of our faith. We can worship regardless
of where we are, at any time.

So what central location of Christianity is our focus? It's not a place, it's
a Person. We don't build our devotion around Jerusalem and its Temple, but
around Jesus and the Temple of His being (John 2:19-21). All of the feasts of
Israel are summed up in Him. All the promises of God are fulfilled in Him.
All of Israel's history points toward Him. When the Word urges us to go up
to the house of the Lord, Jesus is the house. In Him we are redeemed, we are
fulfilled, and we are together. He is our identity as a people.

In Deed

What does your identity revolve around? When someone says to you, "Let us
go to the house of the Lord," does it thrill you? Do you relish the opportunity
to get closer to Jesus, where all God's people dwell, where all His redemptive
work is celebrated, and where all His promises are fulfilled? If somehow your
faith has been distracted or diluted from purity of devotion to Jesus Himself,
take time today to refocus. He's the center of your faith, and even the center
of your life. Rejoice to draw closer to Him.

All God's love and the fruits of it come to us as
we are in Christ, and are one with Him.

—RICHARD SIBBES

Dependence

**Our eyes look to the LORD our God,
till he shows us his mercy.**
PSALM 123:2

In Word

You've asked God something, and you have waited for His answer. It hasn't come yet, or perhaps it hasn't come in the form you wanted. The natural human tendency, in such cases, is to think to yourself, "God must want me to work this out on my own." And you begin crossing that very fine line between expectant faith and willful self-assertion. When you do, you may get results—some sort of resolution to your problem. But it won't be God's resolution if it didn't come from Him.

That's a common problem in the life of faith. We trust God, but when He delays His intervention in our lives, we start making assumptions. Perhaps He wanted us to fend for ourselves, or perhaps He simply said no to our request and we missed it. So we act. We take our eyes off of His provision and put them on whatever we manage ourselves. It's a subtle shift with dramatic implications. Soon we're living on our own, only occasionally acknowledging the God we know is up there, though we're not sure where.

This psalm tells us the right attitude. As a servant looks to his master—for everything, in its time—and as a maid looks to her mistress, so we are to look to God. Our eyes are to stay on Him. If He gives us what we expect, we have it. If He doesn't, we don't. There are no alternatives, no plan B's, no going back to the drawing board. If we truly depend on God, we depend only on Him and not on any other. Not even ourselves.

In Deed

Trust and dependence are single-minded attitudes. If we have them, we have pinned all our hopes on this God, and whatever He does for us, that's what we have. He isn't the first resort before we move on to second, third, and last resorts; He isn't the first bank to which we apply for a loan, or the first school to which we apply for admission, with backup choices waiting just in case. No, He's it. All there is. The trusting heart will wait because it believes there are no other options. And in the end, that's the heart that will be shown mercy.

What is more elevating and transporting than the generosity
of heart which risks everything on God's Word?
—JOHN HENRY NEWMAN

If . . .

If the LORD had not been on our side . . .
PSALM 124:1

In Word

Have you ever thought about all the "ifs" of your life? Not your second-guessing, wondering what life would be like if you'd made different choices; that's pointless. But have you thought about the "ifs" of God? What if He hadn't spared Noah and family when He flooded the earth? What if He had never delivered Israel from Egypt? What if He had let this rebellious race go its rebellious ways, without ever having intervened or restrained the ravages of sin? What if He had never sent Jesus or raised Him from the dead? Even more personally, what if He had never given you any insight into His plan, had never called you to be His child, had never rescued you from the sinful, decaying conditions around you? In other words, what if He had not been on our side?

It's a horrifying thought, isn't it? A fallen world left to its own devices would be a frightening place to be. Just as frightening is the hollow in our own souls. Confronting our lostness, for many of us, was terrifying. And God could have left us in that condition. We're scarcely aware of the high stakes of eternity at this point, but one day we'll see: The difference between complete, ecstatic fulfillment and desolate, eternal separation was a gentle gesture of the merciful God. And if that gesture had never been made . . .

The psalmist speaks of raging torrents engulfing Israel and sweeping away its people. It's a graphic representation of invisible spiritual truths. If God were not a rescuing God, we would be the most pitied creatures in all the universe. Forever.

In Deed

It's good to think about the "ifs" whenever you start to take life for granted. When that attitude of self-sufficiency, complacency, or pride creeps in, ask those "what if" questions. It will drive you to your knees in gratitude.

While you're giving thanks, consider this: The "ifs" are true for those who haven't yet received that gentle, merciful gesture. The "if" that once terrified us may be their reality. Be the gentle gesture of God to someone today.

> Is it not wonderful news to believe that
> salvation lies outside ourselves?
> —MARTIN LUTHER

Unshaken

**Those who trust in the Lord are like Mount Zion,
which cannot be shaken but endures forever.**
PSALM 125:1

In Word

We can be shaken. That's a fact of human nature, proven by plenty of visual
evidence all around us as well as by our own experiences. Sometimes trials
come, problems overwhelm, and turmoil reigns. When that happens, we talk
to family, friends, and counselors; we lie awake at night; we make lists of
pros and cons or of resolutions that will keep us out of similar predicaments;
and we pray our hearts out. None of those things is wrong. They are simply
evidence of one undeniable fact: we can be shaken.

But God gives us a promise not just for the daily troubles that come up
but for the once-in-a-lifetime crises that overwhelm us. Those who trust in
Him cannot be shaken. Our emotions may be shaken, and our thoughts can
be awfully jumbled. But our position in Christ as a child of our Father? Never.
It isn't shaken. His providence is certain and His promises sure. If we belong
to Him, and if we believe in Him—really believe—we will endure forever.
Through anything.

Many people can't say that. That's because they haven't met the condition of this psalm. The implication of verse 1 is that if those who trust in the
Lord cannot be shaken, those who don't trust in Him can. The key is where
we've fixed our faith. Like a mountain climber who fastens himself to a rocky
face with ropes and spikes, those who trust in God have fixed themselves to
an immovable object. Our trust is like the tools of the climber; as long as it
binds us to God, we are secure on the mountain. We can't fall, and we can't
be shaken.

In Deed

Have you considered whether your faith is the kind that binds you to the
mountain? As you go through your trials, are you stepping on sandy slopes or
driving spikes into solid rock? Trust God and never loosen your grip on your
trust. You'll soon find that He never loosens His grip on you.

Oh, how great peace and quietness would
he possess who should cut off all vain anxiety
and place all his confidence in God.
—THOMAS À KEMPIS

Sow in Tears

Those who sow in tears will reap with songs of joy.
PSALM 126:5

In Word

Captives had returned to Jerusalem—probably from a long exile in Babylon—and were absolutely giddy about being back in the homeland. They were
"like men who dreamed" (v. 1), filled with laughter and songs of joy. It was a
celebration that satisfied them to the depths of their souls.

That's the story anytime God redeems. He brings back captives, and they
rejoice. That's why Israel's history and the church's are filled with songs of
victory and gratitude, and it's why God's people are always talking about their
salvation; it's a glorious event. Broken hearts drink in the promise of restoration like dry desert grounds soak up the pouring rain. And God always knows
exactly what to do with broken hearts.

Because God brought His captives back from exile, the prayer of verse 4
and the principle of verses 5-6 are entirely reasonable. Considering who He
is, it is the most rational thing in the world for the destitute and hopeless to
seek His blessing. It should be natural for those of us who have been redeemed
to say, "Restore our fortunes, O LORD." And we must understand His means
for doing so: "Those who sow in tears will reap with songs of joy." That's the
way of the Kingdom.

In Deed

Why is that? Because we live in a fallen world. All around us are deserts, broken dreams, exiles, and hurting hearts. But what begins in sorrow for us ends
in laughter and joy. There's one catalyst that changes everything: God.

"The LORD has done great things for us, and we are filled with joy" (v. 3).
Is that the story of your life? No matter how hopeless your situation, how
difficult your struggles, how distant your exile—or, to be more specific, no
matter how painful your divorce, your bankruptcy, your unemployment, or
your disease—in one way or another, God will bring you back. How do we
know? Because that's what God does.

Perhaps you've felt captive. You've probably sown a few tears too. Don't
worry; God is restoring the homeland—the place of dreams—to His children,
and you will reap with songs of joy. Your troubles will end with celebration.

> Tears have a tongue and grammar and
> language that our Father knows.
> —SAMUEL RUTHERFORD

Vain Labor

**Unless the LORD builds the house,
its builders labor in vain.**
PSALM 127:1

In Word

We bear unnecessary burdens. We worry about finances, relationships, work, health, and just about anything we can think to worry about. We can be anxious about the future, regretful about the past, and oblivious to the present. There is almost no limit to the stresses the human mind can cultivate.

Meanwhile, there is Someone with us, in us, and for us who is a blesser by nature, who in the very center of His being is compassionate and loving. Not only that, He holds all resources in His hand. According to the emphatic witness of Scripture and all who know Him, He is fully willing and fully able to do anything and everything on our behalf.

Why, then, do we insist on building our own houses? Why do we develop our own projects, rely on our own protection, and arrange for our own providence? What do we find lacking in the almighty God of love that convinces us that we must bear our own burdens and fulfill our own plans? Do we enjoy the weight of burdens? Or is it simply that we have lost sight of the God who guards, gives, and builds?

In Deed

This psalm calls our thinking "vanity." It tells us that only God's projects are worth investing in, and only His projects will be blessed. It tells us that all of our anxious stress—our manic early rising and late-night work—is pointless under the watch of the God who grants sleep to those He loves (v. 2). It tells us that our families are places of refuge and blessing, not burdens we must bear.

Dispense with vain thinking. Labor in the things God has ordained and called you to, and not in the things you've devised yourself. He doesn't stretch His people too thin and lay heavy burdens on their shoulders. If you're experiencing overwhelming burdens, they are probably man-made. Protection, provision, and all prospects for your future are in His hand. And His hand is always open.

Hard work is a thrill and a joy when you are in the will of God.
—ROBERT A. COOK

Holy Fear

**Blessed are all who fear the LORD,
who walk in his ways.**
PSALM 128:1

In Word

Fear of the Lord is not a popular subject. Modern revisionists have dismissed Bible verses that speak of fearing God and have adapted hymns that once praised it. God, we are told, is love—an entirely biblical idea; and love, we are told, tolerates anything and everything our heart desires—an entirely unbiblical idea. So while the Bible tells us to fear God, society says He's completely harmless and tame, and will pat us on the back for whatever we do.

But we know better. Fear is appropriate when we come into God's presence. It isn't a fear that dreads impending judgment—perfect love casts that out (1 John 4:18)—but a fear that is overwhelmed with something so awesomely greater than ourselves. If the sight of the Grand Canyon or Niagara Falls can make us tremble, as the power of natural forces can do, the sight of supernatural power is even more terrifying. A quick survey of Isaiah's call, the disciples' frequent reaction to Jesus' miracles, and John's vision on Patmos will confirm it: God is worthy of our fear.

That's important to remember because the fear of God—not just a healthy respect for Him—will constantly remind us that we live sacred lives in a sacred presence. We are always, in a sense, on holy ground. The God who has redeemed us has come to dwell within us, and we can never take sin, obedience, or even life itself casually again. The knowledge of the Holy One is a traumatic experience with powerful results. The presence of God changes us.

In Deed

That's why this psalm tells us that those who fear the Lord are blessed—happy, fulfilled, complete. A sacred awareness of our lives as redeemed servants of the most high God will keep us focused on reality. It will change our behavior and our hearts in remarkable ways. It will keep us believing, praying, and loving because the majesty of the Creator overwhelms us with faith, hope, and love. The psalm is a promise: Blessing and prosperity come to those who do not take God casually.

The fear of God kills all other fears.
—HUGH BLACK

Set Free

**The LORD is righteous; he has cut me
free from the cords of the wicked.**
PSALM 129:4

In Word

Israel rejoiced in the fact that despite years of oppression—despite slavery
in Egypt, domination by foreign powers, captivities in Assyria and Babylon,
and the threat of growing empires—it was a redeemed people with eternal
promises. It could have let its collective psyche be absorbed with a sense
of inferiority and futility, except for one thing: God kept delivering them.
No one can feel inferior and futile when the sovereign Lord keeps interven-
ing. A history of redemption allows people to define themselves not by their
enslaved past but by their liberated future.

Like Israel, we too could be absorbed with our past, dwelling on our
captivities and futility. We could remember the times we've been enslaved,
the times we've been brutalized, and especially the times we've suffered self-
inflicted wounds from our own disobedience. But our history isn't defined by
such failures. It's defined by the God who redeemed us from them.

God has cut us free from the cords of the wicked. In fact, the wicked
never mastered us (v. 2). We may have been dominated, oppressed, enslaved,
and ridiculed in our sinful, fallen condition—the Bible reminds us often that
we were bound by sin. But the wicked and their cords did not gain victory.
Jesus did. A cross and an empty tomb are our assurance of that.

In Deed

If you're like most human beings, you tend to regret aspects of your past
and lament your failures. That's normal, but it's not how God defines us. The
failures exist for one explicit purpose: to highlight the Redeemer. It's the
redemption that defines who we are.

Live by the promise of your future today. It's a glorious future, signaled by
cut cords and the fading wake of wickedness behind you. Whatever your past
failures, you've been cut free from them. They don't have any power over you,
and they never will. The Redeemer trumps the oppressors every time.

*Redemption does not only look back to Calvary. It looks
forward to the freedom in which the redeemed stand.*
—LEON MORRIS

Hope Waits

My soul waits for the Lord more than
watchmen wait for the morning, more than
watchmen wait for the morning.
PSALM 130:6

In Word

The soul has cries we often cannot hear. We meet people daily who are composed on the outside and wounded within. We, too, know how to put on our game face for work, for family, or for our social life, even when deep inside we're in pain. We don't share our pain well because we're afraid of what others will think of the real person inside. So the soul cries—quietly, pitifully, but deeply.

But there is no hiding from God. He hears. His ears of mercy never let cries from the depths go unnoticed. It doesn't matter how deep the depths are, God is close and His hearing is perfect. The soul is bare before Him.

Psalm 130 gives us the appropriate posture of a broken soul. There's no pretense, no positioning—just honesty. And when the soul is so bare, there is nothing left but to wait. We can't pressure God, because we have no leverage against Him. We can't induce Him, because we have nothing to offer. In the depths, broken souls have nothing but hope in the One who hears. And hope waits.

In Deed

You've likely been in the depths, and you'll likely be there again. Perhaps you are there now. Look for God like the watchman looks for the morning. The watchman knows the sun will rise; there's no question in his mind. He may not enjoy the dark of night, but he knows it will end. The night is never permanent, and the daylight never fails to come. Likewise, your depths are not permanent and light will come. God will rise on your behalf at the appointed hour. Like the watchman, you can wait for Him in certain hope.

The psalmist knows such depths, and he also knows such hope. He knows God has "unfailing love" and "full redemption" (v. 7). When He delivers—and "unfailing love" assures us that He will—it will not be a halfway deliverance. You can pray your anguish with absolute certainty that He hears, He loves, and the morning is coming soon.

Hope is the power of being cheerful in circumstances
which we know to be desperate.
—G. K. CHESTERTON

Beyond Formulas

**My heart is not proud, O LORD,
my eyes are not haughty.**

PSALM 131:1

In Word

Religion is an attempt to figure out God. It's natural for us; we want a set of rules and rituals that will get us into His good graces. Even when we've been trained in the principle of salvation by grace through faith, we easily revert to practices that we can follow rather than the Person we need to know. We love formulas.

But God is not a formula God. Proud hearts can't figure Him out and haughty eyes can't see Him. Ambitious spiritual entrepreneurs will never get a handle on Him. The spiritual gymnastics we attempt just to get Him to answer our prayers—every time—and to bless our careers—every time— and to smooth over all our relationships—every time—will never result in what we hope for. We forget that God operates on a basis of our need and His mercy. Methods will always fall short. Desperate cries to a merciful God will always reach Him.

The way to get to know our God is not through intellectual inquiry or self-righteous behavior, but through humility and a still, quiet soul. That has always been the case. The gentle God of grace asks us to acknowledge reality—the true condition of our diseased hearts—so He can act in a way that we will recognize. Mercy travels incognito in the presence of pride, which thinks grace is well deserved; but when humility sees the benevolence of God, it sees clearly.

In Deed

You may have noticed a tendency to approach God through principles and formulas rather than through humble hope. It isn't an arrogant pride, just a misperception. Like all of us, you don't mean to presume upon His presence. You simply forgot: God cannot be figured out, only needed.

Ascend to God on that humble basis, and He'll never disappoint you. He may delay His help and tolerate your pain for a while, but only for a reason. He will never let you down. How could He? He has promised that everyone who is humble will be lifted up. It's the only direction for a humble heart to go.

The door of God is humility.

—JOHN THE SHORT

The Spirit's Home

I will allow no sleep to my eyes, no slumber to
my eyelids, till I find a place for the LORD.
PSALM 132:4-5

In Word

The psalmist ascended to Jerusalem, where God dwells, while meditating on
the origin of the Temple. It began as King David's highest hope—to build a
temple where the Lord could dwell. God did not let him leave that legacy, but
he honored the desire. He promised David that one of his descendants would
forever sit on the throne. We know now who that descendant was and is—
Jesus, the King who will reign for all eternity. But David's desire is in some
ways unfulfilled. The Lord still seeks places to dwell.

We're not called to build temples, of course. But we are told that Jesus
dwells in our hearts through faith and that we are the temple of God. He lives
in His church collectively and individually, and He still seeks a better home.
The house of God is growing, and we are a vital element in its growth. We are
to find other hearts in which He can dwell.

The house of God is to be improving in quality too. No matter how long
He has lived within us, He is not yet perfectly at home there. We still have
clutter that interferes with His living space; desires and dreams that contradict His plans for us; and attitudes that conflict with His character. In theory,
our hearts should be completely clear, the road into them free from debris.
But we know that's not the case. We have tried to crowd into our hearts both
God and ambitions, or God and unhealthy relationships, or God and money
or possessions. The house of God is not the place it ought to be.

In Deed

Look at the depth of David's desire. He would not rest well until he found a
place for God. He brought the Ark and a tabernacle to Jerusalem, and still
he dreamed of a permanent temple. He was deeply unsettled—sleepless and
willing to suffer hardship—until he settled that issue.

Is that your attitude toward the residence of God within your own heart
and within your church? Are you restless until it grows both in quantity and
quality? Is your greatest desire to make sure that God has a fertile, welcoming
place in your life? Learn to see your heart as a dwelling place—and make it
completely His.

Thou, O Spirit, that dost prefer, before all
temples the upright heart and pure.
—JOHN MILTON

The Blessed Fellowship

**How good and pleasant it is when
brothers live together in unity!**
PSALM 133:1

In Word

It's a strange psalm in modern contexts. The oil of Aaron (v. 2) and the dew of Hermon (v. 3) are lost on us. But the images would have been loaded with meaning to the Israelites who first heard them. They would have presented a picture of God's greatest blessings falling upon a united fellowship.

Oil was poured on Aaron's head for his anointing as the father of Israel's priests. Verse 2 describes a thorough covering; he was thoroughly sanctified and powerfully prepared for his priestly work. He was set apart to God for a specific, holy purpose. He was ordained to communicate God to humanity and humanity to God in the prescribed acts of worship. The precious oil on his head, flowing down his beard and onto his robes, was a sign that God was with His people.

The dew of Mount Hermon was abundant; it made the land green and fruitful. What if, as the psalmist suggests, it had fallen on Mount Zion and Jerusalem? It would have blessed the land in amazing ways. The most holy city would have been the most fruitful city.

In Deed

That's what unity does for a fellowship. It turns a common gathering into a priestly community, able to communicate God to humanity and humanity to God. It points to His character for those who don't know Him, and it confirms His presence among us for those who do. Unity is the greatest evidence that God is living, active, and right there where the fellowship is. It is precious.

Unity also makes the fellowship fruitful. It takes the dew—the blessing of God—from one place and pours it on a needy land. It turns a common people into a holy conduit of mercy, where God's character flows and powerfully changes lives. It makes dry land green.

That's how good and pleasant our unity is to God. It isn't a casual matter to Him; it's critical. God desires our unity because our unity shows the world who He is and how He works. If we don't have it, they won't know Him.

Strive for unity. It's a good and pleasant gift, a precious, powerful sign that God is among us.

If we focus on our differences, our focus is on each
other. If we focus on unity, our focus is on God.
—ANONYMOUS

The Offering

**From beyond the rivers of Cush my worshipers,
my scattered people, will bring me offerings.**
ZEPHANIAH 3:10

In Word

The ultimate goal of creation, the purpose for which God designed the world and the human race, is worship. In making people in His own image, breathing life into us, going to extraordinary lengths to redeem us from our horrible, self-inflicted condition, and calling us into intimacy with Him, God has laid the foundation for an eternal Kingdom that rallies around one overriding purpose: adoring Him. We were all made for worship.

We're on the receiving end of adoration as well, so this is no one-sided relationship. God has loved us passionately; that's why our worship is so important to Him. He loves to be loved, and because we're made in His image, we love to be loved too. We crave close communion with Him, desiring to be fully embraced by the One who knows every detail of our lives and loves us anyway.

God desires this close communion too. He doesn't just tolerate us and "love" us because He's obligated to do so. He actually enjoys loving us—emotionally, enthusiastically. He didn't create the human race only to achieve minimal fulfillment from us, like an ill-matched couple whose love has come to feel compulsory over time. No, His design includes deep satisfaction and unrestrained joy—both for Him and for us. And in the end, that fulfillment will be realized on a global scale.

In Deed

Whether God is calling His people into His Kingdom from the far reaches of the ancient Middle East, as in Zephaniah's day, or from every corner of the planet today, His purpose is to be worshiped. His desire is to pour out love on us extravagantly, and to have our love returned to Him extravagantly. We already know He has lived up to His end of the relationship. He invites us to live up to ours.

To love God is the greatest of virtues; to be
loved by God is the greatest of blessings.
—PORTUGUESE PROVERB

Our Kind of Savior

Salmon the father of Boaz, whose mother
was Rahab, Boaz the father of Obed, whose
mother was Ruth, Obed the father of Jesse,
and Jesse the father of King David.
MATTHEW 1:5-6

In Word

They seem boring, these long genealogies. And even though the lineage of
Jesus is extremely special, it still isn't the highlight of our Bible reading. We
know He's traceable to Abraham, but that should matter only to a first-century
Jew, not to a twenty-first-century Christian, right?

But a closer look is revealing. In Jesus' genealogy is Rahab, a woman of
questionable morals who helped the Hebrew spies as they entered the Promised Land. And a generation later, the Moabite Ruth appears. Then, within two
generations, an adulterous king with a murderous bent shows up. What are
a Canaanite prostitute, a Moabite outsider, and a law-breaking king doing in
Jesus' genealogy? Pointing to the hope we have in Christ, that's what.

Think about it: Jesus—the incarnate God, the invisible Creator appearing
in the flesh—is a descendant of sinners. If Jesus could come from the seed
of a prostitute, a foreigner, and an adulterer, He's just the One to represent
sinners to God. While sinless Himself, the holy Son of God came in the form
of fallen flesh, a descendant of sinful humanity in need of salvation. That kind
of God-man could represent us well. In Him we can hope.

In Deed

We forget, with all of Jesus' holiness and perfection, the fallenness of the
world He entered. He didn't take on Garden of Eden flesh; He took on the
flesh that was forced out of the Garden to till the stubborn soil. He took on
the flesh that killed prophets and seduced God's people, the flesh of circum-
cised rebels, foreigners, and outcasts. He took on the flesh of all of us.

That's why Christmas is so astounding. God didn't just become man, He
became man in the form of those who had fallen—miserably. Only that kind
of Savior can give us hope. His descent to save us is greater than we thought.
And our salvation is greater than we imagined.

> Christ became what we are that He
> might make us what He is.
> —ATHANASIUS OF ALEXANDRIA

The Mystery of Christmas

**To us a child is born . . . and he will
be called . . . Mighty God.**
ISAIAH 9:6

In Word

Think of how amazing that is. A son—a tiny little baby—will be called Ever-lasting Father. A child will be called Mighty God. On the surface, that's absurd. Titles of deity and eternal fatherhood are reserved for God Himself, not for babies.

But the absurdity of Isaiah's prophecy came true a few centuries later when a child was born, grew up, and actually lived up to those expectations. Many people who encountered Him simply could not envision Him as an ordinary human, or even a human at all. Others couldn't tolerate those who called Him divine. He was unclassifiable, as all once-in-a-lifetime phenomena are. Uniqueness precludes categories, and people have argued about Jesus' identity ever since He visited us. But Isaiah had it right, years before Jesus came: A child would be called things that only God can be called. People who argue that Jesus isn't God need to go back a few centuries to a Jewish prophet and take up their case with him. A human being would be given divine names, he said, and to this point in world history, Jesus is the only One who has ever truly qualified for them.

That's what's so amazing about Christmas. It isn't just that a Spirit became man—lots of religions talk about incarnations of spiritual beings—but that the uncreated entered creation, the eternal entered the temporal, and the infinite entered finitude. That which was completely "other" to human think-ing expressed Himself in what was familiar to us. It's a case of two different realities merging right before our eyes, and it still stretches our vision.

In Deed

Christmas is a mystery. It doesn't matter how many familiar carols we sing, gifts we give, or traditional dinners we eat. A long time ago, infinite deity and fragile flesh met, and it rocked our world. It still does, and that's okay. Let it. That's what Christmas should be all about.

I need this annual angel visitation . . . to know
the virgin conceives and God is with us.
—EUGENE PETERSON

Opening Treasures

They saw the child with his mother Mary,
and they bowed down and worshiped him.
Then they opened their treasures.
MATTHEW 2:11

In Word

It's a familiar scene, isn't it? We've seen and heard it practically every year in nativity plays, television specials, and our favorite Christmas carols. Wise men—three, we're often told, but the Bible doesn't say how many—came from a great distance to see the new King, and when they saw Him, they gave Him gifts. Pretty pricey stuff too. Gold, incense, and myrrh—things that shine brightly, smell nice, and feel wonderful. Gifts that only kings can afford.

Perhaps this act of giving doesn't resonate with us like it should. Maybe we've heard it so often that our familiarity with it has bred, if not contempt, at least a lack of fascination. Perhaps we assume that rich magi under the patronage of their kings could easily afford such treasures. To them it could have been nothing more than a routine baby-shower gift, as far as we know. But the important thing to notice in this passage is that the wise men gave to Jesus the things they considered most valuable. In a Middle Eastern culture two thousand years ago, these gifts were top of the line. It took them a lot of time and a lot of treasure to make that journey and present these gifts. It was an act of adoration.

In Deed

Such giving ought to characterize our adoration too. We praise God with our tongues, raise our hands to Him, and study His Word. But do we give Him what is most costly to us? Do we take the things we have that are top of the line—our treasures that we value most highly—and offer them to Him? Answering that is a challenge. We have to know ourselves well.

Think of what you value most. It may not be your time on Sunday mornings or your 10 percent tithe. Maybe it's a relationship, a dream, an honor, or an allegiance. Whatever it is, it's your treasure. Lay it at His feet and tell Him it's His. True love always involves deep sacrifice. It certainly did for Him. It does for us as well.

> As they offered gifts most rare, at the manger
> rude and bare, . . . all our costliest treasures
> bring, Christ, to Thee our heav'nly King.
> —WILLIAM DIX

The High Cost of Worship

When Herod realized that he had been outwitted by the Magi, he was furious.

MATTHEW 2:16

In Word

Why did our sovereign, omniscient God allow the tragic events surrounding Jesus' birth? The slaughter of Bethlehem's sons is particularly disturbing. The King of kings had entered this world, and a jealous local ruler had caught wind of it when Magi showed up in Jerusalem with a desire to worship the new King. Herod's prophecy experts pointed to Bethlehem as the place of His birth. The scheme to eliminate his "competition" failed when God warned the Magi not to cooperate. In his rage, Herod slaughtered a whole town's male toddlers and newborns. All Bethlehem wailed.

Jesus "flew in" under Satan's radar. God's enemy missed his chance to kill the dreaded "seed" prophesied way back in Genesis 3:15. His rage flared, and the sound of "Rachel weeping for her children" (Matthew 2:18) filled Bethlehem's skies. And if we think about it, we want to ask one simple question. Why?

Why did God allow Herod to be tipped off to the Messiah's birth? Why did the magi enter Jerusalem with such little discretion about their purpose? God spent so much of the New Testament's first chapters warning people in their dreams. Why didn't He warn the wise men to avoid Herod in the first place? Or even to stay home? Their gifts of gold, frankincense, and myrrh cost painfully more than their asking price. Why did Rachel's babies have to lie dead in the streets?

In Deed

Because of worship, at least in part. For reasons we now know, it was important for representatives of the nations to visit the King and bow before Him. It meant a lot then, and it means a lot today. It tells us that Jesus is more than a Jewish Messiah; He's the Savior of all who come, even from the far reaches of this world. Even Herod's rage—and Satan's—has become a witness to Jesus' identity. Was that witness worth the horrible cost? We believe in an ancient, Middle Eastern Messiah because of such testimonies. They have given us life. And Rachel's children now know: Their lives were lost so that worship of the Child might happen—then and even now. Yes, it cost a lot. And yes, it was worth it.

Once the most holy Child of salvation gently and lowly lived below; now as our glorious mighty Redeemer, see Him victorious o'er each foe.

—MARY MACDONALD

Treasure in a Manger?

**This will be a sign to you: You will find a baby
wrapped in cloths and lying in a manger.**
LUKE 2:12

In Word

Today is one of the best days of the year to express devotion, and yet devotion is so much easier on other days. Why is that? Perhaps because habits are easier to perform on routine days, and today is anything but routine. It's a celebration. Depending on your household, it may be a noisy celebration or a quiet one, a crowded one or a lonely one. But regardless of the noise level and the people around you, it is a special day. One of the most special of the year.

Why? What's so special about an arbitrary winter's day that may or may not be close on the calendar to the time of Jesus' real birth? After all, it's the event that we celebrate, not the day itself. But oh, what an event. It was a once-in-eternity occasion when God clothed Himself in our form and lived among us. Our ancestors saw Him first as a carpenter's boy, then as a precocious teenager, then as a powerful teacher and gifted communicator. Only a few saw what billions would later accept: That this was no ordinary human. He was fully human, yes; but He was—and is—so much more. In an intimate setting in Bethlehem, God got intimately close to His fallen creation. Instead of turning His back on our fallenness, He embraced our need. Our lives have never been the same, nor will they ever be again. Thank God.

In Deed

Look at that baby in the crude manger. His mother's blood has just been wiped from his face. She will one day have to wipe his blood from hers, but forget that for now. See Him in this humble scene, obscured by a dark night in an out-of-the-way town. You have pinned all your hopes on this fragile child. All of them. You have trusted Him with all of your fears and all of your treasures. You have made Him your life, and if He doesn't come through—if He proves to be just a long-ago baby in a faraway land—you have no hope. But He always comes through. He has never disappointed us, and He never will. He is Jesus, Lord at His birth.

> Love's pure light; radiant beams from Thy holy
> face, with the dawn of redeeming grace.
> —JOSEPH MOHR

Precious Offerings

**He refused to drink it; instead, he
poured it out before the LORD.**
1 CHRONICLES 11:18

In Word

David had been on the run from Saul, hiding out in caves and deserts. Now after Saul's death, he was on the attack against Philistines in the same desert near the same caves. And, not surprisingly, David was thirsty. Far from home, he longed for the familiar water of Bethlehem. Three of his warriors decided to do something about it. They broke through Philistine lines and brought back the coveted water to quench David's thirst. David's response? He poured it out to the Lord.

Those of us from capitalist societies cringe at his wastefulness. The water came at such great sacrifice, at such enormous risk, that David could at least show his appreciation by drinking some of it! But David had a higher goal than quenching thirst. His desire was to offer the Lord whatever was most precious to him. And this water was precious. Three of his right-hand men had risked life and limb to get it, even though there were surely closer sources of water than the well at Bethlehem. They did it because they loved David. The water, therefore, was immediately one of David's most treasured possessions. And treasured possessions make the best offerings.

In Deed

We could learn from that. We give generously to God at times, but we save our most treasured possessions for ourselves. The first 10 percent of our income is one thing; the precious items we secure with the rest of it are another. God loves expressions of sacrifice. The greater the sacrifice, the greater the love demonstrated. If we hold things tightly, we love less fully.

Consider the things you give God. Do you give Him not only the first of your income, time, and talents, but also the best of them? Do the things you treasure become the things you most want to honor God with? When you survey your domain, you will see things you hold dear and things that are expendable. Which do you give to God? Do you long to give Him what is most precious to you?

> To sacrifice something is to make it
> holy by giving it away for love.
> —FREDERICK BUECHNER

Heavenly Worship

They were calling to one another: "Holy, holy, holy is
the LORD Almighty; the whole earth is full of his glory."

ISAIAH 6:3

In Word

Every once in a while, Scripture pulls back the curtain that divides time and
eternity, and we get a brief glimpse of heavenly worship. We may crave more
than a glimpse, but that's probably all we can handle; the vision is too overwhelming for inhabitants of a fallen world.

Isaiah's vision of the heavenly throne is one of the more famous. It must
have been an awesome scene, one that mere prophetic words can hardly capture. What we can tell from this passage is that the seraphs are so enamored
with the holiness of God that they can do nothing else but proclaim it; and that
the scene is so powerful and pure that Isaiah is terrified by his own impurity.

The angels worship God for His holiness because that's what they can
see of Him. Isaiah, however, can see that and more. He becomes a redeemed
servant, a proclaimer of both holy judgment and merciful atonement. He has
seen not only the power and majesty, but the grace and mercy. He knows
the gap between perfect God and fallen man, and he's amazed that there's a
remedy. He goes on to prophesy about fallen kingdoms, the coming Kingdom,
and the Intercessor who bridges the gap between them. Isaiah is a man who
has seen heavenly worship and has lived to tell about it.

In Deed

That's the role of every believer. We may not have as dramatic a vision as Isaiah did—the train of God's robe filling the Temple, doorposts and thresholds
shaking, and the voices of angels who are perpetually astounded at God's
holiness—but we know the truth. We've seen that scene by faith, and we've
embraced the Intercessor who bridged the gap. We bring the same message
that Isaiah was given: God is holy, we're not, and there's a solution.

That's an exhilarating mission. Like Isaiah, we stand between a perfect
God and an imperfect world with an imperative: point to the Bridge between
them. Live your mission as your highest act of worship.

Angels, help us to adore Him; ye behold Him face to face.
. . . Praise Him! Praise Him! Praise with us the God of grace.

—HENRY FRANCIS LYTE

The Power of Glory

This was the appearance of the likeness of the
glory of the LORD. When I saw it, I fell facedown.
EZEKIEL 1:28

In Word

Brilliant flashes of light, gyroscopic movements, mysterious faces, and a glowing presence. Those are feeble words describing an awesome vision—"the appearance of the likeness of the glory of the LORD," according to the prophet. In other words, Ezekiel is saying, "This is the best that words can do." But he implies—and we know from his response—that it was more than a strange vision. It was the indescribable presence of majesty.

That sense of majesty—of great glory, unimaginably inspiring and impossible to grasp—is the sense that every believer should live with. It prompts prophets to declare God's truth with superhuman courage, and it drives painfully human worshipers to their knees. If we live without a sense of excitement, going through the routine of our days with rote motion and chilling apathy, we don't have it. We aren't living in the presence of God.

That's an absurd picture: In one realm, there are flashes of lightning, powerful winds, shouting angelic voices, and indescribable fire and motion. In another realm, there are lukewarm people going through stale routines without much enthusiasm, energy, or hope. That's expected of people who have never known God. It's inappropriate for those who have.

In Deed

How can we who dwell in the passionless, visible realm live with the perspective of those who have seen the eternal flames of glory? For starters, we can begin each day in the posture of Ezekiel's response: We can fall facedown. In other words, we can worship. Given enough truth, time, and practice in the art of adoration, we get greater glimpses of God's glory. And if a day begins with that, it is anything but a routine day.

If you are bored with life, lacking energy, and losing hope, try spending more time in God's presence. Ask Him to reveal His glory. Life will never be the same.

God is boundlessly enthusiastic.
—A. W. TOZER

Eternal Dominion

His dominion is an everlasting dominion
that will not pass away, and his kingdom
is one that will never be destroyed.

DANIEL 7:14

In Word

David asked why the nations raged and conspired against God, and then answered that question with an image of God laughing at them (Psalm 2). No matter how many of the earth's kings take their stand against God, their position is an absurd one. God can sit on His throne and laugh, because He knows the futility of their plans and the certainty of their end. Earthly maneuvers are no threat to His purposes.

That's the same image Daniel gives us when he recounts his heavenly vision. The pure and purifying Ancient of Days was on His throne, with a river of fire flowing from Him. Fire destroys filth and makes truer elements glow. And in Daniel's prophecy, a filthy spirit of pride rages against the truest Kingdom. The river of fire resolves the conflict.

The beauty of Daniel's vision is that the pure and holy Ancient of Days has all the majesty of the Holy One in Isaiah's and Ezekiel's visions. He's the same God. But the majesty doesn't just define the difference between God and humanity. In Daniel, it immediately shows us a King and a Kingdom. All of the chaos and corruption of this world will bow in order and obedience to the sovereign God. The evil reports that we read in today's news are temporary travesties. Their destiny is a river of fire; they have no power against God or His people.

In Deed

A vision of God will convince us of that. When our eyes are filled with beasts and headlines, we panic. But if we fill them with the majesty of God, we can hold the human devices in highest contempt. No king can threaten His sovereignty.

As part of your devotion today, read a newspaper. Let the trauma of national and international events sink in. Then open your eyes to God and let Him sink in even more. All of today's trials are on a short leash. They will burn in the river of fire. How do we know? The Ancient of Days says so.

> Faith in the kingdom of God is what
> . . . Christian joy is all about.
>
> —JOHN MAIN

What to Wear

His face was like the sun shining in all its brilliance.
REVELATION 1:16

In Word

John was in exile on a beautiful but isolated Greek island. On one spectacular Lord's Day, he had a visitor. He was "in the Spirit," and a voice like a trumpet spoke to him. When he turned to look, he saw a glorious vision of a "son of man"—the name Jesus used so often for Himself. Was it Jesus? Of course. Who else shines with such brilliance, speaks words as sharp as a sword, and identifies Himself as the First and the Last, the Living One who was dead and is now alive? Yes, it was Jesus. Radiant, spectacular, risen Jesus.

John fell at His feet (v. 17). Wouldn't you? Even so, he remembered Jesus' appearance: a long robe, a golden sash, white hair, blazing eyes, glowing feet, and a face as bright as the sun. In other words, He is purity, perfection, and power.

This radiant Bridegroom once told a story of a man who made it into a wedding banquet without the right clothes (Matthew 22:1-14). The intruder was thrown out. He didn't belong because he wasn't dressed for the occasion.

How do you dress for the kind of groom John describes in Revelation? It would be an act of supreme devotion to clothe yourself in similar apparel, wouldn't it? You want to look like you belong.

In Deed

For fallen human beings with severely deficient wardrobes, that's a problem. Besides, even if we had the cash, we wouldn't know where to look for such radiant attire. But in ancient Middle Eastern weddings, wedding garments were often provided by the hosts. All that was required was to accept them.

This radiant Jesus spoke a few verses later of people from Sardis who would walk with Him dressed in white (Revelation 3:4). Those are the robes of righteousness that God, our Host at the wedding banquet, generously and mercifully provides for us. Why? Because our attire is important to Him. Wear His righteousness—His holiness, His radiant face. You'll need it to look like you belong next to that Groom.

To love Jesus is to love holiness.
—DAVID SMITHERS

Worship Forever

**All nations will come and worship before you,
for your righteous acts have been revealed.**
REVELATION 15:4

In Word

Revelation is filled with songs to God. His judgments are deemed perfect, His mercy gratefully cherished, His holiness reverently honored, and His victory wildly celebrated. When the dust from the last battle clears, we'll be able to see what we should have seen all along: that God was always right, merciful, and loving; and that His archenemy was always distorting our view. All the subterfuge, deception, bogus accusations, and vile injustices will be exposed for what they were. Only God will shine, and though we've spent a lifetime not understanding the suffering and evil in this world, we will understand it then. Everything will make sense.

That's good to know. We forget that our world is full of illusions. The Word of God cuts through the smoke and mirrors of the enemy and sets us straight, but we fall away from it easily. It's important for us to flip to the final chapter from time to time and see how it ends.

In Deed

When you need a spiritual lift, read through all the songs of praise in the book of Revelation. It isn't hard; they are usually indented and set off in quotes, so they should be easy to find. And though the full implications of their words may not be clear just yet, the fact that God is amazingly glorious, spectacularly brilliant, and awesomely praiseworthy will. The multitudes of heaven, the chorus of elders and martyrs, and the intriguingly beautiful songs of angels will convince you that your worship and discipleship today are extremely, eternally worthwhile.

As you read the songs of praise, you may want to memorize one or two of them. Why? Because you might as well get used to them. Like the adrenaline you feel when you cheer a last-second score or witness a triumphant dramatic scene, you'll be captivated. Your attention will be riveted to the glory of God, and your songs will sound uncannily like the words of Revelation. This is a preview of your destiny: eternal, thrilling worship.

> Come, let us offer Him the great, universal sacrifice of our love, and pour out before Him our richest hymns and prayers.
>
> —EPHREM

you've been told not to trust your emotions—

feeling
like
GOD

the emotional side
of discipleship—and why you can't
fully follow Jesus without it

chris tiegreen

to rely on what you know rather than what you feel.

Yet you were created in the image of God, which means that many of your feelings are echoes of his own. In *Feeling like God*, Chris Tiegreen traces the character of God throughout Scripture, showing how God reveals himself as a deeply emotional being who longs to connect closely with you. When men and women like Abraham, Hannah, David, and Paul opened their hearts to him, their lives were radically transformed. Discover how your emotions are a bridge drawing you closer to your Savior—and you'll experience the passion of feeling like God does.

"If you're longing to *feel* God's love—not just *know* it—read this book."—**Chip Ingram**, president, teaching pastor, *Living on the Edge*

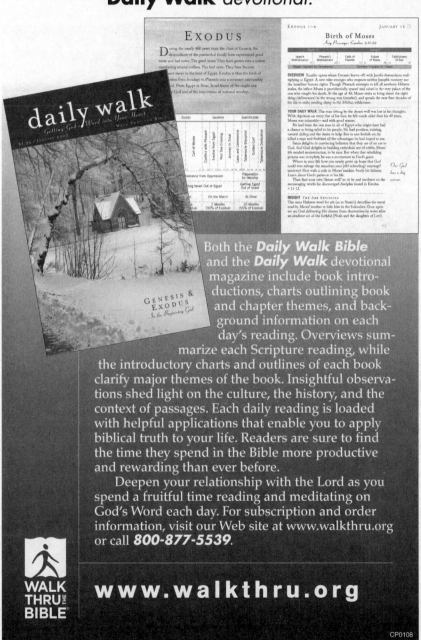

The devotionals in this book come from **_indeed_**—a bimonthly
magazine from Walk Thru the Bible created specifically to help
Christians deepen their relationship with God.

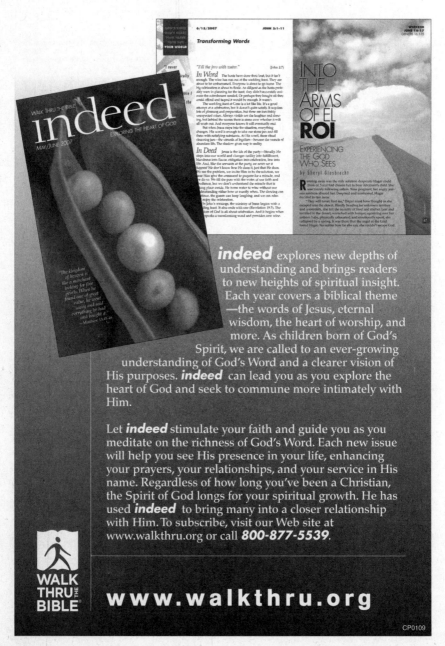

indeed explores new depths of
understanding and brings readers
to new heights of spiritual insight.
Each year covers a biblical theme
—the words of Jesus, eternal
wisdom, the heart of worship, and
more. As children born of God's
Spirit, we are called to an ever-growing
understanding of God's Word and a clearer vision of
His purposes. **_indeed_** can lead you as you explore the
heart of God and seek to commune more intimately with
Him.

Let **_indeed_** stimulate your faith and guide you as you
meditate on the richness of God's Word. Each new issue
will help you see His presence in your life, enhancing
your prayers, your relationships, and your service in His
name. Regardless of how long you've been a Christian,
the Spirit of God longs for your spiritual growth. He has
used **_indeed_** to bring many into a closer relationship
with Him. To subscribe, visit our Web site at
www.walkthru.org or call **800-877-5539**.

**WALK
THRU ᵀᴴᴱ
BIBLE**

www.walkthru.org

CP0109